D1289102

Harness Oil
and
Gas Big Data
with Analytics

Wiley & SAS Business Series

The Wiley & SAS Business Series presents books that help senior-level managers with their critical management decisions.

Titles in the Wiley & SAS Business Series include:

Activity-Based Management for Financial Institutions: Driving Bottom-Line Results by Brent Bahnub

Bank Fraud: Using Technology to Combat Losses by Revathi Subramanian

Big Data Analytics: Turning Big Data into Big Money by Frank Ohlhorst

Branded! How Retailers Engage Consumers with Social Media and Mobility by Bernie Brennan and Lori Schafer

Business Analytics for Customer Intelligence by Gert Laursen

Business Analytics for Managers: Taking Business Intelligence beyond Reporting by Gert Laursen and Jesper Thorlund

The Business Forecasting Deal: Exposing Bad Practices and Providing Practical Solutions by Michael Gilliland

Business Intelligence Applied: Implementing an Effective Information and Communications Technology Infrastructure by Michael Gendron

Business Intelligence in the Cloud: Strategic Implementation Guide by Michael S. Gendron

Business Intelligence Success Factors: Tools for Aligning Your Business in the Global Economy by Olivia Parr Rud

CIO Best Practices: Enabling Strategic Value with Information Technology, Second Edition by Joe Stenzel

Connecting Organizational Silos: Taking Knowledge Flow Management to the Next Level with Social Media by Frank Leistner

Credit Risk Assessment: The New Lending System for Borrowers, Lenders, and Investors by Clark Abrahams and Mingyuan Zhang

Credit Risk Scorecards: Developing and Implementing Intelligent Credit Scoring by Naeem Siddiqi

The Data Asset: How Smart Companies Govern Their Data for Business Success by Tony Fisher

Delivering Business Analytics: Practical Guidelines for Best Practice by Evan Stubbs

Demand-Driven Forecasting: A Structured Approach to Forecasting, Second Edition by Charles Chase

Demand-Driven Inventory Optimization and Replenishment: Creating a More Efficient Supply Chain by Robert A. Davis

The Executive's Guide to Enterprise Social Media Strategy: How Social Networks Are Radically Transforming Your Business by David Thomas and Mike Barlow

Economic and Business Forecasting: Analyzing and Interpreting Econometric Results by John Silvia, Azhar Iqbal, Kaylyn Swankoski, Sarah Watt, and Sam Bullard

Executive's Guide to Solvency II by David Buckham, Jason Wahl, and Stuart Rose

Fair Lending Compliance: Intelligence and Implications for Credit Risk Management by Clark R. Abrahams and Mingyuan Zhang

Foreign Currency Financial Reporting from Euros to Yen to Yuan: A Guide to Fundamental Concepts and Practical Applications by Robert Rowan

Health Analytics: Gaining the Insights to Transform Health Care by Jason Burke

Heuristics in Analytics: A Practical Perspective of What Influences Our Analytical World by Carlos Andre Reis Pinheiro and Fiona McNeill

Human Capital Analytics: How to Harness the Potential of Your Organization's Greatest Asset by Gene Pease, Boyce Byerly, and Jac Fitz-enz

Implement, Improve and Expand Your Statewide Longitudinal Data System: Creating a Culture of Data in Education by Jamie McQuiggan and Armistead Sapp

Information Revolution: Using the Information Evolution Model to Grow Your Business by Jim Davis, Gloria J. Miller, and Allan Russell

Killer Analytics: Top 20 Metrics Missing from Your Balance Sheet by Mark Brown

Manufacturing Best Practices: Optimizing Productivity and Product Quality by Bobby Hull

Marketing Automation: Practical Steps to More Effective Direct Marketing by Jeff LeSueur

Mastering Organizational Knowledge Flow: How to Make Knowledge Sharing Work by Frank Leistner

The New Know: Innovation Powered by Analytics by Thornton May

Performance Management: Integrating Strategy Execution, Methodologies, Risk, and Analytics by Gary Cokins

For more information on any of the above titles, please visit www.wiley.com.

Harness Oil and Gas Big Data with Analytics

Optimize Exploration and Production
with Data-Driven Models

Keith R. Holdaway

WILEY

Published by John Wiley & Sons, Inc., Hoboken, New Jersey.
Published simultaneously in Canada.

For general information on our other products and services or for technical support, please contact our Customer Care Department within the United States at (800) 762-2974, outside the United States at (317) 572-3993 or fax (317) 572-4002.

Wiley publishes in a variety of print and electronic formats and by print-on-demand. Some material included with standard print versions of this book may not be included in e-books or in print-on-demand. If this book refers to media such as a CD or DVD that is not included in the version you purchased, you may download this material at http://booksupport.wiley.com. For more information about Wiley products, visit www.wiley.com.

Library of Congress Cataloging-in-Publication Data:

ISBN 9781118779316 (Hardcover)
ISBN 9781118910955 (ePDF)
ISBN 9781118910894 (ePub)

Printed in the United States of America

10 9 8 7 6 5 4 3 2 1

I dedicate this book to my patient and loving family,
Patricia, my wife, and my children, Elyse and Ian.

Contents

Preface

My motivation for writing this book comes from the cumulative issues I have witnessed over the past seven years that are now prevalent in the upstream oil and gas industry. The three most prominent issues are data management, quantifying uncertainty in the subsurface, and risk assessment around field engineering strategies. With the advent of the tsunami of data across the disparate engineering silos, it is evident that data-driven models offer incredible insight, turning raw Big Data into actionable knowledge. I see geoscientists piecemeal adopting analytical methodologies that incorporate soft computing techniques as they come to the inevitable conclusion that traditional deterministic and interpretive studies are no longer viable as monolithic approaches to garnering maximum value from Big Data across the Exploration and Production value chain.

No longer is the stochastic and nondeterministic perspective a professional hobby as the array of soft computing techniques gain credibility with the critical onset of technical papers detailing the use of data-driven and predictive models. The Society of Petroleum Engineers has witnessed an incredible release of papers at conferences globally that provide beneficial evidence of the application of neural networks, fuzzy logic, and genetic algorithms to the disciplines of reservoir modeling and simulation. As the old school retire from the petroleum industry and the new generation of geoscientists graduate with an advanced appreciation of statistics and soft computing methodologies, we shall evolve even greater application across the upstream. The age of the Digital Oilfield littered with intelligent wells generates a plethora of data that when mined surface hidden patterns to enhance the conventional studies. Marrying first principles with data-driven modeling is becoming more popular among earth scientists and engineers.

This book arrives at a very opportune time for the oil and gas industry as we face a data explosion. We have seen an increase in pre-stack analysis of 3D seismic data coupled with the derivation of multiple seismic attributes for reservoir characterization. With the advent of permanently in-place sensors on the ocean bed and in the multiple wells drilled in unconventional reservoirs across shale plays, coal seam gas, steam-assisted gravity drainage, and deep offshore assets, we are watching a proliferation of data-intensive activity.

Soft computing concepts incorporate heuristic information. What does that mean? We can adopt hybrid analytical workflows to address some of the most challenging upstream problems. Couple expert knowledge that is readily retiring from the petroleum industry with data-driven models that explore and predict events resulting in negative impacts on CAPEX and OPEX. Retain the many years of experience by developing a collaborative analytical center of excellence that incorporates soft skills and expertise with the most important asset in any oil and gas operation: data.

I would like to take this opportunity to thank all the contributors and reviewers of the manuscript, especially Horia Orenstein for his diligent expertise in predictive analytics and Moray Laing for his excellent feedback, expertise in drilling, and contribution with the pictures that illustrate many case studies. Stacey Hamilton of SAS Institute has been an encouraging and patient editor, without whom this book would never have been completed. I would like to acknowledge my colleagues in the industry who have given constructive feedback, especially Mike Pittman of Saudi Aramco, Mohammad Kurdi, David Dozoul and Sebastian Maurice of SAS Institute, ensuring the relevance and applicability of the contents.

1

Fundamentals of Soft Computing

There are more things in heaven and earth, Horatio,
than are dreamt of in your philosophy.

William Shakespeare: *Hamlet*

The oil and gas industry has witnessed a compelling argument over the
past decade to adopt soft computing techniques as upstream problems
become too complex to entrust siloed disciplines with deterministic and
interpretation analysis methods. We find ourselves in the thick of a data avalanche across the exploration and production value chain that is transforming
data-driven models from a professional curiosity into an industry imperative.
At the core of the multidisciplinary analytical methodologies are data-mining
techniques that provide descriptive and predictive models to complement conventional engineering analysis steeped in first principles. Advances in data
aggregation, integration, quantification of uncertainties, and soft computing
methods are enabling supplementary perspectives on the disparate upstream
data to create more accurate reservoir models in a timelier manner. *Soft computing* is amenable, efficient, and robust as well as being less resource intensive than traditional interpretation based on mathematics, physics, and the
experience of experts. We shall explore the multifaceted benefits garnered
from the application of the rich array of soft computing techniques in the
petroleum industry.

CURRENT LANDSCAPE IN UPSTREAM DATA ANALYSIS

What is *human-level artificial intelligence*? Precise definitions are important, but many experts reasonably respond to this question by stating that such phrases have yet to be exactly defined. Bertrand Russell remarked:

> I do not pretend to start with precise questions. I do not think you can start with anything precise. You have to achieve such precision as you can, as you go along.[1]

The assertion of knowledge garnered from raw data, which includes imparting precise definitions, invariably results from exhaustive research in a particular field such as the upstream oil and gas (O&G) disciplines. We are seeing four major trends impacting the *exploration and production* (E&P) value chain: Big Data, the cloud, social media, and mobile devices; and these drivers are steering geoscientists at varying rates toward the implementation of soft computing techniques.

The visualization of Big Data across the E&P value chain necessitates the usage of Tukey's suite of exploratory data analysis charts, maps, and graphs[2] to surface hidden patterns and relationships in a multivariate and complex upstream set of systems. We shall detail these visual techniques in Chapters 3, 4, and 9 as they are critical in the data-driven methodologies implemented in O&G.

Artificial neural networks (ANN), fuzzy logic (FL), and genetic algorithms (GA) are human-level artificial intelligence techniques currently being practiced in O&G reservoir management and simulation, production and drilling optimization, real-time drilling automation, and facility maintenance. Data-mining methodologies that underpin data-driven models are ubiquitous in many industries, and over the past few years the entrenched and anachronistic attitudes of upstream engineers in O&G are being diluted by the extant business pressures to explore and produce more hydrocarbons to address the increasing global demand for energy.

Digital oilfields of the future (DOFFs) and intelligent wells with multiple sensors and gauges are generating at high velocity a plethora of disparate data defining a complex, heterogeneous landscape such as a reservoir-well-facility integrated system. These high-dimensionality data are supplemented by unstructured data originating from social media activity, and with mobile devices proving to be valuable in field operations and cloud computing delivering heightened flexibility and increased performance in networking and data management, we are ideally positioned to marry soft computing methodologies to the traditional deterministic and interpretive approaches.

Big Data: Definition

The intention throughout the following pages is to address the challenges inherent in the analysis of Big Data across the E&P value chain. By definition,

Big Data is an expression coined to represent an aggregation of datasets that are voluminous, complex, disparate, and/or collated at very high frequencies, resulting in substantive analytical difficulties that cannot be addressed by traditional data processing applications and tools. There are obvious limitations working with Big Data in a relational database management system (DBMS), implementing desktop statistics and visualization software. The term *Big Data* is relative, depending on an organization's extant architecture and software capabilities; invariably the definition is a moving target as terabytes evolve into petabytes and inexorably into exabytes. *Business intelligence* (BI) adopts descriptive statistics to tackle data to uncover trends and initiate fundamental measurements; whereas Big Data tend to find recreation in the playgrounds of inductive statistics and concepts from nonlinear system identification. This enables E&P professionals to manage Big Data, identify correlations, surface hidden relationships and dependencies, and apply advanced analytical data-driven workflows to predict behaviors in a complex, heterogeneous, and multivariate system such as a reservoir. Chapter 2 discusses Big Data in more detail and the case studies throughout the book will strive to define methodologies to harness Big Data by way of a suite of analytical workflows. The intent is to highlight the benefits of marrying data-driven models and first principles in E&P.

First Principles

What are *first principles*? The answer depends on your perspective as an inquisitive bystander. In the field of mathematics, first principles reference axioms or postulates, whereas in philosophy, a first principle is a self-evident proposition or assumption that cannot be derived from any other proposition or assumption. A first principle is thus one that cannot be deduced from any other. The classic example is that of Euclid's geometry that demonstrates that the many propositions therein can be deduced from a set of definitions, postulates, and common notions: All three types constitute first principles. These foundations are often coined as *a priori* truths. More appropriate to the core message in this book, first principles underpin the theoretical work that stems directly from established science without making assumptions. Geoscientists have invariably implemented analytical and numerical techniques to derive a solution to a problem, both of which have been compromised through approximation.

We have eased through history starting thousands of years ago when empirical models embraced our thinking to only a few centuries ago when the landscape was populated by theoretical intelligentsia espousing models based on generalizations. Such luminaries as Sir Isaac Newton, Johannes Kepler, and James Clerk Maxwell made enormous contributions to our understanding of Mother Nature's secrets and by extension enabled the geoscientific community to grasp fundamentals that underpin physics and mathematics. These fundamentals reflect the heterogeneous complexity inherent in hydrocarbon reservoirs. Only a few decades have passed since we strolled through the computational branch of science that witnessed the simulation of complex systems, edging toward the current landscape sculpted by a data-intensive exploratory analysis, building models that are data driven. *Let the data relate the story.* Production data, for example, echo the movement of fluids as they eke their way inexorably through reservoir rocks via interconnected pores to be pushed under natural or subsequently fabricated pressures to the producing wells. There is no argument that these production data are encyclopedia housing knowledge of the reservoirs' characterization, even if their usefulness is directly related to localized areas adjacent to wells. Thus, let us surface the subtle hidden trends and relationships that correlate a well's performance with a suite of rock properties and influential operational parameters in a complex multivariate system. Geomechanical fingerprints washed in first principles have touched the porous rocks of our reservoirs, ushering the hydrocarbons toward their manmade conduits. Let us not divorce first principles, but rather marry the interpretative and deterministic approach underscored by our scientific teachings with a nondeterministic or stochastic methodology enhanced by raw data flourishing into knowledge via data-driven models.

Data-Driven Models

> *The new model is for the data to be captured by instruments or to be generated by simulations before being processed by software and for the resulting information and knowledge to be stored in computers.*[3]
>
> Jim Gray

Turning a plethora of raw upstream data from disparate engineering disciplines into useful information is a ubiquitous challenge for O&G companies as the relationships and answers that identify key opportunities often lie buried in mountains of data collated at various scales in depth as well as in a temporal fashion, both stationary and non-stationary by nature.

O&G reservoir models can be characterized as physical, mathematical, and empirical. Recent developments in computational intelligence, in the area of machine learning in particular, have greatly expanded the capabilities of empirical modeling. The discipline that encompasses these new approaches is called *data-driven modeling* (DDM) and is based on analyzing the data within a system. One of the focal points inherent in DDM is to discover connections between the system state variables (input and output) without explicit knowledge of the physical behavior of the system. This approach pushes the boundaries beyond conventional empirical modeling to accommodate contributions from superimposed spheres of study:[4]

- *Artificial intelligence* (AI), which is the overreaching contemplation of how human intelligence can be incorporated into computers.
- *Computational intelligence* (CI), which embraces the family of neural networks, fuzzy systems, and evolutionary computing in addition to other fields within AI and machine learning.
- *Soft computing* (SC), which is close to CI, but with special emphasis on fuzzy rules-based systems posited from data.
- *Machine learning* (ML), which originated as a subcomponent of AI, concentrates on the theoretical foundations used by CI and SC.
- *Data mining* (DM) and *knowledge discovery in databases* (KDD) are aimed often at very large databases. DM is seen as a part of a wider KDD. Methods used are mainly from statistics and ML. Unfortunately, the O&G industry is moving toward adoption of DM at a speed appreciated by Alfred Wegener as the tsunami of disparate, real-time data flood the upstream E&P value chain.

Data-driven modeling is therefore focused on CI and ML methods that can be implemented to construct models for supplementing or replacing models based on first principles. A machine-learning algorithm such as a neural network is used to determine the relationship between a system's inputs and outputs employing a training dataset that is quintessentially reflective of the complete behavior inherent in the system.

Let us introduce some of the techniques implemented in a data-driven approach.

Soft Computing Techniques

We shall enumerate some of the most prevalent and important algorithms implemented across the E&P value chain from a data-driven modeling perspective. Three of the most commonplace techniques are artificial neural networks, fuzzy rules-based systems, and genetic algorithms. All these approaches are referenced in subsequent chapters as we illustrate applicability through case studies across global O&G assets.

Artificial Neural Networks

ANNs show great potential for generating accurate analysis and predictions from historical E&P datasets. Neural networks should be used in cases where mathematical modeling is not a practical option. This may be due to the fact that all the parameters involved in a particular process are not known and/or the interrelationship of the parameters is too complicated for mathematical modeling of the system. In such cases a neural network can be constructed to observe the system's behavior striving to replicate its functionality and behavior.

ANNs (Figure 1.1) are an adaptive, parallel information processing system that can develop associations, transformations, or mappings between objects or data. They are an efficient and popular technique for solving regression and classification issues in the upstream O&G industry. The basic elements of a neural network are the neurons and their connection strengths or weights. In a supervised learning scenario a set of known input–output data patterns are implemented to train the network. The learning algorithm takes an initial model with some prior connection weights (random numbers) and applies an updating algorithm to produce final weights via an iterative process. ANNs can be used to build a representative model of well performance in a particular reservoir under study. The data are used as input–output pairs to train the neural network. Well information, reservoir quality data, and stimulation-related data are examples of input to an ANN with production rates describing the various output bins. Since the first principles required to model such a complex process using the conventional mathematical techniques are tenuous at best, neural networks can provide explicit insight into the complexities witnessed between formation interactions with a stimulation process such as a hydraulic fracture strategy or an acidizing plan. Once a reasonably accurate and representative model of the stimulation processes has been completed for the formation under study, more analysis can be performed. These analyses may include the use of the model in order to answer many *what-if* questions that may arise. Furthermore, the model can be used to identify the best and worst completion and stimulation practices in the field.

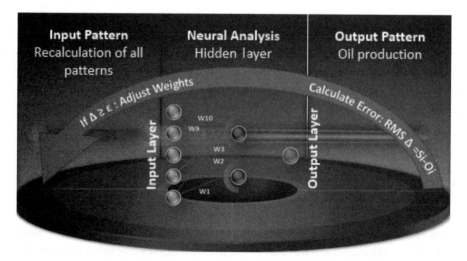

Figure 1.1 Artificial Neural Network

Genetic Algorithms

Darwin's theory of survival of the fittest,[5] coupled with the *selectionism* of Weismann[6] and the genetics of Mendel, have formed the universally accepted set of arguments known as the evolution theory.

Evolutionary computing represents mechanisms of evolution as key elements in algorithmic design and implementation. One of the main types of evolutionary computing is the *genetic algorithm* (GA) that is an efficient global optimization method for solving ill-behaved, nonlinear, discontinuous, and multi-criteria problems.

It is possible to resolve a multitude of problems across the spectrum of life by adopting a searching algorithm or methodology. We live in a world overcome by an almost unlimited set of permutations. We need to find the best time to schedule meetings, the best mix of chemicals, the best way to design a hydraulic fracture treatment strategy, or the best stocks to pick. The most common way we solve simple problems is the *trial-and-error* method. The size of the search space grows exponentially as the number of associated parameters (variables) increases. This makes finding the best combination of parameters too costly and sometimes impossible. Historically, engineers would address such issues by making smart and intuitive estimates as to the values of the parameters.

We could apply an ANN to provide output bins (e.g., 3, 6, 9, and 12 months cumulative production) based on the input to the network, namely, stimulation design, well information, and reservoir quality for each particular well. Obviously, only stimulation design parameters are under engineering control. Well information and reservoir quality are part of Mother Nature's domain. It is essential to implement adjuvant data quality workflows and a suite of *exploratory data analysis* (EDA) techniques to surface hidden patterns and trends. We then implement the genetic algorithm as a potential arbitrator to assess all the possible combinations of those stimulation parameters to identify the most optimum combination. Such a combinatory set of stimulation parameters is devised as being for any particular well (based on the well information and reservoir quality) that provides the highest output (3, 6, 9, and 12 months' cumulative production). The difference between these cumulative values from the optimum stimulation treatment and the actual cumulative values produced by the well is interpreted as the production potential that may be recovered by (re)stimulation of that well.

Fuzzy Rules-Based Systems

How does the word *fuzzy* resonate with you? Most people assign a negative connotation to its meaning. The term *fuzzy logic* in Western culture seems both to realign thought as an obtuse and confused process as well as to imply a mental state of early morning mist. On the other hand, Eastern culture promotes the concept of coexistence of contradictions as it appears in the Yin-Yang symbol, as observed by Mohaghegh.[7]

Human thought, logic, and decision-making processes are not doused in Boolean purity. We tend to use vague and imprecise words to explain our thoughts or communicate with one another. There is an apparent conflict between the imprecise and vague process of human reasoning, thinking, and decision making and the crisp, scientific reasoning of Boolean computer logic. This conflict has escalated computer usage to assist engineers in the decision-making process, which has inexorably led to the inadequacy experienced by traditional artificial intelligence or conventional rules-based systems, also known as *expert systems*.

Uncertainty as represented by fuzzy set theory is invariably due to either the random nature of events or to the imprecision and ambiguity of information we analyze to solve the problem. The outcome of an event in a random process is strictly the result of chance. Probability theory is the ideal tool to adopt when the uncertainty is a product of the randomness of events. Statistical or random uncertainty can be ascertained by acute observations and measurements. For example, once a coin is tossed, no more random or statistical uncertainty remains.

When dealing with complex systems such as hydrocarbon reservoirs we find that most uncertainties are the result of a lack of information. The kind of uncertainty that is the outcome of the complexity of the system arises from our ineptitude to perform satisfactory measurements, from imprecision, from a lack of expertise, or from fuzziness inherent in natural language. Fuzzy set theory is a plausible and effective means to model the type of uncertainty associated with imprecision.

Exploratory wells located invariably by a set of deterministic seismic interpretations are drilled into reservoirs under uncertainty that is invariably poorly quantified, the geologic models yawning to be optimized by a mindset that is educated in a data-driven methodology.

Fuzzy logic was first introduced by Zadeh,[8] and unlike the conventional binary or Boolean logic, which is based on crisp sets of "true" and "false," fuzzy logic allows the object to belong to both "true" and "false" sets with varying degrees of membership, ranging from 0 to 1. In reservoir geology, natural language has been playing a very crucial role for some time, and has thus provided a modeling methodology for complex and ill-defined systems. To continue the stimulation optimization workflow broached under "artificial neural networks," we could incorporate a fuzzy decision support system. This fuzzy expert system uses the information provided by the neural networks and genetic algorithms. The expert system then augments those findings with information that can be gathered from the expert engineers who have worked on that particular field for many years in order to select the best (re)stimulation candidates. Keep in mind that the information provided to the fuzzy expert system may be different from formation to formation and from company to company. This part of the methodology provides the means to capture and maintain and use some valuable expertise that will remain in the company even if engineers are transferred to other sections of the company where their expertise is no longer readily available. The fuzzy expert system is capable of incorporating natural language to process information. This capability provides maximum efficiency in using the imprecise information in less certain situations. A typical rule in the fuzzy expert system that will help engineers in ranking the (re)stimulation candidates can be expressed as follows:

> **IF** the well shows a high potential for an increase 3-, 6-, 9-, and/or 12-month cumulative production
>
> **AND** has a plausible but moderate pressure
>
> **AND** has a low acidizing volume
>
> **THEN** this well is a good candidate for (re)stimulation.

A *truth-value* is associated with every rule in the fuzzy expert system developed for this methodology. The process of making decisions from fuzzy subsets using the parameters and relative functional truth-values as rules provides the means of using approximate reasoning. This process is known to be one of the most robust methods in developing high-end expert systems in many industries. Thus it is feasible to incorporate fuzzy linguistic rules, risk analysis, and decision support in an imprecise and uncertain environment.

EVOLUTION FROM PLATO TO ARISTOTLE

Aristotle's sharp logic underpins contemporary science. The Aristotelian school of thought makes observations based on a bivalent perspective, such as black and white, yes and no, and 0 and 1. The nineteenth century mathematician George Cantor instituted the development of the set theory based on Aristotle's bivalent logic and thus rendered this logic amenable to modern science.[9] Probability theory subsequently effected the bivalent logic plausible and workable. The German's theory defines *sets* as a collection of definite and distinguishable objects.

The physical sciences throughout medieval Europe were profoundly shaped by Aristotle's views, extending their influence into the Renaissance, to be eventually revised by Newtonian physics. Like his teacher Plato, Aristotle's philosophy aims at the universal. Aristotle, however, finds the universal in particular things, which he calls the *essence of things*, while Plato finds that the universal exists apart from particular things, and is related to them as their prototype or exemplar. For Aristotle, therefore, philosophic method implies the ascent from the study of particular phenomena to the knowledge of essences, while for Plato philosophic method means the descent from knowledge of universal forms (or ideas) to a contemplation of particular imitations of these. In a certain sense, Aristotle's method is both inductive and deductive, while Plato's is essentially deductive from *a priori* principles.

If you study carefully the center of Raphael's fresco entitled *The School of Athens* in the Apostolic Palace in the Vatican, you will note Plato, to the left, and Aristotle are the two undisputed subjects of attention. Popular interpretation suggests that their gestures along different dimensions are indicative of their respective philosophies. Plato points vertically, echoing his Theory of Forms, while Aristotle extends his arm along the horizontal plane, representing his belief in knowledge through empirical observation and experience.

Science is overly burdened by Aristotle's laws of logic that is deeply rooted in the fecund Grecian landscape diligently cultivated by scientists and philosophers of the ancient world. His laws are firmly planted on the fundamental ground of "X or not-X"; something *is* or it *is not*. Conventional Boolean logic influences our thought processes as we classify things or make judgments about things, thus losing the fine details or plethora of possibilities that range between the empirical extremes of 0 and 1 or true and false.

DESCRIPTIVE AND PREDICTIVE MODELS

There are two distinct branches of data mining, *predictive* and *descriptive/exploratory* (Figure 1.2), that can turn raw data into actionable knowledge. Sometimes you hear these two categories called *directed* (predictive) and *undirected* (descriptive). Predictive models use known results to develop (or train or estimate) a model that can be used to predict values for different data. Descriptive models describe patterns in existing data that may be found in new data. With descriptive models, there is no target variable for which you are striving to predict the value. Most of the big payoff has been in predictive modeling when the models are operationalized in a real-world setting.

Descriptive modeling involves clustering or segmentation that is essentially the lumping together of similar things such as wells, rock mechanics, or hydraulic fracture strategies. An association is a relationship between two measured quantities that exhibits statistical dependency.

Descriptive modeling techniques cover two major areas:

1. Clustering

2. Associations and sequences

The objective of clustering or segmenting your data is to place objects into groups or clusters suggested by the data such that objects in a given cluster tend to be similar to each other in some sense and objects in different clusters

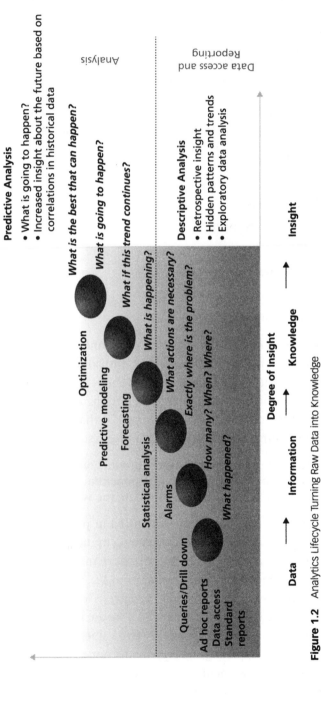

Figure 1.2 Analytics Lifecycle Turning Raw Data into Knowledge

tend to be dissimilar. The term *association* intimates an expansive relationship as opposed to the more limited *correlation* that refers to a linear relationship between two quantities. Thus in quantifying the values of parameters in O&G the term *association* is invariably adopted to underline the non-causality in an apparent relationship.

Predictive modeling appears in two guises:

1. Classification models that predict class membership
2. Regression models that predict a number

There are four main predictive modeling techniques detailed in this book as important upstream O&G data-driven analytic methodologies:

1. Decision trees
2. Regression
   a. Linear regression
   b. Logistic regression
3. Neural networks
   a. Artificial neural networks
   b. Self-organizing maps (SOMs)
4. K-means clustering

Decision trees are prevalent owing to their inherent ease of interpretation. Also they handle missing values very well, providing a succinct and effective interpretation of data riddled with missing values.

An advantage of the decision tree algorithm over other modeling techniques, such as the neural network approach, is that it produces a model that may represent interpretable English rules or logic statements. For example:

> If monthly oil production-to-water production ratio is less than 28 percent and oil production rate is exponential in decline and OPEX is greater than $100,000, then stimulate the well.

With regression analysis we are interested in predicting a number, called the *response* or *Y* variable. When you are doing multiple linear regressions, you are still predicting one number (*Y*), but you have multiple independent or predictor variables trying to explain the change in *Y*.

In logistic regression our response variable is categorical, meaning it can assume only a limited number of values. So if we are talking about binary logistic regression, our response variable has only two values, such as 0 or 1, on or off.

In the case of multiple logistic regressions our response variable can have many levels, such as low, medium, and high or 1, 2, and 3.

Artificial neural networks were originally developed by researchers who were trying to mimic the neurophysiology of the human brain. By combining many simple computing elements (neurons or units) into a highly interconnected system, these researchers hoped to produce complex phenomena such as intelligence. Neural networks are very sophisticated modeling techniques capable of modeling extremely complex functions.

The main reasons they are popular are because they are both very powerful and easy to use. The power comes in their ability to handle nonlinear relationships in data, which is increasingly more common as we collect more and more data and try to use that data for predictive modeling.

Neural networks are being implemented to address a wide scope of O&G upstream problems where engineers strive to resolve issues of prediction, classification or control.

Common applications of neural networks across the E&P value chain include mapping seismic attributes to reservoir properties, computing surface seismic statics, and determining an optimized hydraulic fracture treatment strategy in exploiting the unconventional reservoirs.

THE SEMMA PROCESS

SEMMA[10] defines *data mining* as the process of **S**ampling, **E**xploring, **M**odifying, **M**odeling, and **A**ssessing inordinate amounts of data to surface hidden patterns and relationships in a multivariate system. The data-mining process is applicable across a variety of industries and provides methodologies for such diverse business problems in the O&G vertical as maximizing well location, optimizing production, ascertaining maximum recovery factor, identifying an optimum hydraulic fracture strategy in unconventional reservoirs, field segmentation, risk analysis, pump failure prediction, and well portfolio analysis.

Let us detail the SEMMA data-mining process:

- **S**ample the data by extracting and preparing a sample of data for model building using one or more data tables. Sampling includes operations that define or subset rows of data. The samples should be large enough to efficiently contain the significant information. It is optimum to include the complete and comprehensive dataset for the Explore step owing to hidden patterns and trends only discovered when all the data are analyzed. Software constraints may preclude such an ideal.

- **E**xplore the data by searching for anticipated relationships, unanticipated trends, and anomalies in order to gain understanding and insightful ideas that insinuate hypotheses worth modeling.

- **M**odify the data by creating, selecting, and transforming the variables to focus the model selection process on the most valuable attributes. This focuses the model selection process on those variables displaying significant attributes vis-à-vis the objective function or target variable(s).

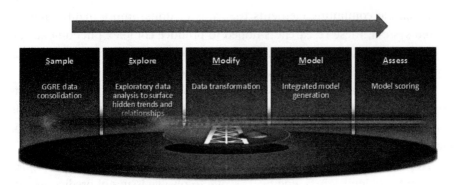

Figure 1.3 SEMMA Process for Data-Mining Workflows

- **M**odel the data by using the analytical techniques to search for a combination of the data that reliably predicts a desired outcome.

- **A**ssess the data by evaluating the usefulness and reliability of the findings from the data-mining process. Compare different models and statistically differentiate and grade those models to ascertain optimum range of probabilistic results, delivered under uncertainty.

It is important to remember that SEMMA (Figure 1.3) is a process, not a methodology. As such, SEMMA is fully compatible with various data-mining methodologies in the IT industry.

HIGH-PERFORMANCE ANALYTICS

High-performance analytics enable O&G companies to be more nimble and confident in their decision-making cycles as they engage in new ventures, generating new value from a tsunami of data. The most challenging fields can be quickly assessed, generating high-impact insights to transform their operations.

With high-performance analytics you can achieve the following:

- Attain timely insights requisite to making decisions in a diminishing window of opportunity.

- Surface insights that once took weeks or months in just hours or days to accelerate innovation.

- Uncover precise answers for complex problems.

- Identify unrecognized opportunities for growth.

- Achieve much improved performance.

In the age of Big Data, O&G companies depend on increasingly sophisticated analysis of the exponential growth in volumes and varieties of data collected at even more frequent rates across the siloed geoscientific community. The velocities of data, coming from intelligent wells equipped with downhole sensors, are adding enormous pressures on upstream thinking. How can we extract maximum knowledge and cultivate optimized information from raw data? How can we impose quality control workflows that filter noise and outliers, impute missing values, and normalize and transform data values? We must strive to yield a robust collection of disparate data in readiness for both the deterministic and stochastic workflows. It is important to understand that the teachings underpinning the philosophy of this book are not deflecting the traditional interpretations so ingrained by our geophysics, geology, petroleum, and reservoir engineering institutions, but simply emphasizing an important supplement based on the data yielding their hidden secrets. A hybrid approach is optimum, marrying both schools of thought.

In-Memory Analytics

In-memory analytics enable analytical workflows on Big Data to solve complex upstream E&P problems in an unfettered manner. You can also explore solutions to problems you have never even considered due to computing environment constraints.

In-memory analytics scale to your business needs, providing concurrent, in-memory, and multiuse access to data, no matter how big or small. The software is optimized for distributed, multi-threaded architectures and scalable processing, so requests to run new scenarios or complex analytical computations are handled blazingly fast.

It behooves O&G upstream geoscientists to implement in-memory analytics technologies to perform analyses that range from data exploration, visualization, and descriptive statistics to model building with advanced algorithms.

When it comes to the most common descriptive statistics calculations, SQL-based solutions have a number of limitations, including column limits, storage constraints, and limited data-type support. In addition, the iterative nature of EDA and data-mining operations, such as variable selection, dimension reduction, visualization, complex analytic data transformations, and model training, require multiple concurrent passes through the data: operations for which SQL and relational technology are not well-suited.[11]

As an example of the power behind an in-memory analytical architecture, look at the simple heat map in Figure 1.4. Invariably you would send data back to the front-end reporting tools to serially perform complex calculations. But when huge amounts of computations are needed to analyze and produce information, bottlenecks can occur. Implementing in-memory technology performs the calculations on the server, on the fly and in parallel. As a result, computations are very fast because you are not moving large amounts of data elsewhere for processing. Processing can take place on the

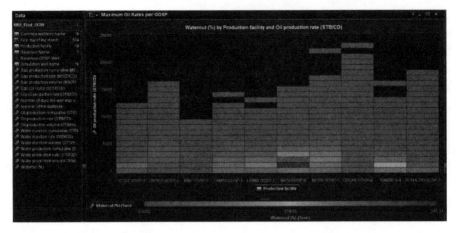

Figure 1.4   Heat Map Highlighting Gas–Oil Separation Plants (GOSPs) and Associated Water Cut

analytic server with the thin results sent back to the client for presentation, rather than for computation.

In-Database Analytics

In-database analytics can execute within database engines using native database code. Traditional processing may include copying data to a secondary location, and the data are then processed using E&P upstream products. Benefits of in-database processing include reduced data movement, faster run-times, and the ability to leverage existing data warehousing investments.[12]

In-database analytics invariably cover two key areas:

1. Develop new products that provide access to and process extant functions within the database.

2. Enhance existing products to leverage database functionality.

In-database processing is a flexible, efficient way to leverage increasing amounts of data by integrating select upstream technology into databases or data warehouses. It utilizes the *massively parallel processing* (MPP) architecture of the database or data warehouse for scalability and better performance. Moving relevant data management, analytics, and reporting tasks to where the data reside is beneficial in terms of speed, reducing unnecessary data movement and promoting better data governance. For upstream decision makers, this means faster access to analytical results and more agile and accurate decisions.

Oil companies operate in a competitive and changing global economy, and every problem has an opportunity attached. Most organizations struggle to manage and glean insights from data and utilize analytic results to improve performance. They often find analytic model development, deployment, and management to be a time-consuming, labor-intensive process, especially when combined with excessive data movement and redundancy.

In-database processing is ideal for two key scenarios. The first scenario is for *Big Data enterprise analytics*, where the sheer volume of the data involved makes it impractical to repetitively copy them over the network. The second scenario is in complex, organizationally diverse environments, where varying business communities need to share common data sources, driving the need for a centralized enterprise data warehouse. Oil companies should implement corporate data governance policies to promote one single version of the truth, minimizing data inconsistency and data redundancy, and aligning data access needs to common business usage.

Grid Computing

As data integration, analytics, and reporting capabilities grow in strategic importance and encompass increasing numbers of users and larger quantities of data, the ability to cost-effectively scale a business analytics system to gain operational flexibility, improve performance, and meet peak demands using grid computing becomes a competitive advantage.

Grid computing enables O&G companies to create a managed, shared environment to process large volumes of data and analytic programs more efficiently. It provides critical capabilities that are necessary for today's business analytics environments, including workload balancing, job prioritization, high availability and built-in failover, parallel processing and resource assignment, and monitoring.

A grid manager provides a central point for administering policies, programs, queues, and job prioritization to achieve business goals across multiple types of users and applications under a given set of constraints. IT can gain flexibility and meet service levels by easily reassigning computing resources to meet peak workloads or changing business demands.

The presence of multiple servers in a grid environment enables jobs to run on the best available resource, and if a server fails, its jobs can be seamlessly transitioned to another server; providing a highly available business analytics environment. High availability also enables the IT staff to perform maintenance on specific servers without interrupting analytics jobs, as well as introduce additional computing resources without disruption to the business.

Grid computing provides critical capabilities that are necessary for O&G business analytics environments, including:

- Workload management and job prioritization
- High availability
- Parallelization of business analytics jobs for improved performance

Workload management allows users to share resources in order to most effectively balance workload and meet service levels across the enterprise. Business analytics jobs benefit by having workflows execute on the most appropriate resource and multiuser workload is balanced within the grid to enable the optimum usage of resources. Grid computing provides the capability to prioritize jobs, which enables critical jobs to start immediately instead of waiting in a queue. Low-priority jobs can be temporarily suspended to enable critical jobs to be immediately processed.

Grid computing provides standardized workload management to optimally process multiple applications and workloads to maximize overall throughput. In addition, grid computing can parse large analytics jobs into smaller tasks that can be run, in parallel, on smaller, more cost-effective servers with equal or better performance than seen on large symmetric multiprocessor (SMP) systems. Parallelization of upstream analytics jobs enables O&G companies to improve processing speeds by orders of magnitude and deliver exceptional improvements in analyst productivity.

Reservoir simulation programs are best suited for parallel processing owing to potentially large datasets and long run-times.

By combining the power of workload management, job prioritization, and high availability, grid computing accelerates performance and provides enterprises with more control and utilization of their business analytics environment.

THREE TENETS OF UPSTREAM DATA

The three tenets of upstream data are:

1. Data management
2. Quantification of uncertainty
3. Risk assessment

These are key issues in petroleum exploration and development. Oil companies are being forced to explore in more geologically complex and remote areas to exploit deeper or unconventional hydrocarbon deposits. As the problems become too complex in areas of intrinsically poor data quality, and the cost associated with poor predictions (dry holes) increases, the need for proper integration of disciplines, data fusion, risk reduction, and uncertainty management becomes very important. Soft computing methods offer an excellent opportunity to address issues, such as integrating information from various sources with varying degrees of uncertainty, establishing relationships between measurements and reservoir properties, and assigning risk factors or error bars to predictions.

Data Management

We discuss in Chapter 2 the methodologies that underpin data management in the upstream. It is paramount to emphasize the corporate benefits behind automated and semi-automated workflows that enable seamless data aggregation, integration of disparate datasets from siloed engineering disciplines, and the generation of analytical data warehouses (ADWs) in preparation for advanced analytical processes.

With the advent of Big Data in the upstream we are witnessing an explosion of data from downhole sensors in intelligent wells distributed across DOFFs. It is becoming even more essential to implement a concrete enterprise data management framework to address some of the current business issues spawned by an O&G company's critical asset: data.

- Data disparity across systems
- Organizational silos with different data
- Multiple customer views
- The need to access unstructured data within your systems
- Overwhelming growth in data volumes

Quantification of Uncertainty

Do you think the quantification of uncertainty across the E&P value chain has improved over the last few years? And has this progress translated into condensed and more effective decision-making cycles? The answer to the first question is a demonstrative "Yes," but the answer to the second is a qualified "No."

What is happening? Uncertainty quantification is not an end unto itself; removing or even reducing uncertainty is not the goal. Rather the objective is to make a good decision, which in many cases requires the assessment of the relevant uncertainties. The O&G industry seems to have lost sight of this goal in its good-faith effort to provide decision makers with a richer understanding of the possible outcomes flowing from major decisions. The industry implicitly believes that making good decisions merely requires more information. To counter this, let us explore a decision-focused uncertainty quantification framework that will aid in the innovation of better decision-making tools and methodologies. We shall discuss quantification of uncertainty as a common theme threaded through several case studies describing advanced analytics and soft computing techniques.

Risk Assessment

Risk assessment enables decisions under uncertainty to post a risk analysis either through a risk ranking of hazard reduction strategies or through comparison to target risk levels and cost-benefit analysis. *Risk* can be defined as the product of the consequences of the potential hazard times the probability of occurrence of scenarios. After the risk is calculated, the results must be compared to either governmental or company criteria to determine if the risk is tolerable. This means that the risk is at a level people are generally willing to accept.

EXPLORATION AND PRODUCTION VALUE PROPOSITIONS

If you imagine the analytical algorithms or techniques as the atoms in a molecular structure (Figure 1.5) held together by covalent analytical methodologies or workflows, you get a sense of how the analogy emphasizes the seamless connectivity of soft computing and nondeterministic approaches to aggregate the functions across the E&P value chain that are invariably performed in geoscientific silos.

Oil companies are striving to attain the hidden knowledge in their key asset: data. These data are exploding in volume, velocity, and variety as real-time data from intelligent wells across DOFFs supplement historical interpretations and generated datasets. It is paramount to gain insight from these multiple datasets and enable engineers and stakeholders to make faster more accurate decisions under uncertainty. By marrying the traditional deterministic and interpretive workflows with a data-driven probabilistic set of analyses, it is possible to predict events that result in poor reservoir or well performance or facility failures. Building predictive models based on cleansed historical data and analyzing in real-time data streams, it is now feasible to optimize production. Controlling costs and ensuring efficient processes that impact positively HSE and resource usage are key benefits that fall out of analytical methodologies.

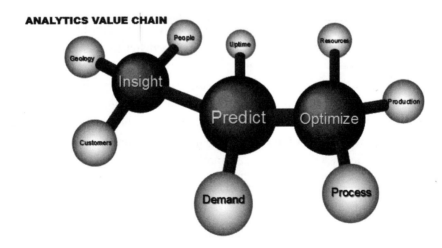

Figure 1.5 E&P Value Propositions

When we think about the lifecycle of an asset, a field or well, there is a business decision that must take place for each phase. That decision must have commercial value and that intrinsic value can be attained by enriching the interpretation from 3D immersive visualization workflows with data-driven models.

Exploration

You could be entering a new play and doing exploration to generate prospects, striving to gain insight from seismic data and to locate exploratory wells in increasingly complex reservoirs.

Appraisal

The appraisal phase of petroleum operations immediately follows successful exploratory drilling. You need to appraise the commercial quantities of hydrocarbons and mitigate risks while drilling delineation wells to determine type, shape, and size of field and strategies for optimum development.

Development

The development phase of petroleum operations occurs after exploration has proven successful, and before full-scale production. The newly discovered oil or gas field is assessed during an appraisal phase, a plan to fully and efficiently exploit it is created, and additional wells are usually drilled. During the development stage a drilling program with optimized completion strategies is enacted as additional wells are located for the production stage. Surface facilities are designed for efficient O&G exploitation. Do we have to consider water production? What cumulative liquid productions do we anticipate? These are some of the questions we need to answer as we design those surface facilities.

Production

The production phase occurs after successful exploration and development during which hydrocarbons are exploited from an oil or gas field. The production phase necessitates efficient exploitation of the hydrocarbons. We have to consider HSE and maintenance schedules. Is the production of hydrocarbons maximized for each well? How reliable are short- and long-term forecasts?

Enhancement

Lastly, enhancement maintains optimal production based on a business decision as to whether an asset is economically viable. How do we identify wells that are ideal candidates for artificial lift? When and how do we stimulate a candidate well?

A well enhancement is any operation carried out on an oil or gas well, during or at the end of its productive life, that alters the state of the well and/or well geometry, provides well diagnostics, or manages the production of the well. There are several techniques traditionally implemented to enhance well production that are categorically termed *enhanced oil recovery* (EOR) or *improved oil recovery* (IOR) artificial lift processes.

OILFIELD ANALYTICS

The oilfield analytics (OA) framework (Figure 1.6) proposes a simple and flexible structure to position data-driven methodologies across the E&P value chain. The profiles of the main actors/stakeholders are then easily associated with the following tenets.

Oilfield Data Management

A robust and consistent suite of data is of utmost importance for successful and credible advanced analytical methodologies. A stable and flexible data management platform is a prerequisite to any soft computing analysis. Once the foundation is established, multiple analytical data marts can be spawned from the master data management (MDM) environment. Over 70 to 80 percent of time is consumed by managing and organizing the upstream data, and with the evolving explosion of data, both historical and real-time, it is a growing business issue in the O&G industry to ensure data integrity. Data flows to/from service providers' popular interpretation tools and products must be integrated into any chosen architecture for a comprehensive solution. We describe O&G data management in Chapter 2.

Oilfield Exploration Analysis

Seismic data are now becoming pivotal as 3D and 4D surveys are accelerated across green- and brownfields. In addition to the customary seismic wavelet data processing, it is becoming more important to fully appreciate the seismic attributes of which there are hundreds and build a seismic data mart for advance analysis. Soft computing methodologies that map seismic attributes to reservoir properties are incredibly important as a means to define more credible and reliable reservoir characterization definitions that underpin field (re) development, supplementing and integrating well logs. The spatial integrity of large areal reservoirs requires high-resolution seismic and a more in-depth understanding of those seismic attributes that can identify both stratigraphic and structural traps. It is essential to attain accuracy, fidelity, and integrity for a seismic data cube containing pre- and/or post-stack traces having been processed with traditional workflows and algorithms such as true amplitude recovery, deconvolution, migration, filtering, and scaling as well as static and

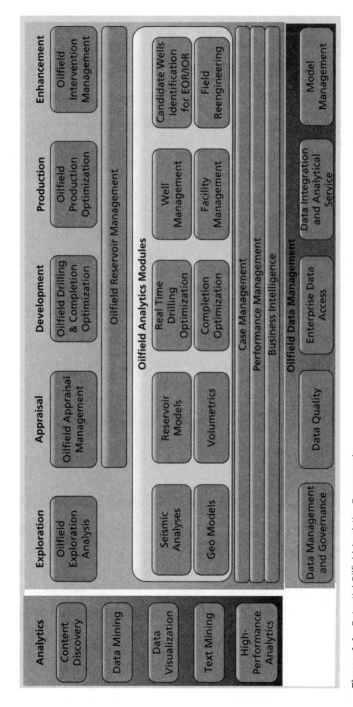

Figure 1.6 Potential Oilfield Analytics Framework

velocity analysis. This is so because these traces are the precursors to the single trace analysis and attribute-derived methodologies described in Chapter 3.

Exploratory drilling is the next step, using drilling rigs suitable for the respective environment (i.e., land, shallow water, or deep water). We cover drilling and completion optimization in Chapter 5.

Oilfield Appraisal Management

The process to characterize the reservoir(s) of a potential or mature field encapsulates the analysis of large datasets collated from well tests, production history, and core analysis results, enhanced by high-resolution mapping of seismic attributes to reservoir properties. It is imperative to capture the more subtle observations inherent in these datasets, to comprehend the structure of the data. Invariably, geostatistical methods can be implemented to accurately quantify heterogeneity, integrate scalable data, and capture the scope of uncertainty. However, between 70 and 80 percent of allotted time for any reservoir characterization study worth its investment should be concentrated on EDA. As an overture to spatial analysis, simulation, and uncertainty quantification, EDA ensures consistent data integration, data aggregation, and data management, underpinned by univariate, bivariate, and multivariate analysis. It is important to visualize and perform descriptive and inferential statistics on upstream data.[13]

If hydrocarbons have been found in sufficient quantities, the development process begins with the drilling of appraisal wells in order to better assess the size and commerciality of the discovery.

It is of paramount importance to undertake the study of uncertainties from engineering design parameters and flow characteristics of the rocks that are not accessible from seismic data. We explore reservoir characterization in Chapter 4.

Oilfield Drilling and Completion Optimization

The target of many operators, particularly in the unconventional assets, is to determine the variables that impact the key performance metric of cost per foot drilled. Other focus areas could be on spud to total depth (TD) and costs of drilling and casing horizontal wells. By using historical drilling data, it is feasible to quantitatively identify best and worst practices that impact the target. The intent is that these insights will improve future drilling operations in unconventional plays and potentially in conventional fields. Advanced analytical methodologies would ultimately develop a predictive model that would provide early warning of deviations from best practices or other events that will adversely impact drilling time or costs. Chapter 5 details some data-driven case studies and workflows to optimize drilling and completion strategies.

The vision of real-time drilling optimization is achievable. Advanced analytical techniques can be applied to gauge how real-time data are analyzed relative to past performance/events to predict downhole tool failures and the ability to do immediate root-cause activities and implement real-time solutions. Some of the benefits gained from establishing consistent drilling methodologies that compare real-time drilling data against previous trends include:

- Avoidance of potential nonproductive time (NPT), by predicting a failure, such as a positive displacement motor (PDM) failure owing to excessive vibration, or in high-pressure and -temperature environments where tool/equipment longevity can be predicted.
- Geo-steering: Able to make real-time adjustments to the well-bore trajectory to achieve maximum reservoir contact based on real-time updates to the geo-modeling data.
- Able to make real-time drilling parameter changes (i.e., weight on bit [WOB], torque on bit [TOB], and flow rate).
- Prevent blowouts: multivariate iterative process to analyze pressures such as formation, mud, and drilling fluid pressures.

Oilfield Reservoir Management

The *reservoir management* component of OA is the nursery or inception of the *digital oilfield of the future* (DOFF). The E&P arena in all O&G companies is taking nontraditional approaches to the more traditional DOFF activities of production optimization and real-time drilling. Ultimately it is a grand design to realize a DOFF and promote the development or evolution of an *analytical center of excellence* (ACE) or event solution center that is at the core of global activities in the upstream environment. Chapter 6 discusses soft computing techniques in reservoir management as well as detailing the requisite steps to establish an ACE.

At the crux of reservoir management are the technologies and methodologies underpinned by advanced analytics that are requisite for a multi-skilled and multidisciplinary control center that enables every aspect of development and production to be handled remotely. When presented with a continuous stream of reservoir, well facilities, and pipeline information, geoscientists and engineers must have automated systems to analyze the data, and help them formulate effective responses to changing surface and subsurface conditions, and the means to implement these responses in real time.

Digital oilfield workflows automate the processes for collection, verification, and validation of the right data so the right people have it at the right time in the right context. However, as investments and capabilities continue to grow, particularly with respect to smarter wells and smarter assets, O&G

companies have new opportunities to turn this information into actionable insights from these efforts. While traditional fit-for-purpose analytic tools function very well for the purpose they were originally designed for, these tools struggle to manage the sheer data growth. And smarter assets produce challenges in how to manage the tremendous growth in data volumes, both structured and unstructured. However, new technologies in real-time analytic processing, complex event processing (CEP), pattern recognition, and data mining can be applied to deliver value from the asset. Chapter 9's section on the early warning detection system studies event stream processing in an analytical workflow.

Oilfield Intervention Management

Intervention optimization remediates wells that have either formation or mechanical issues. It is important to develop a suite of advanced analytical data-mining workflows that implement soft computing techniques such as principal component analysis (PCA), multivariate analyses, clustering, self-organizing maps (SOM), and decision trees to generate descriptive and predictive models that efficiently identify candidate wells for remediation. Implementing an oilfield performance forecasting module to determine robust and reliable probabilistic forecasts for the complete portfolio of wells in an asset is an essential step. Subsequent to this step, real-time production data can be compared to the type curves determined with 90 percent confidence limits to identify wells suitable for intervention. Chapter 7 covers a suite of probabilistic methodologies for forecasting performance across a well portfolio.

Oilfield Performance Forecasting

Analytical workflows can incorporate a decline curve analysis (DCA) step implementing an oilfield production forecasting workflow to identify short- and long-term forecasts for oil, gas, and water production. Implementing mature forecasting models and first principles such as Arps[14] empirical algorithms, you can estimate accurate well performance and estimated ultimate recovery (EUR) and measure the impact, positive or negative, of well remediation techniques.

Comparing real-time production data rates and type curves against forecasted trends, you can:

- Quickly and efficiently identify those wells that require remediation.
- Segment the field via well profile clustering.
- Ratify from a field, reservoir, or well perspective whether current production falls within confidence intervals of expectation and act accordingly.

Oilfield Production Optimization

Advanced analytical methodologies are applicable to perform multivariate analysis on disparate upstream datasets, both operational and nonoperational, to evaluate and determine those variables that either inhibit or improve well performance. Predictive and descriptive analytical workflows combine to explore the data to surface hidden patterns and identify trends in a complex system. Adopting data-driven models in the following areas enables extensive and efficient insight and significant discovery of influential parameters to address issues that adversely impact production, without relying solely on first principles.

There are many production inhibitors, such as skin damage and sanding, that can be predicted by generating models inferred by EDA. Aggregating and integrating datasets from across the geoscientific silos to produce a robust dataset tailored for specific analytical studies are the foundation for all such studies. Analytical workflows can be implemented to attain the following goals:

- Establish variables that are key production indicators.
- Identify critical parameters and their range of values.
- Automate normalization and remediation of all data for missing and erroneous values.
- Identify objective function (i.e., target variable such as recovery factor, liquid carryover, or cumulative non-zero production over a certain period) and determine sensitivity studies to identify key drivers.

Such workflows can identify key performance drivers, and offer strategies and tactics for well completion methods and optimized hydraulic fracture treatment designs. A probabilistic approach helps quantify uncertainty and assess risk for individual field development plans.

Important results from production performance studies adopting aforementioned workflows embrace an automatic methodology to characterize impairment, classify wells as good or bad candidates for well stimulation, predict performance outcomes of particular operational parameters, and increase production with faster decision-cycles. Chapter 8 details advanced analytical workflows to increase production while Chapters 9 and 10 address the range of models and Big Data workflows respectively.

I AM A . . .

Geophysicist

Geophysicists invariably expend a great deal of their time processing and interpreting seismic data to delineate subsurface structure and to evaluate reservoir quality implementing analytical workflows on pre- and post-stack-derived datasets. The industry is currently focused on exploiting more challenging hydrocarbon accumulations, necessitating the need to incorporate a more diverse suite of data types such as electromagnetic and microseismic.

Whether you are solving exploration, development, or production challenges, you need software tools and advanced analytical methodologies to enable you to easily evaluate all your structural and stratigraphic uncertainties.

Chapter 3, *Seismic Attribute Analysis*, details some important soft computing case studies with an emphasis on applying stochastic workflows on the evolving array of seismic attributes derived from 3D seismic cubes.

Geologist

Geology has its roots firmly planted in science, but the geologist harbors a latent artistic talent that can orchestrate the wealth of subsurface knowledge to reenact the geological processes of deposition, erosion, and compaction predisposing the hydrocarbon reservoirs. You may be addressing challenges across the full gamut of the E&P value chain, and so you need the flexibility to harness advanced analytical methodologies with 3D immersive visualization to meet the pressing business needs. Chapter 4, *Reservoir Characterization and Simulation*, Chapter 6, *Reservoir Management*, Chapter 7, *Production Forecasting*, and Chapter 8, *Production Optimization*, showcase several case studies that illustrate a suite of nondeterministic workflows that generate data-driven models.

Petrophysicist

Intricate data acquired from intelligent wells represent an important investment. It is essential to capitalize on that investment and garner significant knowledge leading to accurate reservoir characterization. Chapter 4, *Reservoir Characterization and Simulation*, and Chapter 9, *Exploratory and Predictive Data Analysis*, offer case studies and enumerate workflows to enable petrophysicists to determine the volume of hydrocarbons present in a reservoir and the potential flow regimes from reservoir rock to wellbore.

Drilling Engineer

Wells are expensive and complex, especially with the advent of unconventional reservoirs. It is essential to integrate geosciences and drilling knowledge so as to ensure drilling and completion optimization leading to smarter and higher quality wells, improved risk management, and reduced nonproductive time.

Well control is crucial in challenging environments, particularly high pressure–high temperature (HPHT) and deepwater, to preclude operating risks related to wellbore instability and failure. Chapter 5, *Drilling and Completion Optimization*, discusses analytical workflows and soft computing techniques to provide a thorough understanding of data-driven models to predict real-time drilling issues such as stuck-pipe.

Reservoir Engineer

The O&G industry is inundated with reservoir simulation software to generate a suite of numerical solutions that strive to provide fast and accurate prediction of dynamic behavior. Owing to the array of reservoirs and their inherent complexity in structure, geology, fluids, and development strategies, it is paramount to adopt a top-down workflow that incorporates artificial intelligence and data-driven models. Conventional wisdom assumes that the reservoir characteristics defined in a static model may not be accurate and thus in a history matching workflow can be modified to attain a match. The functional relationships between those characteristics are deemed as constants derived from first principles. However, a reservoir engineer can question the constancy of the functional relationships and adopt an AI and DM methodology that makes no *a priori* assumptions about how reservoir characteristics and production data relate to each other. Chapter 4, *Reservoir Characterization and Simulation*, Chapter 6, *Reservoir Management*, and Chapter 9, *Exploratory and Predictive Data Analysis*, offer some supportive case studies and salient discussion points to enrich a reservoir engineer's toolbox. Chapter 8, *Production Optimization*, discusses methodologies in a case study to optimize hydrocarbon production via maximized well placement strategies implementing data-driven workflows.

Production Engineer

Data-driven models are ideal supplementary methodologies that deliver significant performance improvements across the current E&P landscape that is densely populated by digital oilfields and intelligent wells generating a plethora of disparate raw data. *Data Management* (Chapter 2), integrated production operations, and performance optimization are key goals for any asset. Production engineers can leverage innovative technology capabilities that are scalable and tailored to individual assets. Marry the data-driven and soft computing techniques to traditional models to fully exploit an asset's riches. Chapter 6, *Reservoir Management*, Chapter 7, *Production Forecasting*, and Chapter 8, *Production Optimization*, offer nondeterministic workflows to endorse the soft computing methodology.

Petroleum Engineer

As a petroleum engineer you are concerned with all activities related to oil and gas production. It is imperative to fully capitalize on all available subsurface data to estimate the recoverable volume of hydrocarbons and comprehend a detailed appreciation of the physical behavior of oil, water, and gas within the porous rocks. The low-hanging fruit of the global oilfields have been discovered and gradually depleted. It behooves petroleum engineers to take advantage of the improvements in computer modeling, statistics, and probability analysis as the advent of Big Data across the E&P value chain, and the complexity of sub-surface systems, force the industry to adopt a data-driven analysis. Chapter 4, *Reservoir Characterization and Simulation*, Chapter 7, *Production Forecasting*, and Chapter 8, *Production Optimization*, offer data-driven methodologies focused on production optimization. Chapter 9, *Exploratory and Predictive Data Analysis*, discusses soft computing techniques that are integral to developing models based on subsurface data, driving the analytical solution.

Petroleum Economist

It is essential to harness the technical skills of petroleum engineers with the fore-sight of economists to empower better business decisions in the E&P industry. Chapter 7, *Production Forecasting*, discusses an integrated *decline curve analysis* methodology providing robust short- and long-term forecasts of well performance.

Information Management Technology Specialist

The O&G industry continues evolving to multiple databases, structured (data) and unstructured (documents) data management, web services, and portals, as well as hand-held devices and cloud computing. It is about building on technology advancements to provide an integrated and innovative solution that has real and measurable value to the E&P business. New client problems must now be solved, including the management of disruptive applications and growing data complexity, frequency, and volume. This chapter broaches several topics that impact the IT professional, particularly the sections on high-performance analytics. Chapter 2, *Data Management*, details some of the critical thinking behind the endorsement that data are a key asset, especially in the sphere of data-driven models.

Data Analyst

What is a data analyst? The analysis of data is a multifaceted task that incorporates inspection, cleansing, transformation, and modeling of data. In the world of O&G companies, such a persona adopts artificial intelligence and data-mining techniques on E&P data to pursue knowledge discovery. Essentially this entire book complements the profile of data analysts as they implement exploratory data analysis, descriptive and predictive models through data visualization techniques (Chapter 9) and integrate text analytics (Chapter 10) to garner business intelligence.

NOTES

1. Bertrand Russell, *The Philosophy of Logical Atomism* (London: Fontana, 1972).

2. J. T. Tukey, *Exploratory Data Analysis* (Reading, MA: Addison-Wesley, 1977).

3. Jim Gray, "A Transformed Scientific Method," based on the transcript of a talk given by Jim Gray to the NRC-CSTB in Mountain View, CA, January 11, 2007.

4. D. E. Goldberg, *Genetic Algorithms in Search, Optimization, and Machine Learning* (Reading, MA: Addison-Wesley, 1989).

5. Charles Darwin, *On the Origin of Species*, 4th ed. (London: John Murray, 1866).

6. A. Weismann, *Essays upon Heredity* (London: Oxford Clarendon Press, 1889).

7. S. Mohaghegh, Virtual Intelligence and Its Applications in Petroleum Engineering, Part 3. *Fuzzy Logic, Journal of Petroleum Technology*, November 2000.

8. L. A. Zadeh, "Fuzzy Sets," *Information and Control* 8, no. 3 (1968): 338–353.

9. G. F. L. P. Cantor, "On a Property of the Collection of All Real Algebraic Numbers," *Journal fur die reine und angewandte Mathematik* 77 (1874): 258–262.

10. SAS Institute defines *data mining* as the process of Sampling, Exploring, Modifying, Modeling, and Assessing (SEMMA) large amounts of data to uncover previously unknown patterns.

11. "In-Memory Analytics for Big Data," SAS Institute Inc, White Paper, 2012.

12. Paul Kent, R. Kulkarni, U. Sglavo, "Turning Big Data into Information with High-Performance Analytics," Datanami, June 17, 2013.

13. K. R. Holdaway, "Exploratory Data Analysis in Reservoir Characterization Projects," SPE/EAGE Reservoir Characterization and Simulation Conference, 19–21 October 2009, Abu Dhabi, UAE.

14. J. J. Arps, Analysis of Decline Curves, *Transactions of the American Institute of Mining Engineers* 160 (1945): 228–247.

CHAPTER 2

Data Management

One of the most critical design and architecture decisions adopters of advanced analytics must make is whether to store analytic data in a data warehouse or in a standalone analytic database. Where does the data go? Where is it managed? Where are we going to do our analytical processes?

Philip Russom, Senior Manager, TDWI Research

The integration of disparate data types across siloed upstream engineering disciplines is gaining momentum owing to the demand for accurate predictions and effective field engineering strategies that can address critical business issues across the exploration and production (E&P) value chain. Where the interpretation of a single data type is sufficient to provide insight into variations hidden in a limited set of physical properties or combinations thereof, a multivariate perspective enabled by integration of different data types will have potential for more robust estimates and more astute discrimination of different physical effects.

The oil and gas industry is collecting massive amounts of sensor data from operations spanning exploration, drilling, and production. The velocity and complexity of data growth has put immense strain on application and database performance. This rapid growth necessitates a fundamental change to the way data are collected, stored, analyzed, and accessed to support real-time intelligence and condensed decision-making cycles.

Oil and gas operators are faced with a daunting challenge as they strive to collate the raw data that serve as the very foundation of their business success, transforming that raw data into actionable knowledge. However, with the exponential growth in data volumes and the breadth of siloed, disparate data sources increasing at ever-faster rates, the industry is realizing that data

33

management is fundamental to their success. Let us explore some important concepts in data management that enable geoscientists to become effective data scientists as wardens of an oil and gas (O&G) company's vital asset: data.

EXPLORATION AND PRODUCTION VALUE PROPOSITION

Exploration and production (E&P) is inherently one of the world's most challenging analytical, Big Data industries. The oil and gas industry produces petabytes of data and the data sizes are only increasing.

What is Big Data? Figure 2.1 identifies the three key ingredients to the Big Data amalgam: *volume*, *variety*, and *velocity*. Unfortunately, the methods to analyze data have not kept pace, and so *value* can appear as an unattainable goal.

The oil and gas industry has always managed significant data *volumes*. However, the business climate now favors companies that are positioned to use the entirety of available data (not just spatial or temporal samples) to fine-tune E&P strategies. The emergence of advanced analytics within a high-performance environment enables more companies to take advantage of the descriptive and predictive insights previously locked up in siloed data sources.

We need to establish an integrated environment of solutions, tools, methodologies, and workflows that enable oil and gas companies to manage Big Data as a valued asset, driving both core operational processes and strategic decision making. With established data management capabilities, organizations can make full use of all incoming data to uncover hidden insights and increase the competitive edge.

Over the past decade we have witnessed the adoption of a *digital oilfield* strategy and integrated operations. As these blueprints for automated

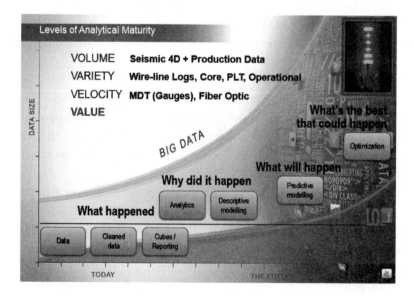

Figure 2.1 Big Data Combined with Big Analytics

and semi-automated processes become more pervasive across the industry, we shall see an ever-increasing frequency of data being generated. This phenomenon translates into high *velocities*. Sometimes high-frequency and low-latency events must be resolved to preclude catastrophic events such as pump failures. We shall investigate some of these case studies in Chapters 5 and 6 when we discuss drilling and completion optimization as well as reservoir management.

It is also critical to adopt an effective geographic information systems (GIS) environment as well as a subsurface management system (GGRE) within the data management (DM) platform. Knowledge garnered from raw disparate data collated from the diverse upstream engineering silos is tantamount to the life-blood of O&G companies. These datasets constitute the *variety* of input sources. Essentially, good GIS and DM protocols and architectures are fundamental to the financial success of the company as it navigates the choppy economic waters that are globally in a constant state of flux.

Invariably, an oil and gas company has multiple information systems, each churning through a plethora of data to expedite and enhance the decision-making cycles. Successful administration of these information systems necessitates professional data management practices. Key responsibilities should include.[1]

- Overseeing data through program coordination
- Integration across systems
- Sound stewardship
- Establishing quality processes
- Developing new systems and support operations

The industry has been impacted by the introduction of Sarbanes-Oxley,[2] catapulting data management into a crucial prerequisite for effective corporate governance. Thus, O&G upper management are more interested than ever in the provenance, fullness, and accuracy of all types of information fundamental to their financial and management accounting statements. Data management processes must, therefore, be clearly defined, repeatable, and auditable, allowing risks to be quantified and ultimately mitigated.

Cadres of engineers, scientists, researchers, and other personnel across the E&P routinely apply their own cleansing routines to manipulate data prior to using them in the processes that can create value and insight. Data cleansing routines and cleansed data are seldom shared between practices and regional groups because of differences in data storage systems and application systems from different vendors.

Bad and duplicate data reduce your efficiency, increase your maintenance costs, and contribute to higher development costs for every IT project. Each project must wade through poorly documented legacy data to determine which data to use for a specific project. Often a onetime "fix" is developed for a particular project and redeveloped in subsequent projects. These "fixes" are continually revisited over time as source or destination systems change or are upgraded, resulting in added costs and inefficiencies. Often changes made in one system trigger unforeseen failures in downstream processes. The lack of unified metadata on the creation, manipulation, and use of data is the reason these events occur.

The most successful E&P companies will have a clear and precise strategy in place that recognizes data as a fundamental cornerstone of their competitive differentiation. Those who succeed by addressing data as a strategic asset will be the leaders who can address all their needs by using one integrated offering, thereby having the flexibility to react to new challenges quickly.

A single integrated offering will shorten learning curves and give decision makers the information and data confidence they really need to support decisions. Correct data will be delivered where and when they are needed with high confidence. Any questions about the lineage of the data will be answered with tools that identify the data origin and all transformations applied to that data. Eliminating the piecemeal approach of linking and managing technologies from different vendors ensures data credibility, reduces risk, and speeds results. O&G customers adopting this strategy will benefit from better decisions that will be measured as faster time to revenue, fewer dry holes, less downtime, and increased reliability.

The single integrated offering must support the needs of the enterprise, spanning both the operational and analytical needs. The use of data for operations can span virtually every department and every workflow within those departments. The data quality needs of each of these workflows must be identified and included in minimal requirements of the data quality solution. Especially important in this analysis is to capture the unique needs of the sciences for O&G companies. Improving the quality of seismic, well logs, and process data involves statistical processes and manual interpretations that are not available in most data-quality solutions.

DATA MANAGEMENT PLATFORM

With a data management (DM) platform, you can create automated and semi-automated workflows for data quality, data integration, and *master data management* (MDM) processes. Such a framework frees valuable time for the geoscientists to devote their energy to interpretive tasks for which they are highly trained, releasing them from the onerous and tedious assignment of collating pertinent datasets.

A well-structured DM platform enables E&P personnel to:

- Correct, standardize, and validate information across the enterprise from a single platform.
- Profile metadata and data to discover errors, inconsistencies, redundancies, and incomplete information.
- Match, merge, or integrate data from a variety of disparate sources.
- Enrich data using information from internal and external data sources.
- Check and control data integrity over time with real-time data monitoring, dashboards, and scorecards.
- Write business rules once and easily reuse them in other workflows.

Inconsistent and disjointed data can put your organization at risk by jeopardizing enterprise resource planning (ERP), customer relationship management (CRM), data warehousing, business intelligence (BI), or any other initiative that relies on accurate data drawn from multiple sources. An effective data integration strategy can lower costs and improve productivity by promoting consistent, accurate, and reliable data across your enterprise.

The DM platform is a single, unified platform that enables real-time, batch, and virtual data integration:

- Match, reconcile, and consolidate multiple data sources to create the best possible view of a well, reservoir, field, asset, gas–oil separation plant (GOSP), operator, facility, or geographical location.
- Gain access to the right data sources at the right time to spur enhanced decision making.
- Ensure that high-quality information arrives at new data targets during data migration or consolidation efforts.
- Access your data on virtually any platform during an integration project.
- Increase the quality of your data before loading it into new systems.

MDM is the creation of a single, accurate, and unified view of corporate data, integrating information from various data sources into one master record. This master data is then used to feed information back to the applications, creating a consistent view of data across the enterprise.

In a challenging economic environment, reactive decision making is not sufficient to sustain a competitive advantage. Oil and gas companies are collecting more data, dealing with more complex business issues, and experiencing heightened global competition. There has never been a greater need to transform data assets into innovation and maximize the productivity of resources to drive sustainable growth. It is plausible to combine grid computing and in-database processing to drive proactive, evidence-based business decisions and promote agile strategies to anticipate and manage change.

Previously large datasets, complexity of data relationships, and modeling such complexity made it impossible to solve the highest-value business analytic computations quickly and efficiently. High-performance computing, which combines in-database processing and grid computing, solves business problems once thought to be unsolvable. With high-performance computing, business users see exponential performance gains, an increase in productivity, and the ability to streamline their analytics processes. Together, in-database processing and grid computing enable a revolution in business analytics and offer customers immediate competitive differentiation and cost savings.

From legacy systems to enterprise resource planning (ERP) applications, data from virtually any hardware platform or operating system can be accessed, cleansed, and processed. New source systems can easily be added and security is managed centrally. This saves time, shortens learning curves, and gives decision makers the complete information they need.

Data are the common factor that enables the best business decisions. Whether you are an executive or an engineer, the best decision you will make is the one based upon data. But decision makers often lack confidence that the data are correct, current, complete, and used correctly. The lack of confidence is the direct result of the difficulties of working with data, the explosive growth in data resulting from numerous sources (digital oilfield), and the haphazard way in which they are typically used in the enterprise. To be effective the data must be considered a corporate asset that must be nurtured and managed to be useful for the creation of value to the enterprise.

Problems with data quality have existed for longer than there have been computers. Initially thought of as an irritant that could be corrected with White-Out, the data quality issue has continued to grow with the proliferation of systems and application of automation in more and more areas of operation. The ERP wave that swept the oil and gas industry in the 1990s held the promise of correcting data issues with a single instance of enterprise data. That promise was never met since the ERP systems seldom held all the enterprise's data, and mergers, acquisitions, and business requirements resulted in multiple instances of ERP applications. Besides duplicity, bad data come from a wide variety of sources, including:

- Source systems' inaccurate data entry
- Typographical and data manipulation errors
- Flawed data entry processes utilizing misunderstood or inaccurate data fields
- Null or blank entries
- Data transmission errors in process data

- Invalid data types
- Noise in seismic data
- Spikes in process data
- Aging of data owing to failure to use latest well logs
- Improper extraction transformation and loading (ETL) jobs
- Loss of granularity commonly found with process data
- Numeric precision
- Incorrect data types
- Incorrect data corrections
- Poorly supervised or executed media transcription intended to extend data lifecycles, corrupting metadata

The analysis of data management requirements sheds insight into the current state of affairs. The following data governance model provides guidance for the journey to world-class data governance.

- Undisciplined
  - Duplication rampant
  - Unintegrated silos of data
  - One-off processing for all initiatives
  - IT-only data quality projects addressing basics like well, reservoir, and field
- Reactive
  - Some cross-functional collaboration
  - Data warehouses for reporting
  - Multiple data sources tapped for one-off initiatives
  - High maintenance and initiative development costs
  - Business users needing to rely on IT for initiatives
- Proactive
  - IT and business group collaborating on targeted domains of data integration and data quality
  - Some enterprise-wide views in certain domains
  - Some data quality standardization
  - Data recognized as corporate asset
  - Enterprise data architecture defined
- Governed
  - Business requirements driving IT efforts
  - Repeatable automated processing of data

- Data consumers helping themselves to integrated extracts of data from multiple sources
- Development of process optimization

To address the emerging issues around managing, governing, and utilizing data, organizations have been acquiring quite a toolbox of data integration tools and technologies. One of the core drivers for these and the subsequently assembled data integration toolbox, has been the ever-evolving world of the data warehouse.

Organizations need tools and technologies that can address new requirements and enable employees to focus on the job at hand instead of spending their time constantly integrating disparate technologies in the toolbox. The need for a single, integrated data management platform that can address all aspects of data integration, data quality, and master data management could be sounding the death-knell for the data integration toolbox. These key areas will be underpinned by adapters and a federation capability, and will share technical and business metadata that aid in collaboration. Ultimately, a single user interface should surface all the capabilities of this platform rather than a disparate set of user interfaces. Let us enumerate the functions a single governance model must provide to move an enterprise into a controlled and quality-conducive environment:

- Movement and integration
  - Migrate to new data stores or implementation of new systems.
  - Reduce data sources.
  - Consolidate from multiple environments.
- Synchronization
  - Ensure consistency between systems where data cannot be moved or combined.
  - Enable data capture or change in low-latency environments.
- Quality
  - Monitor and alert of issues.
  - Inspect and correct data errors.
  - Standardize data values.
  - Validate using custom-defined business rules.
  - Remove redundant data entries.
  - Incorporate reporting, validation, and analytical tools.
- Management
  - Data quality stewards are empowered to control data assets.
  - Data are enhanced with application of business rules.

- Services
  - Maintain metadata linkages to surface the master data as needed.
  - Coordinate and manage maintenance of master data at the source system with real-time updates provided as a called-upon service.

In summary, O&G companies must adopt an *information management* (IM) strategy to underpin an analytical foundation that provides the requisite intelligence—one that is based on both historical and "live" operational data—hence the concept of what is now seen as an "active" data warehouse. An active data warehouse aligns *business intelligence*, "What has happened," and *operational intelligence*, "What is happening," creating active intelligence that allows actionable information, enabling a company to decide "What is going to happen." Analytics underpin these strategies in data management.

We shall retain a consistent thread of discussing the concept of *analytics* throughout the book. Analytics encompass a wide range of techniques and processes for collecting, classifying, and interpreting data to reveal patterns, anomalies, key variables, and relationships. The goal is to derive new insights that drive better decisions and more effective operational processes.

For many users, analytics means little more than slicing, dicing, sorting, filtering, drilling down, and visualizing data to investigate past events. However, a growing number of oil and gas companies are embracing more advanced forms of analytics in a quest to predict the future and adapt to rapid change—especially important capabilities in an unforgiving economy with unpredictable fluctuations in the price of oil and gas.

The opening gambit to all analysis is a data management platform such as the four-tiered architecture discussed in the following section.

Four-Tiered DM Architecture

In order to transform raw data into a viable and effective asset, E&P organizations are pursuing an implementation of a four-tiered platform architecture (Figure 2.2):

1. Information platform
2. Knowledge platform
3. Collaboration and analytical framework
4. Performance platform

Information Platform

The information platform handles the transformation of data into information, assures the consistency and accuracy of the information, adapts it according to the needs of the users, and provides full access to the information. This base

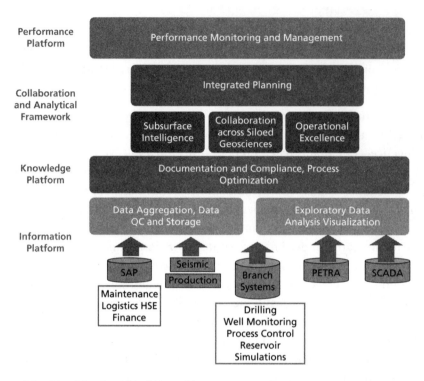

Figure 2.2 Oil and Gas Four-Tiered DM Architecture

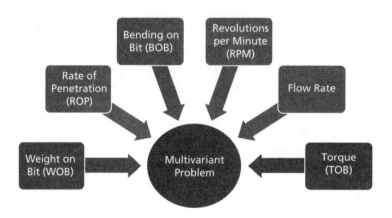

Figure 2.3 Multivariant Perspective

platform ensures that the information, communications, directives, and decisions can flow freely, striving toward a probabilistic range of acceptable outcomes based on a multivariant, multidimensional, multivariate, and stochastic analysis of the aggregated data.

What do these types of data represent in an analytical sense?

Multivariant: Multiple independent variables that affect the outcome of a singularity as depicted in Figure 2.3.

Multidimensional: Dimensions that affect independent variables. For example vibrations can be axial, tangential, and lateral, as illustrated in Figure 2.4. It refers to an input space where several exploratory variables may epitomize the property of collinearity where the values demonstrate an exact or approximate linear relationship. Anisotropy inherent in some rock properties, such as permeability, increases the dimensionality of the input space since it is directionally dependent.

Multivariate: Multiple dependent variables that have to be predicted in order to reach an objective on a singularity. These are typically variables that have interdependencies that can impact the outcome of the singularity. For example, Figure 2.5 shows *torque* impacts RPM; *weight* affects torque and RPM; all three affect *rate of penetration* (the outcome).

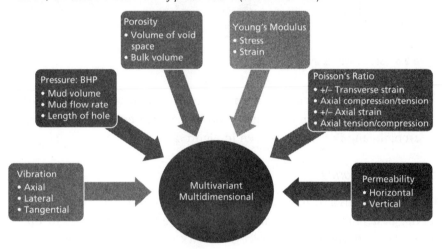

Figure 2.4 Multidimensional Perspective

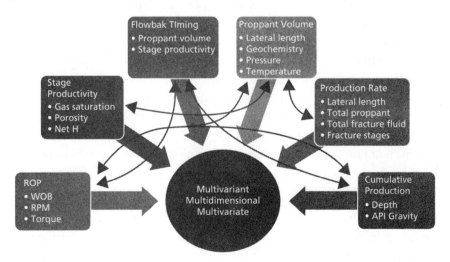

Figure 2.5 Multivariate Perspective

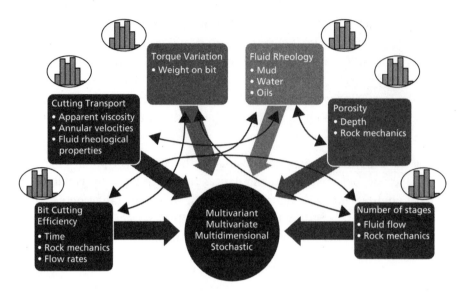

Figure 2.6 Stochastic Perspective

Stochastic: Variability and random behavior of independent variables. For example, the performance of the bit will vary, depending on time, rock strength, and flow rates, as seen in Figure 2.6.

Knowledge Platform

This layer contains a structured collection of rules for the data, decision-making criteria, best practices, corporate standards, event patterns, and so on. The knowledge platform monitors processes, flows, and decision making. It ensures that these comply not only with corporate policy and best practices, but also with government legislation. Geoscientists can implement first principles and engineering concepts, enabling the foundation to garner a rich dataset ideal for hybrid solutions that marry data-driven models with an expert system based on interpretation and deterministic workflows. The essence of this layer is a pool of captured and formalized knowledge, accessible at any time by the organization. With the rigorous introduction of the two layers from above, the organization can preclude tedious and ineffective processes that result in obtuse and muddled data handling tasks. The foundation of business processes from this point on becomes accurate information and formalized knowledge.

Collaboration and Analytical Framework

The collaboration and analytical framework uses the information and knowledge taken from the first two layers to prepare and automate decisions. This enables your organization to get a full understanding of the past and present, as well as a glimpse into the future, by building potential future scenarios and then analyzing and ranking them. This platform includes analytical elements with capabilities such as prediction, forecasting, and optimization. It forms the decision point in the process, providing the environment necessary to integrate and link various disparate processes, such as communications and directives.

In addition, this layer provides the ability to transform decision making throughout all hierarchies and disciplines in an organization into an efficient practice that involves the full alignment of the participants.

Performance Platform

The final platform of the four-layer infrastructure is responsible for setting up the strategic framework, planning the performance metrics in line with the business strategy and then combining the decisions from the previous platforms into plans. The execution of these plans can then be monitored for their progress against the full metrics setup, which can then be established for amendment and improvement.

This layer makes sure that the strategy is consistent, the E&P professionals and management are aligned, and all the operational activities are captured and focused on the targets and improvement efforts. It also ensures that the business plan and the operations continuously adapt to business environment changes.

The good news is this challenge can be overcome by treating data as a critical asset and deploying the right strategies and technologies that enable organizations to make sound business decisions based on trusted data. There is an evolving realization that oil and gas companies require a dedicated suite of software to support an information management infrastructure that offers geoscientists a conducive playpen to aggregate and integrate key data sources.

A focus on enterprise data management can provide unprecedented insights into E&P efficiencies and deficiencies while identifying potential CAPEX and OPEX cost reduction, thereby mitigating risks and maximizing performance.

Robust data leads to improved decision making, which, ultimately, leads to enhanced asset portfolio.

ARRAY OF DATA REPOSITORIES

Let us distinguish between a data warehouse, a data mart, and an analytical database. Oil and gas companies must clarify the definitions for each of these repositories, owing to their inherent variability and appropriateness to support advanced analytics. These data repositories have fundamentally different purposes:

- An *enterprise data warehouse* is an all-encompassing platform that manages data for multiple geoscientific departments and their autonomous functions. It is designed to be the single version of the truth, and a supplementary historian of enterprise performance.

- *Data marts* tend to be more narrowly defined, usually addressing a single subject area, such as seismic data or well log data.

- "An analytical database is kind of a fuzzy term," said Russom.[3] "It can mean a lot of things to different people. As a collection of analytical data, it may be physically located within an enterprise data warehouse. For some, it may look like a data mart. More and more, I've seen people put together a separate database outside of their data warehouse or data marts that contains analytical data specifically for analytic purposes. Wherever it resides physically, an analytical database is not seen as a permanent record of enterprise performance but rather a test bed for exploring change and opportunity."

The three types of data repositories are optimized by different processes. "For instance, a lot of enterprise data warehouses are optimized so you can feed data into them at different update speeds and make high-speed queries against that data," said Russom.

> Data marts have very similar attributes, except smaller. In contrast, analytical databases are optimized for fairly unpredictable data sets, because the data are not nearly as stable as in a data warehouse or mart. When you're trying to figure out business change, the data will change quite a bit.

Online analytic processing (OLAP) enables multidimensional queries by caching data in cubes. "As with reporting, this kind of multidimensional data are carefully cleansed and carefully documented," said Russom. "You would put a lot of effort into metadata, maybe master data. There is transformation through ETL processes and so forth. All the practices that we associate with data preparation for a data warehouse are appropriate for online analytic processing."

With query-based analytics, users often want to begin the analysis very quickly in response to a sudden change in the business environment. The analysis can require large data volumes, often multiple terabytes of raw operational data. The urgency of the analysis precludes opportunities for substantial data transformation, cleansing, and modeling.

"Not that you would want to," said Russom.

> Too much prep at the beginning of an analytical data project may lose some of the "data nuggets" that fuel the discovery. Whether it's query-based or predictive, or some variation of those, you need the detailed source data pretty much intact to do your first pass of discovery. Later you may come back and start transforming the data.

"Some predictive tools or algorithms need specific data structures," said Russom.

> A lot of these tools run fast on a flat record structure, so if you have data hierarchies, these may need to be flattened. If you have

data strewn across multiple tables, maybe related through keys, you might want to combine these into single but very wide records. The analytic tool may prefer range fields, so certain data values may need to be transformed into ranges in a process called binning. Some algorithms demand a flat file (as opposed to in-database processing), so generating a very large flat file is core to data preparation.

Analytic discovery depends on data nuggets found in raw source data. "Both query-based and predictive analytics depend on large amounts of raw source data," said Russom. "It's not just the fact that it is a large sample size, but it's also fairly raw data, which provides details that are essential for discovering facts, relationships, clusters and anomalies."

Analytical data can also be unstructured. Text mining or text analytic tools often feed data into predictive analytics, data mining tools, and statistical tools. Text mining provides a rich additional source of data for the predictive analytics workflows. If you capitalize on unstructured data resources, such as daily drilling reports, you can have more accurate predictive models.

Data from an enterprise data warehouse can be analytical as well. "Although advanced analytics tend to need new data sets, they can also tap the content of a data warehouse," said Russom. "Data from the warehouse provides a historic context for newly discovered facts, plus additional dimensions and other useful details. The insights of analytics should be incorporated into the historic record of the data warehouse."

A common misconception is that preparing data for analytics is the same as preparing them for data warehousing. But, as mentioned earlier, there are perils to "improving" analytic data too much, too soon in the process.

"Often you want to do discovery with pretty raw source data," Russom said. "Standardizing and cleansing the data too much or too soon can inhibit the insights drawn from it." For example, permeability anisotropy is often revealed in nonstandard or outlier data, so you do not want to strip or standardize the data too heavily, the way we would for data warehousing, because that could mask the very problems you are striving to resolve.

What about remodeling data to speed up queries and enable multidimensional views? "Not advisable for advanced analytics," said Russom.

> You may also lose data details and limit the scope of queries. It's the kind of thing you would do eventually, but not at the start of an analytic project. Do only what is required for the analytic tools, such as flattening and binning.
>
> You want to get analysts and data stewards working with the analytic data quickly, when the data is still pretty raw. Then you come back later and start cleaning up the data and maybe remodeling it. You might do similar data preparation work as for data warehousing, but at a later phase, after analysts have worked with the data for a while.

Most organizations have automated processes around their enterprise data warehouse and data marts, but data preparation for analytics has traditionally been done in a very ad-hoc manner, which is inefficient, inconsistent, and unsustainable. As the enterprise becomes more reliant on advanced analytics, it needs to ensure that best practices are applied consistently across analytical applications and in operationalizing the results.

A structured framework for automating data preparation for analytics is critical to enable organizations to:

- Document and automate the analytical data preparation processes, making them more consistent and repeatable, with traceable metadata.

- Incorporate best practices from the organization's data management experts into a shared, standardized, and reusable best practice.

- Schedule the formerly ad-hoc data preparation stages for analytics, such as incremental updates, loading of transactional data, or more frequent refresh of OLAP cube data.

- Automate the process of pushing the results of analytics into operations, either directly into databases or to support fast-acting decisions in the organization.

- Flag suspect data, missing data, and outliers (as determined by predefined range or category variables), without necessarily changing the data before analysis.

- Proactively run "triage" models in the central repository as appropriate, such as customer segmentation, customer lifetime value, and risk scoring, so analysts can begin discovery work more quickly.

- Set up live alerts around analytic data governance that are consistent across the enterprise, such as, "If the well's average high-risk BHP changes by x or y, deliver an alert."

Operational excellence begins with understanding your data. You need to capture, store, contextualize, and visualize real-time information and make it available to the right people at the right time to enable the right decisions.

The oil and gas industry has a voracious appetite for data. Exploration and production value chains acquire terabytes of seismic data that are processed to produce new projects, creating exponential growth of information. Furthermore, these data are increasingly acquired in three or four dimensions, creating some of the most challenging archiving and backup data management scenarios of any industry.

With the rise of the digital oilfield, the oil and gas industry is gathering more data, more often, at every stage of the business lifecycle. Your company is investing millions of dollars to gather, analyze, and interpret that data without any assurance that the data are complete, correct, and contextual.

The lack of a single view of upstream data leads to:

- Delayed projects
- Underutilized production capacity
- Missed revenue opportunities
- Runaway costs
- Regulatory noncompliance

STRUCTURED DATA AND UNSTRUCTURED DATA

Data is widely available; what is scarce is the ability to extract wisdom from it.

Hal Varian, Chief Economist, Google

One way to accelerate decision making is to link structured and unstructured data together to enhance pattern recognition that can improve the optimization of oil and gas operations. For example, real-time data inputs can be compared against patterns mined from a historical database through base analytics or enhanced visualization techniques. Companies are able to identify issues and root causes in massive volumes of information, and then identify and implement appropriate actions that will treat the cause upon detecting the pattern, rather than waiting for a crisis to trigger action.

The challenge in E&P is to provide quick, seamless, and automated access to structured and unstructured seismic data for geophysical interpretation. This linkage enables geotechnical professionals to understand the context in which seismic surveys were conducted, and it makes supplementary information available in real-time to support the decision-making process. Additional benefits are gained when well master data are integrated with unstructured information. Correlating seismic and well production data is critical to enable unified production and profitability analysis.

Integrating and potentially mobilizing this information helps oil and gas firms optimize processes by providing collaborative information and integrating seismic data management with unstructured information. This supports data preservation, data quality, data accessibility, and real-time process refresh.

O&G companies can leverage information gathered at the development site to enhance results obtained during the drilling process. Using complex algorithms that correlate multiple information sources, engineers can identify signatures and patterns associated with undesirable results. Information is then fed back into automated or manual control processes to either capture potential events in real-time or address needed process changes to avoid suboptimal results.

We can identify appropriate signatures through the use of algorithms to analyze information from multiple control systems and data historians. These algorithms are then implemented in appropriate real-time control systems to act automatically, or support manual processes for intervention or process change.

It is feasible to optimize results such as uptime with condition-based maintenance techniques involving the linkage and analysis of real-time operating data with asset maintenance and inspection data. The increased use of mobility solutions, whether based on common mobile devices or sophisticated machine-to-machine systems, provides another set of potential data streams for either analysis or condition-based monitoring activities.

In support of this, the trend toward an integrated operations model that provides common, standardized data for improved processes and enhancing the ability to detect, analyze, and show trends in operational data aberrations helps to significantly facilitate optimizing uptime. For example, by leveraging a predictive/preventative model, oil and gas companies can better determine if a piece of equipment is degrading or requires inspection or maintenance, or should have its primary duty changed based on fatigue or power cycles.

The increased web of local, state, and federal regulations that change and mature with increasing activity of unconventional assets has increased compliance requirements across the oil and gas lifecycle. Documentation and the ability to show traceability across structured and unstructured information help demonstrate what activity happened and when, so it is clear when the energy firm has completed the steps necessary to avoid incidents, mitigate impacts, resolve problems, and prevent similar incidents in the future.

EXTRACTION, TRANSFORMATION, AND LOADING PROCESSES

Loading data warehouses and data marts within allotted time windows, quickly building analytical marts for special projects, and creating extract files for reporting and analysis applications are tasks IT organizations face each day. It is necessary to build logical process workflows, quickly identify the input and output data stores, and create business rules in metadata. This enables the rapid generation of data warehouses, data marts, and data streams. Users can also choose to have many transformations and processes take place inside a connected database, data warehouse, or storage system. This is referred to as ETL, pushdown, or in-database processing, and can substantially speed up overall processing times by reducing unnecessary data movement.

Major Tasks in Data Preparation

The workflows that underpin data processing in preparation for stochastic analytical methodologies fall into five major categories:

1. *Data cleansing* to impute missing values, smooth noisy data, identify and remove outliers, and resolve inconsistencies

2. *Data integration* of multiple datasets be they cubes, flat files, or temporal and spatial in nature

3. *Data transformation* to normalize and aggregate across siloes E&P engineering disciplines

4. *Data reduction* to obtain a minimal representation in dimension and volume as well as retain consistent variance and entropy for similar analytical results

5. *Data discretization* to apply data reduction techniques for numerical data types

Some of the important steps that define data cleansing necessitate focus on data acquisition with an emphasis on the metadata. What are *metadata*? They are essentially data that describe data. The term carries some ambiguity since there are two fundamental types or variations on a theme. Structural metadata concerns the design and specification of data structures and is more succinctly coined as "data about the containers of data," whereas descriptive metadata is more about individual instances of application data (i.e., data content). *Imputation* is the computation of replacement values for missing input values. This can be attained by adopting the attribute mean for all samples belonging to the same class. The most probable value could be induced by adopting an inference-based approach such as a Bayesian formula or decision tree. It is also critical to unify data formats such as dates and convert nominal to numeric type to be conducive with soft computing methodologies such as artificial neural networks, regression, and nearest neighbor. Once outliers are identified, it is an interpretive process to determine whether such values are to be removed or integrated into the sample data under study. Having de-noised the data by applying smoothing algorithms or filtering techniques, we can attain correct, consistent, and robust data in preparation for analytical workflows.

Data integration of multiple datasets from different databases or data marts could result in redundancy as the same attribute may have different names. Correlation workflows can aid in reducing such attribute bloat.

Data transformation can also remove noise inherent in the data as well as perform summarization and data cube construction and development of a concept hierarchy. Normalization strives to ensure that attributes when compared across different temporal or spatial axes retain valid and plausible insight and trends. Perhaps production logging tool (PLT) data are collated at different times across a well portfolio. It is essential to generate a new attribute such as QgN that represents cumulative gas production measured N days after the PLT data were initiated in each well, ensuring a comparative parameter across all wells in the study.

Min-Max Normalization:

$$v' = v - min_A/max_A - min_A(new\_max_A - new\_min_A) + new\_min_A$$

There are several data reduction techniques such as cube aggregation, dimensionality reduction of the input space, numerosity reduction and discretization, and concept hierarchy generation. Dimensionality reduction encompasses feature selection whereby a minimum set of features are ascertained such that the probability distribution of different classes given the values for those features is as close as possible to the original distribution. There are also heuristic methods such as stepwise forward selection and stepwise backward elimination as well as decision-tree induction.

BIG DATA BIG ANALYTICS

Data-driven analytical workflows incorporate "hard data" referred to as factual or measured field data such as well logs (gamma ray, density, sonic, etc.), fluid type, and production rates, as well as "soft data" that refer to interpreted or estimated parameters.

In exploration, the seismic datasets being generated can result in a plethora of soft data by way of seismic attributes.

- Volume
  - Wide azimuth offshore seismic data acquisition
- Velocity
  - Real-time streaming data from drill-heads and equipment sensors
- Variety
  - Structured, unstructured, and semi-structured data
- Value
  - Increased speed to first oil
  - Maximized production
  - Reduced risk and costs

The petroleum industry is no stranger to large volumes of data. Operating in arguably the original sensor-based industry, oil and gas companies have for decades used tens of thousands of data-collecting sensors installed in subsurface wells and surface facilities to provide continuous, real-time monitoring of assets and environmental conditions. These companies closely monitor the performance of their operational assets. They also conduct advanced physics-based modeling and simulation to support operational and business analytics and optimization.

Organizations are capturing a greater volume and variety of data, at a faster velocity, than ever before. In addition to sensor data, these Big Data include large volumes of semi-structured and unstructured data, ranging from high-frequency drilling and production measurements to daily, written operations logs that quickly add terabytes of new data. They also contain a massive collection of business data, such as internal financial results, and news on energy and petroleum competitors bidding on leases and making major capital investments. Those organizations accumulate petabytes of such information with the goal of using it to improve performance and increase their competitive edge.

With the right technology solutions, these companies can move beyond traditional real-time monitoring to more agile real-time prediction. By rapidly analyzing incoming technical and business data and applying that information to complex models in real-time, they can generate tactical insights that help increase drilling and production performance while preventing problems. By quickly searching and analyzing a large volume and variety of competitive intelligence, such as news about mergers, acquisitions, or new investments, they can substantially improve strategic decision making.

Big Data can help companies develop the digital oilfield, integrated operations that unite information technology (IT) with operational technology (OT)[4] to improve decision making and enhance operational and business performance as depicted in Figure 2.7. Adding empirical analytics to existing physics-based analytics can take the industry to a new level of business improvement.

To capitalize on these opportunities, many oil and gas companies will need to adopt new IT solutions designed to address the specific challenges of Big Data. They need technology that can collect, manage, and analyze large and rapidly growing volumes of data, such as the petabytes of production data generated by oilfield sensors. In addition, they need solutions that can analyze a wide variety of data types, including numerical data streaming in from drilling-rig sensors and unstructured data from logs, microseismic, and other sources. New solutions must help integrate business data with technical data, bringing together multiple IT and OT systems. They must enable searches of Big Data

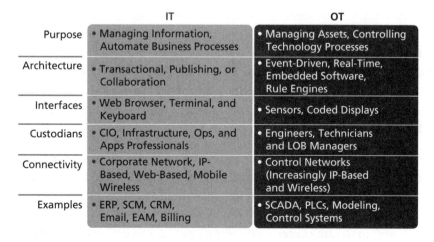

Figure 2.7 Information and Operational Technology Comparison

repositories to help oil and gas companies quickly identify and visualize information among vast quantities of structured and unstructured data, and deliver results to support time-sensitive processes.

STANDARD DATA SOURCES

There are several crucial standards bodies across the E&P industry that identify areas of intersection so as to preclude duplicity or conflict when ascertaining O&G standards in data.

Energistics is a global consortium that enables the development, management, and adoption of data exchange standards for the upstream O&G industry. There is a focus on asset and data management as well as work processes. Their standards portfolio covers the following areas:

- WITSML
- PRODML
- RESQML

These focal points address the transfer of data and hence knowledge across the geosciences, drilling, completions, interventions, production, and reservoir organizations.

PPDM is the Professional Petroleum Data Management association that provides a data model covering multiple subject areas that could essentially act as an MDM. The body strives to evangelize the use of faceted taxonomies to help control the evolving Big Data waves across the disparate engineering silos within E&P.

PODS is an acronym for Pipeline Open Data Standard, providing a scalable database architecture to integrate critical records and analysis data with geospatial location for each component of a pipeline system.

PCA stands for POSC Caesar Association and under its auspices develops open specifications to enable the interoperability of data and software. As a body it participates in research and joint industry projects to develop reference data and semantic technology.

OPC, OPen Connectivity, is a widely accepted industrial communication standard that enables the exchange of data between multivendor devices and control applications without any proprietary restrictions.

Semantic Data

Semantic data standards exist in the oil and gas industry to enable you to integrate different types of data. The O&G industry is striving to add meaning to the data. In Chapter 10, we delve into text analytics to identify ontology management of the upstream data. Such a management system is an organizational lens on your upstream content, providing interfaces to define the relationships between O&G entities such as wells in a portfolio, reservoirs and fields in an asset, and global basin characterization. We can generate semantic terms that codify engineering subject matter expertise in geology, geophysics, petroleum, and reservoir engineering as well as drilling and completions.

Semantic data relates content stores and informational silos with defined terms to help propagate the value of domain experts. It is essential to emphasize that data-driven analytics that are the core subject matter of this book must be married to first principles or at the very least constrained by the empirical and interpretive methodologies. This approach promotes the now-rapid adoption of hybrid solutions in the upstream where we see the combination of a user-driven expert system and a data-driven knowledge capturing system calibrated with historical data.

CASE STUDY: PRODUCTION DATA QUALITY CONTROL FRAMEWORK

Production data in petroleum engineering is often affected by errors occurring during data acquisition and recording. As interventions in the well alter the natural exponential decay of the production curve, the errors made during the data acquisition and recording are concealed. Automatic data validation techniques can help in cleaning production data.

- Detection of outliers in non-stationary signals
- Detection of sudden changes altering the natural trend of the signal
- Detection of rogue values disrupting signal trend in the light of statistically related variables

Data validation is concerned with finding erroneous data in a time series and, when appropriate, suggesting a plausible alternative value. Data validation can be defined as a systematic process in which data are compared with a set of acceptance rules defining their validity. In petroleum engineering, causes for erroneous data include noise, sensor failures, and data manipulation mistakes.

Outliers are observations numerically distant from the rest of data. Surprisingly there is not a standard method for identifying them. Often data are assumed to comply with a Gaussian distribution and a distance criterion (e.g., deviation from the distribution descriptor determines the outlier condition of a data sample). Oil well production data are a non-stationary process, and thus the naïve approach does not suffice. However, upon looking at a sample neighborhood, stationarity can be assumed. Here we propose a local solution for outlier identification.

Atypical sudden changes deviating from the natural trend of the signal often correspond to noise, or failures in data recording. Noise in the context of oil well production can often be associated to well interventions. There already exist a number of approaches for the detection of sudden changes as, for instance, the use of the Laplacian or a Gaussian operator. Here we use Haar wavelets for the detection of sudden changes in the signal, proposing a variant from an existing approach developed for neuroimaging data.

The final validation problem addressed here is the detection of suspicious values that may be in range and agree with the signal trend but that contradict the trend in statistically dependent variables. In order to catch these rogue values we recommend an approach based on Bayesian networks. The use of a Bayesian network for validating data by related variables capitalizes on the following idea: The trend of statistically related variables must grossly follow each other. When this premise is violated, the observation is likely to be a rogue value.

Outliers

Perhaps the easiest form of outlier detection consists of imposing a valid data range within which variable data are allowed, and labeling values outside the range as outliers. Often this range is established from the data distribution as defined by equations 1 and 2:

$$\text{Lower limit} = m - 3\sigma_m \qquad \text{Equation (1)}$$
$$\text{Upper limit} = m + 3\sigma_m \qquad \text{Equation (2)}$$

where m is the distribution median and σ_m is the deviation from the median.

If stationarity does not hold, the above solution is not satisfactory. Notwithstanding, upon accepting that the decay of the oil well production curve is slow, local stationarity holds and the above solution can be reused. A local outlier detection can be constructed upon windowing the data. The basic idea is then to shift the window along the data and compute the lower and upper limits of the data range only for the visible data within the window.

Abrupt Change

The wavelet transform decomposes a signal in its time-scale components re-expressing the original function in terms of the wavelet family basis. The continuous wavelet transform (CWT) of a signal $x(t)$ is defined by equation 3.

$$CWT(a,b) = \frac{1}{\sqrt{a}} \int_{-\infty}^{\infty} x(t) \Psi_{a,b}^* \left(\frac{t-b}{a} \right) dt \qquad \text{Equation (3)}$$

where a and b are the scale and shift parameters respectively, and $\psi(t)$ is the wavelet function used for the decomposition of $x(t)$.

Among the wavelets functions families, Haar wavelets are especially suitable for the detection of discontinuities.

For each time-scale pair represented by (a, b), a wavelet coefficient grasps the similarity of the signal $x(t)$ and a stretched and shifted version of $\psi(t)$. These coefficients discriminate sudden changes in the signal. Application of the median filter to the coefficients independently at each scale endorses the characteristics of the sudden changes in addition to minimizing the influence of white noise. Determining the limit between acceptable and unacceptable changes, a threshold T is imposed in the matrix of coefficients. Thus we set the threshold automatically using the *universal threshold* in accordance with equation 4:

$$T = \sigma * \sqrt{2 * \ln n}$$ Equation (4)

where σ is the absolute deviation over the median and n is the number of coefficients.

BEST PRACTICES

It is imperative to adopt a methodology that supports the entire data integration lifecycle through an integrated phased approach (Figure 2.8). These phases include data profiling, data quality, data integration, data enrichment, and data monitoring. The methodology may be implemented as an ongoing process to control the quality of information being loaded into target information systems.

Additionally, this methodology fits into an overarching three-phase business methodology approach: *analyze, improve,* and *control.* The first phase of this methodology focuses solely on data discovery or assessment to accurately identify the consistency, exactness, and validity of the source data. During this phase, data quality issues are identified and documented, and business rules are created to correct the issues. The second phase, *improve,* supports the flexible correction of the identified data quality issues and, if appropriate, the improvement of core business processes. The last phase, *control,* supports ongoing monitoring and trending of source data to ensure information accuracy and to automatically detect and alert users if data violate defined business rules or corporate data quality standards.

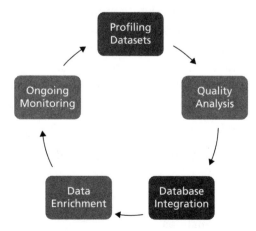

Figure 2.8   Data Integration Management Lifecycle

Data Profiling

The first phase of the methodology, data profiling, includes data discovery and auditing activities that support complete assessment of the validity, accuracy, and completeness of the source data. The profiling functions include profiling the actual record value and its metadata information. Too many organizations embark on data integration projects without first discovering the quality levels of source data. Undiscovered data quality issues typically show up late in the integration lifecycle and often cause project overruns, delays, and potentially complete project failure. By including data profiling at the beginning of the integration lifecycle, users can:

- Immediately identify if the data will fit the business purpose.
- Accurately plan the integration strategy by accounting for all data anomalies up front.
- Successfully integrate the source data using an automated data quality process.

Data Quality

The second phase, data quality, supports the correction of all quality issues discovered during the profiling phase. This often includes eliminating semantic differences found within the source data, breaking apart multi-value fields into discrete elements, moving information into the appropriate location, normalizing patterns, and so on.

For example, during the profiling phase, a data quality issue may be uncovered, such as multiple versions of the same basin name.

This type of advanced analysis is difficult to discover using manual processes, and building the rules to correct the nonstandard versions is extremely time consuming and requires a very data-dependent process. Other issues such as well names or reservoir nomenclature in the wrong field, multiple versions of hydraulic fracture strategy descriptions, and missing geomechanical information can be immediately corrected using out-of-the-box data standardization, parsing, identification, and validation routines.

A proposed data quality solution to furnish aggregated and robust data in an upstream E&P environment must fulfill some rudimentary objectives:

1. Interface seamlessly with *all* identified data sources across the E&P.
2. Access engines to facilitate both real-time and historical data transfer.
3. Automate and semi-automate workflows for exploratory data analysis:
   a. Identify outliers.
   b. Perform transformations.
   c. Impute missing data.

    d. Cleanse data.

    e. Surface hidden patterns.

    f. Identify trends and correlations.

4. Perform factor analysis and/or principal component analysis to reduce input space.

5. Generate metadata.

6. Create data quality assessment reports:

    a. Highlight data quality issues.

    b. Audit trail for data value changes.

7. Update or synchronize values based on *a priori* business rules.

The 80/20 rule[5] (Figure 2.9) means that in anything a few (20%) are vital and many (80%) are trivial. In Pareto's case it meant 20 percent of the people owned 80 percent of the wealth. After Pareto made his observation and created his formula, many others observed similar phenomena in their own areas of expertise. We can ostensibly apply this principle to time consumed when resolving a business problem in E&P—exhausting 80 percent of our time in data management and preparation prior to actually addressing the problem via a suite of invariably deterministic workflows or visual interpretations.

The data management solution must reverse this paradigm and ensure that 80 percent of the geoscientists' time is consumed by interpreting the data and marrying first principles with stochastic and data-driven methodologies.

Data Integration

The third phase, data integration, includes processes for automatically identifying related information within a single data source, or across multiple, disparate data sources. Once these records are identified, the integration phase calls for the records to be either linked or consolidated into one single "best" record. Data integration strategies may vary from simple duplicate detection and removal, to advanced entity resolution in both real-time and batch environments. During this phase, the organization begins to build a unified view of its assets, reservoirs, wells strategies, and tactics or any other type of entity found within source systems.

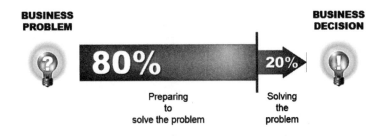

Figure 2.9 Pareto's Principle: The 80/20 Rule

Data Enrichment

The fourth phase, data enrichment, encompasses techniques for enhancing the value of source data using other sources of reference information. By enriching the source information, organizations can populate incomplete fields, as well as append valuable information that will better identify well attributes. Enrichment may include well nomenclature enhancement, geocode enhancement, asset code updates, basin sedimentology information, and other pieces of data that add value to existing information.

Data Monitoring

The final phase of the methodology, data monitoring, supports ongoing data quality analysis and tracking/trending of data quality over time. This phase of the methodology extends data quality processes beyond traditional project-based application and ensures the accuracy and reliability of information sources over time. Monitoring may include simple data profiling trend analysis over time, or it may include specific business rules analysis. By configuring rules that define acceptable data quality values, monitoring can be used to automatically identify records that violate quality standards and alert users of the violations. Monitoring allows the team to take action well before the data anomaly affects business decisions, processes, or projects.

Understanding and leveraging data in the upstream business segment enables companies to remain competitive throughout planning, exploration, delineation, and field development. The downstream segment depends on data to maximize production with regard to maintenance and forecasting. Fortunately, oil and gas companies have access to an abundance of valuable data in both upstream and downstream operations. Unfortunately, this information comes in various and increasingly complex forms, making it a challenge for energy companies to collect, interpret, and leverage the disparate data.

It is of paramount importance to integrate common and disparate datasets to deliver the right information at the appropriate time to the correct decision maker. These capabilities help companies act on large volumes of data, transforming decision making from reactive to proactive and optimizing all phases of exploration, development, and production.

Benefits:

- Reducing time to first oil
- Increasing the productivity of assets across their lifecycles
- Applying advanced business intelligence and embedded analytics
- Ensuring the right information is available to the workforce at the right time
- Improving planning and forecasting results

Figure 2.10 represents a maturity matrix that encapsulates all the requisite steps in data management, quantification of uncertainty in the data, and risk

Maturity Matrix

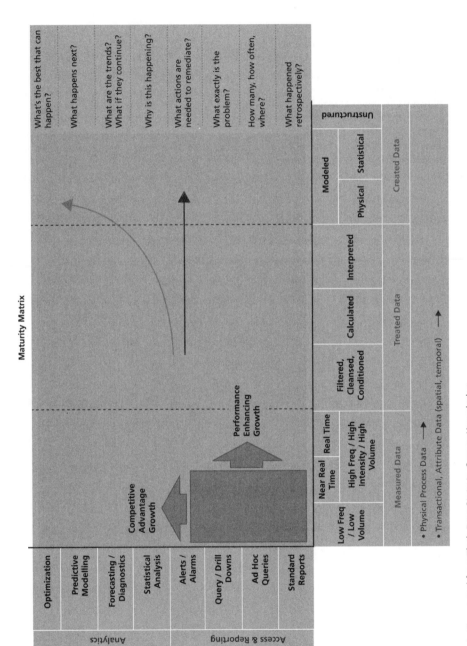

Figure 2.10 Data Converted from Their Raw State to Garner Knowledge

61

assessment resulting from analytical workflows and methodologies based on data stored across upstream repositories.

NOTES

1. J. Cruise and U. Algan, "E&P Information Management: Beyond Web Portals," *First Break* 24 (January 2006).

2. Sarbanes-Oxley (2002) legislated stringent changes to the regulation of financial practice and corporate governance.

3. Philip Russom, Senior Manager of TDWI Research, the Data Warehousing Institute, "Analytical Data Preparation 101: Best Practices for Managing Data for Advanced Analytics," insights from a webinar, May 2010.

4. Edward Evans, Managing Director NDB Ltd., "Controlling the Applications Portfolio: A Beach-Head for IM Strategy," *Finding Petroleum*, London, April 2011.

5. R. Koch, *The 80/20 Principle: The Secret of Achieving More with Less*, (London: Nicholas Brealey, 2001).

CHAPTER **3**

Seismic Attribute Analysis

As far as the laws of mathematics refer to reality, they are not certain, and as far as they are certain, they do not refer to reality.

Albert Einstein (1879–1955)

Traditionally, seismic data have been acquired, processed, and interpreted to identify stratigraphic and structural traps and to act as adjuvant support in reservoir characterization. However, seismic attributes have gained increasing importance as the seismic acquisition and processing techniques have improved over the past decade. The multitude of seismic attributes and the understanding of their relevance have spawned a great deal of interest to explore the correlations between acoustic properties and rock petrophysics.

EXPLORATION AND PRODUCTION VALUE PROPOSITIONS

Seismic data play an increasingly important role in reservoir surveillance, characterization, and integrated history matching. Quantitative use of time-lapse seismic data (4D seismic) requires modeling relationships and correlations between the changes in reservoir saturation, pressures, elastic properties, and seismic attributes.

Seismic data are now becoming pivotal as 3D and 4D surveys are accelerated across green- and brownfields. In addition to the customary seismic wavelet data processing out of scope for this book, it is becoming more important to fully appreciate the extensive array of seismic attributes that can be generated from both pre- and post-stack traces. We shall discuss the value of building a seismic data mart for advance analysis based on these attributes. Soft computing methodologies that map seismic attributes to reservoir properties are incredibly important as a means to define more credible and reliable reservoir characterization definitions that underpin field (re)development. The spatial integrity of large areal reservoirs requires high-resolution seismic and a more in-depth understanding of those seismic attributes that can reflect patterns or signatures indicative of hydrocarbons.

Seismic interpretation techniques have always labored for acceptance across the decades, starting with the introduction of color in seismic analysis married to the idea of temporal seismic rendition converted to a digitally mastered depth perspective in the 1970s. The term *neural network* was disparaged in the 1980s and 1990s on account of a distorted and misrepresented value proposition. Attribute analysis and 3D seismic surveys also both met with resistance from the barrage of entrenched traditional geophysicists. We shall highlight how a combination of principal component analysis (PCA) and neural networks (supervised and unsupervised) can forge an analytical methodology that forms a powerful pattern recognition workflow to identify those attributes that inherently have the most predictive capacity to ascertain geologic and stratigraphic features, pore pressure gradients, and direct hydrocarbon indicators (DHIs).

Let us quantify the value of integrating seismic attribute analysis workflows into traditional 4D seismic processing to build more rich static and dynamic geologic models. How can we improve the mapping of fluid flow through complex heterogeneous reservoirs and identify effectiveness of enhanced oil recovery (EOR) strategies such as *water-alternating-gas* (WAG)?

TIME-LAPSE SEISMIC EXPLORATION

The time-lapse seismic methodology involves acquisition, processing, and interpretation of repeated 3D seismic surveys over a producing hydrocarbon field. The objective is to determine the changes occurring in the reservoir as a result of hydrocarbon production or injection of water or gas into the reservoir by comparing the repeated datasets. A typical final processing product is a time-lapse difference dataset. (The seismic data from Survey A are subtracted from the data from Survey B.) The difference should be close to zero, except where reservoir changes have occurred.

Modifications in the seismic reflection strength at the top of the reservoir are related not only to the saturation change, but also to the original oil-column height. When water replaces oil, the acoustic impedance in the reservoir increases, causing a dimming effect on what used to be a strong response from the top of the reservoir. The strong seismic response from the oil–water contact (OWC) can also be dimmed owing to production.

Time-lapse seismic reservoir surveillance is based on the fact that production or injection significantly changes the reservoir fluid saturations, pressures, and temperatures, which subsequently alter the acoustic response of the reservoir rock, and this can be detected using seismic data. Changes in reservoir saturation and pressure can be derived through high-resolution seismic inversion and subsequent petroelastic calibration.

SEISMIC ATTRIBUTES

A *seismic attribute* is defined as a quantitative measure of a seismic characteristic reflecting a point of interest or focus to explicate a geologic feature. We have been studying seismic attributes since the 1930s when geophysicists picked travel times to coherent seismic reflections across field shot records. But essentially the genesis of complex seismic trace attribute analysis finds its roots in the early 1970s. A vast compendium of technical papers has been written to describe the popular methodology of utilizing seismic attributes as effective discriminators for geological characterization classifications. Attributes are generated from both pre- and post-stack datasets as well as pre- and post-migration implementation. Tables 3.1 and 3.2 enumerate many of the more popular current attributes.

Table 3.1 Curvature Attributes

Primary Outputs	Geometric	High Resolution	Shapes	Semblance
Min. Curvature	Dip Azimuth	Dip Curvature	Dome	Cross Correlation of Real vs. Imaginary
Max. Curvature	Dip Magnitude	Gaussian Curvature	Ridge	Derivative of Total Energy
Most Positive Curvature	Inline Apparent Dip	Strike Curvature	Saddle	Outer Product
Most Negative Curvature	Cross-line Apparent Dip	Angular Unconformity	Bowl	

Table 3.2 Rock Solid Attributes

Instantaneous Attributes	Wavelet Attributes	Geometrical Attributes
Real Part of Complex Trace	Wavelet Phase	Event Continuity
Imaginary Part of Complex Trace	Wavelet Frequency	Sand/Shale Ratio
Trace Envelope	Wavelet Q Factor	Dip Variance
Instantaneous Phase	Dominant Frequency	Instantaneous Dip
Instantaneous Q Factor	Apparent Polarity of Wavelet	Dip Azimuth

There are several schools of thought that classify seismic attributes differently. Let us study the attributes based on a classification determined by domain characteristics inherent in the attributes.

Instantaneous Attributes

When a seismic trace is studied as an analytic signal in the mathematical sense, it can be represented as a complex-valued function. The real part is the actual recorded seismic signal itself. The imaginary part is the quadrature that is the 90-degree phase-shifted version of the real part. The Hilbert transform of the real part is the quadrature trace. It is a simple process to compute the instantaneous attributes of the seismic signal once the complex seismic trace is established. Attributes termed *amplitude envelope* (or instantaneous amplitude), *instantaneous phase*, and *instantaneous frequency* are commonly computed from the complex seismic trace and displayed as colored sections or overlays for interpretational purposes. These attributes can be collectively termed *instantaneous attributes* since they concisely and quantitatively describe the seismic waveform (or character) at any sample point. As such, they can be extremely useful in correlating seismic events.

Instantaneous amplitude measures the reflectivity strength that is proportional to the square root of the total energy of the seismic signal at a particular instant in time. The continuity of the events on a seismic profile is a measure reflected by instantaneous phase and the temporal rate of change of the instantaneous phase is represented as the instantaneous frequency.

The instantaneous amplitude that echoes reflectivity strength is a good indicator of bright and dim spots. The phase attribute is often a robust delineator of pinch-outs, faults, and on-laps, whereas the frequency attribute can aid in describing some condensate reservoirs that have a tendency to attenuate high frequencies.

Once these instantaneous attributes have been generated across a 3D seismic cube, usually post multiple attenuation and random noise suppression, it is feasible to implement an exploratory data analysis set of workflows to surface hidden patterns and correlations explicated by these attributes as the input space. The objective function could be to identify all potential stratigraphic pinch-outs not easily discerned on a low-to-medium-resolution seismic section with poor signal–noise ratio. Those independent variables represented by the generated seismic attributes can be statistically correlated to the objective function to classify the most influential in identifying such features as pinch-outs.

Root Mean Square

The root mean square (RMS), or *quadratic mean*, is a popular statistical measure of the magnitude of variation over a dataset. The RMS proves particularly useful when values run through the positive and negative domain, as in sinusoids or seismic traces. The RMS attribute thus emphasizes the variations in acoustic impedance over a selected sample interval. Generally the higher the acoustic impedance variation of stacked lithologies (with bed thicknesses above the seismic resolution) the higher the RMS values will be. For example, a high RMS in a channel results from either a high acoustic impedance contrast of channel fill with the surrounding lithology or acoustic impedance contrasts within the infill.

Variance

The variance (the opposite of coherency) attribute is calculated in three dimensions and represents the trace-to-trace variability over a particular sample interval and therefore produces interpretable lateral changes in acoustic impedance. Similar traces produce low-variance coefficients while discontinuities have high coefficients. Because faults and channels may cause discontinuities in the neighboring lithologies and subsequently in the trace-to-trace variability, they become detectable in 3D seismic volumes.

Pre-Stack Attributes

During the pre-stack seismic processing sequence we may generate attributes from the common depth point (CDP) or shot gather traces. The critical information to be surfaced from such seismic images is directional or azimuthal and offset-related knowledge. It is apparent that a large amount of data is created in the pre-stack classification cluster of multiple traces.

It is essential to adopt a Big Data, Big Analytics suite of methodologies that can store a plethora of seismic attributes into memory and via a suite of correlation and regression processes perform an exploratory data analysis to surface trends and hidden patterns. The knowledge entrenched in pre-stack attributes is critical to understand fluid content and fracture orientation. Included in this classification of attributes are amplitude versus offset (AVO), velocity, and azimuthal variation.

Post-Stack Attributes

The stacking process eliminates the offset- and azimuth-related knowledge as we smash traces together at a CDP level by applying a velocity model to remove the *normal move-out* (NMO) effects. Time-migrated data obviously retain their temporal relationships so that frequency, for example, reserves its physical dimensions. But depth-migrated data are analyzed from the perspective of wavenumber that is a function of propagation velocity and frequency. Owing to the condensed number of seismic traces in the post-stack arena, it is more manageable to analyze the post-stack seismic attributes.

We can classify further by observing the computational characteristics of attributes.

Norman Neidell[1] suggested the use of a Hilbert Transform as a starting point for complex-trace analysis. Later, Taner and Koehler[2] developed a single mathematical framework for attribute computation. Thus we can determine the seismic trace amplitude as the real part of the complex analytical signal while the imaginary part of the signal is computed by taking its Hilbert transform.

RESERVOIR CHARACTERIZATION

Reservoir characterization is the process of calibrating or mapping reservoir thickness, net-to-gross ratio, porosity, permeability, and water saturation. Well logs have habitually provided the source of the data to generate the maps, but piecemeal seismic attributes have gained popularity when calibrated with extant well control. The seismic data can be used to interpolate and extrapolate between and beyond sparse well control that provides only localized knowledge.

Let us now enumerate those seismic attributes that are most conducive for reservoir characterization. One methodology to classify seismic attributes is to cluster them into the following four categories:

1. *Qualitative attributes* such as coherency and perhaps instantaneous phase or instantaneous frequency are ideal for identifying spatial patterns such as faults or facies changes. It is essentially impossible to map these attributes directly to a reservoir property such as porosity, and consequently these attributes are not implemented to quantify reservoir properties.

2. *Quantitative attributes:* The most fundamental quantitative attribute is amplitude on zero-phase data, relative impedance data, or absolute impedance data. Traditionally, we identify these three attributes as the most pertinent for quantitative reservoir characterization.

3. *Interval attributes* are those that quantify a lens into the seismic data that windows more than one peak or trough. The majority of seismic attributes can be categorized in this manner. Interval attributes include number of zero crossings, average energy, and dominant frequency. These attributes are invariably adopted when a reservoir's seismic reflection is discontinuous as to preclude an obvious "pick" across the same peak or trough on all traces. An interval attribute is analogous to a well log cross-section with a number of thin, discontinuous sands that cannot be correlated with any certainty.

4. *AVO attributes* are those that are generated using a reflection's pre-stack amplitudes. Examples of pre-stack attributes are AVO gradient, AVO intercept, near amplitude, and far amplitude. 3D pre-stack attributes have only become available recently with the advent of affordable pre-stack time migrations.

We explore an array of soft computing data-driven methodologies in Chapter 4 that lend credence to and support reservoir characterization.

RESERVOIR MANAGEMENT

Seismic attribute and wavelet processing analyses have evolved into one of the cornerstones of reservoir management, providing a very critical source of knowledge that sheds light on identifying methodologies to de-risk opportunities. Fundamental to garnering the intrinsic value of the temporal dimension in 4D seismic data is the craft of enumerating analytical methodologies combined with strategies for interpretation. With the advent of Big Data, Big Analytics in the O&G industry it is critical to adopt a broader vision toward seismic data analysis, complementing the traditional interpretation of 3D seismic data cubes with a stochastic or nondeterministic data-driven suite of methodologies.

Geoscientists are entrenched in their upstream bailiwicks as they continue to labor in isolation, drowning in a sea of seismic traces and attendant attributes. Admittedly the multitude of wiggle traces with their peaks and troughs are a daunting prospect with subtle signatures not only influenced by fluid and pressure changes in the rocks' pores but also smeared by convolved responses anchored in first principles.

Studying the seismic amplitudes and time-shifts between 3D datasets may constitute a workflow underpinning important interpretation, but such deterministic approaches often need support in a marriage with a data-driven analytical methodology that can focus very quickly on those correlations and hidden patterns in the vast array of seismic signatures. The 3D responses are non-unique and it is imperative to support an interpretation with additional datasets such as production and injection data and production logging tool (PLT) and tracer information.

Chapter 6 explores the *digital oilfield* and analytical workflows to enhance reservoir management.

SEISMIC TRACE ANALYSIS

Traditionally, geophysicists focus on the amplitude differences and variations in the velocity field that are reflected in time-shifts across seismic 3D data cubes in a temporal dimension. Any amplitude dimming or brightening are invariably correlated to increase in water and gas saturation, respectively. Additionally, a positive time-shift reflects a decrease in pressure and conversely a negative time-shift implies an increase in pressure.

Let us study an analytical workflow that integrates a suite of seismic attributes and additional subsurface data points garnered from well logs and existing production and injector rates from extant wells. Figure 3.1 describes a pictorial methodology that implements soft computing techniques via pattern recognition processing, self-organizing maps (SOMs), and clustering algorithms. The deliverables from such a study are not limited to the outputs depicted in Figure 3.1, as only the limitation in existing software architecture and constraints on thinking outside the box can restrict the engineers' momentum and return on investment.

Single Trace Analysis

- Spectral analysis
- Time series analysis
- Wavelet decomposition
- Fast Fourier transform
- Principal component analysis
- Hilbert transform

Spectral Analysis

Identifying individual subsurface faults in a larger fault system is important to characterize and understand the relationship between microseismicity and subsurface processes. This information can potentially help drive reservoir management and mitigate the risks of natural or induced seismicity. We have evaluated a method of statistically clustering power spectra from microseismic events associated with an enhanced oil recovery operation. Specifically, we were able to provide a clear distinction within a set of events originally designated in the time domain as a single cluster and to identify evidence of *en echelon* faulting. Subtle time-domain differences between events were accentuated in the frequency domain. Power spectra based on the Fourier transform of the time-domain autocorrelation function were used, as this formulation results in statistically independent intensities and is supported by a full body of statistical theory upon which decision frameworks can be developed.

There are many ways to implement a spectral analysis workflow. Some that are suitable particularly for seismic trace data will be presented here together with examples to illustrate how reported outputs may be rendered. All results here are based on a SEG-Y dataset with 390 post-stack traces shot at 4 milliseconds sample period over 4 seconds.

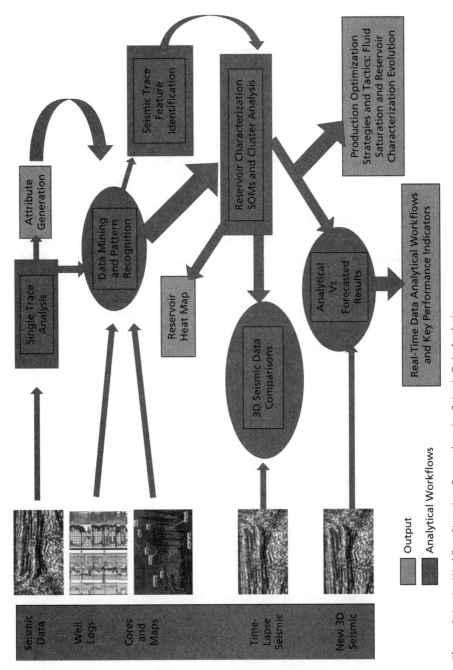

Figure 3.1 Key Workflow Steps in a Comprehensive Seismic Data Analysis

Output

Analytical Workflows

Seismic Data

Well Logs

Cores and Maps

Time-Lapse Seismic

New 3D Seismic

Single Trace Analysis

Attribute Generation

Data Mining and Pattern Recognition

Seismic Trace Feature Identification

Reservoir Characterization SOMs and Cluster Analysis

Reservoir Heat Map

3D Seismic Data Comparisons

Analytical Vs Forecasted Results

Production Optimization Strategies and Tactics: Fluid Saturation and Reservoir Characterization Evolution

Real-Time Data Analytical Workflows and Key Performance Indicators

The following tools will be demonstrated here:

■ A data mining tool with visualization brushing techniques

■ Principal component analysis on SEG-Y data

■ Wavelet trace decomposition

■ Fast Fourier transform (FFT) on trace data

■ Discussion on how seismic data can be statistically analyzed

■ Statistical models to find/group attributes comprising the most interesting features

In Figure 3.2 we see an example of rotation, and zooming of 3D trace plots. Three plots in Figure 3.3 illustrate how the brushing technique can be applied to better understand the relationship between traces. Marking points in one plot highlights respective points in other plots.

Another easy way to find dependencies in trace data is to systematically model or select traces and compare with every other trace. An example, illustrated in Figures 3.4 and 3.5, is based on such a comparison performed in a data mining workflow where clicking on the Play button shows the comparison as it iterates through all traces. It also illustrates a third-degree polynomial fitted to every trace. Traces with closest fit can be depicted and studied.

In Figure 3.6 we see an example of clustering the traces. The dendrogram shows mother clusters and the distances from each other.

Time Series Analysis

Time series analysis comprises two objectives:

1. Comprehend the underlying model that generates the data under study.

2. Forecast future trends and discrete values in the data based on the historical analysis.

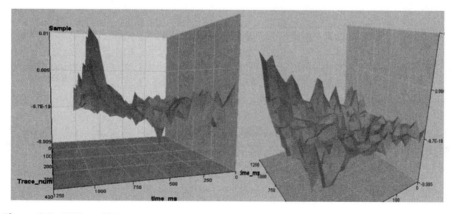

Figure 3.2 3D Trace Plots

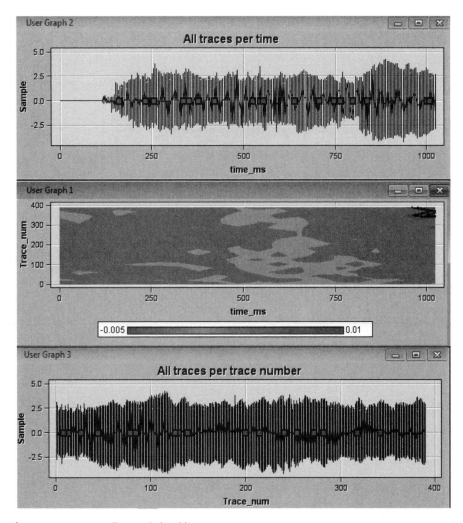

Figure 3.3 Trace Attribute Relationships

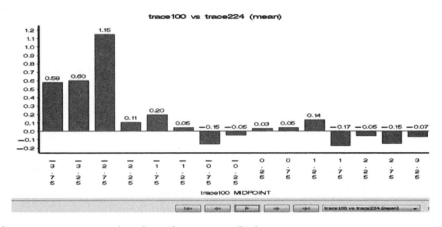

Figure 3.4 Trace Comparison Illustrating Mean Amplitude

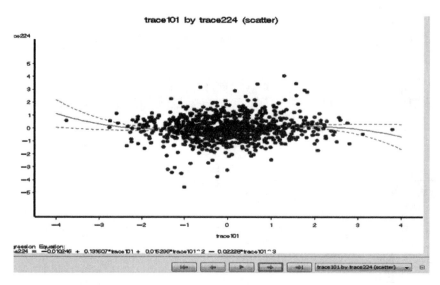

Figure 3.5 Scatter Plot of Amplitudes Comparing Trace 101 and 224

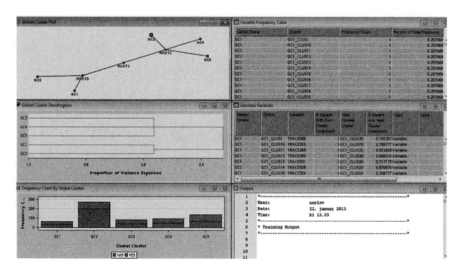

Figure 3.6 Trace Cluster Analysis

The nonstationary nature of seismic data necessitates a segmentation algorithm to rapidly identify quasistationary temporal and contiguous portions.

Wavelet Decomposition

Wavelet analysis is a mathematical technique used to represent data or functions. The wavelets used in the analysis are functions that possess certain mathematical properties and break the data down into different scales or resolutions. Wavelets are better able to handle spikes and discontinuities than traditional Fourier analysis, making them a perfect tool to denoise data.

Traditional applications of wavelet analysis have focused on image compression, but they are also being used to analyze time series, biological processes,

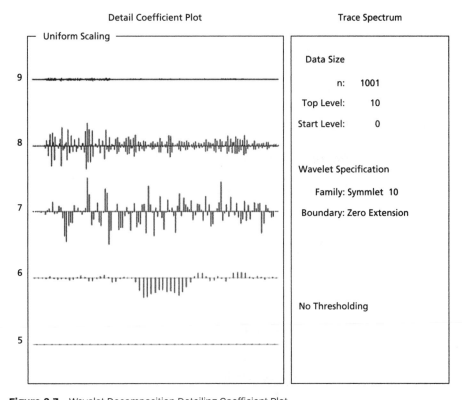

Figure 3.7 Wavelet Decomposition Detailing Coefficient Plot

spectroscopic data of chemical compounds, seismic signals for earthquake prediction, and atmospheric data for weather prediction.

Wavelet analyses based on the Daubechies and Symmlet families are illustrated in Figure 3.7. The examples focus on one trace wavelet decomposition. The analysis includes features such as:

- Multi-resolution decomposition plot
- Wavelet coefficient plot before shrinking
- Wavelet coefficient plot after shrinking
- Wavelet scalogram either with or without shrinking and thresholding, using three different types of thresholding algorithms

Figure 3.8 details graphs that are representative of the results after applying shrinking and zeroing algorithms to clean insignificant coefficients.

The scalogram module amplifies the small wavelet coefficients by scaling the magnitudes of all coefficients to lie in the interval [0, 1], and then raising the scaled magnitudes to a default power of 1/3. The scalogram on the left represents the wavelet coefficients with no thresholding applied. The bar to the left displays the total energy of each level, which is defined as the sum of squares of the wavelet coefficients. The total energy is higher at levels 6, 7, and 8, which is consistent with the results in the detail coefficient plot. The

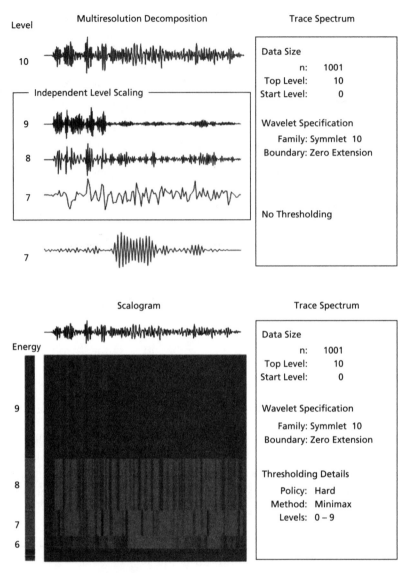

Figure 3.8 Wavelet Decomposition

scalogram represents the wavelet decomposition after applying HardShrink thresholding. Level 9 reflects how HardShrink zeroed out or shrank the small detail coefficients.

Fast Fourier Transform

Discrete Fourier transform is mainly used to transform data from time domain to frequency domain, as in the plot of *single-sided spectrum* in Figure 3.9. Figure 3.10 is the result of cleaning the spectrum by plotting only the 10 most dominant frequencies.

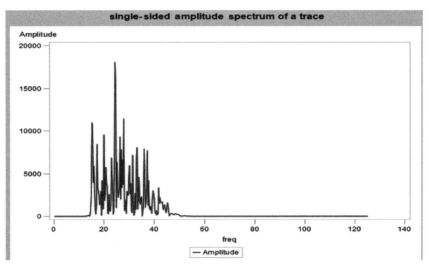

Figure 3.9 Single-Sided Spectrum Analysis

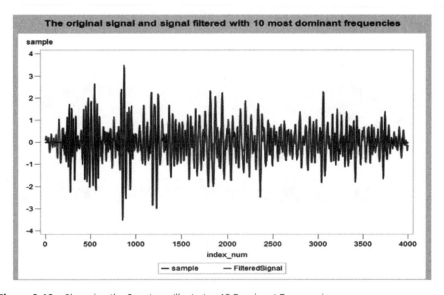

Figure 3.10 Cleansing the Spectrum Illustrates 10 Dominant Frequencies

Principal Component Analysis

The time series PCA is developed especially to enhance the properties of longitudinal data such as spectral or seismic data. The results depicted in Figures 3.11 and 3.12 are performed for 39 traces, trace 352 to 390 (the whole dataset was split into 10 groups) with 971 nonzero seismic shots sampled at 4 milliseconds interval. The results can be used in a twofold way, both as exploratory but also in a later phase, when identified for well locations, as a

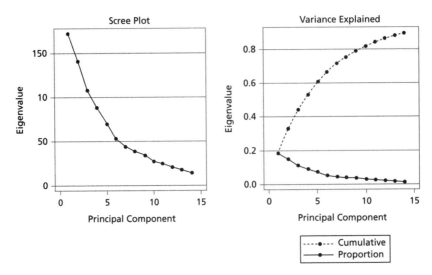

Figure 3.11 Scree and Variance Plots

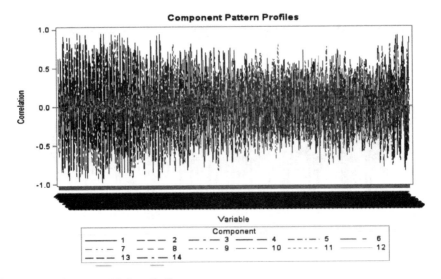

Figure 3.12 Component Pattern Profiles

classification tool for further clustering and correlation analysis. Here the raw amplitude values are under loop, but even the results of the wavelet, scalogram, or spectral densities/frequencies can also be put through the same analytical process and evaluated together, giving some probabilistic measure of porosities.

First we see that 14 principal components built on nearly 1000 shots explain almost 90 percent of variance, due to scree plots in Figure 3.11. Component pattern profile shows the loading parameters' values for all traces. These can be used to depict most dominant amplitudes in the data and thus used as filter.

Next, the spectrum of our data is investigated. The score plot for the 39 traces is presented in Figure 3.13.

We see that it displays a typical worm-like appearance. Components 1 and 2 yield traces 1 and 39 as least important as they lie near the [0, 0] point compared to the opposite value seen in component 3. The score values for these 39 traces can be used to discriminate between patterns of groups of traces with similar or totally different amplitude attributes.

Figure 3.14 displays the Hotteling T2 charts based on 14 PCs. We see that all traces save those at the extremes are not deviating from the mean values of the PCA model.

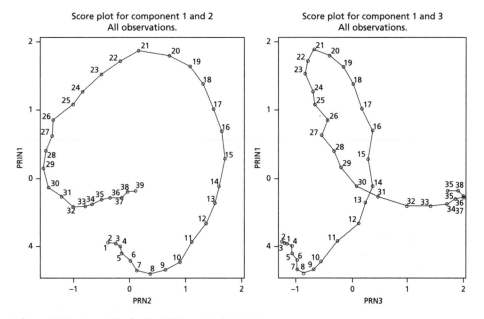

Figure 3.13 Score Plot for the 39 Traces Under Study

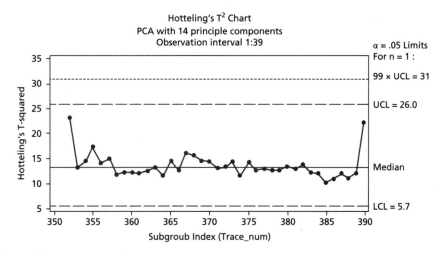

Figure 3.14 Hotteling T² Chart

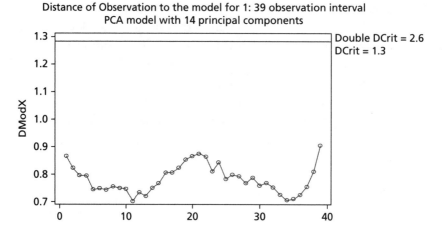

Figure 3.15 Distance-to-Model Valuation

In Figure 3.15 the Distance-to-Model value shows that all traces are well adjusted to the model.

Based on this PCA analysis, if those traces were located on the wells' locations, they are building a good PCA model that can form a pattern or cluster to correlate with other trace groups.

Hilbert Transform

Later on, in the beginning of the twentieth century, German scientist David Hilbert (1862–1943) showed that the function sin() is the Hilbert transform of cos(). This gave us the *phase-shift operator*, which is a basic property of the Hilbert transform.

A real function $a(t)$ and its Hilbert transform are related to each other in such a way that they together create a so-called *strong analytic signal*, as seen in Figure 3.16. The strong analytic signal can be written with amplitude and a phase where the derivative of the phase can be identified as the instantaneous frequency. The Fourier transform of the strong analytic signal gives us a one-sided spectrum in the frequency domain.

Hilbert Transform

$$H[a(t)] = \tilde{a}(t) = \frac{1}{\pi} \int_{-\infty}^{\infty} a(\tau) \frac{1}{t - \tau} d\tau$$

$$= \frac{1}{\pi} a(t) * \frac{1}{t}$$

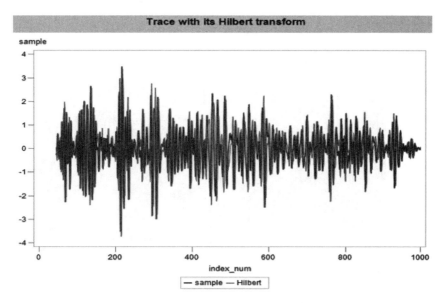

Figure 3.16 Trace with Its Hilbert Transform

The most common attributes are derived from the transform:

Analytic Signal - Descriptors

Magnitude

$$\left|\overset{\triangledown}{a}(t)\right| = \sqrt{a^2(t) + \tilde{a}^2(t)}$$

Instantaneous Phase

$$\theta(t) = \tan^{-1} \frac{\tilde{a}(t)}{a(t)}$$

Instantaneous
Frequency

$$f_i(t) = \frac{1}{2\pi} \frac{d\theta(t)}{dt}$$

where $\tilde{a}$ is the Hilbert transform and a is the signal.

Figures 3.17, 3.18, and 3.19 present plots of signal descriptors of a trace derived with a Hilbert transform.

Data Mining and Pattern Recognition

It is essential to adopt an *exploratory data analysis* suite of workflows that via intuitive visualizations surface hidden patterns, correlations, and trends in the

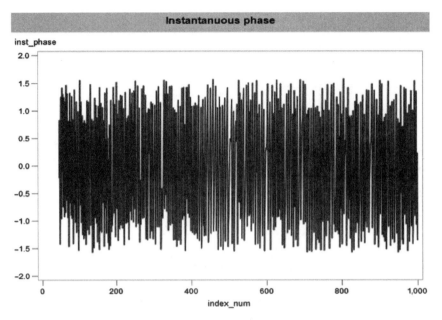

Figure 3.17 Instantaneous Phase Attribute Plot

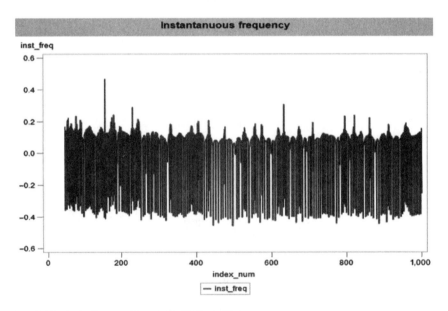

Figure 3.18 Instantaneous Frequency Attribute Plot

underlying datasets. In the case of seismic analysis you could aggregate multiple attributes from a pre- or post-stack perspective dependent on the objective function or business problem under study, for example, production optimization or effectiveness of an enhanced oil recovery technique such as WAG. The data-driven methodology supplements the traditional interpretation of 3D immersive visualization workflows. The key is to ensure that the soft computing

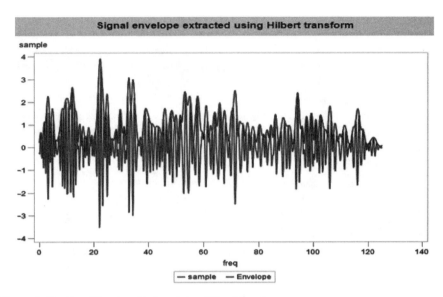

Figure 3.19 Signal Envelope Deduced via a Hilbert Transform

techniques adopted are not mere reincarnations of extant visualizations. What do I mean by that statement? Too often I witness "analytical" software being implemented that advocate multidimensional, multivariate, multivariant, and stochastic algorithms, but if you dip your finger into the shallow streams of the code, you soon come to the realization that complex, heterogeneous subsurface systems are beyond its scope and your finger is relatively dry! Don't just re-image your important asset from multiple perspectives, enriched by different boutique graphs and charts. Enable the data to actually work for you and let it ride the data-driven non-deterministic highway to convert raw data into actionable knowledge.

One simple but very effective methodology that renders intuitive and insightful observations on a 3D seismic cube is predicated on the pattern recognition workflows via principal component analysis and neural networks, both unsupervised (self-organizing maps) and supervised. The "Case Study: Reservoir Properties Defined by Seismic Attributes" section details the PCA analytics step studying amplitudes across a seismic dataset.

Given a volume of 3D seismic data, seismic attributes can be defined that have a numerical value for every point in that volume. Seismic attributes encompass a wide array of measurements derived from seismic traces such as amplitude, spectral decomposition, zones of unconformity, similarity variance, and thin bed indicator. We can calculate multiple attributes for every point across a 3D grid. Generating such a volume of seismic attribute data essentially disables the traditional interpretive workflow for fear of missing the nuances, hidden patterns, and multivariate relationships only surfaced by a soft computing methodology, as depicted in Figure 3.20.

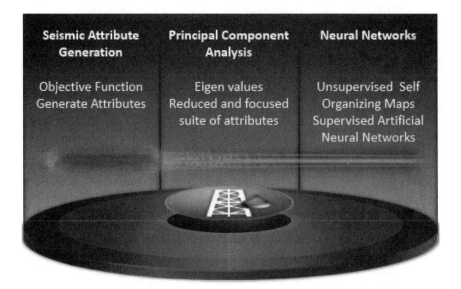

Figure 3.20 Seismic Attribute PCA/SOM/ANN Pattern Recognition Workflow

Having ascertained the objective function, and this includes identification of geologic and stratigraphic features, pore pressure gradients, and direct hydrocarbon indicators (DHIs), we can create a suite of seismic attributes with derived values. The PCA step establishes those attributes that paint the most pertinent picture of the subsurface vis-à-vis the objective function, filtering out those attributes that are essentially carriers of noise, providing little-to-no contribution to the study. If well logs and/or cores are available to train the neural network, then a supervised ANN can be implemented with the localized hard-data readings. The ANN maps the seismic attributes to reservoir properties between the wells. The unsupervised neural network based entirely on seismic response data can be used potentially in reducing exploration risk and resources in a greenfield.

As stated by Dr. Tom Smith of Geophysical Insights:[3]

> In one example, the software was used to evaluate a 3D volume offshore in South America. A well had been drilled in deepwater and encountered unexpected high pressures, which prevented drilling to the originally planned depth. This high pressure zone was not seen in the initial interpretation using a widely adopted interpretation system. An evaluation of the 3D seismic volume suggested there may be facies and stratigraphic variations in the high pressure zone.
>
> After an interpretation of the local geology and putting this into a regional context, 5 different sets of attributes were analyzed. One particular set of 6 attributes was found to distinctly reveal the zone of high pressure area.

The anomalous pressure zone appeared to be associated with a slope facies, a type of marine depositional fill that is often a target for hydrocarbon exploration. Slope facies are typically associated with a slope setting where there have been rapid changes in the deposition, including discontinuous siltstone and mudstone beds, and at times channelized sands with interchannel mudstones.

Seismic Trace Feature Identification

This action is to match the well data parameters with the trace signature to identify the relevant trace features reflected within the attributes and patterns. Almost all wells are logged with conventional logs such as SP, gamma ray, density, and induction upon drilling and completion. Some wells may have *magnetic resonance logs* that have the capability of in-situ measurement of effective porosity, fluid saturation, and permeability. Feature identification and extraction methods are essential so as to tie the seismic signatures with the well logs at local focal points across a reservoir.

Since time series data have a unique data structure, it is not easy to apply some existing data mining tools directly to the data. For example, each time-point is often considered a variable and each time series is often considered an observation in the classification problem. As the time dimension increases, the number of variables also increases proportionally. Therefore, to classify large numbers of time series efficiently, it is critical to apply some feature extraction techniques to render more concise each time series in a form of significantly lower dimension. The most common techniques for dimension reduction in time series are singular value decomposition, discrete Fourier transformation, discrete wavelet transformation, and line segment approximations.

Given a time dimension of size T, the line segment method divides the time dimension into d equal-sized segments (or time intervals). After segmentation, the sum, mean, or other aggregation statistic can be computed for each segment. For example, suppose that we have a time series with 12 time points, say {1, 2, 5, 7, 8, 5, 5, 7, 8, 2, 5, 3}, and we want to have a reduced time series with 3 points. In this case, we can transform the original series into a reduced series {3.75, 6.25, 4.5} with the mean statistic of each segment. Figure 3.21 shows the original series and the transformed series with three means. Keogh and Lin[4] proposed this method first with a mean statistic. They call it *piecewise aggregate approximation*. The biggest advantage of this approach is that it is simple to understand and to implement.

Time series feature extraction can be explained in two different ways:

1. Feature extraction via classical time series
2. Feature extraction for dimension reduction

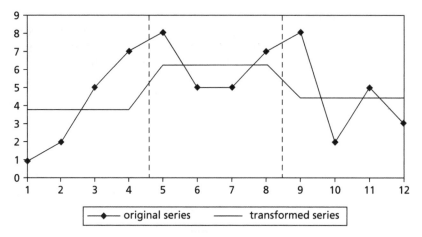

Figure 3.21 Dimension Reduction Using Line Segments with Mean

Some classical time series analysis for feature extraction such as seasonal, trend, seasonal decomposition and adjustments, and correlation analysis are all conducive to identifying critical seismic trace features.

Reservoir Characterization Analytical Model

One of the most effective analytical workflows is cluster analysis and it is an ideal data mining candidate to describe patterns garnered from seismic attributes.

Let us look at two clustering techniques: *hierarchical* and *K-means*.

Hierarchical Clustering

The hierarchical option clusters rows that group the points (rows) of a table into clusters whose values are close to each other relative to those of other clusters. Hierarchical clustering is a process that starts with each point in its own cluster. At each step, the two clusters that are closest together are combined into a single cluster. This process continues until there is only one cluster containing all the points. This type of clustering is good for smaller datasets (a few hundred observations).

The clustering sequence is easily visualized with the help of a *dendrogram* (Figure 3.22), which is a tree diagram listing each observation, and showing which cluster it is in and when it entered its cluster.

The technical details behind hierarchical clustering are enumerated by five methods:

1. Average linkage
2. Centroid method
3. Ward's method
4. Single linkage
5. Complete linkage

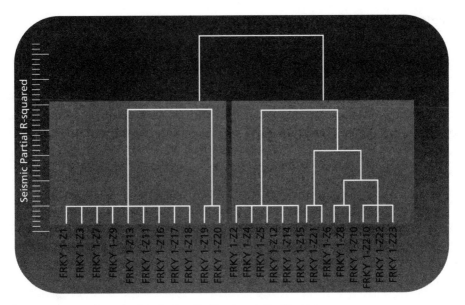

Figure 3.22 Dendrogram of Wells Classified by Cumulative Liquids

Average Linkage

In average linkage, the distance between two clusters is the average distance between pairs of observations, or one in each cluster. Average linkage tends to join clusters with small variances and is slightly biased toward producing clusters with the same variance.

Centroid Method

In the centroid method, the distance between two clusters is defined as the squared Euclidean distance between their means. The centroid method is more robust to outliers than most other hierarchical methods but in other respects might not perform as well as Ward's method or average linkage.

Ward's Method

In Ward's minimum variance method, the distance between two clusters is the ANOVA sum of squares between the two clusters added up over all the variables. At each generation, the within-cluster sum of squares is minimized over all partitions obtainable by merging two clusters from the previous generation. The sums of squares are easier to interpret when they are divided by the total sum of squares to give the proportions of variance (squared semi-partial correlations).

Ward's method joins clusters to maximize the likelihood at each level of the hierarchy under the assumptions of multivariate normal mixtures, spherical covariance matrixes, and equal sampling probabilities.

Ward's method tends to join clusters with a small number of observations and is strongly biased toward producing clusters with approximately the same number of observations. It is also very sensitive to outliers.

Single Linkage

In single linkage the distance between two clusters is the minimum distance between an observation in one cluster and an observation in the other cluster. Single linkage has many desirable theoretical properties.[5] Single linkage has, however, fared poorly in Monte Carlo studies.[6] By imposing no constraints on the shape of clusters, single linkage sacrifices performance in the recovery of compact clusters in return for the ability to detect elongated and irregular clusters. Single linkage tends to chop off the tails of distributions before separating the main cluster.

Complete Linkage

In complete linkage, the distance between two clusters is the maximum distance between an observation in one cluster and an observation in the other cluster. Complete linkage is strongly biased toward producing clusters with approximately equal diameters and can be severely distorted by moderate outliers.

K-Means Clustering

The K-means approach to clustering performs an iterative alternating fitting process to form the number of specified clusters as depicted in Figure 3.23. The K-means method first selects a set of *n* points called *cluster seeds* as a first guess of the means of the clusters. Each observation is assigned to the nearest seed to form a set of temporary clusters. The seeds are then replaced by the cluster

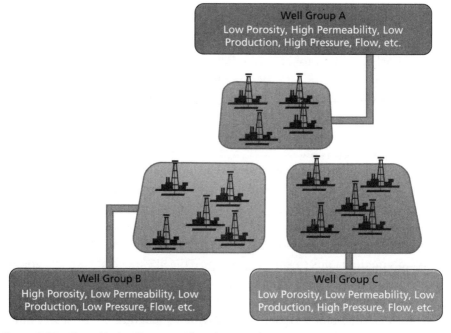

Figure 3.23 Hierarchical and K-Means Clustering to Evaluate EOR

means, the points are reassigned, and the process continues until no further changes occur in the clusters. When the clustering process is finished, you see tables showing brief summaries of the clusters. The K-means approach is a special case of a general approach called the EM algorithm; *E* stands for *expectation* (the cluster means in this case), and *M* stands for *maximization*, which means assigning points to closest clusters in this case.

The K-means method is intended for use with larger data tables, from approximately 200 to 100,000 observations. With smaller data tables, the results can be highly sensitive to the order of the observations in the data table.

K-Means clustering only supports numeric columns. K-Means clustering ignores model types (nominal and ordinal), and treats all numeric columns as continuous columns.

Once the clustering methodology has been implemented, it is then feasible to segment the reservoir or field based on the results. For example, by clustering the seismic attributes and those rock properties that can be mapped via artificial neural networks from the attributes, you can identify those wells that are good and bad from a producer or an injector perspective.

From the trace features combined with the production data it is now possible to generate an analytical model that can be visualized on a map and identify the sweet-spot to advise on future exploration/appraisal wells and reduce likelihood of dry wells.

3D Seismic Data Comparisons

The magic of 3D is best conveyed by considering how we capture measurements of a returning wavefield. When we introduce acoustic energy in the earth, it is like dropping a large bag of Ping-Pong balls from the ceiling of a large room. The balls will bounce erratically from inhomogeneities in the room (chairs, desks, and people). Many of the balls will return to the ceiling where their return could be observed and measured. By analyzing the timing and position of the returning balls, we can infer what irregularities may exist in the room. In oil and gas exploration, we are trying to image reservoirs and traps. Our image and reconstruction of the subsurface will be limited if we only receive the "Ping-Pong balls" in distinct 2D lines. However, if we observe the reflected wavefield (Ping-Pong balls) over a large area, we will have much more useful information to construct our subsurface images. Thus, if we have two 3D wavefields separated by time, it is conceivable to subtract one from the other and note the difference in seismic attribute patterns such as amplitude and phase. Note the subtle changes in time-shifts as seismic trace signatures differ between the two 3D datasets. These comparisons surface patterns and relationships that are indicative of hydrocarbon movements through the reservoir. Such questions as, How effective is my WAG strategy?, can be measured and quantified.

The enormous amount of seismic samples and generated attributes must be correlated to identify those areas of the seismic wavefield that necessitate further investigation.

Analytical versus Forecasted Results

By comparing new seismic time-lapse data with original traces/model we could evaluate injection/production wells' efficiency, locate where the injection flows, and quantify fluid saturation changes during the reservoir life. By comparing new seismic data (from a different location) with reservoir model/seismic trace expectations we could identify deviation from model and hence achieve real-time data quality during seismic acquisition.

It is critical during the seismic exploration phase of the E&P value chain to capture as much knowledge as possible that is germane to understanding the deposition, generation, migration, and entrapment of hydrocarbons in the subsurface. Thus, one of the most important tasks for geophysicists is to identify geologic features that can be mapped to the oil and gas lifecycle. Both the static and dynamic characteristics inherent in the reservoirs must be surfaced from the plethora of seismic wiggle traces. These characteristics are enumerated by Cosentino as a lexicon of parameters:[7]

1. *Structure:* horizon depth, reservoir thickness, faults, and so on

2. *Internal architecture:* heterogeneity

3. *Petrophysical properties:* permeability, porosity, and so on

4. *Hydrocarbon properties:* product, thermodynamics, and so on

Obviously, the traditional collection of information by way of well logs provides only localized and thus sparsely sampled datasets in a one-dimensional perspective. It is apparent that we need to generate seismic attributes to enhance and supplement the seismic knowledge garnered from interpretation of the subsurface seismic sections. We need to fill the knowledge gap that sits between adjacent well locations. Geostatistics can interpolate and extrapolate between and beyond the collected well logs by way of advanced soft computing algorithms. We discuss multivariate geostatistics in more detail in Chapter 10's "Multivariate Geostatistics." Another methodology is the derivation and analysis of seismic attributes.

CASE STUDY: RESERVOIR PROPERTIES DEFINED BY SEISMIC ATTRIBUTES

A principal component analysis (PCA) workflow implements statistical steps to gain insight into reservoir property characterization. Studying a 3D seismic dataset with derived amplitude values, it is feasible to offer a predictive capability to understand reservoir properties across a heavily faulted sand reservoir with shale inclusions.

As we are applying PCA to a single seismic attribute, namely amplitude, we must sample the 3D volume with a sliding window that encapsulates many contiguous amplitude samples from adjacent seismic traces. This enables us to populate vectors of sampled amplitude values for multiple windows across the 3D seismic volume. These vectors act as an input space for the PCA statistical algorithm, producing an output space that consists of a cube of clustered principal components (PCs) that act as a categorical variable when predicting reservoir properties distant from localized well control cores and wireline logs.

In areas of accelerated lateral stratigraphic variation within the reservoir, this methodology proves to be an efficient and accurate predictive workflow that enables geoscientists to build rigorous reservoir models. Traditional geostatistics adopt a variogram-based workflow implementing a suite of *kriging* and simulation steps. However, such workflows cannot capture in detail the lithofacies' distributions owing to the limitations inherent in the sampling bias of the hard-data at each control location.

The implementation of multivariate analysis to surface stratigraphic anomalies in seismic data has been discussed since 1969. But the adoption of predictive analytical workflows in geophysics has accelerated recently with the advent of commonly attainable high-fidelity 3D seismic data and subsequent derivation of pre- and post-stack seismic attributes.

A seismic attribute is any property derived from the seismic reflection signal and as such can be utilized as a means to predict a primary reservoir property distant from well control. There are several soft computing techniques that can be used as vehicles of a predictive nature. The stochastic landscape is littered with methodologies such as a basic linear multiplier (single attribute), multivariate and multivariant analysis using canonical correlation techniques, geostatistical approaches, nonlinear and fuzzy methods, and artificial neural networks.

It seems the number and variation of derived seismic attributes has been more expeditious than the uptake of implementing soft computing techniques embracing said attributes to ascertain areal reservoir properties outside of deterministic processes.

Of course, the first principles that invisibly link attributes to specific reservoir properties are well defined but the relationships from a data-driven perspective are shrouded in uncertainty. That uncertainty must be quantified to constrain the confidence in the results. However, unambiguity may never be attained; but to balance the argument can we state that scientists have not demonstrably proven beyond doubt those physical processes now coined as empirical truths?

There are also the age old questions when delving into the realm of statistics that find their roots in black-box logic. Can we trust the results based on pushing an input space of high dimensionality through an algorithm that could easily be deceived if overly trained? It has been shown that there is a distinct possibility that a false correlation is feasible, if not anticipated, when the number of attributes in the input space reaches a certain limit, inviting the unwelcome guests: redundancy and colinearity.

Lendzionowski, Walden, and White suggest that the maximum number of independent attributes to comprehensively represent a trace segment can be designated by a simple equation:[8]

2BT: B = bandwidth (Hz) and T = trace segment length (seconds)

The implication is that the majority of the common attributes are redundant. And this redundancy highlights the potential for collinearity between multiple seemingly independent seismic attributes that bear similar correlations to a target or dependent variable.

We need to transform the input space that consists of the suite of seismic traces into a unique set of attributes representative of the singularity in the signal's characteristics. PCA is ideal to uncover both the smooth time trends and any sudden time-shifts in a multivariate dataset. Additionally, we also gain an understanding of the relationships among the attributes' values. Which contribute similar information to the PCA model and which provide unique information about the observations? PCA describes the correlation structure between input variables. Essentially, initial PCA analysis reveals groupings among observations and invariably two or three major groups of observations are not uncommon.

Recall we are striving to identify via a PCA application the "most comprehensively descriptive understanding of the signal" that is both "unique and mutually independent." These two definitions are à propos since they map to the nomenclature that explicates the essence of PCA: *maximally variant* and *mutually orthogonal*, respectively.

The first step in the PCA workflow is to compute all the covariances for N-input components. The second step provides the inversion of the covariance matrix so as to create a set of N-orthogonal eigenvectors and corresponding eigenvalues. Each eigenvector–eigenvalue pair represents a distinct principal component (PC). All N-PCs are solitarily and concurrently calculated from the set of input vectors. Inversion of the covariance matrix guarantees the unique identification of the "maximally variant" component (highest-eigenvalue PC). All secondary PCs, ranked in order of decreasing eigenvalue, are mutually orthogonal (the eigenvector ensures this).

We then derive an unabridged set of seismic attributes represented as PCs and this process attains the following important characteristics for the attributes under study:

- Maximally descriptive of the signal
- Mutually independent, and therefore maximally unique

PCA requires multiple (N) inputs, even though we are applying PCA against only one seismic attribute: amplitude. But recall we are analyzing many adjacent amplitude values simultaneously via a sampling window.

The seismic methodology inherently disperses subsurface reflector knowledge throughout a larger volume of recorded amplitude data outside the immediate scope of a localized reflector. The seismic wavelet has a limited bandwidth of spectral components and is dominated by long wavelengths (low frequencies), resulting in its dispersive nature. Thus, the wavelet ambiguously images any localized, tightly grouped features.

It is necessary to design a sampling window to encapsulate the dispersed signal resulting from a small-scale feature in the subsurface, but ensure exclusion of as much unrelated signal as possible.

The sampling-window selects all the amplitude values (N-samples) as an ordered N-dimensional vector that acts as an input to the PCA algorithm. By sampling the entire 3D seismic data volume with multiple evenly sized windows, we generate the statistical array of vector samples requisite for computation of covariances. This step immediately precedes the inversion of the covariance matrix. The size of the sampling window is calculated by identifying the number of grid samples above and below a relative reference point that is at the center of each window. It was decided to limit the size of the window in the vertical dimension to approximately the seismic wavelet's mean-period, ~34 milliseconds in this dataset. Thus, by limiting the sampling window to approximately the size of the impulse wavelet, we capture the signal that is directly related to any given reflector while minimizing the influence of signal generated by other, unrelated reflectors.

We are primarily interested in the stationary components correlating to localized reflectors and to render this knowledge it is necessary to calibrate the PCs with well logs.

The process whereby we calibrate the PCs to the well data strives to "smash" the dispersed fine-scale knowledge back to the initial physical locus of the reflectors, by comparison with the highly resolved reservoir property data at the wells. The ultimate goal is to attain a highly resolved and unequivocal reservoir property representation in 3D directly from the decomposed seismic signal. A clustering algorithm is first applied to the principal components. Subsequently we ascertain a predicted reservoir property (effective porosity) on the grid, by implementing the statistics of the reservoir property at the wells for each cluster.

In Figure 3.24 the first PC with the highest eigenvalue contains the most knowledge about the trace and each subsequent PC steadily has less information about the studied trace. This reflects progressively smaller variance contributions of the total signal volume.

In the scree plot depicted in Figure 3.24 we note a simple line segment plot that shows the fraction of total variance in the amplitude data as explained or

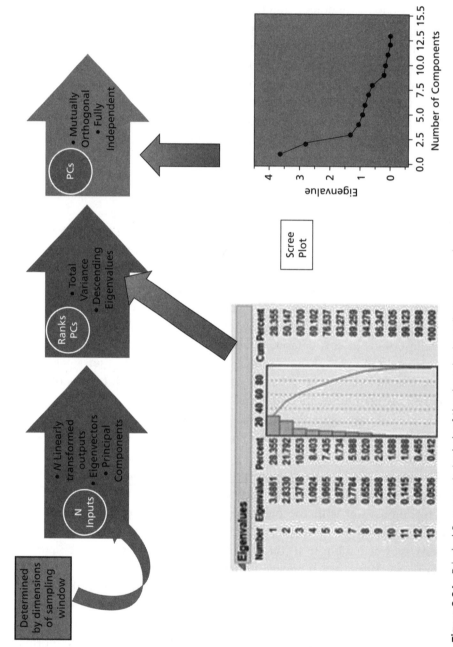

Figure 3.24 Principal Components Analysis of Singular Seismic Attribute

represented by each PC. The PCs are ordered, and by definition are therefore assigned a number label, by decreasing order of contribution to total variance. The PC with the largest fraction contribution is labeled with the label name from the preferences file. Such a plot when read left-to-right across the abscissa can often show a clear separation in fraction of total variance where the "most important" components cease and the "least important" components begin. The point of separation is often called the "elbow."

The *fully independent* characteristic is adopted as the premise for clustering and classifying the population of transformed input vectors.

The dimensionality of the input space was reduced not by factor analysis but accomplished through the use of a clustering approach. Clustering allows us to produce a volume of discrete classes that are computed directly, using all significant PCs in an objective way. This strategy combines the signifi-cant information contained in all the PCs with compactness of a categorical description.

The mutually orthogonal principal components inherently occupy a world of N-orthogonal spatial dimensions (so-called *principal component-space*). Understanding its eigenvector coefficients in this multidimensional space, it is plausible for each sample vector to be located uniquely. With all sample vectors (seismic sample windows) containing unique loci in this PC-space, a proximity-based clustering scheme (K-means method) can be implemented. This cluster approach jointly clusters and classifies each window of the seismic data. It is reasonable to assume that the same cluster index will be associated to those sample vectors that are located proximal to one another in PC-space. Having resolved cluster membership for a given sample, the cluster index can be posted on the original seismic grid at each sample-window's reference point. The resulting cube populated by PCA cluster indexes represents a suite of unique categorical properties. Thus the PC clustering component in the workflow depicted in Figure 3.25 retains the characteristic uniqueness of all the PCs, but reduces the dimensionality of the problem space by forming a single categorical variable that we use for calibration to well data.

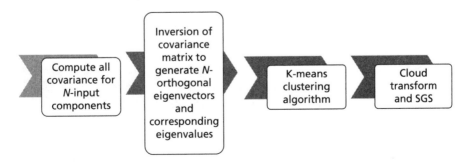

Figure 3.25 PCA Workflow

It is necessary to determine the parameter representative of the number of clusters prior to executing the clustering algorithm. Ultimately, we must calibrate the clusters by comparing them to spatially corresponding reservoir property values at the wells, and the number of clusters retained will determine in part the success of this operation. There are two influential considerations to be evaluated that compete for the ideal setting of the number of clusters parameter:

1. Selection of a higher number of clusters diminishes the average sampled volume per cluster. This addresses the concept behind producing as finely resolved a characterization as possible, in an attempt to capture fine reservoir detail.

2. To calibrate the clusters with greater statistical weight necessitates catching as many well data points within each cluster as is possible. This objective results in selecting fewer clusters, increasing the sampled volume per cluster.

It was decided to elect 50 clusters as optimal to attain a balance between these two competing objectives. Experimentation and some subjective analysis is required to arrive at the optimal choice of cluster number, and usually retaining multiple choices of cluster numbers will serve to capture the uncertainty imposed by this step.

The categorical variable (cluster index) enables the implementation of a geostatistical estimation (simulation) defined as a *categorical cloud transform*. This generates multiple realizations of the property estimates based on the co-located well and cluster properties.

We use this technique to populate the seismic grid with effective porosity (PHIE) by using the PCA clusters as a guide. PHIE is the proportion of fluids in the matrix (Figure 3.26). It is generally accepted that PHIT should preferably be used to compute water saturation and hydrocarbon volumes. Unfortunately, no logs currently enable direct calculation of PHIT. Coring and laboratory measurements are required before PHIT can be accurately calculated from logs. PHIE should therefore be used in exploration wells or where insufficient laboratory measurements are available.

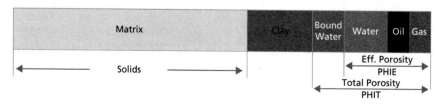

Figure 3.26 Distribution of Fluids and Formation Solids

A cloud transform is a stochastic estimation technique that enables geoscientists to simulate a variable from another variable using the scatter diagram between them and is based on matching a cross-plot (*cloud*) of points relating the two variables. The cloud is simply the physical bivariate plot of soft- versus hard-data at the wells' sampling locations. In order to apply the transform ubiquitously, the soft-data must be located everywhere. The hard-data must exist at the sampled well locations and are intended for estimation over the entire grid, guided by the soft-data. Here the PCA clusters are the soft-data and PHIE values are the hard-data.

The cloud transform is a derivative of the commonly used sequential Gaussian simulation (SGS) methodology of property estimation and is capable of generating multiple unique estimations of property values. All such estimated volumes obey the imposed spatial geostatistical model (variogram structure) and honor the hard-data.

SGS creates a property estimate using the following five steps as depicted in Figure 3.27:

Step 1. A random travel path is determined to pass through the unpopulated cells of the grid. Once established, the first cell can be populated.

Step 2. Compute the local kriging solution constrained by the PHIE values and populate the first cell on the path.

Step 3. A random selection is made from the univariate Gaussian population limited by the mean and variance for that location from step 2.

Step 4. The value selected in step 3 is posted to the first grid location and becomes a member of the hard-data.

Step 5. The algorithm then moves ahead to the next random-path location, repeating steps 1–4 until the entire grid is filled.

It must be noted that since previously simulated points influence the subsequently simulated values, each choice of random path will essentially generate a distinctly unique, yet equally valid, realization of the property.

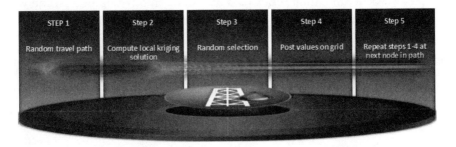

Figure 3.27 Sequential Gaussian Simulation Workflow

Synopsis

Amplitude anomalies associated with both free gas and light oil in the sandstone sections can be observed within the data. These effects show up as high-amplitude values on the right side of the amplitudes at the contacts. The presence of hydrocarbon-related amplitude effects presents a problem for conventional attribute analysis, in that PHIE generally varies independently of hydrocarbon saturation. A characterization of PHIE that is affected by hydrocarbon saturation can be typically unreliable. Our results using PCA clusters seem to be largely unaffected by these hydrocarbon anomalies thanks to the calibration method that is used.

Singular Spectrum Analysis

Singular spectrum analysis (SSA) is a relatively new approach to modeling time series data. The SSA method of time series analysis applies nonparametric techniques to decompose time series into principal components. SSA is particularly valuable for long time series, for which patterns (such as trends and cycles) are difficult to visualize and analyze.

Time series data often contain trends, cycles, anomalies, and other components. For long time series, these patterns are often difficult to visualize and discover. Singular spectrum analysis (SSA) applies nonparametric techniques that adapt the commonly used principal components analysis (PCA) for decomposing time series data. These components can help the analyst discover and understand the various patterns contained in the time series. Once these components are understood by the analyst, each component series can be modeled and forecasted separately; then, the component series forecasts can be aggregated to forecast the original series under investigation.

To illustrate the use of SSA in geophysics, 3D seismic data acquired from a marine environment are analyzed to discover significant patterns.

Basic Time Series Analysis

The post-stack seismic time series data are representative of a cross-line with 390 traces shot at 4 milliseconds sample period over 4 seconds.

Singular Spectrum Analysis

Next, singular spectrum analysis is applied using a threshold value for the eigenspectrum. The time series is analyzed using the TIMESERIES procedure as follows:

```
proc timeseries data=noaa out=_NULL_ plot = (series cycles SSA);
     SSA / LENGTH=120 THRESHOLD=80;
```

```
   id trace interval=ms;

   var amplitude;

run;
```

The SSA statement LENGTH=120 option specifies a window length of 120 (ten years), and the THRESHOLD=80 option specifies an eigenspectrum threshold value of 80 percent. Including SSA as one of the values in the PLOT= option requests that the SSA analysis be plotted.

Figure 3.28 illustrates the eigenspectrum plot. The first graph illustrates the eigenspectrum, and the second graph illustrates the cumulative percentage of the eigenspectrum on the *Y*-axis, and the *X*-axis represents the window lags. As you can see from this graph, the eigenspectrum decreases rapidly after the fourth lag. Close inspection reveals that there are two steps of equal value in the eigenspectrum plot: (1 2) (3 4).

Next, singular spectrum analysis is applied using grouping of the eigenspectrum. The time series is analyzed using the TIMESERIES procedure as follows:

```
PROC timeseries data=noaa out=_NULL_ plot = (series cycles SSA)

OUTSSA=SSA;

   ssa / length=120 GROUP = (1 2)(3 4);

   id trace interval=ms;

   var amplitude;

run;
```

The SSA statement GROUP = (1 2) (3 4) specifies that the series be decomposed into two spectral groups. The first group contains the first lag and the second lag; the second group contains the third and fourth lags. Since two spectral groups are requested, the dataset contains two variables (GROUP1 and GROUP2).

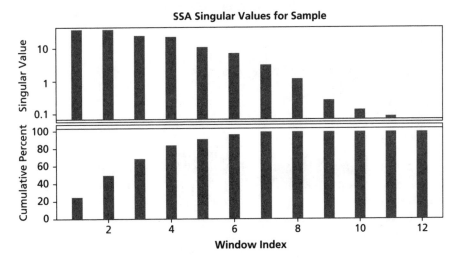

Figure 3.28 Single Value and Cumulative Percentage Eigenspectrum

As you can see from the plot, the first group represents the dominant short-term cycle in the amplitude anomaly series. From this plot, it appears that amplitude variation is small for the time window 2400 milliseconds to 3000 milliseconds.

Figure 3.29 illustrates the first and second group. In the first graph, the black line represents the original series and the blue line represents the first group. In the second graph, the blue line represents the second group.

Figure 3.30 illustrates the first group. In the first graph, the black line represents the original series and the blue line represents the first group. In the second graph, the blue line represents the first group.

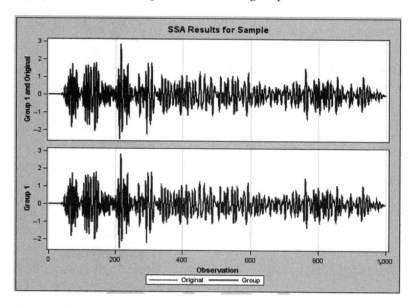

Figure 3.29 Singular Spectrum Analysis Results

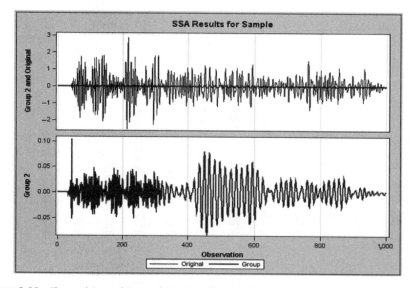

Figure 3.30 First and Second Spectral Group of the Amplitude Anomaly

As you can see in Figure 3.30, the second group represents the dominant medium-term cycle in the amplitude anomaly series. From this plot, it appears that amplitude variation is very large for the time window 1600 Ms to 2400 Ms.

Figure 3.31 depicts the periodogram and spectral density for the 390 traces.

The preceding analysis decomposed the time series into additive components. Multiplicative components can be achieved by taking the log transform of the (positive-valued) time series.

Unobserved Component Model Analysis

Now that the time series has been effectively decomposed into spectral groups, the first spectral grouping is analyzed using a basic trend model (state space model) using the *unobserved component model* (UCM) procedure:

```
proc ucm data=SSA;
    id trace interval=ms;
    model GROUP1;
    LEVEL;
    SLOPE PLOT=SMOOTH;
run;
```

The DATA= option of the PROC UCM statement specifies the input dataset. The ID statement specifies that the time ID variable is TRACE and the time interval is milliseconds. The MODEL statement specifies that the variable under analysis is GROUP1 (the first spectral group). The LEVEL statement specifies that a time-varying level component be included in the state-space model, and

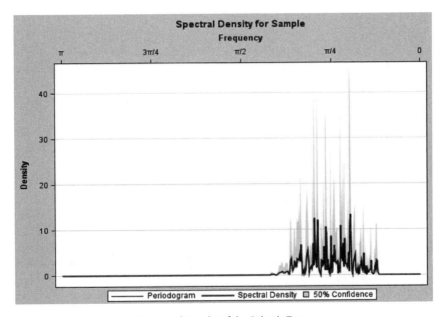

Figure 3.31 Periodogram and Spectral Density of the Seismic Traces

the SLOPE statement specifies that a time-varying slope component be included in the state space model. Figure 3.32 illustrates the slope component over time.

Figures 3.32 and 3.33 illustrate the distribution of the slope component. The results of this analysis (not shown) indicate that the mean/median filtered slope component is 0.00081 degrees per millisecond (about 1 degree per 1.25 seconds) with standard deviation of 0.00125 per millisecond and that the final

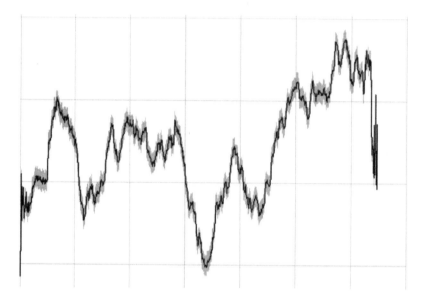

Figure 3.32   Slope Component of the Amplitude Anomaly

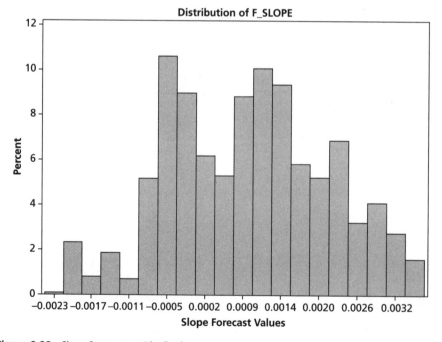

Figure 3.33   Slope Component Distribution

filtered slope component is (−0.0031) degree per millisecond (about −3 degrees per second).

Other analyses can be applied to each of the spectral groups: time domain analysis, frequency domain analysis, component analysis, distribution analysis, forecasting, and others.

Singular spectrum analysis (SSA) is a very powerful tool for detecting patterns in long time series with few model assumptions. SSA effectively decomposes time series into spectral groupings. These spectral groupings can be individually analyzed using time series analysis techniques such as forecasting and state-space component analysis.

Unsupervised Seismic Analysis

Estimating reservoir properties away from localized well control is a hazardous and invariably arduous task. However, adopting a workflow that is predicated on derived seismic attributes being analyzed via pattern recognition algorithms enables a data-driven methodology to supplement the traditional deterministic interpretation of geophysicists.

Owing to any scarcity in geological knowledge we are often found groping in the dark as we depend heavily on empirical assumptions to determine facies changes and seismic attribute associations to our objectives.

Let us propose two methodologies based on soft computing techniques. The Kohonen *self-organizing maps* (SOMs) enable geophysicists to create facies maps, and wavelet transforms aid in the identification of seismic trace singularities.

We know that variations in lithology and fluids result in changes in amplitude, instantaneous phase and frequency, lateral coherence, and other seismic attributes. Thus seismic attributes play an adjuvant role in the building of reservoir models. It is feasible to surface lateral changes in the reservoir through seismic attribute analytical workflows, with subsequent calibration with well information and experience garnered from geophysical interpreters. Implementing seismic data and pattern recognition techniques has been positioned by several scientific publications.[9]

The temporal and spatial segmentation of the reservoir is riddled with inherent uncertainties. Seismic stratigraphy enables geophysicists to identify and evaluate seismic facies vis-à-vis the geologic heterogeneity.[10] The analysis is undertaken by studying seismic traces to surface the characteristics of a window or cluster of seismic reflections comprised of amplitudes, phases, frequencies, continuity, and configuration of said reflections. Can we predict under uncertainty the stratigraphy and depositional environment?

Let us initiate a seismic facies study following the workflow depicted in Figure 3.34. This workflow implements the SOM soft computing technique.

The SOM is closely related to vector quantization methods. It is assumed *a priori* that the input variables (i.e., the seismic attributes) can be represented by

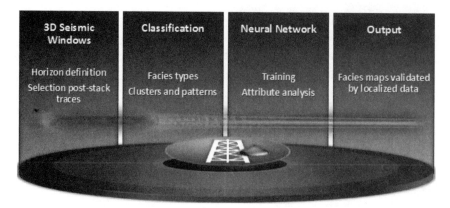

Figure 3.34 Seismic Facies Workflow

vectors in the space R^n, $x = [x_1, x_2, \ldots, x_n]$. The intention is to arrange the input dataset consisting of seismic attributes into a geometric structure known as the SOM. Each SOM unit, defined as a vector prototype, is connected to its neighbors, which in 2D usually forms hexagonal or rectangular structural maps.

Let us estimate the number of seismic facies through SOM visualization. Initially we select a number for the SOM prototype vectors that is larger than the number of anticipated groups in the data. Even though only qualitative information is generated, by using concepts of geomorphology, this procedure can be quite a powerful interpretation tool. To obtain a more quantitative clustering of data properties, SOM groups could be visualized using the U-matrix and chosen manually.

Agglomerative, or *partitive*, SOM clustering or U-matrix segmentation using image processing algorithms provides an automated means of clustering. A clustering methodology known as *K-means partitive* is employed as the algorithm. As opposed to traditional K-means, it classifies the prototype vectors instead of the original data. Thus, very large datasets formed by the SOM prototype vectors can be indirectly clustered. This approach not only furnishes a better understanding about the group formations, but it is also computationally more dynamic. An additional benefit inherent in this methodology is noise suppression owing to the prototype vectors that represent local averages of the original data without any loss of resolution. An optimal clustering algorithm should minimize the distance between the elements of each group and, at the same time, maximize the distance between the different clusters.

The model used as input to generate the convolutional synthetic dataset is illustrated in Figure 3.35. The reservoir is represented by three different seismic facies characterized by their P-wave propagation velocities of 3240 m/s (meters per second), 3300 m/s, and 3375 m/s.

The study used the seismic amplitudes within a 30-sample window around the reservoir base. The contiguous seismic trace amplitudes adopted as input attributes is equivalent to a waveform classification in the zone of interest.

The analysis results are shown in Figure 3.36. The U-matrix, the DBI, and the resulting facies map can be seen, respectively. In this example, three groups

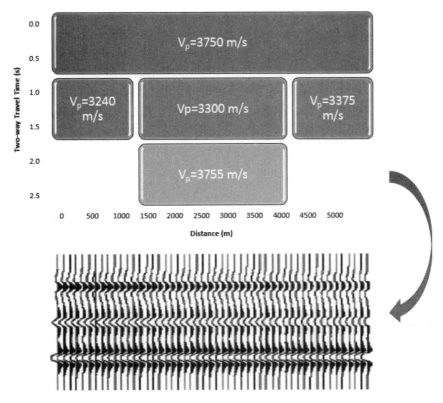

Figure 3.35 Geologic Velocity Model and Seismic Response

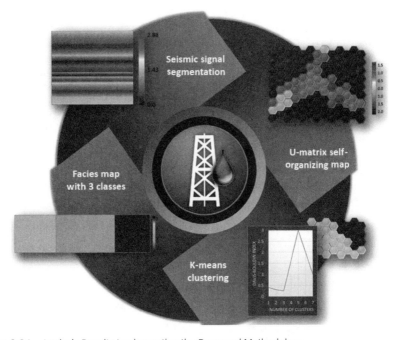

Figure 3.36 Analysis Results Implementing the Proposed Methodology

or facies are easily identified from the U-matrix, and the classification result was excellent. However, the minimum DBI of 4 did not correspond to the number of existing facies. Therefore, the choice of the number of facies should, whenever possible, be done in a semiautomatic way; in other words, the estimate of the facies number should be confirmed by the U-matrix visualization.

Such a result is related to the chosen seismic attribute, which is known to be sensitive to time displacements.[11] Therefore, the choice of the seismic attributes for the classification of seismic patterns is fundamental to obtain coherent results.[12]

NOTES

1. Norman S. Neidell, "Stratigraphic Modeling and Interpretation," AAPG Department of Education, 1979.

2. M. T. Taner, F. Koehler, and R. E. Sheriff, "Complex Seismic Trace Analysis," *Geophysics* 44 (1979): 1196–1212.

3. T. Smith, "Seismic Data: Time to Reconsider Neural Networks?" *Digital Energy Journal* 45 (Nov./ Dec. 2013): 8–9.

4. J. Lin, E. Keogh, S. Lonardi, J. P. Lankford, and D. M. Nystrom, "Visually Mining and Monitoring Massive Time Series," in *Proceedings of the Tenth ACM SIGKDD International Conference on Knowledge Discovery and Data Mining*, Seattle, WA, Aug. 22–25, 2004, KDD '04, New York, ACM Press, pp. 460–469.

5. See N. Jardine and R. Sibson, *Mathematical Taxonomy*, London, Wiley, 1971; L. Fisher and J. W. Van Ness, "Admissible Clustering Procedures," *Biometrika* 58 (1971): 91–104; and J. Hartigan, *Clustering Algorithms* (New York: John Wiley & Sons, 1975).

6. See G. W. Milligan, "An Examination of the Effect of Six Types of Error Perturbation on Fifteen Clustering Algorithms," *Psychometrika* 45 (1980): 325–342.

7. L. Cosentino, *Integrated Reservoir Studies* (Paris: Editions Technip, 2001).

8. V. Lendzionowski, A. Walden, and R. White, "Seismic Character Mapping Over Reservoir Intervals," *Geophysical Prospecting* 38 (1990): 951.

9. J. Dumay and F. Fournier, "Multivariate Statistical Analyses Applied to Seismic Facies Recognition," *Geophysics* 53, no. 9 (1988): 1151–1159; F. Fournier and J. Derain, "A Statistical Methodology for Deriving Reservoir Properties from Seismic Data," *Geophysics* 60, no. 5 (1995): 1437; and M. M. Saggaf, M. N. Toksöz, and M. I. Marhoon, "Seismic Facies Classification and Identification by Competitive Neural Networks," *Geophysics* 68 (2003): 1984–1999.

10. J. Dumay and F. Fournier, "Multivariate Statistical Analyses Applied to Seismic Facies Recognition," *Geophysics* 63, no. 9 (1988): 1151–1159.

11. E. C. Rankey and J. C. Mitchell, "That's Why It's Called Interpretation: The Role of Horizon Uncertainty on Seismic Attribute Analysis," *The Leading Edge* (2003): 820–828.

12. M. Poupon, T. Coléou, and K. Azbel, "Unsupervised Seismic Facies Classification: A Review and Comparison of Techniques and Implementation," *The Leading Edge* (2003), 22: 942–953.

CHAPTER 4

Reservoir Characterization and Simulation

Simplicity is the ultimate sophistication.

Leonardo da Vinci

Reservoir characterization is the process whereby a model of a subsurface body of rock is defined, incorporating all the distinguishing features that are pertinent to the reservoir capacity to accumulate hydrocarbons. One of the critical roles in traditional reservoir management is reservoir characterization as it enables the upstream engineers to make sound decisions regarding the exploitation of both oil and gas stored in these assets. The models strive to explain through simulation the behavior of fluids as they flow through the reservoir under a variable set of natural circumstances. The ultimate goal is to establish a suite of optimal strategies to maximize the production of the black gold.

Across the exploration and production (E&P) value chain the scope of success in drilling, completion, and production strategies hinges on the quantifiable accuracy of the reservoir characterization. An ever-increasing number of Society of Petroleum Engineers technical papers (Figure 4.1) are positioning data-driven models, analytics, and the range of soft computing techniques (neural networks, fuzzy logic, and genetic algorithms) as demonstrable processes to enhance the reservoir models.

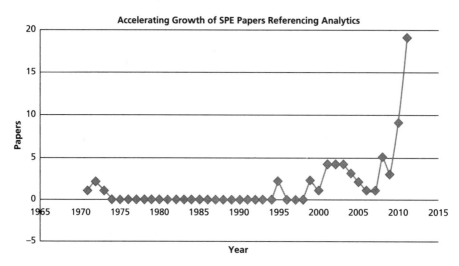

Figure 4.1 Accelerated Uptake of Soft Computing Technical Papers

EXPLORATION AND PRODUCTION VALUE PROPOSITIONS

Often well data are deficient in regular quantity, and seismic data exhibit poor resolution owing to fractured reservoirs, basalt intrusions, and salt domes. Easy oil is a thing of the past and we are led to explore in uncharted frontiers such as deepwater environments and the unconventional reservoirs that house tight gas and oil-bearing shales. During the exploration, development, and production phases of such resources it is apparent that business strategies become more problematic and that perhaps the traditional approach that entails a deterministic study necessitates a supplementary methodology. The E&P value chain (Figure 4.2) opens multiple opportunities to garner knowledge from the disparate datasets by advocating a data-driven suite of workflows based on advanced analytical models and by establishing more robust reservoir models. Thus it is vital to adopt a hybrid stance that marries interpretation and soft computing methodologies to address business problems such as quantifying the accuracy of reservoir models and enhancing production performance as well as maximizing location of both production and injector wells.

The oil and gas industry devotes a great deal of resources and expenditures in the upstream E&P domain. When we think about the lifecycle of an asset such as a well or reservoir, there is a business decision that must take place during each phase. That decision must have commercial value. You could be entering a new play and doing exploration to generate prospects, striving to gain insight from seismic and to locate exploratory wells in increasingly complex reservoirs. You need to appraise the commercial

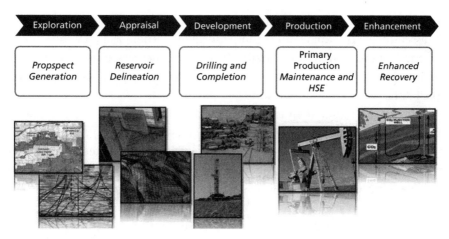

Figure 4.2 Exploration and Production Value Chains

quantities of hydrocarbons and mitigate risks while drilling delineation wells to determine type, shape, and size of reservoir and strategies for optimum development.

During the development stage, a drilling program with optimized completion strategies is enacted as additional wells are located for the production stage. Surface facilities are designed for efficient oil and gas exploitation. Do we have to consider water production? What cumulative liquid productions do we anticipate? These are some of the questions we need to answer as we design those surface facilities.

The production phase necessitates efficient exploitation of the hydrocarbons. We have to consider health, safety, and environment (HSE) commitments and maintenance schedules. Is the production of hydrocarbons maximized for each well? How reliable are short- and long-term forecasts?

Maintaining optimal field production necessitates business decisions that determine whether an asset is economically viable. How do we identify wells that are ideal candidates for artificial lift? When and how do we stimulate a candidate well?

We have to be aware of the three major challenges across the E&P value chain:

1. Data integration and management

2. Quantification of the uncertainty in a multivariate subsurface system

3. Risk assessment

These three tenets have recently been addressed by focusing a tremendous amount of effort to uncover innovative methodologies that can remediate the issues inherent in the traditional deterministic model-building exercises. The E&P

problems are evolving into complex and undeterminable constraints on effective asset discovery, exploitation, and performance. There is a growing need for efficient data integration across all upstream disciplines as we strive to turn raw data into actionable knowledge by quantifying uncertainty and assessing from a probabilistic perspective a set of strategies that mitigate risk.

Soft computing techniques that entail descriptive and predictive analysis and adoption of data-driven analytics to mine ever-increasing volumes of disparate data force us to move from reactive to proactive management of oil and gas assets. The degree of comprehension moves from raw data through information and insight to actionable knowledge.

The analytical methodology must always start with an exploratory data analysis (EDA) step that surfaces hidden trends and relationships in the multivariate complex system that is a hydrocarbon reservoir. Do not model raw data; determine a suite of hypotheses worth modeling through an exploration of your key asset: data.

Let us concentrate on the soft computing techniques at our disposal to understand how reservoir characterization can be enhanced as we strive to quantify the uncertainty in the rock properties. We must ultimately mitigate risks associated with the field engineering tactics and strategies that evolve from a compressed decision-making cycle. We can accelerate this process by data-driven methodologies that employ advanced analytics.

As a field matures over age with production performance declining owing to natural pressure changes in the reservoir, it behooves a reappraisal step that again studies the hydrocarbon lifecycle through a dynamic body that is the reservoir. Reservoir characterization calibrated by history matching offers a more substantial geologic model to underpin that reappraisal step.

Reservoir characterization of a brownfield that has been producing for decades necessitates the analysis of invariably very large datasets aggregated from well logs, production history, and core analysis results enhanced by high-resolution mapping of seismic attributes to reservoir properties. It is imperative to surface the more subtle relationships inherent in these datasets, to comprehend the structure of the data, and identify the correlations in a complex multivariate system.

To accurately quantify the uncertainty in subsurface variables it is necessary to appreciate the heterogeneity of a complex system such as a hydrocarbon reservoir. How best to achieve this goal? We need to move away from the singular traditional deterministic modeling of data that are invariably raw with little or no quality control. Between 50 and 70 percent of time attributed to a reservoir characterization study should be invested in an analytical methodology that starts with a suite of data management workflows. You then design an iterative process implementing a data exploration to surface hidden patterns and comprehend correlations, trends, and relationships among those variables, both operational and nonoperational, that bear the most statistical influence on an objective function.

EXPLORATORY DATA ANALYSIS

EDA encompasses an iterative approach and enhances the process toward consistent data integration, data aggregation, and data management. EDA is achieved by adopting a suite of visualization techniques from a univariate, bivariate, and multivariate perspective.

Let us enumerate some of the common visualization techniques and build a logical sequence that underpins the methodology for efficient reservoir characterization projects during the exploration, development, and production stages in the E&P value chain. It is important to stress the positive impact behind the EDA school of thought that is often forgotten or even precluded prior to any traditional spatial analysis such as kriging, simulation, and uncertainty quantification steps. Figure 4.3 reflects a flowchart that typically engages the EDA methodology.

It is imperative to reduce the dimensionality of an engineering problem as complex systems invariably consist of a multivariate suite of independent and dependent variables. Which parameters are most sensitive statistically and hence most dominant or relevant vis-à-vis an objective function that can be identified as one or more dependent variables? We can address dimensionality

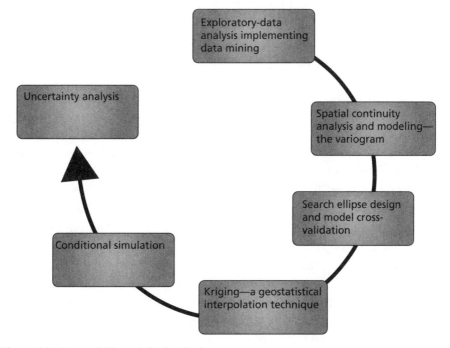

Figure 4.3 Reservoir Characterization Cycle

and consequently formulate more realistic models by adopting a suite of analytical workflows that implement techniques such as principal component and factor analyses.

EDA[1] is a philosophy for data analysis that employs a variety of techniques (mostly graphical) to achieve the following:

- Maximize insight into a dataset.
- Uncover underlying structure.
- Extract important variables.
- Detect outliers and anomalies.
- Test underlying assumptions.
- Develop parsimonious models.
- Determine optimal factor settings.

The main objective of any EDA study is to maximize insight into a dataset. Insight connotes ascertaining and disclosing underlying structure in the data. The significant and concrete insight for a dataset surfaces as the analyst aptly scrutinizes and explores the various nuances of the data. Any appreciation for the data is derived almost singularly from the use of various graphical techniques that yield the essence of the data. Thus, well-chosen graphics are not only irreplaceable, but also at the heart of all insightful determinations since there are no quantitative analogues adopted in a more classical approach. It is essential to draw upon your own pattern-recognition and correlative abilities while studying the graphical depictions of the data under study, and steer away from quantitative techniques that are classical in nature. However, EDA and classical schools of thought are not mutually exclusive and thus can complement each other during a reservoir characterization project.

In an EDA, workflow data collection is not followed by a model imposition; rather it is followed immediately by analysis and a goal of inferring what model would be appropriate. The focus is on the data, their structure, outliers, and models suggested by the data, and hence hypotheses that are worth pursuing. These techniques are generally graphical. They include scatterplots, character plots, box plots, histograms, probability plots, residual plots, and mean plots. EDA techniques do not share in the exactness or formality witnessed in the classical estimation techniques that tend to model the data prior to analysis. EDA techniques compensate for any paucity of rigor by adopting a very meaningful, characteristic, and insightful perspective about what the applicable model should be. There are two protocols that are imposed on the reservoir data and are model driven: deterministic modeling, such as regression models and analysis of variance (ANOVA) models, and probabilistic models that tend to assume that the errors inherent in deterministic models are normally distributed. Such a classical approach, quantitative in nature, is in contrast to the EDA methodology that does not impose deterministic or probabilistic models on the data, preferring the data to suggest acceptable models that reveal optimum fit to those data.

EDA techniques are thus instinctive and rely on interpretation that may vary across a broad scope of individual analysis, although experienced analysts invariably attain identical conclusions. Instead of adopting a classical filtering process that tends only to focus on a few important characteristics within a population by determining estimates, EDA exploits all available data to ensure that such inherent data characteristics such as skewness, kurtosis, and autocorrelation are not lost from that population. Also, unlike any intrinsic assumptions such as normality that are made in a classical approach, EDA techniques make few if any conjectures on upstream data, instead displaying all of the data. EDA strives to pursue as its goal any insight into the engineering or scientific process behind the data. Whereas summary statistics such as standard deviation and mean are passive and historical, EDA is active and futuristic. In order to comprehend the process and improve on it in the future, EDA implements the data as an *aperture* to delve into the core of the process that delivered the data.

Exploratory data analysis is used to identify systematic relationships between variables when there are no (or incomplete) *a priori* expectations as to the nature of those relationships. In a typical exploratory data analysis process, many variables are taken into account and compared, using a variety of techniques in the search for systematic patterns.

The basic statistical exploratory methods include examining distributions of variables (e.g., to identify highly skewed or non-normal, such as bimodal patterns), reviewing large correlation matrixes for coefficients that meet certain thresholds, or studying multi-way frequency tables (e.g., "slice-by-slice," systematically reviewing combinations of levels of control variables). Multivariate exploratory techniques designed specifically to identify patterns in multivariate (or univariate, such as sequences of measurements) datasets include:

- Cluster analysis
- Factor analysis
- Discriminant function analysis
- Multidimensional scaling
- Log-linear analysis
- Canonical correlation
- Stepwise linear and nonlinear regression
- Correspondence analysis
- Time series analysis
- Classification trees

RESERVOIR CHARACTERIZATION CYCLE

It is essential to scrutinize the plethora of data across all upstream domains, integrating cleansed data from the geophysics, geology, and reservoir engineering fields. The effort afforded to this task is critical to the ultimate success of uncertainty analysis, and it is appropriate to adopt workflows to streamline the requisite EDA. Collating many different types of data across all geoscientific domains and applications can be contained in one analytical framework.

EDA itself can be partitioned into four discrete component steps:

Step 1. Univariate analysis

Step 2. Multivariate analysis

Step 3. Data transformation

Step 4. Discretization

The univariate analysis profiles the data and details traditional descriptors such as mean, median, mode, and standard deviation. Multivariate analysis examines relationships between two or more variables, implementing algorithms such as linear or multiple regression, correlation coefficient, cluster analysis, and discriminant analysis. The data transformation methodology encompasses the convenience of placing the data temporarily into a format applicable to particular types of analysis; for example, permeability is often transferred into logarithmic space to abide its relationship with porosity. Discretization embraces the process of coarsening or blocking data into layers consistent within a sequence-stratigraphic framework. Thus well-log data or core properties can be resampled into this space.

TRADITIONAL DATA ANALYSIS

EDA is a data analysis approach. What other data analysis approaches exist and how does EDA differ from these other approaches?

Three popular data analysis approaches are:

1. Classical
2. Exploratory (EDA)
3. Bayesian

These three approaches are similar in that they all start with a general science and engineering problem and all yield science and engineering conclusions. The difference is in the sequence and focus of the intermediate steps.

For classical analysis the sequence is:

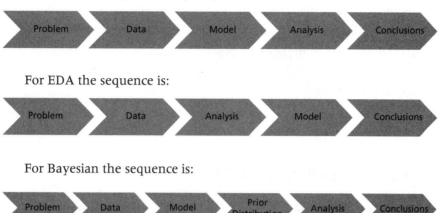

For EDA the sequence is:

For Bayesian the sequence is:

Thus for classical analysis, the data collection is followed by the imposition of a model (normality, linearity, etc.) and the analysis, estimation, and testing that follow are focused on the parameters of that model. For EDA, the data collection is not followed by a model imposition; rather it is followed immediately by analysis with a goal of inferring what model would be appropriate. Finally, for a Bayesian analysis, the analyst attempts to incorporate scientific and engineering knowledge and expertise into the analysis by imposing a data-independent distribution on the parameters of the selected model; the analysis thus consists of formally combining both the prior distribution on the parameters and the collected data to jointly make inferences and/or test assumptions about the model parameters.

The purpose of EDA is to generate hypotheses or clues that guide us in improving quality or process performance. Exploratory analysis is designed to find out "what the data are telling us." Its basic intent is to search for interesting relationships and structures in a body of data and to exhibit the results in such a way as to make them recognizable. This process involves *summarization*, perhaps in the form of a few simple statistics (e.g., mean and variance of a set of data) or perhaps in the form of a simple plot (such as a scatterplot). It also involves *exposure*, that is, the presentation of the data so as to allow one to see both anticipated and unexpected characteristics of the data. Discover the unexpected prior to confirming the suspected in order to elucidate knowledge that leads to field development decisions.

In summary, it is important to remember the following tenets that underpin successful reservoir characterization from an EDA perspective:

- EDA is an iterative process that surfaces by trial-and-error insights and these intuitive observations garnered from each successive step are the platform for the subsequent steps.

■ A model should be entertained at each EDA step, but not too much onus should be attributed to the model. Keep an open mind and flirt with skepticism regarding any potential relationships between the reservoir attributes.

■ Look at the data from several perspectives. Do not preclude the EDA step in the reservoir characterization cycle if no immediate or apparent value appears to surface.

■ EDA typically encompasses a suite of robust and resistant statistics and relies heavily on graphical techniques.

RESERVOIR SIMULATION MODELS

Habit is habit and not to be flung out of the window by any man, but coaxed downstairs a step at a time.

Mark Twain

A reservoir simulation is the traditional industry methodology to comprehend reservoir behavior with a view to forecasting future performance. On account of the complexities in the multivariate system that is the reservoir, a full-field simulation integrating both static and dynamic measurements yields a plausible model in the hands of expert engineers. However, this bottom-up approach starting with a geo-cellular model leading to a dynamic reservoir model is entrenched in first principles and fluid flow concepts that are solved numerically despite the inherent array of uncertainties and non-uniqueness in a calibration process such as history matching.

Top-down intelligent reservoir modeling (TDIRM), as postulated by Shahab Mohaghegh[2] in several SPE papers and commentaries, offers an alternative methodology that strives to garner insight into the heterogeneous complexity by initiating workflows with actual field measurements. This approach is both complementary and efficient, especially in cost-prohibitive scenarios where traditional industry simulation demands immense time and resource investment to generate giant field simulations. In short, TDIRM and similar philosophical workflows implement AI and data mining techniques that are the themes threading this book together across the E&P value chain.

A rich array of advanced analytics provides efficient and simple approaches to flexible workflows to address exploratory data analysis, uncertainty analysis, and risk assessment in typical reservoir characterization projects. Adopting a visualization of analytics reduces the time to appreciate the underlying structure of the disparate upstream data that are prerequisites to making accurate reservoir management strategies.

Rich web-based solutions also enable efficient distribution to decision makers of the vital information and knowledge mined from the enormous amounts of data: well logs, core data, production data, seismic data, and well test data.

Analytical Simulation Workflow

Let us explore a logical suite of processes to enable more insight into reservoir simulation.

- *Dividing fields into regions:* Allowing for comparisons of well performance.
- *Assisted and/or optimized history matching:* Reducing uncertainty with reservoir characteristics.
- *Identifying critical uncertainty factors:* During the analysis of production data, screen data to identify and rank areas of potential production improvement.
- *Analysis of history matching simulation runs:* Targeting an understanding of how these several specific runs are different from each other (or what they have in common).
- *Cluster analysis:* Applying cluster analysis with segment profiling can give an additional insight into differences between history match simulation runs.
- *Interactive data visualization:* Visualization software allows very complex interactive visualizations owing to customization ability with proprietary scripting language that enhances analytic effectiveness for faster insights and actions.
- *Benefits realization:* The complex problem of the uncertainty assessment in performance forecasting is done with analytics using reservoir simulation models with extensive production history.
- *Well correlations:* Sophisticated data access and automated analyses of field data, such as well correlations, can now be processed in a significantly reduced amount of time.
- *Decline curve analysis:* Rather than blindly using all attributes of inputs for modeling, it is necessary to carry out an analysis to determine those attributes that bring a significant amount of useful information of the problem.

Let us explore the first three processes.

Dividing Fields into Regions

Leveraging nonlinear multivariate regressions, interpolation and smoothing procedures, principal component analysis, cluster analysis, and discrimination analysis, it is feasible to divide a field into discrete regions for field reengineering tactics and strategies. The methodology classifies the wells according to the production indicators, and divides the field into areas.

The statistical results can be mapped to identify the production mechanisms (e.g., best producers, depletion, pressure maintenance, and to identify and locate poorly drained zones potentially containing remaining reserves). Field reengineering can also be optimized by identifying those wells where the productivity can be improved.

The following list provides a short summary of the steps in wells classification process:

- Production statistics data preparation:
  - Oil produced daily, water cut percent, gas produced daily.
- Decline curve analysis:
  - Modeling daily production with nonlinear regressions.
- Data noise reduction and data interpolation:
  - Implementation of smoothing methods that are most applicable to available data. For instance, in case of non-equally-spaced data you can use LOWESS (locally weighted least squares) smoothing methodology. Use resulting smoothed curves to interpolate missing data points for water cuts and GOR curves.
- Wells clustering:
  - Principal component analysis:
    - Used to create low-dimensional approximation to production dataset. This technique is often used before cluster analysis.
  - Cluster analysis:
    - Applied to condensed dataset with fewer factor scores (principal component analysis transformation of original variables).
    - Analysis of clusters with different methods: segment profiling and dendrograms.
- Appraisal of wells representation:
  - It can be useful for subsequent studies to have only a limited set of representative wells and to avoid intensive processing.
  - Discriminant analysis:
    - Performed to provide the probabilities of each well belonging to the obtained clusters.

Assisted and/or Optimized History Matching

The *history matching* process is conducted to reduce uncertainty regarding reservoir characteristics. This is done by matching simulation outputs with observed historical data (pressures, water cuts, etc.) by means of varying uncertainty matrix variables. Quality of the match is a statistical measure that identifies how close the simulation run matched the history (zero value would mean ideal match). It is beneficial to implement algorithms to semi-automate the process of searching for solution (Quality = 0) in a multidimensional space defined by the uncertainty matrix variables ranges. We define three main steps for this process:

Step 1. *Perform scoping runs:* To explore relationships between uncertainty matrix variables and simulation outputs (response variables) and train initial estimates based on the information. Employ an Estimator, also called *proxy* or *response surface model*.

Step 2. *Perform most informative runs:* Try to improve quality of the match by exploring solution space in the places that are the most promising according to currently available information in the Estimator.

Step 3. *Perform best match runs:* Global optimization by all uncertainty matrix variables to fit Estimator (response surface model) to historical production data.

It is plausible to suppose that quality will converge to some value close to zero, which is not always true during a history matching process. By analyzing runs (using quality convergence, bracketing, and other types of runs analysis) we can determine if the simulations moved in the wrong direction and searched in the wrong place. In such a case the uncertainty matrix will be adjusted according to the reservoir characteristics knowledge already surfaced and the history matching process will be restarted from the beginning (scoping runs).

The main challenges in the process are:

1. *Identifying critical uncertainty factors:* Which variables have the most impact on quality convergence?
2. *Analysis of simulation runs:* Pattern discovery and comparison of simulation runs to reveal important differences.
3. *Adjusting uncertainty matrix:* How to avoid human judgment errors.

Let us explore a functional history matching methodology that establishes a suite of models that fall above a level of quality imposed by reservoir engineers. Thus we tend to identify those models that have an objective function value under a predefined value. We are not then focused on optimization issues such as local minimum, convergence, and rapidity but more interested in how the quality of the model is measured. It is critical to define the objective function that measures the quality. Functional history matching is invariably coupled with uncertainty analysis that comes with an inflated price when addressed by traditional numerical simulations. We can demonstrate usage of simplified models known as *proxies*, touching on surface response models and artificial neural networks. The functional history matching approach is based on the work initiated by Reis, who proposes a process illustrated in Figure 4.4.

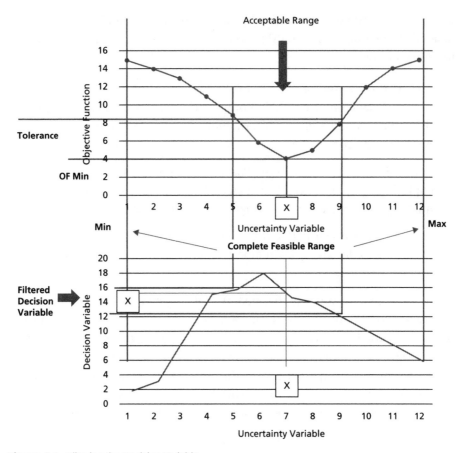

Figure 4.4 Filtering the Decision Variable

Let us assume that all input variables are known except one, so the *objective function* (OF) then depends on one single uncertainty variable. Considering the entire possible range of the values the uncertainty variable could represent, we would search for the minimum value of OF and then identify the "optimum" value *x*. In Figure 4.4 the value *x* correlates to the value *y* of the decision variable (e.g., NPV). However, this is the best model (uncertainty variable value) for the available information, but this model is not necessarily true. Instead of attaining the best model, a suite of models should be under investigation for subsequent analyses. This set of probabilistic models are within an acceptable range as constrained by the objective function and correspond to OF values above the minimum one in accordance to a tolerance threshold previously established by reservoir engineers.

Identifying Critical Uncertainty Factors

There are several tools that can help to resolve the problem of identifying *critical factors* from different perspectives:

- *Decision tree analysis:* automated or supervised learning.

- *Variable importance* based on statistical correlations and other measures.

- *Regressions* can additionally reveal interactions between uncertainty variables.

These techniques are applied to production data, well log data, and core data. Appreciating the stationarity assumptions along both the spatial plane and the temporal axis is important. During the analysis of production data it is necessary to screen the data to identify and rank areas of potential production improvement.

A decision tree represents a segmentation of the data that is created by applying a series of simple rules. Each rule assigns a simulation run to a segment based on the value of one input variable. One rule is applied after another, resulting in a hierarchy of segments within segments. The hierarchy is called a *tree*, and each segment is called a *node*. The original segment contains the entire dataset and is called the *root node of the tree*. Implementing such a technique identifies those reservoir properties that have most predictive power and hence most influence on a determinant or object variable such as OOIP or water cut.

An uncertainty matrix can have hundreds of potential variables that correspond to history match quality response (by means of simulator model). There are a number of statistical approaches to reduce the number of variables, which can be considered as determining variable importance in their power of predicting the match quality.

From a statistical standpoint this can be done by using R-square or Chi-square variable selection criterion (or their combination).

Surrogate Reservoir Models

Traditional proxy models such as the range of response surfaces or reduced models are piecemeal being replaced by *surrogate reservoir models* (SRMs) that are based on pattern recognition proficiencies inherent in an artificial intelligence and data mining school of thought. The numerical reservoir simulation model is a tutor to the SRM, training it to appreciate the physics and first principles of fluid flow through porous media of a specific reservoir as well as the heterogeneous and complex nature of the reservoir characteristics as depicted by the static geologic model. Fluid production and pressure gradients across the reservoir are instilled into the education of the SRM that is defined as a smart replica of a full-field reservoir simulation model.

SRMs offer a feasible alternative to the conventional geostatistical methodologies reflected by response surface and proxy models. As the objective function in uncertainty analysis, SRMs are effective in generating stochastic simulations of the reservoir, quantifying the uncertainty and thus mitigating some of the risks in performance prediction and field reengineering strategies. Additional benefits can be witnessed in real-time optimization and decision making based on real-time responses from the objective function.

Striving to resolve an inverse problem is a methodology that is a common denominator in building E&P models that have an ostensible analytical solution. The numerical solutions associated with traditional reservoir simulation practices are not ideal candidates to solve the inverse problem. SRMs provide the requisite tools to address the inverse problem in addition to furnishing a ranked suite of reservoir characteristics determined by *key performance indicators* that measure or quantify the influence or statistical impact each reservoir characteristic has on the simulation outcome, such as GOR or water cut.

CASE STUDIES

Predicting Reservoir Properties

Let us study a multivariate analytical methodology that incorporates a suite of soft computing workflows leading to a solution for the inverse problem of predicting reservoir properties across geologic layers in the absence of core data at localized wells.

One of the first steps is to implement a set of quantile–quantile (Q-Q) plots on the available data. The Q-Q plot is an exploratory graphical device used to check the validity of a distributional assumption for a dataset. The basic idea is to compute the theoretically expected value for each data point based on the distribution in question. If the data indeed follow the assumed distribution, then the points on the Q-Q plot will fall approximately on a straight line, as illustrated by the *gamma ray* variable in Figure 4.5.

The majority of the multivariate statistical techniques make the assumption that the data follow a multivariate normal distribution based on the experience that sampling distributions of multiple multivariate statistics are approximately normal in spite of the form of the parent population. This is due to the central-limit effect that in probability theory states that, given certain conditions, the mean of a sufficiently large number of independent random variables, each with a well-defined mean and well-defined variance, will be approximately normally distributed. The histogram and the cumulative distribution function (CDF) may be used to assess the assumption of normality by describing whether each variable follows a bell-shaped normal density (Figure 4.6).

Post Q-Q plots we can use principal components, factor analysis, and fuzzy logic concepts to identify the dominant variables and the optimum number of independent variables from the core and well logs that are available. It is imperative to reduce the dimensionality of the input space so as to reduce irrelevant variables that will cause the model to behave poorly. The neural

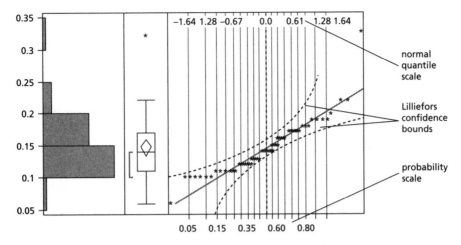

Figure 4.5 Gamma Ray Variable Displayed in a Q-Q Plot

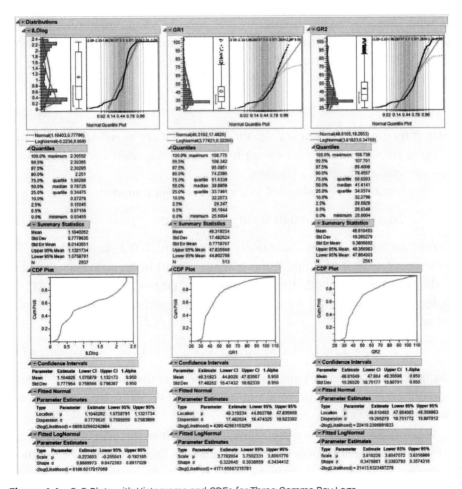

Figure 4.6 Q-Q Plots with Histograms and CDFs for Three Gamma Ray Logs

network, for example, is somewhat undermined by addressing an input space of high dimensionality since we wish to avoid the neural network using almost all of its resources to represent irrelevant sections of the space.

In the subsurface the majority of reservoir characterization algorithms are nonlinear. Soft computing techniques have evolved exponentially during the recent decade to enable identification of nonlinear, temporal, and non-stationary systems such as hydrocarbon reservoirs.

If we are studying more than one regressor variable, it is plausible to scale the input data prior to creating the multiple regression model coefficients since scaling will ensure all input regressors will have equal variance and mean. Thus the subtle differences in the corresponding multiple regression coefficients will be indicative of the value ascertained for each regressor on the model. Let us consider, for example, the logarithmic value of permeability within a particular formation. Assume this logarithm is a function of porosity and gamma ray reading (lithology) that reflects a high and low influence on permeability, respectively.

What does this mean? It suggests that porosity has a more critical role to play in a multiple regression model than the gamma ray reading reflecting lithology differences. Let us define an algorithm (equation 1) that reflects an inoperative model:

$$\text{Log } K\text{core} = 10 \times \text{GR}_{(API)} + 10 \times \varnothing_{(Fraction)} \qquad \text{Equation (1)}$$

There is no input or output scaling and the gamma ray in API units has more influence on the permeability owing to the scale of gamma ray and porosity, the latter being defined as a fraction.

Equation 2 may be positioned as a valid and logical model:

$$\text{Log}(K\text{core})_{(Scaled)} = 0.01 \times \text{GR}_{(Scaled)} + 10 \times \varnothing_{(Scaled)} \qquad \text{Equation (2)}$$

We now see both variables, gamma ray and porosity, at the same scale. Owing to the coefficient of porosity, it has a more critical influence upon the permeability. By scaling both the regressors and targets in the range [−1, 1] implementing equation 3 we are embracing the principle of equal variance and mean:

$$X_{(Scaled)} = (2 \times (X - X(\text{Min})/X_{(Max)} - X_{(Min)})) - 1 \qquad \text{Equation (3)}$$

In equation 3, X represents any variable and reflects the importance of scaling to accurately model in a complex and multivariate system such as a hydrocarbon reservoir.

We can also reduce the dimensionality and reduce the effects of collinearity by adopting the technique of cross-correlation. The coefficients determined via cross-correlation are indicative of the extent and direction of correlation. By modeling any target variable that is representative of an objective function such as production rate or plateau duration, we can implement an analytical workflow that incorporates as input variables those that have a high correlation with the identified target or dependent variable.

If you want to see the arrangement of points across many correlated variables, you can use principal component analysis (PCA) to show the most prominent directions of the high-dimensional data. Using PCA reduces the dimensionality of a set of data and is a way to picture the structure of the data as completely as possible by using as few variables as possible.

For n original variables, n principal components are formed as follows:

- The first principal component is the linear combination of the standardized original variables that has the greatest possible variance.

- Each subsequent principal component is the linear combination of the variables that has the greatest possible variance and is uncorrelated with all previously defined components.

Each principal component is calculated by taking a linear combination of an eigenvector of the correlation matrix (or covariance matrix) with a variable. The eigenvalues show the variance of each component and since the principal components are orthogonal to each other there is no redundancy.

Principal components representation is important in visualizing multivariate data by reducing them to dimensionalities that are able to be graphed as the total variance represented by the original variables is equal to the total variance explicated by the principal components.

Once the input space has thus been reduced, we can implement a fuzzy logic process. Recall from Chapter 1 the logic behind fuzzy thinking and the historical commentary on Aristotle and Plato.

Aristotle formulated the Law of the Excluded Middle. It states that for any proposition, either that proposition is true, or its negation is true. The principle was stated as a theorem of propositional logic by Russell and Whitehead in *Principia Mathematica*.[3] There is no middle or anything between the two parts of a contradiction where one proposition must be true and the other must be false.

However, human thought processes suggest otherwise, where the real world moves away from the bivalent black-and-white into the area that is somewhat gray! Is that why we refer to human brains as gray matter? How do we explain the variation in a curve that reflects a function of mineral volume in a specific rock based on gamma ray readings? Fuzzy logic rescues us from the Aristotelian manacles of Boolean logic. Essentially the world of fuzzy logic embraces four constitutional components:

1. Fuzzification of input/output variables

2. Fuzzy if–then rules

3. Weighting factors

4. De-fuzzification

Fuzzy logic is ostensibly a human appendage of conventional Boolean logic. As members of *homo sapiens sapiens* we tend to think as modern members of the human race, not in zeros and ones but in partial truths: those values that hover inexorably between "completely true" and "completely wrong."

Aristotle's laws of logic are founded on "*X* or not *X*"; it is either true or false. Inevitably we judge and classify in accordance to this stricture. We have an innate desire to categorize everything as it ameliorates our conventional thinking to drop something into a black or a white box. Of course the advent of computers only managed to reinforce this Boolean logic as a binary system underpins their natural reasoning mechanism.

But think about the constraints imposed by the Boolean logic in our thinking as we strive to establish analytical methodologies to help resolve business issues in the upstream E&P value chain. The continuous evolution of the multivariant, dynamic, and complex reservoir, for example, can only be described in a coarse approximation. Thus we are bereft of the essential details required to comprehend the possible solutions to a nondeterministic system. Let us not dismiss the range of probabilities established under uncertainty and described by confidence limits as we assess answers to subsurface questions. Not only does truth exist fundamentally on a moving scale, it is also discerned to change piecemeal by uncertainties in measurements and interpretations. Ironically, E&P engineers must move from the world of black-and-white into the "shadows" where gray predominates. This is the mathematics of fuzzy logic.

The multitude of possibilities that characterize this gray terrain must be tamed by quantification of the grayness or fuzziness. Probabilistic theory is the branch of mathematics concerned with probability, the analysis of random phenomena. The central objects of probability theory are random variables, stochastic processes, and events: mathematical abstractions of nondeterministic events or measured quantities that may either be single occurrences or evolve over time in an apparently random fashion. A random event can be described as an individual toss of a coin or the roll of dice, and if repeated many times, the sequence of these random events will exhibit certain patterns that can be studied and predicted.

Fuzzification of Input–Output Variables

Adopting applicable fuzzy sets controlled by membership functions, we can determine each variable's degree of affiliation.

$$A = \{z, \mu_A \mid z \, \varepsilon \, Z\} \qquad \text{Equation (4)}$$

In equation 4, the elements expressed by z are in the universal set Z, and the fuzzy set A in Z is defined as a set of ordered pairs. The $\mu_A(z)$ is the membership function of z in A and maps each element of Z to a membership value between 0 and 1.

The calculation of the volume of clay in a specific rock such as limestone, for example, can be depicted by a curve based on gamma ray readings to identify inter-bedding occurrences. Such a calculation can be explicated by fuzzy logic as the gamma ray values (z) in the clay-volume (Z) in equation 4 where the membership function maps each gamma ray reading to a membership value between 0 and 1.

Fuzzy If–Then Rules

The rules are essentially statements of expression to embrace the imprecision inherent in the human thinking process. Here is one example of such a statement:

If the gamma ray value is high, then the clay-volume is large.

Note the lingual articulation of gamma ray and clay-volume associated with high and large labels. Of course we could adopt multiple parts to the antecedent and apply fuzzy logic operators AND, OR, and NOT to describe minimum, maximum, and complementary membership values of a variable.

Weighting Factors

If a single rule is inadequate, then multiple rules can be adopted, one playing off another. The fuzzy set that is an output from each rule can be amalgamated with other output fuzzy sets into a single output fuzzy set. As to the relative contributions of each output fuzzy set into the combined fuzzy set, a suite of weighting factors can be assigned to dictate the blended fuzzy output set. Engineering expertise and experience are salient designs on the weighting factors to abide by the different situations in a fuzzy inference system.

De-fuzzification

The fuzzy set or aggregated fuzzy set is input to a de-fuzzification process that generates a succinct value.

The next step in the methodology is application of a neural network. The human brain consists of a multitude of connected neurons. *Artificial neural networks* are adaptive, parallel information processing systems that can develop associations, transformations, or mappings between objects or data. They are thus efficient and popular techniques for solving regression and classification issues in the upstream oil and gas industry. The basic elements of a neural

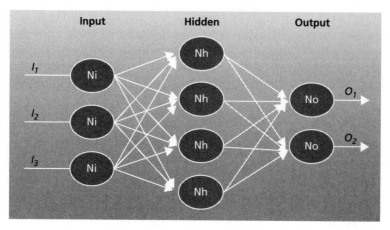

Figure 4.7 Artificial Neural Network

network are the neurons and their connection strengths or weights. In a supervised learning scenario a set of known input–output data patterns are implemented to train the network. The learning algorithm takes an initial model with some prior connection weights (random numbers) and applies an updating algorithm to produce final weights via an iterative process. Artificial neural networks (Figure 4.7) are used to build a representative model of predicting reservoir properties. The data are used as input–output pairs to train the neural network. Well information, reservoir quality data, and related data are used as input and are coupled with another category, production data, as output. Since first principles to model such a complex process using the conventional mathematical modeling techniques are tenuous at best, neural networks can provide an explicit insight into the complexities witnessed in characterizing reservoir properties in a spatiotemporal dimension. Once a reasonably accurate and representative neuro-model of the reservoir processes has been completed for the formation under study, more analysis can be performed. These analyses may include the use of the model in order to answer many *what-if* questions that may arise.

Maximizing Recovery Factors

Reservoir characterization studies necessitate an objective function be defined that drives the appropriate datasets aggregation and ultimately underpins the analytical methodologies to achieve accurate models. It is a continued industry problem to accurately forecast reservoir performance and classify assets as proved, probable, or possible. The reserves are directly tied to the recovery factor. Let us examine a probabilistic approach to qualify and quantify those variables that have a major influence on the recovery factor. The current world average recovery factor from oil fields is 30 to 35 percent (versus 20 percent in 1980).

This parameter ranges from a 10 percent average of extra heavy crude oils to a 50 percent average of the most advanced fields in the North Sea. Increasing the recovery factor boosts reserves even without the discovery of new fields. Increasing by only 1 percent the recovery rate can increase reserves by 35 billion to 55 billion barrels—about one or two years of world oil production. In order to increase the hydrocarbon recovery factor it is necessary to improve the knowledge of oil fields and to use advanced technologies to drill wells and to produce hydrocarbons.

Future earnings are based upon the barrels of recoverable oil and/or gas described as a fraction of the size of the reservoir, and this is referred to as the *recovery factor*. However, there is an inherent degree of uncertainty as regards recoverability and economic viability of any proven reserves. The financial position of any public company depends on the amount of reserves located, the rate at which the reserves are recovered, and the economic and engineering principles and strategies incorporated by the company to optimize efficient reservoir.

An advanced analytical suite of workflows was implemented using multiple linear regression techniques to develop equations to elevate the recovery of hydrocarbons in terms of applicable reservoir rock properties and reservoir fluid properties. However, the first step on the road to determining appropriate algorithms for attaining improved recovery factors is to run an exploratory data analysis that entails techniques that are both graphical and quantitative in nature.

Most EDA techniques are graphical in nature with a few quantitative techniques. Graphics or visualizations provide unparalleled power to entice the data to reveal their structural secrets and surface correlations and trends that point the engineer in the right direction.

The particular graphical techniques employed in this case study are often quite simple. A 3D scatterplot shown in Figure 4.8 reveals relationships or associations among three variables. Such relationships manifest themselves by any nonrandom structure in the plot. Scatterplots can provide answers to the following questions:

- Are variables X and Y and Z related?
- Are variables X and Y and Z linearly related?
- Are variables X and Y and Z nonlinearly related?
- Does the variation in Z change depending on X or on Y?
- Are there outliers?

To help visualize correlations, a scatterplot for each pair of response variables displays in a matrix arrangement, as shown in Figure 4.9. By default, a 95 percent bivariate normal density ellipse is imposed on each scatterplot.

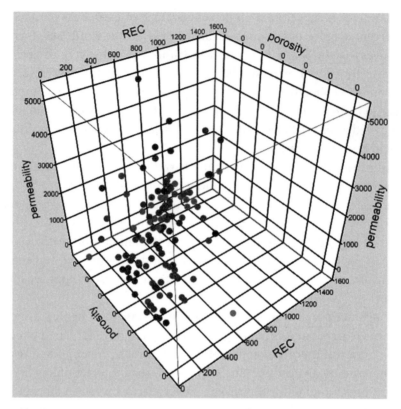

Figure 4.8 3D Scatterplot Surfacing Relationship among Porosity, Permeability, and the Objective Function Recovery Factor

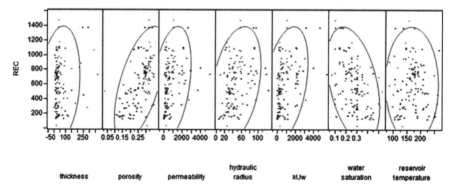

Figure 4.9 Scatterplot Matrix Illustrating Degrees of Correlation with the Recovery Factor

If the variables are bivariate normally distributed, this ellipse encloses approximately 95 percent of the points. The correlation of the variables is seen by the collapsing of the ellipse along the diagonal axis. If the ellipse is fairly round and is not diagonally oriented, the variables are uncorrelated.

Thus it can be noted that the recovery factor has a strong correlation with the *original oil in place* (OOIP)—note the narrow and angled ellipse, a weaker correlation with porosity, permeability, and a lognormal distribution of water saturation—and even less correlation with the reservoir temperature, *T*.

	REC	permeability	water saturation	OOIP	porosity
REC	1.0000	0.3490	-0.4061	0.7485	0.5977
permeability	0.3490	1.0000	-0.1415	0.3839	0.3865
water saturation	-0.4061	-0.1415	1.0000	-0.3478	-0.0227
OOIP	0.7485	0.3839	-0.3478	1.0000	0.6934
porosity	0.5977	0.3865	-0.0227	0.6934	1.0000

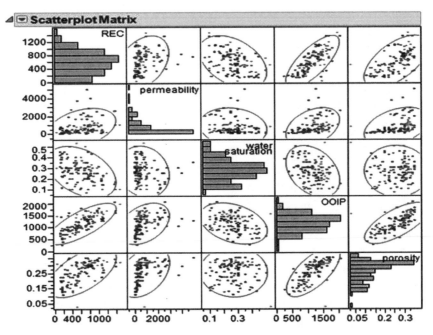

Figure 4.10 Multivariate Correlations of Influencing Reservoir Parameters

With the wide spectrum of reservoir properties and the plethora of observations or rows of data, to guard against including any variables that have little contribution to the predictive power of a model in the population, a small significance level should be specified. In most applications many variables considered have some predictive power, however small. In order to choose a model that provides the best prediction using the sample estimates, we must guard against estimating more parameters than can be reliably estimated with the given sample size.

Consequently, a moderate significance level, perhaps in the range of 10 to 25 percent, may be appropriate, and the importance of thorough exploratory data analysis is underlined.

In Figure 4.10 a correlations table is depicted, which is a matrix of correlation coefficients that summarizes the strength of the linear relationships between each pair of response (Y) variables. This correlation matrix only uses the observations that have non-missing values for all variables in the analysis. It can be seen readily that the recovery factor has strongest correlations with both OOIP and porosity with Pearson correlation values of 0.7509 and 0.6089, respectively.

The multivariate simple statistics (mean, standard deviation, minimum, and maximum) provide a template for focused attention when considering the structure of data. These statistics can be calculated in two ways that differ when

Multivariate Simple Statistics

Column	N	DF	Mean	Std Dev	Sum	Minimum	Maximum
REC	123	122.00	606.398	320.907	74587.0	30.0000	1470.00
permeability	123	122.00	773.536	885.245	95144.9	7.0000	5000.00
water saturation	123	122.00	0.2677	0.0981	32.9290	0.0700	0.5300
OOIP	123	122.00	1166.85	353.409	143523	242.000	2062.00
porosity	123	122.00	0.2579	0.0666	31.7240	0.0310	0.3500

Color Map On Correlations

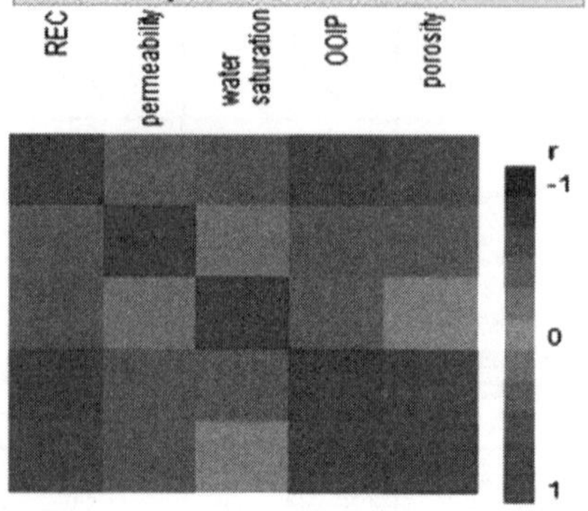

Figure 4.11 Color Map Depicting Correlations and the Analysis from a PCA

there are missing values in the data table. Multivariate simple statistics are calculated by dropping any row that has a missing value for any column in the analysis. These are the statistics that are used by the multivariate platform to calculate correlations. Generating a color map on correlations as in Figure 4.11 produces the cell plot showing the correlations among variables on a scale from red (+1) to blue (−1).

PCA is a technique to take linear combinations of the original variables such that the first principal component has maximum variation, the second principal component has the next most variation subject to being orthogonal to the first, and so on. PCA is implemented across a broad spectrum of geoscientific exploratory data in reservoir characterization projects. It is a technique for examining relationships among several quantitative variables. PCA can be used to summarize data and detect linear relationships. It can also be used for exploring polynomial relationships and for multivariate outlier detection. PCA reduces the dimensionality of a set of data while trying to preserve the structure, and thus can be used to reduce the number of variables in statistical analyses. The purpose of principal component analysis is to derive a small number of independent linear combinations (principal components) of a set of variables that retain as much of the information in the original variables as possible.

The PCA study calculates eigenvalues and eigenvectors from the uncorrected covariance matrix, corrected covariance matrix, or correlation matrix of input variables. Principal components are calculated from the eigenvectors and can be used as inputs for successor modeling nodes in a process flow. Since interpreting principal components is often problematic or impossible, it is much safer to view them simply as a mathematical transformation of the set of original variables.

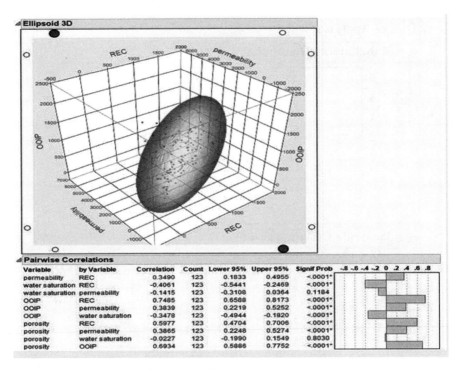

Figure 4.12 Pairwise Correlations Report with a 3D Scatterplot

A principal components analysis is useful for data interpretation and data dimension reduction. It is usually an intermediate step in the data mining process. Principal components are uncorrelated linear combinations of the original input variables; they depend on the covariance matrix or the correlation matrix of the original input variables. Principal components are usually treated as the new set of input variables for successor modeling nodes.

In PCA a set of dummy variables is created for each class of the categorical variables. Instead of original class variables, the dummy variables are used as interval input variables in the principal components analysis. The Ellipsoid 3D Plot toggles a 95 percent confidence ellipsoid around three chosen variables. When the command is first invoked, a dialog asks which three variables to include in the plot. The Pairwise Correlations table lists the Pearson product-moment correlations for each pair of Y variables, using all available values. The count values differ if any pair has a missing value for either variable. These are values produced by the Density Ellipse option on the Fit Y by X platform. The Pairwise Correlations report also shows significance probabilities and compares the correlations with a bar chart, as shown in Figure 4.12.

Using a jackknife technique the distance for each observation is calculated with estimates of the mean, standard deviation, and correlation matrix that do not include the observation itself. The jackknifed distances are useful when there is an outlier as depicted in Figure 4.13. The plot includes the value of

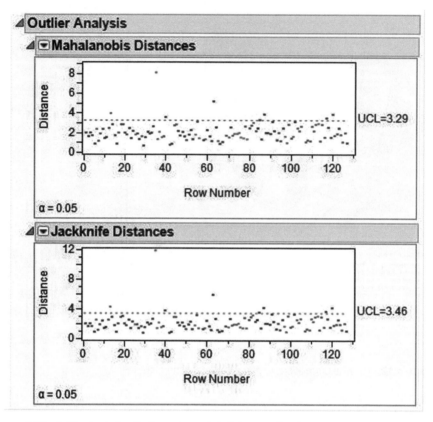

Figure 4.13   Outlier Analysis with Upper Control Limit (UCL) Defined

the calculated T2 statistic, as well as its *upper control limit* (UCL). Values that fall outside this limit may be an outlier.

Figure 4.14 illustrates three possible distributions for porosity: normal, lognormal, and Weibull. The normal fitting option estimates the parameters of the normal distribution based on the analysis sample. The parameters for the normal distribution are μ (mean), which defines the location of the distribution on the X-axis, and σ (standard deviation), which defines the dispersion or spread of the distribution. The standard normal distribution occurs when μ = 0 and σ = 1. The Parameter Estimates table for the normal distribution fit shows mu (estimate of μ) and sigma (estimate of σ), with upper and lower 95 percent confidence limits.

Figure 4.14 also shows an overlay of the density curve on the histogram for porosity using the parameter estimates from the data. The lognormal fitting estimates the parameters μ (scale) and σ (shape) for the two-parameter lognormal distribution for a variable Y where Y is lognormal if and only if $X = \ln(Y)$ is normal. The Weibull distribution has different shapes depending on the values of α (scale) and β (shape). It often provides a good model for estimating the length of life, especially for mechanical devices and in biology.

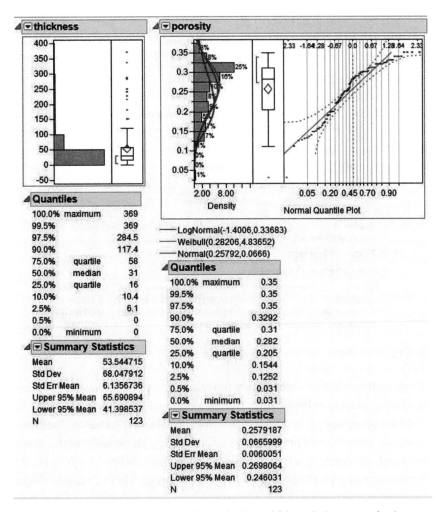

Figure 4.14 Distributions of Thickness and Porosity that Exhibit Predictive Powers for the Recovery Factor

The two-parameter Weibull is the same as the three-parameter Weibull with a threshold (θ) parameter of zero.

The Smooth Curve option fits a smooth curve to the continuous variable histogram using nonparametric density estimation. The smooth curve displays with a slider beneath the plot. One can use the slider to set the kernel standard deviation. The estimate is formed by summing the normal densities of the kernel standard deviation located at each data point.

By changing the kernel standard deviation you can control the amount of smoothing. Thus, the results depicted graphically in Figures 4.14 and 4.15 provide a feel for the distribution of each reservoir property and associated structure of the underlying population data that have to be modeled. It is a necessary step in order to identify an appropriate model for the reservoir.

◢ ⊟ **Confidence Intervals**

Parameter	Estimate	Lower CI	Upper CI	1-Alpha
Mean	0.257919	0.246031	0.269806	0.950
Std Dev	0.0666	0.059189	0.076149	0.950

◢ ⊟ **Fitted LogNormal**

  ◢ **Parameter Estimates**

Type	Parameter	Estimate	Lower 95%	Upper 95%
Scale	μ	-1.400635	-1.460629	-1.340641
Shape	σ	0.3368304	0.2987516	0.3837425

-2log(Likelihood) = -263.188576320613

◢ ⊟ **Fitted 2 parameter Weibull**

  ◢ **Parameter Estimates**

Type	Parameter	Estimate	Lower 95%	Upper 95%
Scale	α	0.2820643	0.271271	0.2929888
Shape	β	4.8365201	4.1413971	5.5978322

-2log(Likelihood) = -325.661873885796

◢ ⊟ **Fitted Normal**

  ◢ **Parameter Estimates**

Type	Parameter	Estimate	Lower 95%	Upper 95%
Location	μ	0.2579187	0.246031	0.2698064
Dispersion	σ	0.0665999	0.0591889	0.0761492

-2log(Likelihood) = -318.367850916324

Figure 4.15 Continuous Parameters with Fitted Estimates

The partition platform recursively partitions the reservoir data according to a relationship between the X and Y values, creating a tree of partitions. It finds a set of cuts or groupings of X values that best predict a Y value. It does this by exhaustively searching all possible cuts or groupings. These splits of the data are done recursively, forming a tree of decision rules until the desired fit is reached.

Variations of this technique go by many names and brand names: decision tree, CARTTM, CHAIDTM, C4.5, C5, and others. The technique is often taught as a data mining technique, because

- It is good for exploring relationships without having a good prior model.
- It handles large problems easily.
- The results are very interpretable.

Each step of a partition tree analysis depicted in Figure 4.16 tries to split the reservoir data into two parts: a part with high mean value of REC (*recovery factor*) and a part with low mean value. At the first step, the high mean value of REC is "all observations such that OOIP has the value greater than or equal to 1032." The other observations make up a set with low mean values of REC. At the second step, each of the sets in the first step is further subdivided. The "low mean value" group is split into a group where porosity < 0.282 and a second group where porosity > 0.282. The "high mean value" group is split into a group where Sw < 0.28 and the complement of that group.

This process continues. The interpretation is a set of rules that predict high or low values of the REC variable or recovery factor. To find the largest values

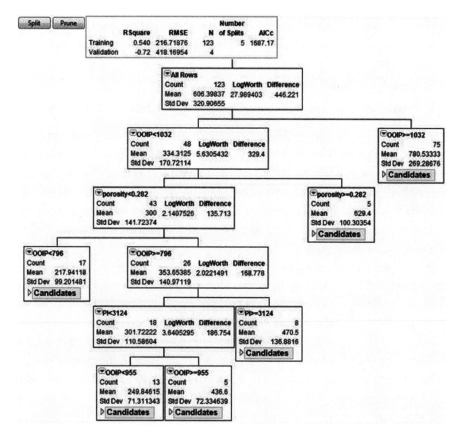

Figure 4.16 Partition Tree Classification

of REC, first choose observations where OOIP >= 1032. Within those, pick observations where Sw < 0.28. Continue for as many splits as one so desires. This *partition tree model* underlines the import of such parameters, OOIP and Sw, when determining an equation for the recovery factor of the reservoir.

Thus, it can be concluded from partition tree analysis that the most influential reservoir parameters and their associated values are: OOIP >= 1032, connate water saturation < 0.28, oil formation volume factor at abandonment pressure >= 1.234, and porosity > 0.256.

An empirical tree represents a segmentation of the data that is created by applying a series of simple rules. Each rule assigns an observation to a segment based on the value of one input. One rule is applied after another, resulting in a hierarchy of segments within segments. The hierarchy is called a *tree*, and each segment is called a *node*. The original segment contains the entire dataset and is called the *root node of the tree*. A node with all its successors forms a *branch* of the node that created it. The final nodes are called *leaves*. For each leaf, a decision is made and applied to all observations in the leaf. The type of decision depends on the context. In predictive modeling, the decision is simply the predicted value.

One can create decision trees that:

- Classify observations based on the values of nominal, binary, and ordinal targets.
- Predict outcomes for interval targets.
- Predict appropriate decisions when specifying decision alternatives.

An advantage of the decision tree is that it produces a model that may represent interpretable English rules or logic statements. Another advantage is the treatment of missing data. The search for a splitting rule uses the missing values of an input. Surrogate rules are available as backup when missing data prohibits the application of a splitting rule. Decision trees produce a set of rules that can be used to generate predictions for a new dataset. This information can then be used to drive business decisions.

If an observation contains a missing value, then by default that observation is not used for modeling by nodes such as neural network, or regression. However, rejecting all incomplete observations may ignore useful or important information that is still contained in the non-missing variables.

How can we deal with missing values? There is no single correct answer. Choosing the "best" missing value replacement technique inherently requires the researcher to make assumptions about the true (missing) data. For example, researchers often replace a missing value with the mean of the variable. This approach assumes that the variable's data distribution follows a normal population response. Replacing missing values with the mean, median, or another measure of central tendency is simple, but it can greatly affect a variable's sample distribution. You should use these replacement statistics carefully and only when the effect is minimal.

Another imputation technique replaces missing values with the mean of all other responses given by that data source. This assumes that the input from that specific data source conforms to a normal distribution. Another technique studies the data to see if the missing values occur in only a few variables. If those variables are determined to be insignificant, the variables can be rejected from the analysis. The observations can still be used by the modeling nodes.

Thus, exploratory data analysis should embrace a technique to identify missing data, so as to diligently handle such occurrences in light of the reservoir characterization project's ultimate goal.

NOTES

1. J. W. Tukey, *Exploratory Data Analysis* (Reading, MA: Addison-Wesley, 1977).
2. S. Mohaghegh, A. S. Popa, and S. Ameri, "Intelligent Systems Can Design Optimum Fracturing Jobs," SPE 57433, in *Proceedings, 1999 SPE EasRegional Conference and Exhibition*, Charleston, WV, October 21–22.
3. Alfred North Whitehead and Bertrand Russell, *Principia Mathematica*, Vol. I (London: Cambridge University Press, 1963).

CHAPTER 5

Drilling and Completion Optimization

*Statistics are like a bikini. What they reveal is
interesting. But what they hide is vital.*

Aaron Levenstein

Drilling is one of the most critical, dangerous, complex, and costly operations in the oil and gas industry. While drilling costs represent nearly half of well expenditures, only 42 percent of the time is attributed to drilling. The remaining 58 percent is divided between drilling problems, rig movement, defects, and latency periods.

Some rigs are not fully automated and no single service company provides the full set of data operators need to comprehensively understand drilling performance. Unfortunately, errors made during the drilling process are very expensive. They occasionally damage reputation and result in hefty civil and government lawsuits and financial penalties (consider the 2010 BP Horizon deepwater fire and oil spill in the Gulf of Mexico). Inefficient drilling programs can have an even greater aggregate financial impact, causing delays in well completions or abandonments, unexpected shutdowns, hydrocarbon spills, and other accidents. There is a pressing need not only to improve drilling efficiency but also to predict hazardous situations that could have a negative impact on health, safety, and the environment.

Intelligent completions obtain downhole pressure and temperature data in real time to identify problems in the reservoir or wellbore and optimize production without costly well intervention. Sensing, data transmission, and

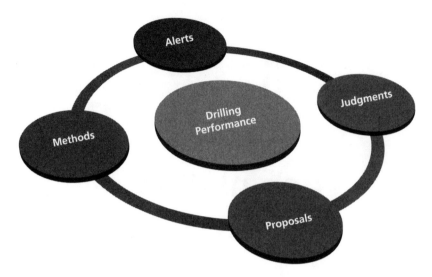

Figure 5.1 Real-Time Drilling Engineering Methodology

remote control of zonal flow to isolate the formation from completion fluids help operators minimize fluid loss, manage the reservoir, maintain well integrity, and maximize production.

It is imperative for drilling personnel to understand the technical aspects of drilling and completion operations of a wellbore, to further enhance productivity of drilling and work-over projects, given the increasing demand for oil and natural gas.

The real-time drilling engineering process consists of four key stages to mitigate risks and preclude major issues, improve efficiency, and establish best practices, as depicted in Figure 5.1. It is paramount to integrate engineers' experience and extant advanced technologies to generate business value within these stages:

Stage 1. Alerts: Prevent operational problems from unexpected trend changes analyzing surface or downhole parameters.

Stage 2. Judgments: Provide suggestions about hydraulic, torque and drag, and directional in order to improve the drilling performance of the well.

Stage 3. Proposals: Propose significant changes on the well design, such as sidetrack, fishing options, unexpected high formation pressure analysis, total lost circulation, and casing point correlation.

Stage 4. Methods: Adjust well program to improve the drilling performance.

EXPLORATION AND PRODUCTION VALUE PROPOSITIONS

Drilling performance optimization is a knowledge-rich domain. It involves the application of drilling-related knowledge to identify and diagnose barriers to drilling performance and to implement procedural and/or technological changes to overcome these barriers. The overall objective of drilling performance optimization is that the well is drilled in the most efficient manner possible.

The knowledge required to execute drilling performance optimization is drawn from a multidisciplinary skillset within the drilling domain. Such skills include: fluids engineering, borehole pressure management, bottom-hole assembly (BHA) and drill-string design, drill bit selection, vibration management, and rock mechanics.

It necessitates a solution to provide a holistic view of the entire drilling system and gives near-real-time insight into parameters that can improve drilling efficiency, from planning through execution and completion.

- *Uncover hidden patterns in data.* Link data from nonoperational variables (rock properties, reservoir characteristics) with drilling operational parameters (weight on bit and revolutions per minute) and drilling system designs (drill bit models).

- *Quantify drilling success.* Data mining techniques applied to a comprehensive dataset identify potential correlations between drilling activity and incremental rate of penetration (ROP). This calculates drilling success in real time, under specific geomechanical conditions and constraints.

- *Rely on root-cause analysis to guide decisions.* Advanced analytical techniques gauge how to analyze real-time data relative to past performance or events so you can predict downhole tool failures and immediately determine which operational parameters to adjust.

- *Improve drilling efficiency through its broad expertise in data integration, data quality, and advanced analytics, including optimization and data mining.* Our solutions encourage collaboration and help operators make trustworthy, data-driven decisions.

- *Identify key performance indicators (KPIs) behind efficient drilling operations.* It is imperative to analyze the statistical relationship between data on relevant drilling incidents (e.g., equipment failures, well control issues, losses, stuck-pipes) and KPIs (e.g., ROP, cost per foot, and foot per day), given geomechanical constraints.

- *Reduce nonproductive time with holistic data integration and management.* Collects and analyzes key data from the entire drilling ecosystem, validates it with quality control processes, and then integrates it with an analytical data mart.

- *Visualize and analyze drilling performance in near real time.* Visualization offers quick-and-easy access to view the latest data on drilling parameters, events, and analytical results.

The system (Figure 5.2) combines multivariate, multidimensional, multivariant, and stochastic analytical workflows. Approaches using multivariate and/or multidimensional analysis fall short of representing a complex and heterogeneous system.

- *Multivariant:* Multiple independent variables that impact the outcome of a singularity.

- *Multidimensional:* Dimensions that affect the independent variables. For example, vibrations can be axial, tangential, and lateral.

- *Multivariate:* Multiple dependent variables that have to be predicted in order to reach an objective on a singularity. These are typically variables that have interdependencies that can affect the outcome of the singularity. For example, *torque* affects RPM, *weight* affects torque and RPM, and all three affect *rate of penetration* (the outcome).

- *Stochastic:* Variability and random behavior of independent variables. For example, the performance of the bit will vary depending on time, rock strength, flow rates, and so on.

WORKFLOW ONE: MITIGATION OF NONPRODUCTIVE TIME

The industry's most common performance-quantifying metrics—cost per foot (CPF), foot per day (FPD), and rate of penetration (ROP)—are strongly influenced by *mechanical specific energy* (MSE), but MSE must not be equated to drilling efficiency alone. It is but one of several parameters that influence drilling productivity.

It is of paramount importance to analyze trends in all drilling performance-quantifying metrics to identify possible drilling inefficiencies, thereby learning from them and making adjustments to drilling parameters to attain an optimized drilling process. To achieve drilling efficiency, certain basic requirements and conditions must be met.

The ultimate objective must be geared toward confirming that the lowest cost per section and the construction of usable wells are the most critical factors in drilling performance and, if this is the case, defining the strategic initiatives and operational solutions that will lead there. In this regard, the sources of nonproductive time (NPT), namely *visible lost time* (VLT) and *invisible lost time* (ILT), must be analyzed in detail. Their contribution to the drilling performance has to be described analytically. Identification of other potential critical contributors to reduced drilling performance has to be performed analytically. Ultimately, the causes of these critical parameters along the drilling process need to be identified, and elimination of those primary inefficiency causes must be described as well.

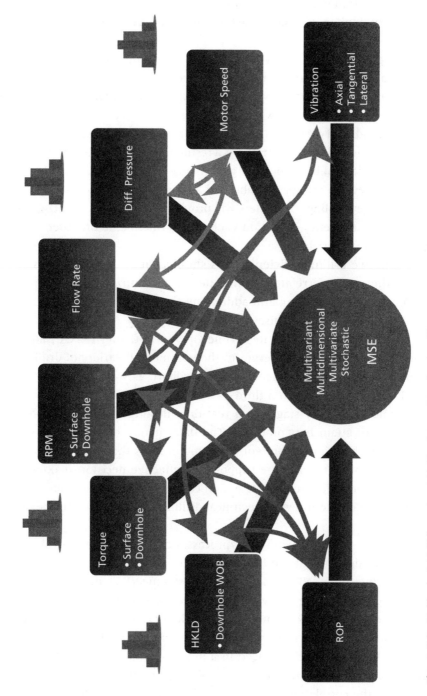

Figure 5.2 Multivariant, Multidimensional, Multivariate, and Stochastic Drilling

143

To achieve this goal, drilling efficiency and ROP must both be defined, and factors influencing ROP and drilling efficiency must be identified. Most importantly, drilling efficiency's different influencing factors, which include but are not limited to ROP, must be analyzed based on specific project objectives.

Drilling efficiency will have the desired effects on costs when all critical operational parameters are identified and assessed. These parameters, referred to as *performance qualifiers* (PQs), must be analyzed and quantified through an exploratory data analysis (EDA) methodology that surfaces hidden patterns and identifies trends and correlations in a multivariate complex system. Hypotheses worth modeling will be enumerated as a result of the EDA processes. The results will lead to a factual basis to allow governance over the drilling process, with performance evaluation logic established as business rules. Normalization and cleansing of key drilling parameters will provide a sound basis for EDA, leading to operational efficiency definition via business rules based on observations of scale and pattern variability.

To improve drilling efficiency, PQs should not be analyzed in isolation because they are interrelated. Consequently, maximization of any particular PQ, without identifying and addressing the effects the effort has on the other PQs, always compromises drilling efficiency.

The implementation of a Real-Time Operation Center (RTOC) addresses the increased complexity inherent in the volume and variety of drilling data currently collected from sensors in the wellbore as well as surface parameters, LWD, MWD, PWD, and third-party mud-logging data. Figure 5.3 illustrates some of the key stages in a real-time drilling engineering workflow that strives to attain best practices. The data management framework that encapsulates the information workflow and ensures the quality of the information generated in real time supports an effective decision-making cycle. Real-time information echoes the extant condition of the well under study. It is then a formality to integrate technical drilling applications into the process in real time.

Advanced analytical workflows/processes can establish and evaluate key performance drivers that are fundamental to identification and reduction of nonproductive time (NPT) and invisible lost time (ILT) during drilling. By performing multivariate analysis on discrete data sources, analytical workflows can determine unknown patterns to identify trends in a drilling system. Through a suite of data cleansing, transformation, and exploratory data analysis (EDA) methodologies packaged in a new operational process for problem identification, selection, diagnosis, and solution finding, we will create models that define the correlations, trends, and signatures that predict stuck-pipe in an operationalized format that will enhance the drilling surveillance and control process.

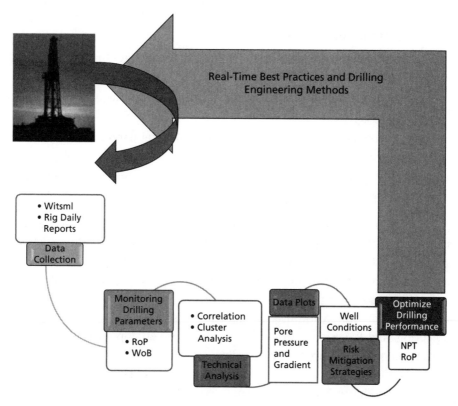

Figure 5.3 Real-Time Drilling Methodology

There are multiple variables and components that comprise a drilling system, and therefore, many potential areas that may create challenges from an optimization perspective. By aggregating all of the relevant data (e.g., offset information, rock mechanics, mud properties, BHA design, rig capabilities, etc.) we are able to generate models that can predict potential points within the drilling system that could be optimized. Analytical workflows/processes can then be developed to achieve many goals, including:

- Continuous levels of improvement through the automation of the entire workflow
- Data validation to build accurate advanced analytical models
- Root-cause analysis to identify key performance indicators and their range of operational values covering different functions in the drilling process, including the following:
  - *Wellbore quality:* Avoid potential issues such as stuck-pipe associated with borehole cleaning activities.
  - *Rig performance:* Why specific rigs perform better than others in the same asset/play.

- *Optimize drilling operations* by gathering and analyzing both static and real-time drilling data.
- *Wellbore stability:* Establish a suite of methodologies to model and forecast borehole stability.
- *Real-time identification* of wellbore instability and associated modes of failure.
- *Forecasting workflows* that encapsulate drilling parameters to preclude unstable wellbore designs.
- *Well pressure management:* Methodologies to analyze and monitor various pressures.

In addition to a data-driven system that translates raw data into tangible and effective knowledge, we see the juxtaposition of a user-driven system underpinned by expert knowledge garnered through experience as completing a hybrid approach. This composition of different or incongruous data sources underpins a soft computing technique driven by a methodology based on advanced analytical workflows implementing self-organizing maps (SOMs), clustering, and Bayesian approaches. The data-driven approach necessitates a robust and quality-assured stream of data.

A solution architecture to realize and estimate events leading to NPT is illustrated in Figure 5.4. We must analyze the historical frequency and probability of occurrence, cross-matching faults with service companies and resources to enhance early decision making. It is necessary to establish a workflow to identify critical wells with higher probability of experiencing NPTs as candidates for remediation and rank a comparison of NPT events between wells.

The NPT identification solution can iterate through several layers of integrated and logical workflows that form a top-down methodology (Figure 5.5) that ultimately morphs into a catalog of historical events with associated diagnoses and best practices for remediation.

Segment wells in accordance with the tactics/strategies and NPT events, as illustrated in Figure 5.6. Business objectives determine a well segmentation

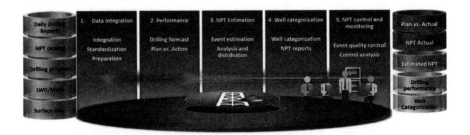

Figure 5.4 Solution Architecture to Reduce NPT

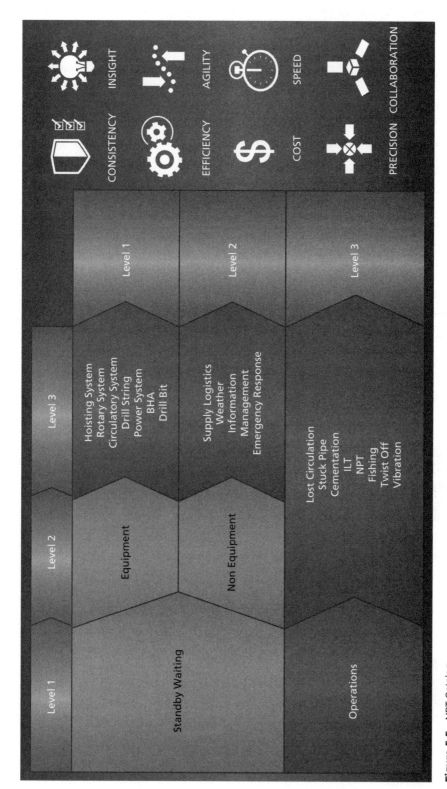

Figure 5.5 NPT Catalog

via a clustering module to characterize on a geographical basis. Relate NPTs to specific drilling companies and crews.

Pareto charts help to identify the most important NPTs by well and/or field, considering their impact by length of time delays. They endorse the definition of priorities for quality improvement activities by identifying the problems that require the most attention. And control graphs by well and fault category enable the identification of critical faults and their impact in drilling depth and performance times as well as the recognition of out-of-control faults. Both forms of visualization underpin the NPT methodology depicted in Figure 5.7.

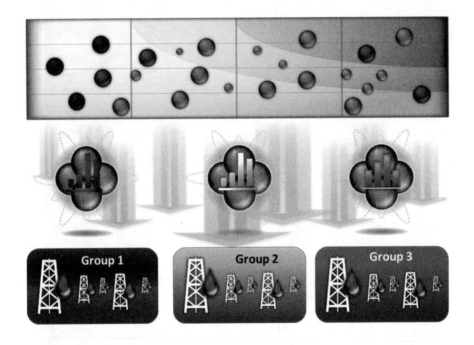

Figure 5.6 Cluster Analysis to Identify Similar Classes by Tactics/Strategies and NPT

Figure 5.7 NPT Methodology

Let us develop a workflow based on a best practice methodology to reduce NPT by minimizing the occurrences of stuck-pipe events.

Stuck-Pipe Model

What is stuck-pipe, and what are the benefits to obviate the effects of such an occurrence? During the drilling operation the drill string sticks while drilling, making a connection, performing logging, or any operation that involves the equipment being left in the hole. Stuck-pipe issues invariably fall into two categories: mechanical and differential. The former occurs while the drill string is mobile and an obstruction or physical constraint results in the sticking event. Such conditions are realized in wellbore instability situations such as poor hole cleaning that triggers high torque, excessive drag on the drill string, and hole pack-off, leading to stuck-pipe. The latter occurs due to a higher pressure in the mud than in the formation fluid. Differential sticking is witnessed when the drill collar rests against the borehole wall, sinking into the mudcake. The area of the drill collar that is not embedded into the mudcake has a pressure acting upon it that is equal to the *hydrostatic pressure (Ph)* in the drilling mud, whereas that area embedded exhibits a pressure equal to the *rock formation pressure (Pf)* acting upon it. Figure 5.8 illustrates the hydrostatic pressure in the wellbore being higher than the formation pressure, resulting in a net force pushing the collar toward the borehole wall.

Thus, a stuck-pipe incident is a pervasive technical challenge that invariably results in a significant amount of downtime and increase in remedial costs.

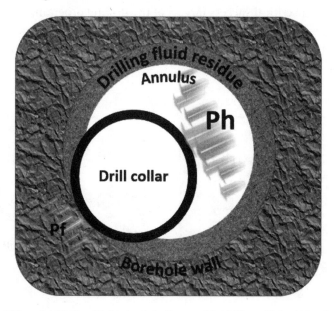

Figure 5.8 Differential Sticking: Ph (Hydrostatic Pressure) Exhibiting a Higher Value than Pf (Pore Pressure of a Permeable Formation)

The drilling of oil and gas wells is a process fraught with potential issues and the multiple mechanisms that can contribute to a stuck-pipe situation have to be discriminated in order to identify those operational and nonoperational parameters that have a major impact on each mechanism. To preclude the adverse impact of attaining critical success targets in a drilling program and in light of recent increases in drilling activity in high-risk assets compounded by an ever-increasing shortage of experienced drilling personnel, it is imperative to introduce an advanced analytical suite of methodologies that deploy a hybrid solution to address such drilling issues. Such a hybrid solution, delivered around a combined user-centric system based on experience and a data-driven component that captures historical data, enables engineers, both young and old, to gain crucial time-critical insights to those parameters that have a major statistical impact on a stuck-pipe incident.

Understanding and anticipating drilling problems, assessing their causes, and planning solutions are necessary for overall-well-cost control and for successfully reaching the target zone. Thus the benefits are both tangible and economically viable to identify methodologies, both deterministic and stochastic, that mitigate the risk and even predict the occurrence of the sticking event and ultimately ensure wellbore integrity that precludes wellbore instability (Figure 5.9) leading to stuck-pipe.

There are multiple mechanisms that can contribute to a stuck-pipe situation. One of the major technical challenges of the drilling program is the frequency of stuck-pipe incidents. Such occurrences invariably result in a significant amount of downtime and increase in remedial costs, adversely impacting the attainment of the critical success targets of the drilling program. Unfortunately, with the recent increase in drilling activity and shortage of experienced drilling personnel, drilling in high-risk assets has augmented the potential of stuck-pipe events.

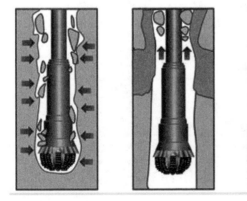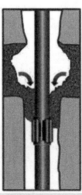

Figure 5.9 Wellbore Instability Is Prone to a Stuck-Pipe Event, Leading to NPT

How do we identify the onset of stuck-pipe in all its forms, find the most critical and frequent stuck-pipe scenarios, diagnose them, and find an operational solution that prevents or mitigates their occurrence? In order to do this it is necessary to analyze and quantify the parameters most influential for all stuck-pipe mechanisms, segment scenarios by signature of behavior of groups of parameters, rank these scenarios by frequency and criticality, select the few top-ranking scenarios, perform causal analysis in order to detect early indicators, and at the same time issue a predictive model to be used operationally. At the end of this process, and under the assumption that the predictive indicators offer a lead time long enough for operators to act, a decision needs to be made on operational actions to be taken in order to prevent or significantly mitigate the analyzed scenario.

Thus, the long-term goal is to identify preventative or mitigating measures in light of warning signs hidden in the appropriate operational and nonoperational parameters deemed necessary for each stuck-pipe mechanism.

The principal data required are:

- Rock mechanics data
- Fluids data
- Lithological data
- BHA dynamics data
- Vibration data
- MWD/LWD data
- Surface equipment data

WORKFLOW TWO: DRILLING PARAMETER OPTIMIZATION

In order to attain minimum cost per foot with an understanding of uncertainty quantification and controlled risk assessment, a drill bit optimization methodology identifies the optimum drill bit for the drilled interval. Incorporate offset well data to select appropriate drill bit and associated critical characteristics. The advanced analytical workflows embrace a thorough analysis of offset well data, including well logs, formation tops, mud logs, core analysis, rock mechanics, drilling parameters, bit records, and dull bit conditions.

Adopting tailored analytical workflows that incorporate disparate datasets it is feasible to attain minimum cost per foot with an understanding of uncertainty quantification and controlled risk assessment in a drill bit optimization methodology. Such an evaluation process would include such steps as:

- Evaluation of expected formation types
- Offset well data gathering

- Determination of unconfined compressive rock strength, effective porosity, abrasion characteristics, and impact potential
- Identification of potentially optimal bit types and various applicable characteristics
- Prediction of cost per foot for each potential bit
- Optimal drill bit recommendation

Post-run, analysis evaluates bit performance from available data such as real-time ROP, RPM, torque, and drill bit conditions. Such analytical results offer design and application feedback to engineers for an iterative and continuous-improvement process.

Well Control

The methodology typically requires multiple iterations of analytical cycles to monitor the various pressures in real time: drilling fluid pressure in the well, gas, oil, and water under pressure (formation pressure), and mud pressure. If the formation pressure is greater than the mud pressure, there is the possibility of a blowout.

Drilling Optimization Analytical Project:

- An automated process to measure both *actual* and *theoretical* drill bit performance and detect abnormal deviations.
- Creation of a multivariate statistical model that automatically identifies and quantifies the drivers of drill bit performance.
- Daily reports facilitate event detection and alerting in drilling surveillance.
- Insight into the performance functions and their drivers one by one and in combination: This enables engineers in surveillance, reliability, process, and operations to understand the drivers' significance in abnormal performance states, detect patterns of performance deviation and their indicators, find causes, improve the patterns with analytical cause indicators, determine short-term performance and long-term reliability risks, and develop prevention measures.

By aggregating all relevant data (such as offset information, rock mechanics, mud properties, BHA design, rig capabilities, etc.) we are able to generate models that can predict potential points within the drilling system that could be optimized. Analytical workflows/processes can be developed to achieve many goals, including:

- The validation of data to build accurate advanced analytic models.
- Continuous levels of improvement through the automation of the entire workflow.

- Root-cause analysis to identify key performance indicators and their range of operational values covering different functions in the drilling process, including the following:

  - *Wellbore integrity/quality:* Avoid potential issues, such as stuck-pipe, associated with hole-cleaning activities.

  - *Rig performance or rig-state detection:* Examine why specific rigs perform better than others in the same asset/play. Optimize drilling operations by gathering and analyzing both static and real-time drilling data during execution and post-drilling operations.

  - *Wellbore stability:* Establish a suite of methodologies to model and forecast borehole stability. In real time, identify wellbore instability and associated modes of failure to minimize cost and optimize drilling regimes. Create a forecasting workflow that encapsulates and analyzes drilling parameters to preclude expensive and unstable wellbore designs.

  - *Well control:* Methodology to analyze and monitor various pressures.

By taking a holistic view of the entire drilling system, analytic models are able to determine the key performance attributes within each discrete component and determine the correlation between multiple variables.

Real-Time Data Interpretation to Predict Future Events

Advanced analytical techniques can be applied to gauge how real-time data are analyzed relative to past performance/events to predict downhole tool failures and the ability to do immediate root-causal activities and implement real-time solutions.

Comparing real-time drilling data against previous trends allows for the following:

- Avoid potential NPT by predicting a failure, such as a PDM due to excessive vibration.

- *Geo-steering:* Able to make real-time adjustments to the wellbore trajectory (i.e., unforeseen transition zones).

- Able to make real-time drilling parameter changes (i.e., WOB, TOB, flow rate).

- *Prevent blowouts:* Multivariate iterative process to analyze pressures such as formation, mud, and drilling fluid pressures.

Statistical analysis uses predefined patterns (parametric model) and compares measures of observations to standard metrics of the model, testing hypotheses. We implement a model to characterize a pattern in the drilling data and match predetermined patterns to data deductively following the Aristotelian path to the truth. We then build a model with the drilling data and thus do not start with a model. Patterns in the data are used to build a model and discover patterns in the data inductively following a Platonic approach to the truth.

- Data management
- Data quality
- Predictive modeling and data mining
- Reporting of results

It is necessary to develop workflows for each of the above capabilities to preclude significant amounts of manual intervention and provide efficient and streamlined processes that are consistent and repeatable across multiple disparate global assets. As your drilling problems become too complex to rely on one discipline and as you find yourselves in the midst of an information explosion, multidisciplinary analysis methods and data mining approaches become more of a necessity than professional curiosity. To tackle difficult problems in drilling unconventional plays, you need to bring down the walls built around traditional disciplines and embark on true multidisciplinary solutions underpinned by advanced analytical workflows.

CASE STUDIES

Steam-Assisted Gravity Drainage Completion

With the production of bitumen and heavy oils becoming economically viable, Dr. Roger Butler's SAGD[1] (*steam-assisted gravity drainage*) technique has become an oilfield norm in such assets. As with all unconventional oil production, SAGD is a complex and dynamic operational process where subsurface influences are managed from a surface control location. This blend of mechanical systems and subsurface heterogeneity creates a stochastic system riddled with uncertainty. Attaining a reduction in the variable production costs and an increase in recovery rate necessitates a decrease in *steam–oil ratio* (SOR). In turn SOR is optimized by reducing the steam injection rates and/or increasing oil production.

The emergence of *downhole distributed sensing* (DTS) combined with the artificial lift and reservoir properties provides a rich multivariate dataset. In this case study we shall present a data-driven approach where observed behaviors from a SAGD operation are used to model a dynamic process constrained by first principles, such that we can leverage the large volumes and varieties of data collected to improve operational effectiveness of the SAGD process. Finally, let us demonstrate how an analytical model for SAGD can be placed into a closed loop system and used to automate heavy oil production in a predictable and predetermined manner, ensuring consistent and optimized completion strategies in such assets.

In the SAGD process, two parallel horizontal oil wells are drilled in the formation, one about four to six meters above the other. The upper well injects steam, and the lower one collects the heated crude oil or bitumen that flows out of the formation, along with any water from the condensation of injected steam. The basis of the process is that the injected steam forms a "steam chamber" that grows vertically and horizontally in the formation. The heat from the steam reduces the viscosity of the heavy crude oil or bitumen, which allows it to flow down into the lower wellbore. The steam and gases rise because of their low density compared to the heavy crude oil below, ensuring that steam is not produced at the lower production well. The gases released, which include methane, carbon dioxide, and usually some hydrogen sulfide, tend to rise in the steam chamber, filling the void space left by the oil and, to a certain extent, forming an insulating heat blanket above the steam. Oil and water flow is by a countercurrent, gravity-driven drainage into the lower wellbore. The condensed water and crude oil or bitumen is recovered to the surface by pumps such as progressive cavity pumps, which work well for moving high-viscosity fluids with suspended solids.

A key measure of efficiency for operations using SAGD technology is the amount of steam needed to produce a barrel of oil, called *steam-to-oil ratio* (SOR). A low SOR allows us to grow and sustain production with comparatively smaller plants and lower energy usage and emissions, all of which results in a smaller environmental footprint.

The data-driven methodology strives to ascertain the optimal values for those control variables that lead to maximum oil production:

- Pump speed
- Short injection string
- Long injection string
- Casing gas
- Header pressure
- Produced emulsion

There are three potential workflows that constitute a multivariate methodology:

Workflow 1: Assumptions are made on the predetermined behavior on the data.

a. Implement linear regression models.

    i. Dependent variables:

        1. Water

        2. Oil

    ii. Independent variables:

        1. Production to header pressure

        2. Casing gas to header pressure

        3. Pump speed

        4. Injection steam to short tubing

        5. Injection steam to long tubing

Workflow 2: No assumptions are made on any predetermined behavior on the data.

    a. Implement neural networks models.

        i. Output variables:

            1. Water

            2. Oil

        ii. Input variables:

            1. Production to header pressure

            2. Casing gas to header pressure

            3. Pump speed

            4. Injection steam to short tubing

            5. Injection steam to long tubing

Workflow 3: Does not assume any predetermined behavior on the data and assumes no model formulation.

    a. Implement association rules.

        i. Surfaces IF/THEN-type rules in the data.

The analytical workflows aggregated data from two well pads with focus on two well pairs: P1 and P3. We separated the dependent variables, water and oil, from the production emulsion based on the water-cut values across the input domain. The input data did not include any nonoperational parameters such as reservoir properties or geomechanics. We set aside 75 percent of the extant data for training purposes to build the models; the remaining 25 percent was used for validation purposes.

Workflow One

The left-hand side of Figure 5.10 details the linear regression model for water production, whereas the right-hand side represents the results applied to oil production data. Note that oil was overpredicted and conversely water was underpredicted. The values of R-squared for water and oil are 0.7188 and

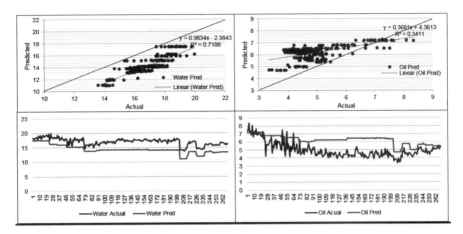

Figure 5.10   Study Results for Well Pair 1

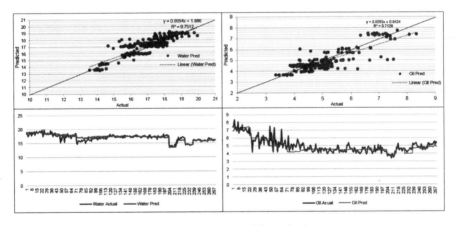

Figure 5.11   Neural Network Models for Water and Oil for Well Pair 3

0.3411, respectively. The value R-squared is the *coefficient of determination* and reflects how well the data points fit the regression line.

Workflow Two

The neural network implemented was a *feed-forward* adaptation with a supervised learning mode with back-propagation to perform sensitivity analysis that determines how each input parameter influences the output (water and oil production; see Figure 5.11). Thus there were five input variables for each neural network modeling water and oil production. The hidden nodes were constrained to two or three.

The *R*-squared values for water and oil are comparable, each about 0.7, thus illustrating a pretty good correlation. It appears that the multivariate analysis workflow implementing the artificial neural network provides a very good methodology to predict the production of either water or oil.

Workflow Three

The final approach utilized five association rules as detailed in Figures 5.12 and 5.13 for well pairs 1 and 3, respectively.

Rule	IF	THEN	Left Side Occurs	Right Side Occurs	Confidence
1	Oil_Well_Pair_1='(6.6-6.9]'	Steam_to_Long_Tubing_Flow='(-inf-191.8]'	15	14	93%
2	Oil_Well_Pair_1='(5.4-5.8]'	Steam_to_Long_Tubing_Flow='(1342-1534]'	85	68	80%
3	Oil_Well_Pair_1='(2.7-3.1]'	Steam_to_Long_Tubing_Flow='(3644-3835]'	82	62	76%
4	Oil_Well_Pair_1='(6.4-6.9]'	Wellbore_Subcool_Temperature_1119A='(24.1-25.1]'	18	12	67%
5	Wellbore_Subcool_Temperature_1119A='(18.4-19.4]'	Oil_Well_Pair_1='(3.4-4.1]'	72	39	54%

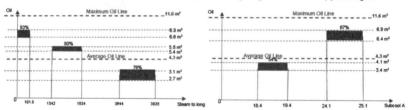

Oil production tends to be higher when less steam is injected in the long tubing and the Toe subcool (A) is held higher.

Figure 5.12 Association Rules Implemented on SAGD Dataset for Well Pair 1

Rule	IF	THEN	Left Side Occurs	Right Side Occurs	Confidence
1	Oil_Well_Pair_2='(8.9-9.9]'	Steam_to_Long_Tubing_Flow='(4076-4524]'	38	33	87%
2	Steam_to_Long_Tubing_Flow='(4524-4972]'	Oil_Well_Pair_2='(4.9-5.9]'	24	18	75%
3	Steam_to_Long_Tubing_Flow='(3627-4076]'	Oil_Well_Pair_2='(3.9-4.9]'	128	77	60%
4	Pump_Subcool_Temperature='(25.8-28.5]'	Oil_Well_Pair_2='(2.9-3.9]'	17	15	88%
5	Pump_Subcool_Temperature='(20.6-23.2]'	Oil_Well_Pair_2='(8.9-9.9]'	20	13	65%

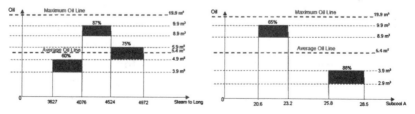

Oil production tends to be higher when more steam is injected in the long tubing and the Toe subcool (A) is held lower.

Figure 5.13 Association Rules Implemented on SAGD Dataset for Well Pair 3

Conclusions

Selecting optimal control variables for well pairs 1 and 3 we concluded that a three-step diagnosis was applicable:

Step 1. Implement the estimated coefficients from workflow 1 or the weights ascertained in workflow 2.

Step 2. Adopt the ranges suggested for the control variables by the association rules in workflow 3 and implement them as constraints for a nonlinear programming model.

Step 3. Establish an objective function.

Perusing the outputs from the three workflows we derived the following functional relationships for each well pair that could subsequently be operationalized in a closed loop process to maximize hydrocarbon production via a suite of operational parameters controlled in the SAGD completion.

Well Pair 1:

Objective Function: MAX Oil =

0.000117*Well_Production_to_Header_Pressure

– 0.000732*Well_Casing_Gas_to_Header_Pressure +

0.0976*Pump_Speed_Reference_in_Hertz

– 0.000034*Steam_to_Short_Tubing –

0.000299*Steam_to_Long_Tubing

   Subject to (Figure 5.14):

2396 < Well_Production_to_Header_Pressure <= 2403

626.5 < Well_Casing_Gas_to_Header_Pressure <= 677.8

Optimal Control Variable Choices	Estimate
Well_Production_to_Header_Pressure	2403
Well_Casing_Gas_to_Header_Pressure	626.5
Pump_Speed_Reference_in_Hertz	63
Steam_to_Short_Tubing	98.15
Steam_to_Long_Tubing	0

Figure 5.14 Optimal Control Variable Values for Well Pair 1

62.5 < Pump_Speed_Reference_in_Hertz <=63

98.15 < Steam_to_Short_Tubing <= 10516

0 < Steam_to_Long_Tubing <= 191.8

Well Pair 3:

Objective Function: MAX Oil = –

0.003300*Well_Production_to_Header_Pressure

+ 0.001091*Well_Casing_Gas_to_Header_Pressure +

0.2674*Pump_Speed_Reference_in_Hertz

– 0.000226*Steam_to_Short_Tubing +

0.0000133*Steam_to_Long_Tubing

   Subject to (Figure 5.15):

2289 < Well_Production_to_Header_Pressure <= 2307

1172 < Well_Casing_Gas_to_Header_Pressure <= 1211

64 <Pump_Speed_Reference_in_Hertz <= 65

10969 < Steam_to_Short_Tubing <= 11229

4076 < Steam_to_Long_Tubing <= 4524

For well pair 1, the average oil production from the training data is 4.3m³/hour; but using the optimal control variables resulted in a maximized oil production of 5.97m³/hour, an increase in performance of 39 percent.

Conversely, for well pair 3, the average oil production from the training data is 5.4m³/hour; but using the optimal control variables resulted in a maximized oil production of 8.73m³/hour, an increase in performance of 62 percent.

Optimal Control Variable Choices	Estimate
Well_Production_to_Header_Pressure	2289
Well_Casing_Gas_to_Header_Pressure	1211
Pump_Speed_Reference_in_Hertz	65
Steam_to_Short_Tubing	10969
Steam_to_Long_Tubing	4524

Figure 5.15 Optimal Control Variable Values for Well Pair 3

In summary, we noted inherent heterogeneities between the well pairs and different analytical approaches were needed to accurately predict oil and water production. The neural network approach was more accurate in predicting oil and water production than the linear regression workflow. Association rules can add further insights and guide operational adjustments in control variables. Nonlinear programming can help to further suggest optimal control variable choices to maximize oil production for the data analyzed.

Drilling Time-Series Pattern Recognition

Improving the drilling process relies on performance analysis that is primarily based on daily activity breakdowns. Drilling a wellbore can be segmented into several distinct operations such as drilling, rotating, and making a connection. Each operation generates detailed information about the status on the rig site. Drilling time-series data are inherently multidimensional leading to very slow access times and expensive computation. Applying machine learning techniques on raw time-series data is not a practical solution. What is needed is a higher-level representation of the raw data that allows efficient computation, and extracts higher-order features.

An innovative analysis of drilling time-series data aggregates trend-based and value-based approximations. This consists of symbolic strings that represent the trends and the values of each variable in the contiguous time-series.

There are multiple studies employing exploratory data analysis to surface hidden patterns in a time-series. Lambrou[2] employs mean, variance, skewness, kurtosis, and entropy as statistical features to classify audio signals. Visual analytics techniques[2] can be utilized to explore the statistical features of sensors' measurement. Statistical features are important in detecting different scenarios in the underlying drilling process. Furthermore, identifying characteristic skewness and entropy can lead to determining precursors of critical events such as stuck-pipe.

Raw sensor-generated data are used as input. Mud-logging systems provide time-series data streams that identify important mechanical parameters. Table 5.1 lists the commonly used data parameters.

In other words, the input is a multivariate time series with nine variables:

$$\{T_1, T_2, \ldots T_9\}$$

where T_i is a series of real numbers $\{X_1, X_2, \ldots X_n\}$ recorded sequentially over a specific temporal period.

The sensor-generated data are not directly ready for building the classification models. These data contain, in most cases, outliers and missing values that will influence the accuracy of the features calculation.

Table 5.1 Standard Data Input Parameters

Data	Description
Flowinav	Average mud-flow-rate
Hkldav	Average hook load
Mdbit	Measure depth of the bit
Mdhole	Measured depth of the hole
Prespumpav	Average pump pressure
Ropav	Average rate of penetration
Rpmav	Average drill string revolutions
Tqav	Average torque
Wobav	Average weight on bit

Data cleansing is an elementary phase that should precede all other machine-learning phases. In data-cleansing task, two subtasks were executed, which are:

- Identification and handling of missing values
- Identification and handling of outliers

An *outlier* is a numeric value that has an unusually high deviation from either the mean or the median value. Although there are numerous sophisticated algorithms for outlier detection, a simple statistical method is used in this work. This method is based on *inter-quartile range* (IQR), which is a measure of variability of the data. IQR was calculated by this equation:

$$IRQ = Q_3 - Q_1 \ldots 1$$

Here, Q_1 and Q_3 are the middle values in the first and the third half of the dataset, respectively. An outlier is any value X that is at least 1.5 interquartile ranges below the first quartile Q_1, or at least 1.5 interquartile ranges above the third quartile Q_3. One of these equations should be satisfied:

$$X < Q_1 - 1.5 * IQR \ldots 2$$

$$X > Q_3 - 1.5 * IQR \ldots 3$$

Box-and-whisker plots were implemented as a graphical representation to show the dispersion of the data, highlighting the values deemed as outliers.

Figure 5.16 shows that there are no outliers in the "mdbit" data taken from one drilling scenario and illustrates the outliers in "mdhole" and "hook load" data taken from the same drilling scenario.

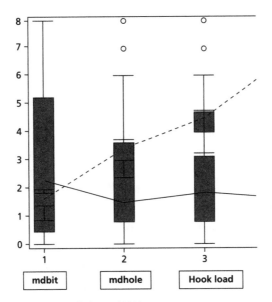

Figure 5.16 Box Plot for mdbit, mdhole, and hkldav

The length of the box equates to the difference between Q_3 and Q_1, which is IRQ. The line drawn inside the box is the median value. All data points above the top horizontal line or below the bottom horizontal line are treated as outliers.

Data were normalized to reduce unwanted variation between datasets. Normalization also enables data represented on different scales to be compared by converting them to a common scale.

As the total depth of each well drilled varies across the well portfolio, all parameters that are related to the depth (e.g., "hkldav," "mdbit," and "mdhole") were normalized by dividing by the total depth of the chosen well. The unrelated parameters (e.g., "ropav") were not normalized.

The second step of the approach is feature extraction, which is the transformation of patterns into features that are considered as a compressed representation.

As drilling time-series data represent a multidimensional input space, it is challenging to analyze owing to the large number of features that can be extracted from the raw data.[3] To reduce the dimensionality of the data, a high-level representation is built where a set of significant features are calculated. These features provide an approximation of the original time-series data.

For each time-series variable $T_i = \{X_1, X_2, \ldots, X_n\}$, $i = 1..10$ many statistical features were calculated to measure different properties of that variable. The main groups of the calculated statistical measures were:

- *Measures of central tendency:* mean, median, and mode
- *Measures of variability:* variance, standard deviation, IRQ, and range

- *Measures of shape:* skewness, kurtosis, and second moment
- *Measures of position:* percentiles
- *Measures of impurity:* entropy

High-dimensional data can contain a high degree of redundancy that adversely impact the performance of learning algorithms.[4] Therefore, feature selection is an important step in the workflow. The initial step in the feature selection phase is removing the correlated features (*collinearity*) in order to reduce the dimensionality of the data and increase the computational efficiency. The most efficient method for feature selection is ranking the features with some statistical test, and then selecting the k features with the highest score or those with a score greater than some threshold t. Such univariate filters do not take into account feature interaction, but they allow a first inspection of the data and most probably provide reasonable results.[5]

Although the algorithms in Table 5.2 did not produce identical results, there was about 70 percent of similarity between these results. For example, most

Table 5.2 Feature-Ranking Algorithms

Algorithm	Description
SAM	Calculates a weight according to "Significance Analysis for Microarrays"
PCA	Uses the factors of one of the principal components analyses as feature weights
SVM	Uses the coefficients of the normal vector of a linear support vector machine as feature weights
Chi-Squared	Calculates the relevance of a feature by computing for each attribute the value of the chi-squared statistic with respect to the class attribute
Relief	Measures the relevance of features by sampling examples and comparing the value of the current feature for the nearest example of the same and of a different class
Gini Index	Calculates the relevance of the attributes based on the Gini impurity index
Correlation	Calculates the correlation of each attribute with the label attribute and returns the absolute or squared value as its weight
Maximum Relevance	Selects Pearson correlation, mutual information, or F-test, depending on feature and label type
Uncertainty	Calculates the relevance of an attribute by measuring the symmetrical uncertainty with respect to the class

algorithms put flowin-p90, wobav-skewness, rpm-variance, and prespumpav-range features in the top of the ranking list.

The resulting question now is: How many features should be used to get the best model in terms of accuracy? To answer this question, it was imperative to conduct multiple tests. Many models with different numbers of features were developed, and subsequently an accuracy indicator was ascertained for each model.

A Principal Components Analysis (PCA) algorithm was used to rank the features. Features were added one at a time, starting with the top feature identified by the corresponding eigenvalues.

Once the most informative features have been extracted, the classification process is initiated. Five classification techniques were used in this study. These techniques are: Support Vector Machine (SVM),[6] Artificial Neural Network (ANN),[8] Rule Induction (RI), Decision Tree (DT), and Naïve Bayes (NB).

The performance of the classifiers was evaluated by using the cross-validation method. The worst classifier is invariably the NB, and the optimum classifiers are SVM and RI.

Unconventional Completion Best Practices

The objective of the study is to identify a completion strategy for an optimized hydraulic fracture treatment plan. Which variables will play the greatest part and impose an impact on hydrocarbon production volumes and post-treatment performance?

Workflows and models were developed capable of classifying a completion strategy and enumerating similar treatment plans previously performed in order to help engineers preclude potential challenges (similarity-based design). Additionally, the main factors influencing the treatment success or failure are identified.

- *Prepare data:* The dataset provided included multiple reservoirs and hydraulic fracture completion strategies. Owing to the inherent variability driven by reservoir parameters, a set of indicators have been developed to normalize the measurements with respect to reservoir parameters and other uncontrollable variables.

- *Qualify completions:* The treatments are grouped into bins of similarity to enable an exploration of the trends and hidden patterns that underpin the subsequent generation of models. Moreover, the grouping of completions serves to identify wells that are atypical for a cluster or cannot be assigned to a specific cluster and hence are deemed as outliers. These are then diagnosed as candidates for future investigation.

- *Quantify completion grouping:* Based on the indicators as defined in the first step, each completion can be classified to one of the bins as defined in the second step of the study. This allows engineers to classify new treatments based on analogs during the planning phase into their most likely bin in order to be able to identify similarities and foresee potential challenges.

- *Deduce completion performance:* Predictive models were developed to infer the most probable completion outcome in those bins where the number of measurements was sufficiently comprehensive to surface trends and relationships under uncertainty. The workflows and models are implemented for planning future wells by comparing the target reservoir properties to those in the extant completions data warehouse. We can then formulate a list of the most similar wells with the best performance to aid in the planning of new treatments.

The objectives of a data-driven model are common for both the planning and operational phases of a hydraulic fracture treatment strategy:

- Minimize total skin.
- Optimize fracture fluid volume.
- Optimize acid volume.
- Optimize proppant volume.
- Maximize cumulative hydrocarbons stage performance.
- Minimize sand and water stage production.

During the planning and operational phases we are studying those geologic parameters that characterize location optimization of a wellbore for maximum reservoir contact and hydrocarbon drainage:

- Perforation area and length
- Fracture dimensions
- Gross formation pay thickness
- Number of stages
- LaPlacian second derivative
- Dip

The planning phase must additionally consider the reservoir geomechanics and rock properties such as permeability and porosity. However, the study is primarily focused on identifying those controllable parameters that can be measured and understood to be effective to attain the previously listed objectives.

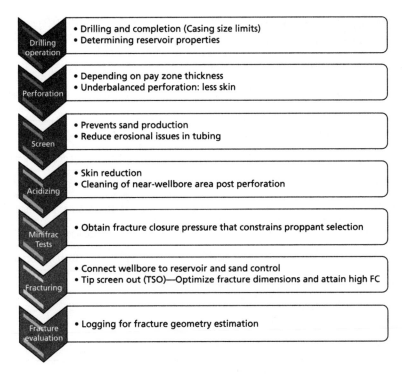

Drilling operation
- Drilling and completion (Casing size limits)
- Determining reservoir properties

Perforation
- Depending on pay zone thickness
- Underbalanced perforation: less skin

Screen
- Prevents sand production
- Reduce erosional issues in tubing

Acidizing
- Skin reduction
- Cleaning of near-wellbore area post perforation

Minifrac Tests
- Obtain fracture closure pressure that constrains proppant selection

Fracturing
- Connect wellbore to reservoir and sand control
- Tip screen out (TSO)—Optimize fracture dimensions and attain high FC

Fracture evaluation
- Logging for fracture geometry estimation

Figure 5.17 Complexity of a Hydraulic Fracture Completion Strategy

The fracture completion strategy is a multistage operation composed of several complex processes that can each result in failure or success. Figure 5.17 provides an overview of the complexity of a common fracture completion strategy.

For high-permeability reservoirs short conductive fractures are ideal. When fracturing a high permeability formation, the fracture should be designed to extend beyond the external radius of the damaged region. Fractures that fail to extend beyond the damaged region will not improve production to optimum levels and will not significantly decrease the potential for sand production. Fractures that significantly extend beyond the damaged region will not significantly impact the productivity, but will result in higher stimulation costs.

Methodology

The investigated database contained 105 fracture pack completion treatments from 12 different reservoirs. The treatments were carried out on different well types (oil producer, gas producer, water injector). In this study we only focused on the treatments of the 67 oil producer wells, and divided the data into three

During Completions Operations		
Static Inputs	**Operationally Controllable**	**Objective Outputs**
Perforation Area and Length	Acid Fluid Volume	Minimize Total Skin
Fracture Height, Width, and Length	Acid Fluid Rate	Optimize Frac Fluid Volume
Gross True Startigraphic Thickness	Frac Pad Fluid Volume	Optimize Acid Fluid Volume
Fracture Conductivity	Frac Pad Fluid Rate	Optimize Proppant Volume
Avg Reservoir Permeability	Flowback/Surge Volume	Optimize Cumulative Production
Avg Reservoir Porosity	Flowback/Surge Rate	Optimize Stage Performance
Water Saturation	Flowback/Surge Time	Minimize and Production
Transmissability	Proppant Volume	Minimize Water Production
Perf OB/UB Gradient MD and TVD	Pumped Proppant Mesh Size by Stage	
Initial BHP Gradient	Initial Oil Rate	
Acid Treatment Pressure Gradient	Net Pressure Gain	
Final Pad and Frac Treatment Pressure Gradient	Initial Adding Index	
BHPi Gradient	Final Injectivity Index Acidizing	
TVD	Final Injectivity Index by Perf Rate Oil Rate and Transmissibility	
Number of Stages		
Planned Proppant Mesh Size by Stage		
Laplacian		
Dip		
Youngs Modulus		
Poissons Ratio		

Figure 5.18 Examples of the Datasets Studied

buckets: static inputs, operationally controllable, and objective outputs as illustrated in Figure 5.18. Each treatment had 280 parameters grouped into the following sections:

- General
- Well and reservoir data

- Perforating information
- Post-perforating information
- Gravel pack (GP) packer information
- GP screen information
- Acidizing information
- Step rate test information
- Mini-fracture information
- Fracturing information
- Post-job analysis
- Completion and performance information
- Reservoir properties

During the first step we differentiated between input and output parameters and filtered out those that have a minor or zero influence on the overall treatment success. Step rate and mini-fracture tests are essential for planning the treatment but do not directly impact the objective function.

SOMs are carried out with five variables at a time to investigate how reservoir parameters influence the fracture geometry. The examined variables are reservoir permeability, porosity, fracture length, fracture width, and fracture height. The goal was to figure out what kind of relationship exists between reservoir and fracture properties.

Based on the ontology, correlation matrixes were created to find an association between various input and output variables, and also among the output variables. The only strong correlation found was between flow efficiency and total skin, which resulted from the fact that the field engineers calculated the flow efficiency from the total skin. In Figure 5.19 the correlation matrix of the most important output variables is depicted.

To reduce the complexity and variance only the treatments on the oil producer wells were taken into account. The whole PCA analysis was done for 77 wells with 86 variables. With the first nine PCs 71 percent of the whole data behavior could be explained and the data complexity was reduced by 88 percent. However, the variables are not sorted by the criteria from the ontology.

During the first step the variables were normalized so that they were comparable to each other. The variable-importance workflow predicts those variables that play a significant role by evaluating the principal components.

Indicators were created to make observations comparable across different reservoirs in order to enable the extraction of patterns and rules. First we distinguished between controllable, uncontrollable, and output variables or objective functions.

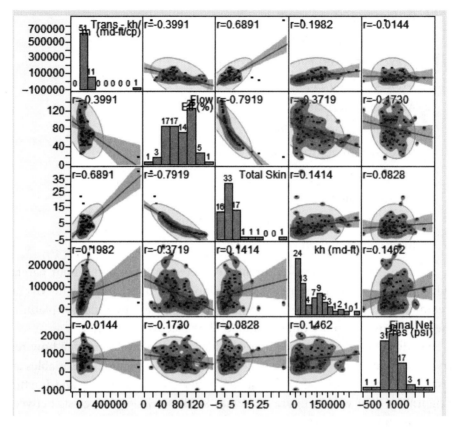

Figure 5.19 Correlation Matrix

For each stage of the completion strategy there are input indicators, which are the normalized design parameters. The output indicators are split in two main groups indicated by the color code. They represent the normalized reservoir response on each treatment stage and on the overall (total) success.

These indicators are listed below:

1. Input indicators:
   a. Perforation
      i. In Perforation A = Perforation Length/Gross True Stratigraphic Thickness
   b. Acidizing
      i. In Acid A = Fluid Volume/(avg. Permeability*Perforation Length MD)
      ii. In Acid B = Acid Treating Pressure Gradient

    c. Fracturing

        i. In Fracture A = Final Pad Treating Pressure Gradient/BHPi Gradient

        ii. In Fracture B = Final Fracture Treating Pressure Gradient/BHPi Gradient

        iii. In Fracture C = Fracture Pad Fluid Volume/(avg. Perm*Perforation Length MD)

        iv. In Fracture D = Fracture Total Fluid Volume/(avg. Perm*Perforation Length MD)

        v. In Fracture E = Fracture Pad Fluid Volume/Fracture Total Fluid Volume

        vi. In Fracture F = Nr. of Stages

        vii. In Fracture G = Max. Proppant Concentration

2. Output indicators:

    a. Perforation

        i. Out Perforation A = (Perforation. OB/UB Pressure)/TVD

    b. Acidizing

        i. Out Acid B = (Final Injectivity Index-Initial Injectivity Index)/(Perforation Area*(Initial Oil Rate/Transmissibility))

    c. Fracturing

        i. Out Fracture A = lbs/ft in TST Perforations

        ii. Out Fracture B = Est Fracture Height

        iii. Out Fracture C = Est Fracture Width

        iv. Out Fracture D = Est. Fracture Length

        v. Out Fracture E = Est. CFD

    d. Total

        i. Total A = Initial Oil Rate/Transmissibility

        ii. Total B = Net Pressure Gain/BHPi

        iii. Total C = Flow Efficiency

        iv. Total D = Total Skin

The PCA was repeated to qualify the correlations among the indicators. The first eight principal components were deemed as being an adequate representation of the variability. At this point, the first two principal components derived from the PCA on the indicators were taken to build the clusters so that the relationship among indicators and treatments can be qualified.

There are two main groups that can be identified easily as depicted in Figure 5.20. The one on the upper-right side behaves completely differently

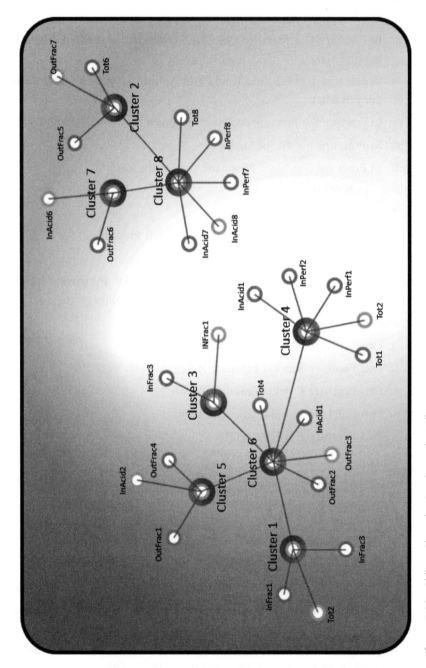

Figure 5.20 Oblique Clustering Results on the Indicators

from the one on the bottom-left side. On the upper-right side are indicators that are mainly influenced by the fracturing design parameters. On the bottom-left side the main cluster can be divided into two further subclasses. The one with Clusters 3 and 5 includes the indicators that are mainly volume-related indicators and the other ones (Clusters 1 and 4) are mainly pressure related.

Next, the oblique clustering was repeated, but now the treatments are also taken into account to see which treatment is best described by which indicator. After analyzing the result the same domination types could be discovered as in the first oblique clustering. However, there are some wells that could not be grouped into these domination types according to the first two principal components. They are the outliers and are neglected during subsequent investigation and model building.

A classification decision tree was built to quantify the domination types. The decision tree indicates that only three indicators (In Acid A, In Fracture E, and In Fracture A) are requisite to differentiate among the domination types.

In Acid 1, we see the strongest rule. It shows that if the relative acid volume pumped is over 1.6, then the well will reflect a volume domination type.

After that, the In Fracture E and In Fracture B differentiate between design- and pressure-dominated treatments. Note that there are two subgroups of design-dominated and three subgroups of pressure-dominated treatments.

After analyzing the data and merging with expert knowledge from the oil industry a model was built that classifies the existing treatments into several categories according to their design and performance. The outcome is a list of type wells for each category. This model can be used for planning future wells by comparing its reservoir properties to the ones in the existing database. It can then generate the list of the most similar wells (based on the uncontrollable variables) with the best performance. The scheme of the type of wells can be used as a design outline by the planning engineers.

Chapter 8's "Pinedale Asset" details another example of a completion optimization strategy ascertained via an advanced analytical methodology. This examination was carried out in the unconventional asset known as the Pinedale in Western Wyoming.

NOTES

1. Tom Keyser, "Roger Butler: Father of SAGD," *Business Edge* (May 2, 2005).
2. T. Lambrou and P. Kudumakis, "Classification of Audio Signals Using Statistical Features on Time and Wavelet Transform Domains," IEEE, 2002.
3. A. Arnaout, B. Esmael, R.K. Fruhwirth, G. Thonhauser, "Diagnosing Drilling Problems Using Visual Analytics of Sensors Measurements," 2012 In Proc. of IEEE International Instrumentation and Measurement Technology Conference I2MTC, Graz, Austria, 2012.
4. C. A. Ratanamahatana, J. Lin, D. Gunopulos, E. Keogh, M. Vlachos, and G. Das, "Mining Time Series Data," in Data Mining and Knowledge Discovery Handbook, 2nd ed., ed. O. Maimon and L. Rokach (New York: Springer, 2010), 1049–1077.

5. L. Yu and H. Liu, "Feature Selection for High-Dimensional Data: A Fast Correlation-Based Filter Solution," Twentieth International Conference on Machine Learning (ICML-2003), 2003.

6. B. Schowe, "Feature Selection for High-Dimensional Data with RapidMiner," Technical University of Dortmund, 2010.

7. Adriane B. S. Serapiao, Rogerio M. Tavares, Jose Ricardo P. Mendes, and Ivan R. Guilherme, "Classification of Petroleum Well Drilling Operations Using Support Vector Machine (SVM)," in Proceedings of the International Conference on Computational Intelligence for Modelling, Control and Automation (CIMCA 2006), IEEE Computer Society, Sydney, Australia, 2006.

8. R. Fruhwirth and G. Thonhauser, "Hybrid Simulation Using Neural Networks to Predict Drilling Hydraulics in Real Time," SPE Annual Technical Conference and Exhibition, San Antonio, TX, September 24–27, 2006.

CHAPTER **6**

Reservoir
Management

Knowledge makes you free from the chains of igno-
rance, and revives your heart; knowledge takes you
out from the darkness of suspicions and superstitions,
and gives a new light to your eyes.

Hazrat Abu Ali Saqfi

The goal of reservoir management is to maximize the economic profitability or net present value of the asset (hydrocarbon reserves) while minimizing CAPEX and OPEX.[1] Controlling operations to maximize both short- and long-term production predicates a lifecycle optimization based on reservoir model uncertainties together with model updating by production measurements, time-lapse seismic, and other available data. Time-lapse seismic data, for example, help to determine reservoir changes that occur over time and can be used as a new dimension in history matching since they contain information about fluid movement and pressure changes between and beyond the well. How can we process and use the huge amount of information in an efficient way and ensure that the reservoir models are kept up to date and consistent with the data? We shall explore some of the data and associated analytical methodologies appropriate to reservoir management in the case studies.

Reservoir management tasks can broadly fall into one of four buckets:[2]

1. Classification
2. Estimation
3. Segmentation
4. Description

175

The *classification* task essentially puts labels on everything deemed important for a study. Thus, to identify ideal well candidates for a stimulation workflow, we could through classification stipulate a predefined set of labels as good, moderate, or bad. The process then attributes wells based on incoming characteristics into the appropriate class. The *estimation* suite of workflows imputes missing data values and performs transformations. These functions can be geared on statistical regressions and complex numerical simulation models that are entrenched in first principles. In reservoir management determining the wells that are good candidates for stimulation is a classification process but predicting the post-stimulation well performance is an estimation task. Often during the application of soft computing techniques, such as neural networks, the input space is characterized by a multidimensional population that captures examples of collinearity. This phenomenon refers to an exact or approximate linear relationship between two explanatory variables; *multicollinearity* extends the concept to more than two input variables. It is beneficial then to sub-populate the original input space into smaller groups that have similar characteristics or profiles. This task is *segmentation*. A suite of clustering techniques enable this task. Soft computing methodologies that implement exploratory data analysis to surface hidden trends and relationships, as well as predictive models such as neural networks, furnish the reservoir engineers with a better *description* of the disparate data aggregated for a study.

It is critical to marry the data-driven workflows with first principles in reservoir management. There are a variety of deterministic or parametric models such as reservoir simulation that rely on input parameters ascertained *a priori*. The soft data generated are then evaluated and compared to the measured data. Domain knowledge ostensibly controls the complexity inherent in deterministic model changes, the assumption being that the complexity is too intricate to rely on automated model tuning to match measured data.

In reservoir management arbitrarily complex multivariant models can be produced by a data-driven methodology while parametric models tend to be limited by human comprehension. Do reservoir managers depend too much on empirical observations? As the industry generates more varieties of data and deals with an avalanche of real-time data from sensors in intelligent wells, it is evolving into an environment that necessitates a data-driven suite of soft computing techniques.

Halbouty[3] stated in 1977: "It is the duty and responsibility of industry managers to encourage full coordination of geologists, geophysicists, and petroleum engineers to advance petroleum exploration, development, and production." However, the adoption of the integrated and collaborative processes echoed by this sentiment has been done haphazardly and at a very slow pace. Haldorsen and Van Golf-Raachtl[4] presented a philosophy of managing reservoirs from exploration to abandonment. The process of designing economically optimum field developments was discussed at great length, with emphasis on reservoir description and the interaction of disciplines.

EXPLORATION AND PRODUCTION VALUE PROPOSITIONS

A reservoir's life begins with exploration, leading to discovery; reservoir delineation and field development; production by primary, secondary, and tertiary means, and inexorably the final phase of abandonment (Figure 6.1).

Sound reservoir management necessitates constant monitoring and surveillance of the reservoir performance from a holistic perspective. Is the reservoir performance conforming to management expectations? The important areas that add value across the E&P value chain as regards monitoring and surveillance involve data acquisition and management:

- Oil, water, and gas rates and cumulative production
- Gas and water injection
- Static and flowing bottom-hole pressures
- Production and injection well tests
- Well injection and production profiles
- Fluid analyses
- 4D seismic surveys

Determine a suite of reservoir performance and field planning workflows:

- Reservoir surveillance:
  - Well management
  - Well reliability and optimization

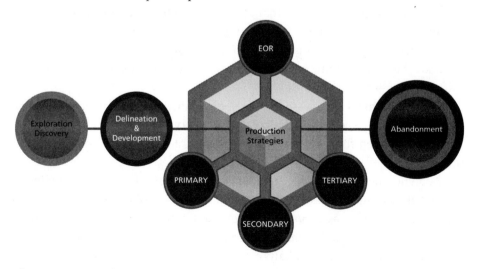

Figure 6.1 Reservoir Management Cogs

- Field management
- Reservoir modeling
- Reservoir performance:
  - Injection production ratio (IPR) monitoring
  - Pressure maintenance
  - Sweep efficiency
  - Water and gas entry detection and diagnostics

Each of these selected workflows has activities that could be categorized as data-driven activities and/or model-driven activities. The *data-driven* activities are intimately involved in the areas of monitoring and event detection, and partially in diagnostics and analysis. The *model-driven* activities are more related to the optimization aspects of the various workflows and involve reservoir models and optimization algorithms.

Automated analytics, be they univariate or multivariate, are essential to render the data robust for the workflows that marry first principles with soft computing techniques to ensure reliable quantification of uncertainty and risk assessment throughout the lifecycle of the reservoir.

Reservoir characterization and simulation as discussed in Chapter 4 plays a vital role in field development and modern reservoir management. It helps to make sound reservoir decisions and improves the asset value of the oil and gas companies. It maximizes the integration of multidisciplinary data and knowledge and improves the reliability of the reservoir performance prediction. The ultimate product is a reservoir model with realistic tolerance for imprecision and uncertainty.

Soft computing is a collection of various intelligent techniques that now plays a crucial role in performance enhancement. The objective of soft computing, compared to traditional "hard" computing, is to exploit the tolerance for imprecision, uncertainty, approximate reasoning, and partial truth. Thus, deterministic model building and interpretation *must* be complemented by stochastic and soft computing–based methods.

The upstream oil and gas sector has some of the largest unmanaged repositories of vertically specialized data of any industry. The major IT hurdles E&P companies face en route to the digital oil field are the integration and validation of data.

Analytics help companies make better decisions; in-database analytics help companies make those decisions more quickly, providing information in seconds and minutes as opposed to weeks and months. In a traditional environment, data are copied from the enterprise data warehouse (EDW) and converted for niche products to analyze and process. With the massive quantities of data O&G companies deal with today, analytic processes can require a great deal of time-consuming data movement within the organization. Running those processes inside the EDW greatly reduces the amount of data that must be copied, moved, and converted.

As a result, redundancy and latency issues decrease, data quality and data consistency improve, and total cost goes down, since the business is no longer required to do all of that extra data management.

In addition to technology there are two other important areas to align:

1. *People:* Effectively incorporate change and knowledge management into your integrated operations for effective collaboration and optimized operations.
2. *Processes:* Improve decision making and boost operational efficiency by effectively linking each component of your digital oilfield.

DIGITAL OILFIELD OF THE FUTURE

The digital oilfield is a strategy for improving a specific area of an oil company's business by deploying people, technology, and knowledge effectively. The digital oilfield initiative, however, is transforming the way people work. A key ingredient of the digital oilfield is quick, easy, and timely access to quality data: Companies must shift the burden of orchestrating data from people to systems.

Achieving the digital oilfield requires innovation in computer software and hardware and in telecommunications to effectively "educate" and "equip" almost every aspect of upstream oil and gas activity into an integrated, real-time operation. And this innovation impacts domain experts and technology to surface one collaborative perspective on the knowledge accrued from all facets of upstream data.

Like Londoners minding the Underground gap, why don't we mind the gap in intelligence deployment—that abyss that has to be bridged in order to ask the right questions and determine more timely and strategic answers? As the demand for intelligence and knowledge augments, one has to mine the exabytes or soon-to-be *petabytes* of data extant in the upstream silos to garner value from the assets, making near real-time decisions and strategies to exploit the reserves in reservoirs.

Plugging the Technological Capability Gap

The oil and gas industry needs to plug the capability gap with pertinent technology that embraces the current trends to improve productivity. The cost implied by poor predictions has to be mitigated by improved integration of disciplines and data fusion by adopting soft computing methods such as neural networks, fuzzy logic, and probabilistic reasoning instilled into efficient workflows.

In reservoir management it is critical to develop models containing any meaningful combination of data types to formulate a spatiotemporal dataset from the following classes:

- Depth-related data (well logs, drilling parameters, core data, etc.)
- Well properties (PI, skin factor, and location, etc.)
- Time series data (pressures, production history, well tests, etc.)
- Areal distributions (OOIP, permeability etc.)

These data classes differ as regards the "pattern" being fed into a neural network for training and calibration of a model ready for prediction.

One pattern could be:

- *Depth-related data:* all data collated at a certain depth
- *Well properties:* all data collected at a specific periodicity (daily or monthly)
- *Areal distributions:* all data from one geographic location

Advanced Analytical Methodologies

There are five main hurdles to overcome in data management in order to achieve the true digital oil field of the future:

1. *Data availability:* Satellite communications have come a long way; however, their reliability and availability will need to be improved to ensure that the 'digital oil field' can maintain its heterogeneous levels of use.
2. *Accessibility:* Ease of use. In most cases, very few people actually send out data entry personnel to the rigs; the system has to be user-friendly to the operators.
3. *Information aggregation:* This is to ensure that global situation awareness is provided, for the operator to facilitate proper flow of information so as to allow the service companies to work closer and thus to reduce human data entry where possible.
4. *Information availability:* Users may be geographically dispersed and will require remote delivery methods (web technology) to get at the data they will need to make decisions or to report on.
5. *Flexibility:* The oilfield operates with many variables that affect the operational progress for each project. The IT system has to deal with changes from the field without losing its place on the map.

Data Management

Data management architectures provide organizations with a flexible and reliable solution for meeting their basic data integration needs while preserving the option of upgrading to more complete capabilities as their situations change. It eliminates delivery delays and high costs associated with having IT building custom code for each integration project or having to piece together myriad nonintegrated technologies by providing a single, integrated, and easy-to-use solution. It eliminates the need for organizations to acquire new tools and learn new skills as they take on new and more complex data integration projects. There are vendors that can establish a single solution to accommodate basic data integration activities now, which can expand to a complete solution later, fully leveraging the skills, processes, and rules that an organization has previously developed.

Are you tasked with building and loading data warehouses and data marts within an allotted time window, quickly building an analytical mart for a special project or creating extract files for reporting and sampling applications? It is imperative to attain an intuitive point-and-click process design desktop that allows designers to easily build logical process workflows, quickly identify the input and output data stores, and create business rules in metadata, enabling the rapid generation of data warehouses, data marts, and data streams. In addition, one needs an easy-to-use transformation language that supports collaboration, reuse, and shared metadata.

Data cleansing and enrichment provides clean, credible, and correct knowledge. From duplicating database information, to cleaning up data before storage in the data warehouse, to looping back to the operational data with the same quality improvements via real-time transaction cleansing, there should be an enterprise approach that lets you develop and share a library of data rules and processes between projects and across the entire data integration solution. A seamless environment takes users from profiling and rules creation, through data integration processing, to monitoring the results. Data quality rules can be built quickly while profiling data and then automatically incorporating them into the data transformation process. A workflow design environment makes it easy to augment existing data with information from new sources, increasing the value of your data.

Creating a master data environment enables organizations to provide a single source of truth around which enterprise systems can be synchronized. This requires extracting key data from diverse operational environments to create a system of record files, establishing links to keep that system and operational system files in sync, and providing fast access across all operational systems to master data without degrading operational performance. With the ability to read from and write to virtually any data on any technology platform in batch and real-time, this is the goal to provide unsurpassed data access.

Data are a strategic asset of any oil company, not primarily owned by the domain that harvests the data. Data integration and master data management are key to enterprise knowledge.

Organizations must create processes for managing their data, or they run the risk of having it misplaced or lost. In a world of real-time accessibility, inaccessibility of any magnitude can cause great damage. The damage is compounded if the data are corrupt or fall into the wrong hands. This leads to another issue: federal legislation.

Federal Legislation

Many organizations are mandated by law to report to federal organizations, such as the Minerals Management Service. If data are compromised or lost, this can result in serious complications. Furthermore, publicly traded companies or those that conduct business with them have the added responsibility of complying with legislation such as Sarbanes-Oxley, further increasing the risk.

Architecture

O&G companies are now housing thousands of different datasets, exponentially more than any other time in history. Each discipline within the organization, whether it's a geophysicist or a drilling engineer, must have easy access to the data to efficiently process, manage, and optimize these discrete datasets.

We should focus on a service-oriented architecture (SOA): An upstream SOA will dramatically augment the flexibility of the IT environment and reduce the maintenance of the IT integration software. SOA is an approach to distributed computing that abstracts complex and heterogeneous IT systems into composite, business-oriented services. Some applications are consumers and some providers. Avoid point-to-point system evolution. The O&G architecture must entertain interoperability to support the plethora of standards such as XML interchange engine, APIs, J2EE compatibility, .NET, and the disparate protocols such as HTTP, SOAP, and T3. It defines how one can plug-and-play. Adhering to interoperability standards precludes or at least obviates somewhat the creation of digital silos of information. Data should go in once and be usable throughout the asset's lifecycle and by various applications.

The DOFF architecture encapsulates the well and reservoir management paradigm that reflects the art of extracting maximum value from oil and gas assets by understanding and optimizing the performance of the reservoirs, wells, and facilities all the way from the pores of the reservoir rocks through the reservoir to the wells, through the wells to the flow-lines and facilities, and then on to the downstream outlets: refineries and gas stations.

The pith and core of any DOFF integrates a version of the lifecycle illustrated in Figure 6.2. It consists of five steps:

Step 1. Gathering and managing the data required to understand our reservoirs, wells, and facilities.

Step 2. Using this data to visualize, interpret, and model the fluid flows and pressures in the asset.

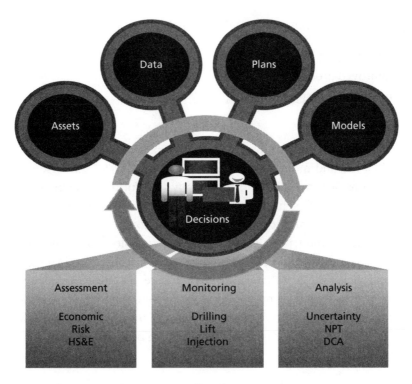

Figure 6.2 Well and Reservoir Management Lifecycle

Step 3. Carrying out a set of structured reviews to efficiently turn these analyses into a robust multidisciplinary understanding of both the components and the whole of the asset.

Step 4. Translating this understanding into a concrete set of actions designed to improve the performance of the reservoir, wells, and facilities.

Step 5. Executing these actions in the field to enhance the performance of the physical asset and tracking the financial performance of these actions.

Real-Time Analytical Workflows

It appears the industry is still pursuing this abstraction of reservoir management. In response to the plethora of real-time data from sensors deployed in intelligent wells, a reservoir management solution embraces advanced technical tools as well as automated and semi-automated analytical workflows. Remote work practices promote collaborative centers of excellence.

Continuous improvement is critical to sustain any tangible success across the oil and gas industry E&P value chain. You must focus your DOFF efforts with continuous improvement to empower the asset teams as they garner support and entice investment from senior management.

What are the documented DOFF benefits?

- Increased reservoir recovery
- Improved production rates
- Reduction in OPEX
- Lower CAPEX

Total asset awareness coupled with timely execution and right-time analysis enable faster and more effective decision-making cycles. Endorsed by data-driven analysis, it is plausible to substantially transform people by establishing workflows and optimized processes underpinned by advanced technology. These DOFF initiatives inexorably open up opportunities for increased recovery factors, enhanced hydrocarbon production rates with tangible savings in operational costs and capital expenditure. It is essential to move from individual technology applications across the DOFF landscape to cross-asset optimization post functional integration in an asset-wide optimization implementation. What are some of the technologies that are ostensibly the major contributors to a DOFF portfolio?

Let us enumerate those technologies that can be reliant on soft computing techniques:

- Electric wellbore sensors
- Intelligent completions
- Real-time data management
- Predictive analytics
- 4D seismic data acquisition/processing
- Wired drill pipes
- Geo-steering
- Artificial lift
- Rotating equipment
- Flow assurance
- Integrated planning
- Zonal optimization
- Drilling
- Planning and logistics
- Maintenance and reliability
- Collaborative centers of analytical competence

There are multiple examples of DOFF initiatives implemented across the O&G global assets; some are more successful than others. Let us explicate in detail one such initiative executed in one of the North Sea fields.

Figure 6.3 DOFFs Integrated Actions Threaded by Analytical Workflows

The key elements of the DOFF program, as depicted in Figure 6.3, that implement advanced analytical methodologies include:

- Integrated planning (IPL)
- Remote project management and surveillance
- Real-time production optimization

These characteristics highlight some of the operational and subsurface complexities that asset personnel are hoping to better manage through their DOFF initiatives.

ANALYTICAL CENTER OF EXCELLENCE

Joseph Warren[5] notes that the success of an individual team can be variable when he states, "The fundamental idea of cross-functional teams and goals appears to surface about every ten years with a new label. Usually, attempts to implement this concept in the E&P business ended with utter failure for a variety of reasons."

To enable real synergy among all team members, easy-to-use yet powerful software is required. Study synergy and parallel workflows can be achieved only if all the team members can at least browse all applications. As an example, all disciplines should be able to browse the geological model (structure, properties, etc.), simulation results (i.e., flood front with time), facilities layout, and well production profiles, regardless of their respective disciplines. To enable this ease of use, customized templates were created to ease study browsing capability without the need to know every application in detail.

Rather than placing a core team of experts in a room with a simple mandate to "go get results," the Analytical Centers of Excellence utilizes a facilitator that leads the team to rapidly identify and focus on key study issues.[6] These key issues are reinforced by the *extended* and *decision teams*. Each team member works in parallel on several tasks. Every day, the results are rolled up and summarized by the facilitator for review and debate by the *core team*. As this routine continues, the entire team, regardless of their discipline, converges on a common understanding of the Big Picture, and the true importance of various issues begins to surface.

The Analytical Centers of Excellence process (Figure 6.4) is very involved and includes 10 steps from project start to completion.

Following are the 10 steps for the Analytical Centers of Excellence process:

Step 1. Gather data and models into one shared drive.

Step 2. Understand the reservoirs, cleanup models, and update.

    a. This stage may include many mechanistic and deterministic models to assist early understanding of the reservoir characterization and behavior.

Step 3. Develop a static and dynamic uncertainties matrix for all variables and notion of critical ones.

Step 4. Evaluate OOIP and its uncertainty (static uncertainties).

    a. *Output:* the *most likely* OOIP along with estimates of the practical low and high uncertainties. The parameters affecting that uncertainty are identified and key parameters noted. The uncertainty matrix (static part of the matrix) that was used initially as a guideline for this step is fine-tuned, showing critical factors and narrowed-down ranges.

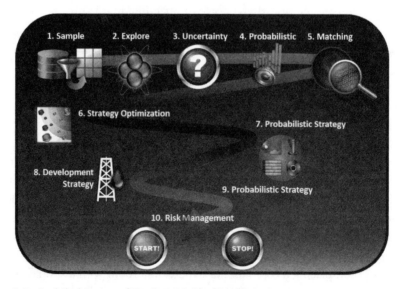

Figure 6.4 Analytical Centers of Excellence Suite of Workflows

Step 5. Achieve history match and its critical factors.

   a. *Output:* multiple history-matched models and a list of critical parameters and their ranges that were required to achieve that match.

Step 6. Construct development strategy analysis.

   a. List the development criteria (plateau, estimated ultimate recovery, drilling/facilities constraints, well types, etc.).

   b. Construct alternative development strategies. These strategies typically include water injection, gas injection, water-alternate-gas, peripheral or pattern floods, etc.

   c. Rank alternatives with deterministic reservoir simulation runs based on the most likely history match.

   d. *Output:* a list of selected alternative strategies and their ranking.

Step 7. Test the most promising alternatives under uncertainty.

   a. In this step, reservoir simulation is performed to the critical factors listed from step 5 to select the preferred development strategy(s).

   b. *Output:* the selection of the most robust alternative, termed the *preferred development strategy* (PDS).

Step 8. Optimize the team focus on the PDS. More detailed optimization is included at this point and typically includes lateral design, work-over strategy, perforation targets, injection/production ratios, and complex well design (equalizers, downhole control values, etc.).

   a. *Output:* an Optimized Field Development Plan (OFDP).

Step 9. Determine the impact of uncertainty on the OFDP and list the information plan required to narrow down the uncertainty range of the critical uncertainty factors.

Step 10. List project risk based on step 9, and list the mitigation plans for the OFDP.

The Analytical Centers of Excellence is a novel study[7] approach that integrates a new process with new tools, synergizing stakeholders from all domains to quickly resolve important problems during a special team event that lasts for two months rather than years. This new approach is flexible and scalable enough to cover problems ranging from one reservoir to an entire business unit with multiple assets, infrastructure areas, and marketing issues, if needed. The Analytical Centers of Excellence is the step beyond conventional asset teams, where the study has been distinctively designed to create better synergy among all stakeholders (asset teams, managers, decision makers, and partners), and enable faster decisions that fully encompass the complex uncertainties associated with current projects.

Implementing this new approach does not require reorganization. Simply assemble a team for each study, and dissolve it when the study is over. The Analytical Centers of Excellence includes a new and successful approach for handling uncertainty and project risks. The Analytical Centers of Excellence is a proven success in projects that have spanned the entire spectrum of asset numbers, complexity, and maturity.

ANALYTICAL WORKFLOWS: BEST PRACTICES

It is essential to develop analytical workflows that are conducive to the software architecture and customary work habits found in the disparate engineering silos. Not only will the processes enable effective data-driven models but it will also break down the walls that barricade the experienced geoscientists as raw data streams into tangible and actionable knowledge. The analytical workflows must address the business problem(s) to be resolved. There is natural evolution for the workflows from identifying the objective function(s) and enumerating those independent variables that are statistically most influential on the identified objective function(s). Let us explore two analytical workflows that detail methodologies as best practices for the use of soft computing techniques to surface value propositions.

Shale Production Management

Neoteric advances across the communications, instrumentation, and oilfield technologies have enabled that once-intangible dream of total asset appreciation to come more into focus. It is important to consider three complex systems,

1. Reservoir
2. Well
3. Surface facilities

and to integrate the disparate datasets that constitute each system, contemporaneously understanding the influence of each upon the others. It is critical to leverage each field's real-time data for continuous monitoring and right-time response during the full field lifecycle across the E&P value chain.

Right-time response has essentially two components:

1. Effective interventions based on intra-process optimization
2. Strategic interventions predicated on minute understanding of detailed models

The O&G industry has adopted various nomenclatures to define their digital surface and subsurface technologies: smart fields, intelligent fields, digital oilfield of the future (DOFFs), integrated fields, and heuristically integrated operations or integrated planning and logistics.

No matter the tag or label assigned to the solution, it is critical to appreciate that the pith and core of such a solution must be achieved through four fundamental activities:

1. Real-time drilling operations
2. Real-time geo-steering
3. Intelligent field data sources
4. Centers of excellence that attain seamless collaboration

Thus the keystones are integrating and leveraging multidisciplinary engineers across all geoscientific schools of thought and threading the methodologies with real-time data across all phases of field development and lifecycle reservoir management.

Figure 6.5 depicts an implementation architecture that consists of four major tiers:

1. Surveillance
2. Integration
3. Optimization
4. Innovation

Surveillance Tier

The surveillance layer provides continuous monitoring and collates real-time data that are fed into a data management platform implementing automated and semi-automated data quality workflows.

Figure 6.5 Implementation Architecture

Integration Tier

The integration layer interrogates real-time data on a continuous basis to identify and surface hidden trends and anomalous relationships. In a multivariate system any anomalies are alerted for subsequent analysis.

Optimization Tier

The optimization layer provides streamlined optimization capabilities and recommendations.

Innovation Tier

The innovation layer preserves knowledge of events that trigger the optimization process and correlates actions throughout each of the business processes. The innovation layer is a knowledge-management and lessons-learned layer that captures and injects "intelligence" into each process.

Surrogate Reservoir Models

A *surrogate reservoir model* (SRM) is a recently introduced technology that is used to tap into the unrealized potential of the reservoir simulation models. High computational cost and long processing time of reservoir simulation models limit our ability to perform comprehensive sensitivity analysis, quantify uncertainties and risks associated with the geologic and operational parameters, or to evaluate a large set of scenarios for development of greenfields. SRM accurately replicates the results of a numerical simulation model with very low computational cost and low turnaround period and allows for extended study of reservoir behavior and potentials. SRM represents the application of artificial intelligence and data mining to reservoir simulation and modeling.

Steps involved in developing the SRM are identifying the number of runs that are required for the development of the SRM, making the runs, extracting static and dynamic data from the simulation runs to develop the necessary spatiotemporal dataset, identifying the key performance indicators (KPIs) that rank the influence of different reservoir characteristics on the oil and gas production in the field, training and matching the results of the simulation model, and finally validating the performance of the SRM using a blind simulation run.

SRM for this reservoir is then used to perform sensitivity analysis as well as quantification of uncertainties associated with the geological model. These analyses that require thousands of simulation runs were performed using the SRM in minutes.

Advantages of the SRM over the response surface and other reduced-order models are: Response surface and other reduced-order models that are developed using statistical approaches use predetermined functional forms that must be identified in advance. Then the results of hundreds of simulation runs are fitted to these predetermined functional forms hoping that the observed behavior from the reservoir simulation model follows a predetermined, well-behaved functional form. During the training and matching of the SRM, no predetermined functional forms are identified. SRMs are developed using universal function approximation technology that will adapt and fit an infinite set of functional forms that may change from one set to another many times within the time and space domain that is the subject of our analysis.

When a simulation run is completed there are two sets of information that can be extracted from it. First are pressure or production profiles at each well and the second are pressure and saturation changes throughout the reservoir that have resulted from the production/injection process. While the pressure and production profiles are presented at each individual well, the changes in pressure and saturation throughout the reservoir are identified at each grid block. Unlike response surface and reduced models that are only capable of reproducing a version of pressure and production at each well, SRM provides accurate replication of simulation results not only at each well but also at each grid block. By using well-based SRMs, one can reproduce rate and pressure profiles at each well in seconds, and while using grid-based SRMs one can reproduce pressure and saturation distribution at each grid block location at each time-step.

SRMs are developed using data extracted from simulation runs. Therefore, the first step in any SRM project starts with developing a representative spatiotemporal database. The extent to which this spatiotemporal database actually represents the fluid flow behavior of the reservoir that is being modeled determines the potential degree of success in developing an accurate model.

The term *spatiotemporal* defines the essence of this database. It is inspired from the physics that controls this phenomenon and is described by the diffusivity equation. The main objective of modeling a reservoir is to be able to know the value of pressure and saturation at any location in the reservoir and at any time. Therefore, data collection, compilation, organization, and processing must be performed with such needs in mind.

An extensive data mining and analysis process should be conducted at this step to fully understand the data that is housed in this database. The data compilation, quality control, and preprocessing is one of the most important and time consuming steps in developing the SRM. The "curse of dimensionality" is one of the issues that is associated with SRM and must be handled eloquently during this step of the process. Proper handling of this important issue can make or break the entire modeling process.

One of the most important steps in the development of the SRM is the identification of KPIs. The spatiotemporal database that was developed in the previous step includes a very large number of parameters that need to be analyzed and possibly included in the predictive model. It is a fact that not all of the parameters have an equal impact on the oil and gas production throughout the reservoir. Using a large number of input parameters in developing a predictive model will result in a system with serious tractability issues. Therefore, it is very important, and even vital to the success of the training, matching, and validating of the SRM to be able to efficiently identify the KPIs of a given model.

The process of building (training) the SRM and matching its performance with that of the reservoir simulation model is performed simultaneously. During this process the SRM is trained to learn the reservoir model and the fluid flow behavior in the specific reservoir simulator being modeled. The spatiotemporal database developed in the previous step is the main source of information for building and matching the SRM. Please note that the SRM may be a collection of several models that are trained, matched, validated, and finally used in concert to generate the desired results.

SRM can be developed for both brown- and greenfields, as long as a numerical reservoir simulation model for a given asset exists. SRM can be built to replicate the results of the numerical reservoir simulation model with high accuracy while having the advantage to run at speeds that can be compared with the real time (fractions of a second). This high-speed and minimal computational footprint coupled with high accuracy (in replicating numerical reservoir simulation model results) make SRM an ideal tool for real-time reservoir management, design of master development plans, as well as uncertainty assessment.

CASE STUDIES

Let us detail two case studies that apply advanced data-driven methodologies to understand the influence of water and how effective management can be garnered from marrying traditional interpretation with soft computing techniques.

Water Flood Optimization

During a water flood, large amounts of injected water are used to maintain and/or increase oil production from a petroleum reservoir. This case study shows how comparing the changes in oil, gas, and water production (relative to the water injection changes) helps assess fluid communication through a reservoir.

The communication parameters are integrated with other geological parameters and used to develop predictive models. These predictive models help estimate the production capacity or production probability in water flooded reservoirs.

This case study also shows how decision tree models support a two-to-four-times more accurate selection of high-production wells than historically implemented selections. It is based on our developments for analyzing injection responses in vertical and horizontal patterns for water flood optimization. The injection responses are estimated from nonparametric correlations between changes in the injection rates and the corresponding changes in the production rates (oil, water, gas, and total fluid). In addition, we estimate the time lag of the above responses.

A water flood response is estimated as a rank correlation between two series of rate changes for all of the injector-producer pairs. Specifically, the nonparametric Spearman rank correlation coefficient is calculated based on ranks of the injection and production rate changes.

Figure 6.6 shows a perfect correspondence or correlation between two time series (the injection rate and the oil production rate). However, the oil rate is shifted in time, which characterizes the water flood response time lag. In this case the water flood response (based on the oil rate) would have a correlation equal to one. In practice, we calculate a set of lagged correlations at time lags from zero to 12 or more months.

Then, we find the highest correlation and the corresponding time lag. Water, gas, and total fluid responses are calculated in the same fashion. The correlation and the time lag between the injection and the associated production rate changes allow us to compress a series of rates into a pair of simple parameters: the correlation (response strength) and the time lag for every produced fluid.

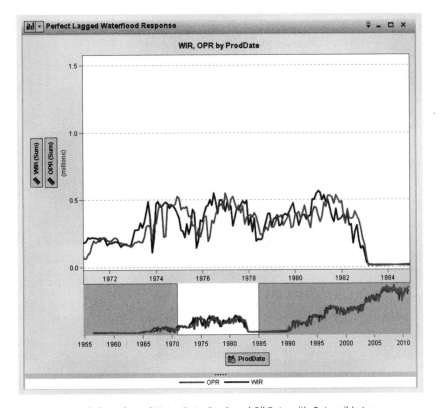

Figure 6.6 Correlation Injected Water Rate, Produced Oil Rate with Ostensible Lag

Injection-production correlations and the corresponding time lags for oil, gas, water, and the total fluid can be integrated with geological parameters at local and global scales. Both the water flood response parameters and geological datasets are noisy and account for a relatively small portion of the total variance in the target variables (e.g., production). Predictive modeling helps summarize these multivariate datasets and relates them to geological and production events. In addition, it helps identify the most important factors, which are then used to develop the predictive models. These models can be quantified, and used to select the development efforts in areas with the highest possible potential.

A numerical integration of geological, completion, treatment, and water flood response parameters is the ultimate technique for predicting oil production during enhanced recovery processes. Predictive models can be developed for a continuous target variable (production) or for a binary target variable (poor or good well). These models can be based on regression, neural networks, and decision trees. A model that has the best predictive powers and stability can be implemented to predict well performance in a specific area or the whole field.

Figure 6.7 shows a decision tree that classifies wells into two groups of *good* and *poor* performers. The target variable was predicted based on the net pay (P_Net_Oil), and the non-lagged gas response (C_Oil_0). An indicator variable (Y/N for Good/Poor well) was derived from the normalized oil production and

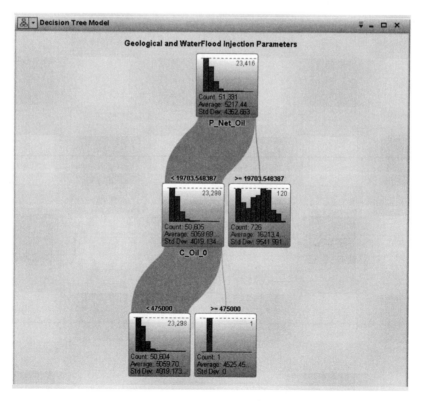

Figure 6.7 Decision Tree Model

identified the best 25 percent of all wells in the whole field. The normalized oil production was characterized by a well's production relative to the whole field's production.

An advantage of the decision tree model over other types of models is that it utilizes interpretable English rules. For example, "If net pay is greater than 6 m and the lag zero gas response is negative, then oil production will be in the top 25 percent of the best production with a probability of 80 percent." In the above case, the model-based well selection resulted in a success rate of two to four times better than by traditional methods and historically observed in the field.

The analysis is based only on the available injection and production history (publicly available data). Furthermore, the same methodology can be used to predict water flood communication paths based on the primary production from interaction between producers.

Water Cut and Fracture Distribution in Carbonate Reservoirs

Meeting the objectives of better reservoir management and identifying a range of strategies ascertained under uncertainty is a tremendous challenge owing to the probabilistic nature of the problem. Let us study a large carbonate reservoir in the Middle East to ascertain a more insightful comprehension of water cut behavior and its relative descriptive power of neighboring fracture networks (Figure 6.8).

There are inherently myriad uncertainties related to the fractures, the scope of the network, and the many structural properties in close proximity. By profiling the individual wells according to certain criteria such as water cut (Sw), minimum free water level distance (FWL), cumulative liquid, wellbore type within different time phases, and incremental geographic regions, it is possible to classify those wells and appreciate through the analytical indicators

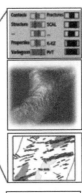

- **Number of uncertainties especially related to the**
  - **Fractures**
  - **Area of the reservoir**
  - **Structural properties**
- **All known parameters are only available for a very small percentage of the whole area**
- **Well production data are temporal and must be normalized across the well portfolio where production initiated at different times**

During history matching process a good amount of time is invested in understanding the water cut behaviors of the wells.

This behavior is important and has a potential of describing fractures close by.

Figure 6.8 Water Cut and Fracture Distribution

of similarity/dissimilarity a potential segmentation of the field. The goal of the analytical process is to understand the distribution of the Sw values in relationship to the cumulative liquid production across the field (Figure 6.9). This appreciation of the statistical results can be mapped to identify the production mechanisms such as best producers, depletion, and pressure maintenance, and thus locate poorly drained zones and potentially lucrative field reengineering tactics and strategies based on a more complete understanding of the distribution of water throughout the field.

The first step is to aggregate the requisite datasets to establish an analytical data warehouse customized to the objective function. The exploratory data analysis suite of visualizations identifies those parameters that have statistical impact on the objective function or dependent variables. Figure 6.10 illustrates some of these important workflows.

Figure 6.9 Extracting Hidden Knowledge

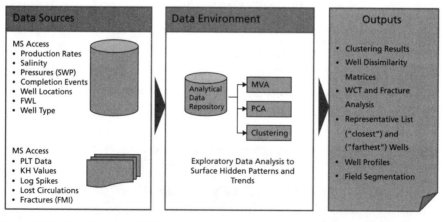

Figure 6.10 Data Sources and EDA for Study

The methodology adopted for a fractured reservoir embraces the sensitivity of those independent parameters that bear a correlation or trending relationship with *water cut and cumulative liquid production* across the array of wells in the field under study. It is very well known that in a fractured reservoir, water cut and the cumulative liquid production relationship may show a significantly different characteristic. Hence, with the objective of generating new insight about the fractures of the carbonate field we started analyzing the distribution of the water-cut values.

Figure 6.11 shows different water cut behaviors in homogeneous and highly fractured reservoirs. Thus a plot of water cut versus cumulative oil production can be used to indicate fracture intensity near the wellbore. In a given reservoir, wells located at different locations may encounter different fracturing intensity, and therefore, may exhibit different water cut against cumulative oil production characteristics.

The modeling parameters were designed according to the criterion that it was necessary to normalize the water cuts based on cumulative liquid production owing to the wide temporal range of wells being spudded during the long history of the producing carbonate reservoir. The spatial distribution was also a factor taken into consideration, dividing the extensive field into three distinct areas. The analytical workflows were also dictated by the temporal aspect, segmenting the analysis into different time periods. The *distance of the free water level* was a contributing factor and thus considered as an influencing independent parameter. We also identified the wellbore types (horizontal and vertical) when ascertaining the results of the study.

Normalization

In order to make valid comparisons between well datasets it is necessary to perform a remediation step that entails a robust quality control work process to identify outliers and impute for missing and erroneous values. A water cut

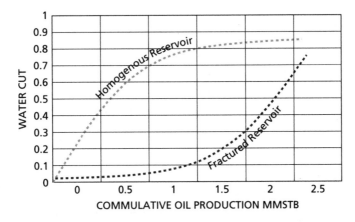

Figure 6.11 Typical Water Cut Behaviors

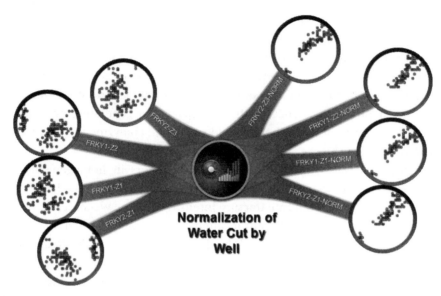

Figure 6.12 Water Cut Normalization Step

normalization step was implemented based on cumulative liquid production (Figure 6.12). That approach helps to eliminate the temporal aspect of the data to some extent.

Spatial Distribution

Spatial location of the well will play an important role in the clustering analysis. We assessed the location with respect to geographical increments across the field. The field was divided into three increments; however, increments are correlated with production time windows. We analyzed the distributions of the wells across the spatial increments in different time windows, and finally consolidated the results into one categorization where the clustering analysis should be focused.

Time Windows

The wells under investigation came into production across different decades, the first in the early 1960s. Thus cumulative production amounts span varying scales across the temporal variance in age since spud-in occurred. The inherent well performance behaviors will also diverge in the depletion, injection, and post-injection phases.

Water Distance

The minimum distance to free water level is an important factor to understand water cut behavior of each well (Figure 6.13). The majority of the wells were distributed within a 4,000–6,600-foot interval (mean: 5,533 ft; median: 5,388 ft).

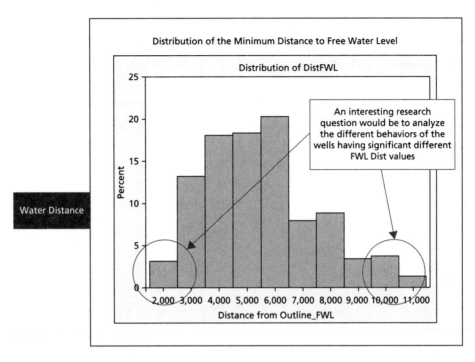

Figure 6.13 Distance to Free Water Level Influences the Water Cut

Wellbore Types

The majority of the wells were horizontal and were analyzed in Time Window 3. There were also a small number of wells having a deviated configuration. Table 6.1 illustrates the distribution of wellbore types in the study.

After normalizing the water cut curves with the cumulative liquid produced, the problem of uncovering similarities between wells essentially evolves into a search for a similarity between the water cut and cumulative liquid production scatterplots (Figure 6.14).

Computing the similarities between the water cut values across the array of wells under study was initiated thus by normalizing the water cut and cumulative liquid curves with the same axis definition for all wells. We defined a grid [0, 1] × [0, 1] for each scatterplot, and if there was an observation in a specific cell, we would record a "1" value. We entered a "0" value otherwise, as illustrated in Figure 6.15. Finally, all data for each well were generated and plotted and subsequently transformed according to the Boolean logic defined on observations. Then with the transformed data we were able to perform a similarity analysis using different metrics proposed in the pattern-recognition literature.

There is a wide variety of distance and similarity measures used in cluster analysis, but as the well data are in now in a coordinate form it is appropriate to use a non-Euclidean distance for clustering, computing a distance matrix. Similarity measures are then converted to dissimilarities before being used in

Table 6.1 Distribution of Wellbore Type Considered in the Study

Time Window	# Horizontal Wells	# Vertical Wells	# Deviated Wells
1: 1963–1996	NA	42	1
2: 1996–2003	88	55	5
3: 2003–2010	138	9	2

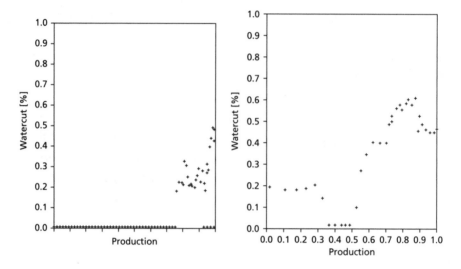

Figure 6.14 How Similar Are These Two Scatterplots?

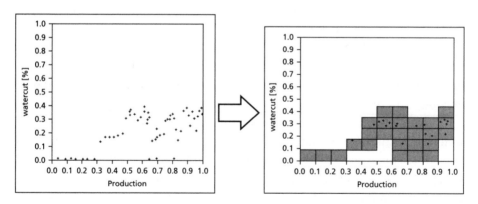

Figure 6.15 Illustrates the Data Transformation Step

a cluster algorithm. We computed the Jaccard coefficient between each pair of wells. The Jaccard coefficient is defined as the number of variables that are coded as 1 for both wells divided by the number of variables that are coded as 1 for either or both wells. Since dissimilarity measures are required by the cluster algorithm, the Jaccard coefficient was adopted. A small value represents two wells that are similar with respect to the water cut (Figure 6.16).

The hierarchical cluster analysis algorithm successively joins data points to form groups with similar behavior until all records are coalesced into one group. The default graphical result of the hierarchical cluster analysis is illustrated in Figure 6.17. It is similar to a tree structure, starting with the single records at the bottom and finishing with all records joined into one single group at the top. This scales the graph based on the distances of the groups and makes dissimilarities more visible. The higher the distance is to the next join (represented

	A	B	C	D	E	F	G	H	I	J	K	L
	WellBoreh	Well01	Well02	Well03	Well04_A	Well05_B	Well06	Well07	Well08	Well09_01	Well09_02	Well10
2	Field_100	0										
3	Field_107	0.642857	0									
4	Field_109	0.758621	0.92	0								
5	Field_112	0.75	0.8565	0.612903	0							
6	Field_120	0.352941	0.733333	0.7142								
7	Field_124	0.870968	0.96	0.8378								
8	Field_130	0.592593	0.84	0.789								
9	Field_133	0.631579	0.692308	0.4074					0			
10	Field_138	0.75	0.894737	0.6285					0.833333	0		
11	Field_140	0.214286	0.545455	0.777					0.5625	0.772727	0	
12	Field_140'	0.703704	0.818182	0.696					0.730769	0.724138	0.666667	0
13	Field_140	0.214286	0.545455	0.7777					0.5625	0.772727	0	0.666667
14	Field_140	0.2	0.615385	0					0.611111	0.791667	0.153846	0.692308
15	Field_140	0.3125	0.615385	0.7037					0.529412	0.791667	0.153846	0.692308
16	Field_140	0.52381	0.705882						0.619048	0.68	0.444444	0.642857
17	Field_140	0.1875	0.666667	0.6785					0.65	0.708333	0.266667	0.714286
18	Field_140	0.214286	0.545455	0.7777					0.5625	0.772727	0	0.666667
19	Field_140	0.214286	0.545455	0.777778	0.72	0.4375	0.896552	0.6	0.5625	0.772727	0	0.666667
20	Field_1409	0.214286	0.545455	0.777778	0.72	0.4375	0.896552	0.6	0.5625	0.772727	0	0.666667

Dissimilarity measure represents the similarity between two wells [140 and 02] based on Water Cut values: high values such as 0.818182 reflect a high dissimilarity.

Figure 6.16 Dissimilarity Matrix Computed Using Jaccard Metric

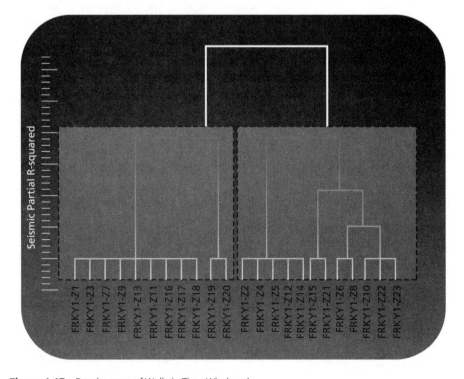

Figure 6.17 Dendrogram of Wells in Time Window 1

by the lines in the graphs that join previous groups), the larger the distance between the groups and the more dissimilar the groups. From the dendrogram it can be concluded that there are two distinct groups in the data based on the water cut and cumulative liquid behavior for the 43 wells clustered in Time Window 1, thus generating two clusters. It is then possible to profile the two clusters to identify the main characteristics of each group. The analysis resulted in 2, 4, and 5 different clusters for Time Windows 1, 2, and 3 respectively.

The clusters are obtained using a Ward algorithm for minimum variance. The highlighted area represents the two different clusters. This methodology delivered a time continuum perspective of the carbonate reservoir across the distributed wells. It identified using the average values of the production indicators in those compartments of the field that had a low or high water cut.

Since the clustering is based on different water cut behavior of the wells, you can establish an understanding of the average predicted "water cut picture" for each clustered region. Figure 6.18 defines the expected behavior of a random well belonging to a specific cluster.

Distribution of well configuration is defined to be either horizontal or vertical in the clusters as illustrated in Figure 6.19. As can be seen the distribution is characteristic for some clusters. Clusters are represented by their numbers.

In the early years of the production both clusters are following the overall trend of the wells in the time window. After 2003, the annual SWP average for the wells in cluster 2 starts increasing and surpasses that of cluster 1, although the SWP trend of both clusters is positive (probably due to injection) as depicted in Figure 6.20.

As in Figure 6.20, we see in Figure 6.21 in the early years of the production that both clusters are following the overall trend of the wells in Time Window 2.

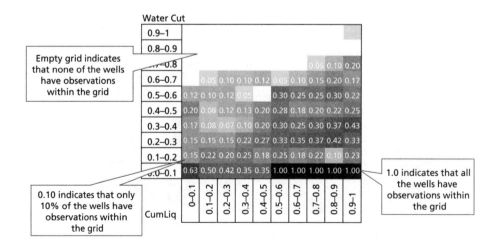

Figure 6.18 Average Water Cut with Color Intensity Yielding Observation Frequency

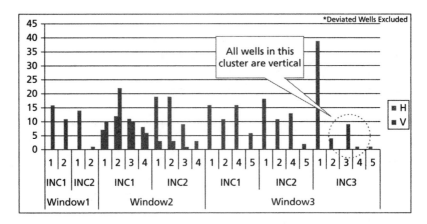

Figure 6.19 Well Configuration Defined as Horizontal or Vertical

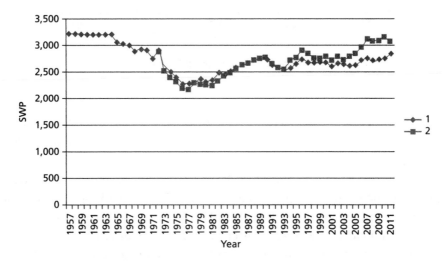

Figure 6.20 Annual Average SWP for the Two Clusters in Time Window 1

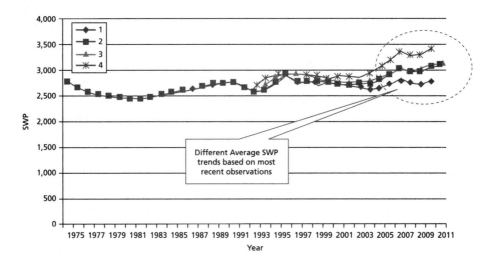

Figure 6.21 Annual Average SWP for the Four Clusters in Time Window 2

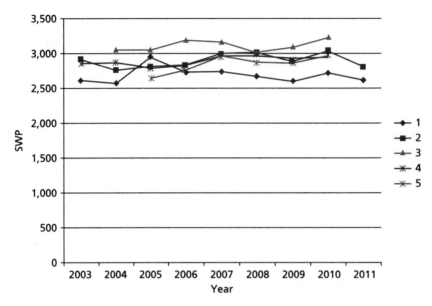

Figure 6.22 Annual Average SWP for the Five Clusters in Time Window 3

After 2003 and injection period, the pressure is measured differently for the wells in cluster 4. That cluster has the largest pressure. It is almost 3500 on average.

Since the wells in Time Window 3 are relatively new and the production started in 2003, the pressure curve follows a steady trend, as illustrated in Figure 6.22. However, it can be noted that the first and second clusters are in the declining phase, whereas clusters 3, 4, and 5 are increasing.

There were 40 wells having Formation MicroImager data (FMI) and their fracture characteristics have been identified, as shown in Figure 6.23. Unfortunately, FMI was not available for the rest of the wells. Clustering results have been analyzed with respect to the distribution of the fractures that were known.

The product of formation permeability (k) and producing formation thickness (h) in a producer well is one of the key factors in the flow potential of a well (Figure 6.24). Besides the missing values for 106 wells, the distribution of the clusters reflects five clusters (1-1, 2-3, 2-4, 3-1, and 3-5) having higher KH value than the overall average.

KH is used for a large number of reservoir engineering calculations such as prediction of future performance, secondary and tertiary recovery potential, and potential success of well-stimulation procedures. Obtaining the best possible value of this product is the primary objective of transient well tests.

Strong correlation of lost circulations and log spikes was visible among the clusters. However, there were significant differences between log spikes and

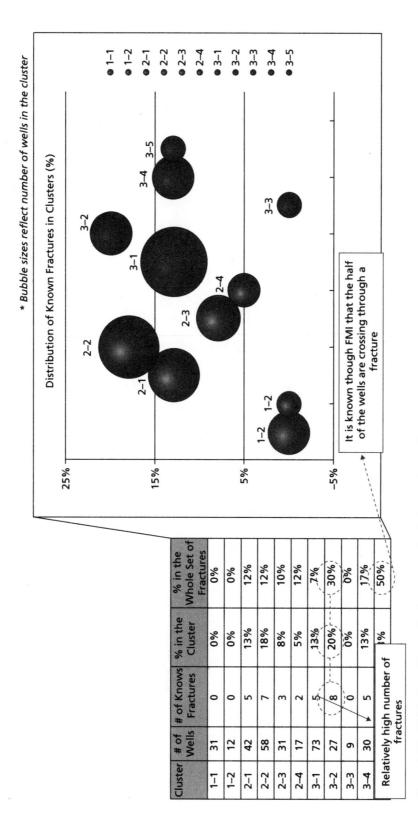

Figure 6.23 Distribution of Known Fractures across the Carbonate Reservoir

205

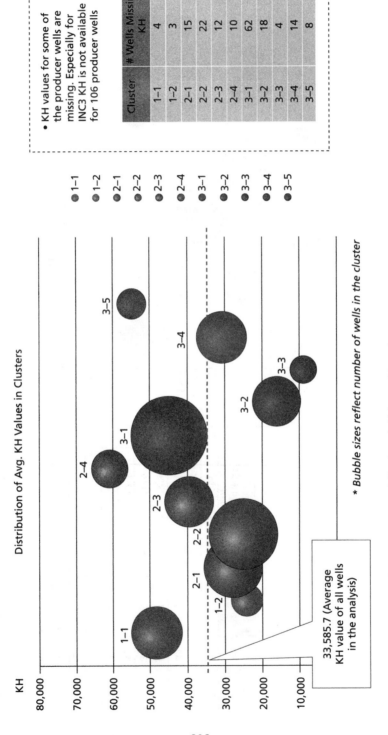

Figure 6.24 Distribution of Formation Permeability (*k*) and Thickness (*h*) Product

Distribution of Avg. KH Values in Clusters

KH

80,000
70,000
60,000
50,000
40,000
30,000
20,000
10,000

1–1
1–2
2–1
2–2
2–3
2–4
3–1
3–2
3–3
3–4
3–5

33,585.7 (Average KH value of all wells in the analysis)

* *Bubble sizes reflect number of wells in the cluster*

● KH values for some of the producer wells are missing. Especially for INC3 KH is not available for 106 producer wells

Cluster	# Wells Missing KH
1–1	4
1–2	3
2–1	15
2–2	22
2–3	12
2–4	10
3–1	62
3–2	18
3–3	4
3–4	14
3–5	8

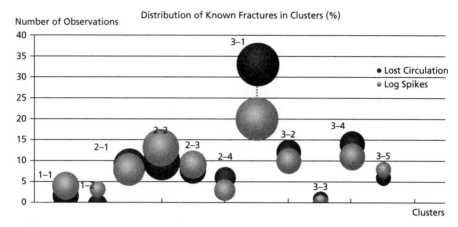

Number of Observations   Distribution of Known Fractures in Clusters (%)

Figure 6.25 Distribution of Known Fractures across the Clusters

lost circulation observations for the 3-1 cluster (LC: 33, LS: 20) as depicted in Figure 6.25.

Studying the cluster analysis results from each time window enabled the engineer to potentially map the fault network across the field from water cut observations across the discrete clusters. Studying Time Window 3 clusters it was apparent that the nine wells that constitute cluster 3 have limited cumulative liquid production with an average value of 10.7 and thus very low water-cut values averaging 0.001.

Plotting those nine wells onto the map it was feasible to deduce a distribution pattern confined to increment zone III that was outside the distribution of the wells in the same increment zone and in the same time window but in cluster 1. Such visualizations enhanced the understanding of geologic facies changes, potential high-permeability layers, or a fault network in this zone when observing the wells in cluster 1 that have a magnitude higher cumulative liquid production rate.

Many such deductions can be easily made by simple visual analysis of the clustering methodology that successfully segmented the field into distinct areas characterized by well clusters or groups underpinned by similar production indicators. By studying the water cuts and cumulative liquid production rates of both water and oil across the time windows and in different geographical regions a much better sense of the water model and potential precursors of the water cuts across the field could be appreciated.

In addition, the tactical well definition, either horizontal or vertical, and the distribution across the various time windows and clusters told another story that perhaps would have been missed if the patterns were not surfaced. For example, it could be noted that the cluster 3 in time window 3 that showed the lowest cumulative oil production rate and cumulative liquid production for the 9 wells identified were *all* vertical.

The exploratory data analysis workflows and subsequent hierarchical clustering analysis workflows to segment the field in both a spatio- and temporal manner offered insights and deductions in a visual manner that could be corroborated with other studies. These analytical results as seen thus far were important to offer signs for further interpretation and areas of concentrated study.

Understanding water income may be deemed a viable expectation if the study subsequently included a further attribute based on the relative time to obtain certain water-cut-level values. For example, the attribute could define the initial and final water-cut values, and the time to attain different levels such as 1, 10, 25, and 50 percent of water. To determine a water cut evolution model the engineer could have applied a smoothing methodology such as the Lowess algorithm and, in tandem with a similar approach with GOR, generate additional indicators of production as both water cut and GOR attain certain values relative to a time continuum for each time window.

To take this study to another level it would behoove the engineers to introduce further datasets such as PLT and rock properties to suggest other important production indicators and influential parameters to further explicate the water model across the time and geographical boundaries.

Figures 6.26 and 6.27 summarize the output results from the methodology, offering insight as regards the water cut and fracture networks across the carbonate reservoir under study.

Augmenting the study with reservoir properties and geomechanics calibrated by wireline logs and cores, it is feasible to ascertain via advanced data-driven methodologies those rock characteristics and fluid properties that are influential drivers controlling the performance of the field studied in the first phase to map fracture network distributions and water-cut values.

Rock and fluid properties are ostensibly the critical controlling factors dictating the performance of hydrocarbon reservoirs. Owing to the multivariate, multidimensional, multivariant, and stochastic complexity inherent in hydrocarbon reservoirs, it is essential not only to identify the salient datasets but also to adopt data-driven models to complement the first principles that underpin the variation in both the rock and fluid properties.

Defining a roadmap for rock–fluid characterization for reservoir management necessitates a multidisciplinary and integrated methodology. We must determine accurate volumes in place, predictable recovery factors, and attainable field development strategies that mitigate risks and maximize economic returns—all quantified under uncertainty to offer a probabilistic range in an effective decision-making cycle.

The performance of hydrocarbon reservoirs is controlled largely by the rock and fluid properties, their spatial and temporal variations, and rock–fluid interactions. Rock characterization involves quantification of porosity, permeability, capillary pressure, and relative permeability associated with various

Time Window	1	1	2	2	2	2	3	3	3	3	3
CLUSTER	1	2	1	2	3	4	1	2	3	4	5
NumWells	31	12	42	58	31	17	73	27	9	30	10
Well Type Distribution	V: 30, D:1	V: 12	V: 13, H: 26, D: 3	V: 25, H: 31, D: 2	V: 11, H: 20	V: 6, H: 11	H: 73	H: 26, D: 1	V: 9	H: 30	H: 9, D: 1
OilProd.Rate	2,819	2,291	3,505	2,851	1,528	605	6,010	3,900	10	2,567	1,052
Water Prod.Rate	19	219	56	250	496	525	59	323	0	679	726
Liq.Prod.Rate	2,838	2,509	3,561	3,101	2,023	1,130	6,069	4,223	11	3,246	1,778
Wcut Level	0.005	0.076	0.012	0.069	0.134	0.142	0.012	0.090	0.001	0.179	0.166
Gas/Oil	236	242	218	218	179	132	579	274	21	273	140
Cum,Oil	20,973,552	15,459,458	7,997,081	7,671,604	4,460,064	1,912,835	5,365,364	4,173,721	5,005	2,411,088	1,303,041
Cum, Water	22,359	530,982	88,036	422,965	1,203,621	1,475,594	39,286	210,114	149	534,486	785,278
Cum, Gas	10,048,218	7,680,695	2,638,489	2,526,009	1,565,037	691,384	1,815,321	1,183,415	1,686	744,618	437,890
Salinity	40,378	44,047	56,376	59,816	44,319	46,083	42,249	48,090	98,200	42,196	37,356
FWL Dist	8,224	5,850	5,138	4,562	4,432	3,648	5,927	6,245	2,824	5,785	6,203
KH	48,297	24,129	27,801	25,210	39,462	60,787	44,741	16,338	8,918	30,886	54,893
Fractures (FMI)	N/A	N/A	5	7	3	2	5	8	N/A	5	5
Lost Circulations	2	N/A	9	10	8	6	33	12	1	14	6
Log Spikes	4	3	8	13	9	3	20	10	N/A	11	8
Dry	52%	0%	55%	2%	0%	6%	81%	4%	100%	0%	30%
Fracture	16%	8%	17%	26%	13%	29%	5%	4%	0%	30%	30%
Strataform	6%	50%	19%	36%	58%	47%	11%	70%	0%	57%	40%
Matrix	26%	42%	10%	36%	29%	18%	3%	22%	0%	13%	0%

Figure 6.26 Tabulated Results by Cluster and Temporal Windows

Time Window 1 (. . .-Jan' 96)		Time Window 2 (Jan'96 – Oct'03)				Time Window 3 (Oct'03 - . . .)				
1-1	1-2	2-1	2-2	2-3	2-4	3-1	3-2	3-3	3-4	3-5
■ Low water production rate ■ V wells distant to the FWL ■ Mostly dry wells ■ ¼ being matrix producer	■ V wells having significantly high water productions (relatively) ■ Mostly strataforms (1/2) and matrix producers (40%)	■ Low water productions rates ■ Dry wells (55%) ■ Fracture signature seen for 17% ■ 1/5 strataforms	■ Biggest cluster of wells in 2nd time window ■ Similar gas prod to 2-1 ■ Equally likely distribution of strataforms and matrix producers	■ Mix of V and H wells having high water production levels ■ Mostly strataforms ■ ~1/3 matrix producers	■ High KH values ■ Significant water production ■ High WCT levels ■ ~1/3 showing almost half being strataforms ■ Fracture signatures ■ (Few observations)	■ Highest gas-oil ratio ■ Largest cluster, all H wells ■ Most of the lost circ. identified for those clusters ■ Majority dry (81%)	■ Low water production rates ■ H wells ■ Mostly strataforms (70%)	■ Small number of new vertical wells, practically there is no water nor prod oil yet ■ High salinity ■ Closeness to FWL	■ High water production ■ Highest WCT levels ■ Horizontal wells ■ ~30% showing fracture signatures ■ Complex WCT behavior	■ Highest water production rate ■ Low salinity ■ ~30% showing fracture signatures ■ 40% strataforms, no matrix formation identified

Figure 6.27 Tabulated Data by Time Window

recovery processes. Similarly, fluid characterization quantifies the reservoir phase behavior, fluid compositional changes throughout the reservoir, and changes in fluid properties as a result of production and injection processes. The process of data gathering begins with exploration and continues through the life of the reservoir.

A rock-and-fluid properties study that underpins reservoir management is predicated on the quality and quantity of both hard and soft datasets. The former embraces direct measurements on reservoir core and fluid samples to quantify reservoir physical and flow properties. The latter defines such measurements from well testing and petrophysics that infer the physical and dynamic properties of the reservoir through the interpretation of formation response to an applied perturbation by use of selected models. These models must be calibrated with rock and fluid data for validation.

The proposed methodology for rock and fluid characterization for reservoir management is depicted in Figure 6.28.

Once the business objectives are identified and the value propositions defined, the relevant datasets are aggregated for the study. The program involves a set of clear objectives, a comprehensive data-collection and testing plan, experimental protocols, rigorous QC/quality-assurance (QA) procedures, and a sound data-management platform. We need to integrate the results of the water study and fracture network determination as these input points act as constraints on the data-driven methodology geared around rock-and-fluid parameter analysis.

The basic and critical rock and fluid data are required for evaluation of various reservoir-depletion strategies. The rock and fluid characterization derived

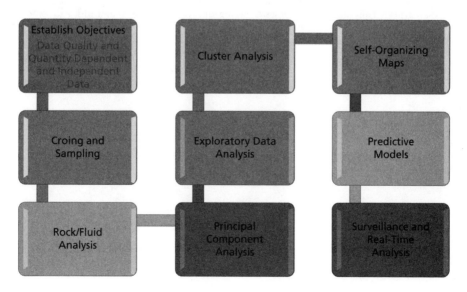

Figure 6.28 Rock–Fluid Characterization for Reservoir Management

from the rock–fluid properties form the basis for the design of any recovery process, calibration of wireline logs, and evaluation of potential compaction and subsidence. The specific rock–fluid data requirements are further classified under three major reservoir-fluid classes: viscous or heavy oils, light oils, or gas and gas condensates. The recovery processes involving light oils are grouped into three processes: immiscible, miscible, and tertiary gas injection, including water-alternating-gas (WAG) injection. Other recovery processes, such as thermal methods, will require customized rock–fluid characterization as well.

Cluster analysis, EDA, PCA, and SOMs are requisite to building a predictive model that can be operationalized in the field. Real-time data from intelligent wells and batch datasets across the E&P value chain deemed pertinent to the objective function(s) can be fed into the model to ensure a dynamic perspective and the extant model is not static. KPIs are established and via a surveillance and monitoring business intelligence platform it is feasible to identify production issues across the well portfolio for remediation strategies.

NOTES

1. A. Satter, "Reservoir Management Training: An Integrated Approach," SPE 20752, presented at the SPE Annual Technical Conference and Exhibition, New Orleans, September 23–26, 1990.

2. G. C. Thakur, "Implementation of Reservoir Management Program," SPE 20748, presented at the SPE Annual Technical Conference and Exhibition, New Orleans, September 23–26, 1990.

3. M. T. Halbouty, "Synergy Is Essential to Maximum Recovery," *JPT* (July 1977): 750.

4. H. H. Haldorsen and T. Van Golf-Racht, "Reservoir Management into the Next Century," NMT 890023, presented at the Centennial Symposium at New Mexico Tech., Socorro, October 16–19, 1989.

5. J. E. Warren, "In My Opinion," *JPT* (December 1994): 1016.

6. Dr. Emad Elrafie, Jerry P. White, and Fatema H. Al-Awami, "The Event Solution: A New Approach for Fully Integrated Studies Covering Uncertainty Analysis and Risk Assessment," Spring 2009 *Saudi Aramco Journal of Technology*.

7. J. A. Masters, "Creating, Managing, and Evaluating Multidisciplinary Teams," *AAPG* Special Publication 164 (1991): 335.

CHAPTER 7

Production Forecasting

I have seen the future and it is very much like the present, only longer.

Kehlog Albran, *The Profit*

The art of predicting production and estimating the ultimate recovery in oil and gas reservoirs has stimulated much debate among upstream engineers across recent decades. The literature in the early years of the twentieth century immersed itself in the study of percentage decline curves or empirical rate-time curves that found credence in expression of production rates across successive units of time, framed as percentages of production over the first unit of time. W. W. Cutler[1] opined that a more robust methodology defining a straight-line relationship was achievable when using log-log paper, the implication being that decline curves that reflected such characteristics were of a hyperbolic geometric type as opposed to an exponential.

We use the decline curve equations to estimate future asset production:[2]

1. Hyperbolic decline:

$$q = q \ (1 + D \, bt)^{-1/b}$$

2. Exponential decline:

$$q = qi \ \exp^{(-Dt)}$$

In the equations, b and D are empirical constants that are determined based on historical production data. When $b = 1$, it is a harmonic model, and when $b = 0$, it yields an exponential decline model.

There are a number of assumptions and restrictions applicable to conventional decline curve analysis (DCA) using these equations. Theoretically, DCA is applicable to a stabilized flow in wells producing at constant flowing bottom-hole pressure (BHP). Thus data from the transient flow period should be excluded from DCA. In addition, use of the equation implies that there are no changes in completion or stimulation, no changes in operating conditions, and that the well produces from a constant drainage area.

The hyperbolic decline exponent b has physical meaning in reservoir engineering, falling between 0 and 1. In general, we think of decline exponent b as a constant. But for a gas well, b varies with time. Instantaneous b decreases as the reservoir depletes at constant BHP condition and can be larger than 1 under some conditions. The average b over the depletion stage is indeed less than 1.

It is also critical to surface the statistical properties of a time-series that are stationary or immutable from a temporal perspective: correlations, autocorrelations, levels, trends, and seasonal patterns. Then we can predict the future from these descriptive properties.

Thus the implementation of data-driven models and automated and semi-automated workflows that feed into a data mining methodology is crucial in order to determine a probabilistic suite of forecasts and estimates for well performance. This chapter will walk through a case study that explicates such an approach in a giant field in the Middle East.

EXPLORATION AND PRODUCTION VALUE PROPOSITIONS

Analytical workflows can incorporate a decline curve analysis step implementing a web-based performance forecasting solution to identify short- and long-term forecasts for oil, gas, and water production. Implementing mature forecasting models and first principles such as Arps' empirical algorithms, you can estimate accurate well performance and estimated ultimate recovery (EUR) and measure the impact, positive or negative, of well remediation techniques.

Estimating reserves and predicting production in reservoirs has long been a challenge. The complexity of data, combined with limited analytical insights, means that some upstream companies do not fully understand the integrity of wells under management. In addition, they take weeks or months to establish and model alternative scenarios, potentially missing an opportunity to capitalize on market conditions.

The importance of performing accurate analysis and interpretation of reservoir behavior is fundamental to assessing extant reserves and potential forecasts for production. DCA is traditionally used to provide deterministic estimates for future performance and remaining reserves. Often, however, the deterministic prediction of future decline is far from the actual future production trend and, thus, the single deterministic value of reserves is not an accurate indication of the true reserves. The *deterministic* estimate in fact contains significant uncertainty. Unlike deterministic estimates, probabilistic approaches quantify the uncertainty, thus improving EUR.

Comparing real-time production data rates and type curves against forecasted trends, you can:

- Quickly and efficiently identify those wells that require remediation.
- Segment the field via well profile clustering.
- Ratify from a field, reservoir, or well perspective whether current production falls within confidence intervals of expectation and act accordingly.

Since the assumptions and conditions required for rigorous use of the Arps decline curve equations rarely apply to actual wells over significant time periods, there is potentially much uncertainty in reserves estimation using conventional DCA. With probabilistic approaches, confidence intervals can be provided for the reserves estimates.

In the petroleum industry, reserves' values are typically calculated at three *confidence levels*, P90, P50, and P10. There is a 90 percent probability that the actual reserves are greater than the P90 quantile; there is a 50 percent probability that the actual reserves are greater than the P50 quantile; and there is a 10 percent probability that the actual reserves are greater than the P10 quantile. The interval between P90 and P10 represents an 80 percent confidence interval. The confidence interval is a probabilistic result and so there is an 80 percent probability that the actual value will fall within the range of values specified.

What this really means is that, if we were to make a large number of independent predictions with 80 percent confidence intervals using a similar methodology, we would expect to be right (the true value falls within the range) about 80 percent of the time and wrong (the true value falls outside the range) about 20 percent of the time.

For probabilistic reserves estimation, an important question remains that is rarely addressed. Do 80 percent confidence intervals truly correspond to 80 percent probability? Since confidence intervals are probabilistic results, we cannot determine the reliability of a single confidence interval, since the test of the estimate using a confidence interval yields only a single result, or sample.

After time passes and we determine the true value, we can establish that the true value is either within the predicted range or outside the range. As Capen[3] illustrated, it is only by evaluation of many predictions (by letting time pass and comparing the true values to the predicted ranges) made using a similar methodology that we can determine the reliability of our estimations of uncertainty and, thus, our methodology for estimating uncertainty. These evaluations are difficult in the petroleum industry because of the long times associated with oil and gas production. Thus we seldom verify the reliability of uncertainty estimates in our industry.

WEB-BASED DECLINE CURVE ANALYSIS SOLUTION

Reservoir engineers are faced with an expanding portfolio of wells to analyze in order to establish EUR and identify candidates for stimulation and/or shut-in. Owing to the data volumes collated from each well, solutions invariably limit the number of wells that may be included in the analysis, thus requiring a deterministic sampling process that increases the uncertainty of forecasts. Data errors and outliers also have to be flagged manually, which is a time-intensive task for engineers.

It is ideal to work with a targeted web-based solution that helps an oil and gas company to:

- Aggregate, analyze, and forecast production from wells and reservoirs.
- Automatically detect and cleanse bad data.
- Publish and share results of analysis throughout the company.

The three important composite engines (Figure 7.1) are data mining, cluster analysis, and bootstrapping:

1. The *bootstrapping* module will help engineers to build reliable confidence intervals for production rate forecast and reserves lifetime estimates.
2. The *clustering* module will help engineers to deal with large numbers of wells by providing a means for grouping wells and finding similar wells.
3. The *data mining* module enables the development of advanced analytical workflows. Via exploratory data analysis it is feasible to identify hidden patterns and correlations that facilitate the evolution of the data-driven predictive models.

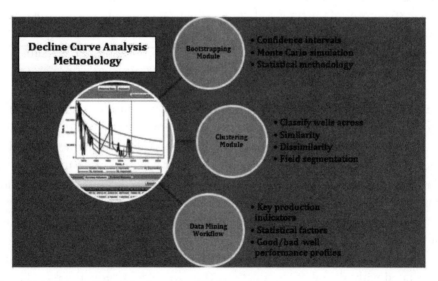

Figure 7.1 Process Diagram Implementing Key Components

Bootstrapping Module

Implementing probabilistic approaches to evaluate the uncertainty in reserves estimates based on DCA is not innovative, but the various methodologies hitherto have failed to take that extra step of developing a suite of analytical processes to mine the DCA results constrained by other upstream data.

Historical production data invariably possess significant amounts of noise, and the empirical postulates that underpin the traditional DCA workflow bestow upon the process to estimate reserves and forecast performance much uncertainty. Probabilistic approaches regularly provide a distribution of reserves estimates with three confidence levels (P10, P50, and P90) with an analogous 80 percent confidence interval. How reliable is the 80 percent confidence interval? To put it another way: Does the *bona fide* estimate of reserves fall within the interval 80 percent of the time? Investigative studies[2] have shown that it is not uncommon for true values of reserves to be located outside the 80 percent confidence interval much more than 20 percent of the time when implementing the traditional methodology. Uncertainty is thus significantly underestimated.

The majority of engineers are ingrained with the philosophy that quantifying uncertainty of estimates is primarily a subjective task. This perspective has taken the oil and gas industry along the perpetual road that bypasses effective probabilistic workflows to assess reserves estimation and quantify uncertainty of those estimates. It seems that prior distributions of drainage area, net pay, porosity, formation volume factor, recovery factor, and saturation are prerequisites to performing Monte Carlo simulations. And invariably we impose several distribution types such as log-normal, triangular, or uniform from an experienced or subjective position. To preclude any assumptions derived from adopting prior distributions of parameters, let us investigate the value inherent in the bootstrap methodology.

The first adventure into application of the bootstrap method for DCA adopted ordinary bootstrap to resample the original production data. This enabled the generation of multiple pseudo-datasets appropriate for probabilistic analysis. However, there are inherent assumptions that are deemed improper for temporal data such as production data, since the ordinary bootstrap method takes for granted the original production time series data as independent and identically distributed. And there are often correlations between data points in a time series data structure.

To avoid assuming prior distributions of parameters, the bootstrap method has been used to directly construct probabilistic estimates with specified confidence intervals from real datasets. It is a statistical approach and is able to assess uncertainty of estimates objectively. To the best of our knowledge, Jochen and Spivey[4] first applied the bootstrap method to decline curve analysis for reserves estimation. They used ordinary bootstrap to resample the original production dataset so as to generate multiple pseudo-datasets for probabilistic analysis. The ordinary bootstrap method adopted assumes that the original production data are independent and identically distributed, so the data will be independent of time.

However, this assumption is usually improper for time series data, such as production data, because the time series data structure often contains correlation between data points.

The purpose of the bootstrapping module is to automate the time series selection process to build reliable confidence intervals for *rate-time* and *rate-cumulative predictive models*. It is done by means of multiple scenarios optimization and Monte Carlo simulation for block residuals resampling.

Bootstrapping statistically reflects a method for assigning measurements or metrics of accuracy to sample estimates. Conventional bootstrap algorithms assume independent points of reference that are identically distributed. The modified bootstrap method (Figure 7.2) essentially generates a plethora of independent bootstrap realizations or synthetic datasets from the original production data, each pseudo-dataset being of equal dimension as the original dataset. A nonlinear regression model is fit to each synthetic dataset to ascertain decline equation parameters and subsequently extrapolated to estimate future production and ultimate recovery. The complete suite of synthetic datasets is used to determine objectively the distribution of the reserves.

To obviate the assumptions that production data contain points that are independent and identically distributed, the modified bootstrap methodology adopts a more rigorous algorithm to preserve time series data structure:

Step 1. It implements the hyperbolic and exponential equations to fit the production data for a given time period and determines residuals from the fitted models and observations.

Step 2. The workflow generates multiple synthetic data realizations using block resampling with modified model-based bootstrap, and to determine the size of the blocks the autocorrelation plot of residuals is used to surface any randomness or potential correlations within the residual data.

Step 3. We implement a backward analysis methodology using a more recent sample of production data to address issues of forecasting owing to periods of transient flow and variable operational conditions.

Step 4. Calculate confidence intervals for production and reserves.

Iterations of steps 1 through 4 provide a scheme to determine automatically the "best forecast" based on analysis of recent historical data during specific time periods.

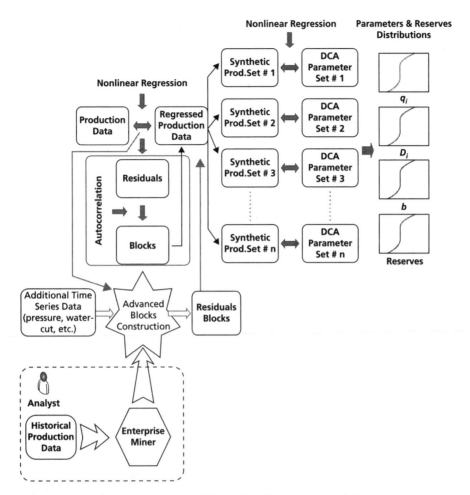

Figure 7.2   A Modified Bootstrap Methodology and Exploratory Data Analysis

An exploratory data analysis step is recommended as a parallel workflow to surface hidden trends and identify correlations and relationships in the production data enriched by additional operational (well tactics and completion strategies) and nonoperational (geomechanical and reservoir characteristics) parameters.

On the first step, the algorithm optimizes backward scenarios to find the three best prediction curves for the past 6 months (short-term), the past 12 months (mid-term), and the past 18 months (long-term). Figures 7.3 and 7.4 schematically detail this step.

The result of the first step is three curves, which could be *linear, exponential, harmonic,* or *hyperbolic.* Note the similarity between the mid-term and long-term curves.

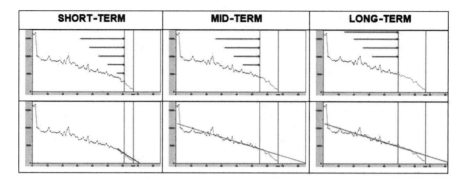

Figure 7.3 Bootstrapping Underpins Automated Time Series Selection

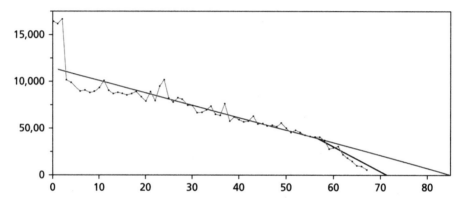

Figure 7.4 Type Curves Fit the Temporal Data

On the second step, the algorithm runs Monte-Carlo simulation (Figure 7.5) to generate 10th-, 50th-, and 90th-percentile confidence intervals for these three curves and the final prediction.

The algorithm should be able to work with monthly data and real-time data (daily or hourly).

Cluster Analysis Module

The purpose of the clustering module in Figure 7.6 is to develop a methodology that enables engineers to easily classify wells into groups (called *clusters*) so that the wells in the same cluster are more similar (based on selected properties) to each other than to those in other clusters.

Cluster analysis can improve engineer convenience in analyzing wells by separating them into groups based on decline curve shapes (patterns) and other properties.

Clustering is a data mining tool for categorizing and analyzing groups of data dimensions having similar attribute characteristics or properties. For analyzing

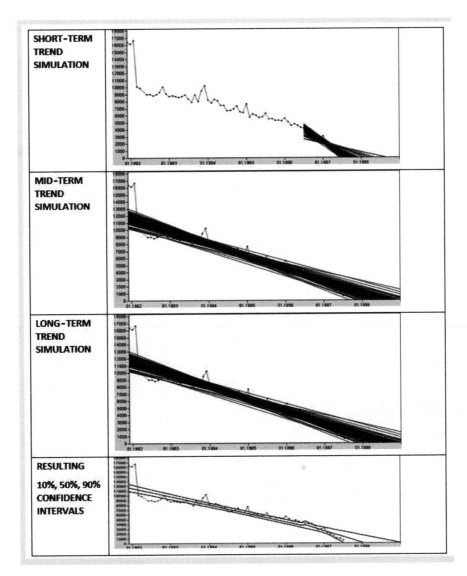

Figure 7.5 Monte Carlo Simulation

well profiles this methodology consists of classifying wells by dividing the field into areas.

This method determines the most similar wells and generates a first set of clusters; then it compares the average of the clusters to the remaining wells to form a second set of clusters, and so on. There are several ways to aggregate wells but the hierarchical method is more stable than the K-means procedure and provides more detailed results; moreover, a displayed dendrogram (Figure 7.7) is useful for results interpretation or to choose the number of clusters.

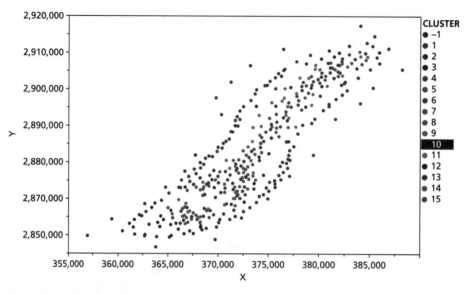

Figure 7.6 Cluster Analysis Results on a Scatterplot

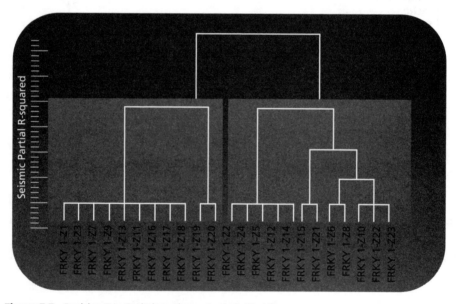

Figure 7.7 Decision Tree Optimizes Cluster Analysis Workflow

The following properties for wells could be used as parameters for clustering:

- Cumulative liquid production
- Cumulative oil or gas production
- Water cut (percentage determined by water production/liquid production)
- B exponent (decline type curve)
- Initial rate of decline

- Initial rate of production
- Average liquid production

There are a number of different ways to visualize cluster analysis results. For instance, the Segment Profile window in Figure 7.8 shows all clusters (segments) and variables that best separate runs in the cluster from all other runs. There are two histogram charts shown for each variable. The red-colored histogram for each variable is based on the whole run dataset; the blue histogram is based on the runs in a specific cluster.

Leveraging nonlinear multivariate regressions, interpolation and smoothing procedures, principal component analysis, cluster analysis, and discrimination analysis, it is feasible to divide a field into discrete regions for field reengineering tactics and strategies. The methodology classifies the wells according to the production indicators, and divides the field into areas.

The statistical results can be mapped to identify the production mechanisms, for example, best producers, depletion, and pressure maintenance, ultimately to identify and locate poorly drained zones potentially containing remaining reserves. Field reengineering can also be optimized by identifying those wells where the productivity can be improved.

What follows is a short summary of the steps in the classification process.

- Production statistics data preparation:
  - Oil produced daily, water cut percent, gas produced daily.
- Decline curve analysis:
  - Modeling daily production with nonlinear regressions.
- Data noise reduction and data interpolation:
  - Adoption of smoothing methods that are most applicable to data. For instance, in case of inordinately spaced data you can use the LOWESS (locally weighted least squares) smoothing method. Use the resulting smoothed curves to interpolate missing data points for water cuts and GOR curves.
- Well clustering:
  - Principal component analysis:
    - Use to create low-dimensional approximation to production dataset. This technique is often used before cluster analysis.
  - Cluster analysis:
    - Applied to condensed dataset with fewer factor scores (principal component analysis transformation of original variables).
    - Analysis of clusters with different methods: segment profiling, dendrograms, and others.

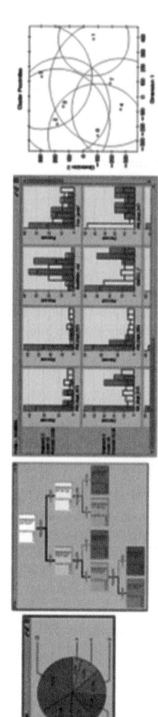

Figure 7.8 Cluster Analysis Visualization

224

- Appraisal of wells representation:
  - It can be useful for subsequent studies to have only a limited set of representative wells and to avoid intensive processing.
- Discriminant analysis:
  - Perform to provide the probabilities of each well to belong to the obtained clusters.

The clustering module should allow assigning wells into clusters based on the following properties:

- Well production history:
  - Cumulative oil production
  - Cumulative water production
  - Cumulative gas production
  - Oil production rate
  - Water production rate
  - Total liquid production rate
  - Gas production rate
  - Water cut
  - Gas–oil ratio
- Well properties:
  - Reservoir name
  - Well position (X, Y)
  - Completion type
  - Completion/tubing string (inner diameter)
  - ESP (Y/N)
  - Choke size
  - Wellbore configuration
  - Reservoir contact
- Reservoir properties:
  - Porosity
  - Permeability
  - Reservoir pressure
  - Surface wellhead pressure
- Well test properties (similar to wells production properties):
  - Oil production rate
  - Water production rate

- Total liquid production rate
- Gas production rate
- Water cut
- Gas–oil ratio

The temporal datasets such as production rates (oil, gas, and water) are automatically cleansed, enabling selection of robust values that are driven by rules established *a priori* by the experienced reservoir engineers. For example, do not take into account months with the number of operating days below 20. The solution can optionally select a 12 months' moving average set of values rather than those last observed.

Data Mining Module

These workflows are based on a SEMMA process (Figure 7.9) that systematically and logically walks through a suite of analytical nodes that *S*ample the data to capture a population applicable to the objective function and thus enables *E*xploration to uncover trends and surface hidden patterns. Subsequent nodes initiate a *M*odify workflow on the selected data to ensure a robust and cleansed version that has been transformed and imputed to preclude the adage "garbage in, garbage out," followed by *M*odeling from a predictive perspective implementing soft computing workflows based on regression, neural networks, decision trees, genetic algorithms, and fuzzy logic. Finally, an *A*ssessment node focuses on the relative merits of the implemented models, resulting in the statistically sound analysis that identifies the optimized model or range of

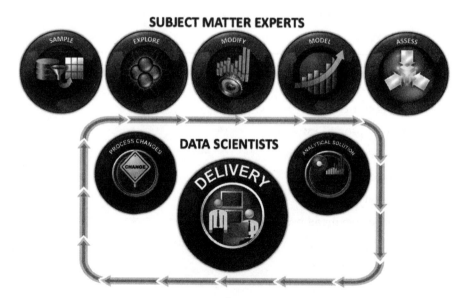

Figure 7.9 SEMMA Process That Underpins a Data Mining Workflow

probabilistically valid models given a range of acceptable confidence intervals. The SEMMA workflows are constrained by prior knowledge provided by subject matter or domain experts (SMEs) to ensure valid interpretations throughout the process. A robust data input space with reduced dimensionality is also paramount to ensure valid results. The data analyst (DA) evolves the analytic solution that is underpinned by the SEMMA process for delivery of a solution that can be operationalized against real-time data feeds from sensors in intelligent wells.

Turning increasing amounts of raw data into useful information remains a challenge for most oil companies because the relationships and answers that identify key opportunities often lie buried in mountains of data. The SEMMA process streamlines the data mining methodology to create highly accurate predictive and descriptive models based on analysis of vast amounts of upstream data gathered from across an enterprise.

The data mining methodology applicable for a well optimization workflow implemented aspects of the SEMMA process:

Sample:

- *Appended* appropriate geomechanical logs, GR logs, and sonic logs with rock properties garnered from core analysis; seismic attributes (instantaneous amplitude, phase, and curvature) contributed supporting knowledge. The results from the DCA aggregated with production data rates and cumulative liquids as well as pressures and fluid saturation generated an *analytical data warehouse* (ADW). Operational parameters that described the tactics and strategies of the completion enriched the ADW for the data-portioning phase in the Sample node.

- *Data Partition* enabled the integrated dataset to be divided into training, test, and validation datasets. The training dataset is used for preliminary model fitting. The validation dataset is used to monitor and tune the model weights during estimation and is also used for model assessment. The test dataset is an additional holdout dataset that you can use for model assessment. This node used simple random sampling, stratified random sampling, or user-defined partitions to create partitioned datasets.

- The *Filter* node applied a filter to the training dataset in order to exclude outliers or other observations that you do not want to include in your data mining analysis. Outliers may greatly affect modeling results and subsequently the accuracy and reliability of trained models.

- The *Sample* node took random, stratified random, and cluster samples of datasets. Sampling is recommended for extremely large databases because it can significantly decrease model training time. If the sample is sufficiently representative, then relationships found in the sample can be expected to generalize to the complete dataset.

■ The *Time Series* node surfaced trends and temporal variations in the production data.

Explore:

■ The *StatExplore* node is a multipurpose node and examined variable distributions and statistics in the datasets. We computed standard univariate statistics, standard bivariate statistics by class target and class segment, and correlation statistics for interval variables by interval input and target. We also rejected variables based on target correlation.

■ We implemented a *SOM/Kohonen* node to perform unsupervised learning by using Kohonen vector quantization (VQ), Kohonen self-organizing maps (SOMs), and batch SOMs with Nadaraya-Watson or local-linear smoothing. Kohonen VQ is a clustering method, whereas SOMs are primarily dimension-reduction methods.

■ The *Variable Selection* node evaluated the importance of input variables in predicting or classifying the target variable. The node implemented either an R-square or a Chi-square selection (tree based) criterion. The R-square criterion removed variables that have large percentages of missing values, and class variables that are based on the number of unique values. The variables that are not related to the target are set to a status of *rejected*. Although rejected variables are passed to subsequent tools in the process flow diagram, these variables are not used as model inputs by modeling nodes such as the neural network and decision tree tools.

Modify:

■ The *Impute* node replaced missing values for interval variables with the distribution-based replacement, and we explored the replacement M-estimator such as Tukey's biweight and Huber's and Andrew's Wave. Missing values for class variables were replaced with the tree-based imputation.

■ The *Principal Components* node performed an analysis for data interpretation and dimension reduction. The node generated principal components that were uncorrelated linear combinations of the original input variables and that depend on the covariance matrix or correlation matrix of the input variables. In data mining, principal components are usually used as the new set of input variables for subsequent analysis by modeling nodes.

■ The *Rules Builder* node created ad-hoc sets of rules for the data to constrain the process by adopting engineer-definable outcomes. For example, you might use the Rules Builder node to define outcomes named Good Well and Bad Well based on rules such as the following:

```
IF Water_Cut > 0.5 then do
    EM_OUTCOME-"Bad";
IF RateCum < 100000 then
    EM_OUTCOME="Review";
            END;
```

- The *Transform Variables* node created new variables that were transformations of existing variables in the aggregated data. Transformations can be used to stabilize variances, remove nonlinearity, improve additivity, and correct non-normality in variables.

Model:

- The *Neural Network* node constructed, trained, and validated multilayer feed-forward neural networks.

- The *Partial Least Squares* node modeled continuous and binary targets and produced data step score code and standard predictive model assessment results.

- The *Regression* node fit both linear and logistic regression models to the data. You can use continuous, ordinal, and binary target variables. You can use both continuous and discrete variables as inputs. The node supports the stepwise, forward, and backward selection methods. A point-and-click interaction builder created higher-order modeling terms.

- The *Rule Induction* node improved the classification of rare events in the modeling data. It created a Rule Induction model that used split techniques to remove the largest pure split node from the data. Rule Induction also created binary models for each level of a target variable and ranked the levels from the rarest event to the most common.

Assess:

- The *Model Comparison* node provided a common framework for comparing models and predictions from any of the modeling tools (such as regression, decision tree, and neural network tools). The comparison is based on standard model fits statistics as well as potential expected and actual performance that would result from implementing the model.

- The *Segment Profile* node assessed and explored segmented datasets. Segmented data are created from data BY-values, clustering, or applied business rules. The Segment Profile node facilitated data exploration to identify factors that differentiate individual segments from the population, and to compare the distribution of key factors between individual segments and the population.

The assumption that key factors resulting in the historical decline continue unchanged throughout the forecast period is fundamental to traditional DCA. These factors include both reservoir conditions and operating conditions. As long as these conditions do not change, the trend in decline can be analyzed and extrapolated to forecast future well performance. If these conditions are altered, for example, through a well work-over, then the decline rate determined pre-work-over would not be applicable to the post-work-over period.

Thus, it is vital to determine the period of a well history that could be used for decline curve analysis and subsequent forecasting and estimation. The data mining module provides a means to facilitate an automated selection of such time periods for accurate decline curve analysis.

The input space for the data mining module may include some of the following salient parameters and data points.

- Well production properties and history:
  - Cumulative oil production
  - Cumulative water production
  - Oil production rate
  - Water production rate
  - Water cut

- Current well properties (well master data):
  - Reservoir name
  - Current well type (wet or dry)
  - Deviated well flag
  - Single lateral well flag
  - Multilateral well flag
  - Maximum reservoir contact well flag
  - Well current status
- Well events history;
  - Event date
  - Event type
  - Event result
- Well work-overs information:
  - Work-over type
  - Work-over description

- ■ Work-over start date
- ■ Work-over end date
- ■ Well activity information:
  - ■ Record effective start date
  - ■ Record effective end date
  - ■ Record is current flag (Y or N)
  - ■ Well status
  - ■ Completion status
  - ■ Completion zone top depth
  - ■ Completion zone bottom depth
  - ■ Completion total footage
  - ■ Multilateral flag
  - ■ Laterals count
  - ■ Active laterals count

Rate-Time Analysis

The solution enables rate-time analysis for two phases, oil and water, to estimate production rates based on production history in three different models in the same time-frame (exponential, hyperbolic, and harmonic). It is beneficial to detail the analysis output in a tabular format to ascertain the quality/accuracy of the historical and forecasted data values.

Rate-Cum Analysis

The solution also provides the ability to perform rate-cumulative analysis for oil and water phases to estimate oil in place based on production history in three different models in the same time-frame (exponential, hyperbolic, and harmonic).

P/Z Analysis

The *web-based decline curve analysis* solution aids reservoir engineers in their estimation of the original gas in place (OGIP) and provides different forecasting models for P/Z analysis including the following models:

- ■ No-Water-Influx, Shilthuis
- ■ Hurst-simplified
- ■ Von Everdingen-Hurst

Automated Time Series Selection

An important step in the process of decline curve analysis is the selection of production data used for the forecast. Besides the decline of the reservoir, there can be technical or economic reasons to cut back production for a well or a group of wells. The engineer must decide based on his or her knowledge which data to use for the forecast. An automated filtering and selection of data can support their decision process.

Normally the reservoir engineer would select a time period where a constant production rate and decline is visible. Sometimes the minimum number of valid data points of month-on-month production rates for a time series analysis cannot be represented with the data available. An automated data selection could support the engineer to solve the following two basic issues:

- Replacing or excluding zero production rates
- Smoothing extreme variance in the data (e.g., production cuts due to economic reasons or well tests)

While excluding zero production rates is straightforward, the detection of outliers is done with the help of mathematics. In probability theory and statistics, the standard deviation of a statistical population or a probability distribution is the square root of its variance. A data point is statistically considered an outlier if the value differs more than twice the standard deviation from the mean. An automatic treatment of detected outliers in a given data population could be:

- Filtering out of all records with outliers
- Filtering out records with zero production rates only
- Replacing all outliers with the mean or median production rate

The value of mean and median of the data selected has been calculated excluding zero production rates. That ensures that the result of the mean and median calculation creates equal results with or without removing the zero production rates first. For time series data used for forecasting, the identity and order of the observations are crucial. A time series is a set of observations made at a succession of equally spaced points in time. If records have been filtered out, this rule-of-thumb has been violated. The simple solution to the problem is to keep the order of the observations and to adjust the time ID of the records in the data population. The system provides interpolation methods in its analytical software that could be used to interpolate missing values or to generate lower frequency output from higher frequency data (e.g., generating quarterly estimates from monthly production data).

The system provides an intelligent application environment in which data from unrelated systems can be gathered, stored, analyzed, and distributed in a simple and timely manner. These technologies allow disparate systems to contribute data and information to an integrated, enterprise-wide business intelligence strategy. This ensures the production data and all requisite reservoir data can be aggregated to provide a robust forecasting experience.

In the future, the addition of grid computing will offer a cost-effective solution for customers who want to accelerate the forecasting process or increase the scale or scope (number of users, size of datasets, and the frequency of analysis) of the DCA.

Unlike single-point deterministic estimates, probabilistic approaches provide a measure of uncertainty in the reserves estimates. They provide a range of estimates within prescribed confidence levels and, thus, attempt to bracket the true value. Probabilistic reserve estimates are able to fulfill multiple purposes of internal decision making and public reporting. However, many engineers have long had the indelible impression that quantifying uncertainty of estimates is largely subjective. This impression has led the industry to be reluctant to search for appropriate probabilistic methods for reserves estimation and use probabilistic methods to quantify uncertainty of estimates. Existing practices for probabilistic estimation of reserves often assume prior knowledge of distributions of relevant parameters or reservoir properties. For example, prior distributions of drainage area, net pay, porosity, hydrocarbon saturation, formation volume factor, and recovery factor are needed to run Monte Carlo simulations when the volumetric method is used in probabilistic reserves estimation.

Data mining is most effective when it is part of an integrated information delivery strategy that includes data gathered from diverse enterprise sources, including unstructured data in the form of daily engineer reports, time series data, production data, production logging tool (PLT), rock properties from cores, well logs, and seismic attributes.

Let us walk through the methodology implemented to achieve the automated well management solution depicted in Figures 7.10 and 7.11.

It is essential to aggregate disparate data across the upstream engineering silos to enable a single ADW to furnish the subsequent analytical processes as we work toward a data-driven approach to supplement the traditional interpretive or deterministic behavior of geoscientists.

Once the objective function or functions for the study have been determined, we can surface hidden trends and correlations in an EDA step, impute missing values, identify outliers in the dataset, and perform a quality control suite of workflows based on first principles to ensure a robust dataset for advanced analytics.

The first probabilistic workflow automatically selects optimum contiguous production data to perform DCA and establish a set of type curves to best

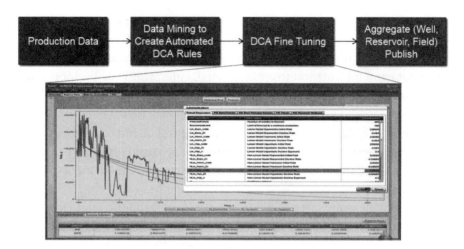

Figure 7.10 Data Mining Methodology with DCA Output to Enhance Models

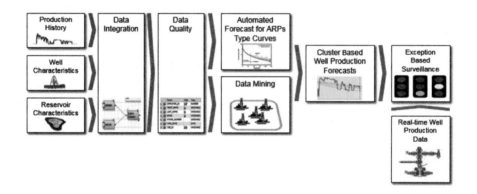

Figure 7.11 Well Optimization Workflows

provide a short- and long-term forecast for each well in the field. The results of the modeling and application of Arps' equation produce additional data points as input to a cluster analysis.

Introducing further data elements from the ADW we can through a hierarchical and iterative cluster algorithm identify key production indicators for each well and thus profile important characteristics that segregate good and poorly performing wells.

We then establish a suite of KPIs that can be used to monitor and survey real-time production data. Any new data readings that fall above or below the confidence limits that constrain good performance are then alerted via a dashboard. Adopting either an *exception-based surveillance* methodology or a *predictive* model, we can respectively identify a set of actionable items to best address an event identified via the KPI alerts or predict via event signatures an impending situation that should be addressed to prevent deferment or poor performance.

Let us enumerate some of the key benefits that are garnered from such a methodology incorporating an automated time series selection process via a bootstrapping module, executing a clustering module to characterize profiles for best- and worst-performing wells, and aggregating key outputs of exploratory data analysis and descriptive models into a SEMMA process for data mining:

- Identify which wells are not performing as expected.
- Focus investigation efforts of reservoir engineers.
- Target investments to improve future well performance.
- Improve recovery factors and minimize costs.

UNCONVENTIONAL RESERVES ESTIMATION

Reliably estimating recoverable reserves from low-permeability shale-gas formations is a problematic exercise owing to the nature of the unconventional reservoir and inherent geomechanical and rock properties.[5] Employing the Arps hyperbolic model, for example, invariably results in an overoptimistic forecast and estimation. Alternative DCA models based on empirical considerations have been positioned:

- The Duong power-law model
- The Valko stretched-exponential-decline model (SEDM)
- Weibull growth curve

Projecting production-decline curves is ostensibly the most commonplace method to forecast well performance in tight gas and shale-gas assets. The potential production and EUR are determined by fitting an empirical model of the well's production-decline trend and then projecting this trend to the well's economic limit or an acceptable cutoff time. Forcing Arps' hyperbolic model to fit production data from shale-gas wells has invariably resulted in overoptimistic results of EUR, stemming from physically unrealistically high values of the decline exponent to force the fit. There have been a few alternatives proposed for the analysis of decline curves in tight gas wells. One preference constrains the tardy decline rate to a more realistic value on the basis of analogs. Another methodology determines empirical decline-curve models that impose physically relevant parameter definitions and finite EUR values on model predictions. A key issue associated with the use of multiple models is how to discriminate between them with limited production periods, and how to combine the model results to yield an assessment of uncertainty in reserves estimates.

Production decline analysis of tight gas and shale-gas wells with this method typically results in a best-fit value of greater than unity for the decline-exponent parameter. The result often is physically unrealistic in that cumulative production becomes unbounded as time increases.

Stretched-Exponential Decline Model

The *stretched-exponential decline model* (SEDM) is a more plausible physical explanation than the assumption of boundary-dominated flow that is inordinately long to develop in tight and shale-gas reservoirs. Unlike the hyperbolic model, the SEDM yields a finite value for ultimate recovery. The SEDM appears to fit field data from various shale plays reasonably well and provides an effective alternative to Arps' hyperbolic model.

Duong Model

Because tight gas and shale-gas reservoirs generally are produced after massive hydraulic fracturing, it is reasonable to assume that flow toward wells in such systems will exhibit fracture-dominated characteristics. For finite-conductivity fractures, the flow will be bilinear, which manifests as a quarter-slope line on a log-log graph of production rate q versus time, whereas flow in infinite-conductivity fractures will be linear and be characterized by a half-slope line on the same graph. Under both conditions, it has been shown that a log-log graph of q/Gp versus time should have a slope of -1.

However, analysis of field data from several shale-gas plays has shown that the relationship between these variables is described better by an empirical model that also appears to fit field data from various shale plays very well, providing an effective alternative to Arps' hyperbolic model.

Weibull Growth Model

Many mathematical algorithms have been implemented to describe population growth (or decline) effectively under an expansive range of conditions. The Weibull growth curve is a generalization of the widely used Weibull distribution for modeling time to failure in applied-engineering problems. A three-parameter Weibull model can be reduced to two unknowns if the q/Gp ratio is taken as the dependent variable. Nonlinear-regression analysis can estimate the observed ratio against time.

Uncertainty Assessment: The GLUE Model

Previous studies of decline-curve analysis by use of multiple models have shown that fits of comparable quality can be obtained for short data windows, but they will yield very different 30-year EUR estimates.

If multiple models are used for generating reserves estimates, it is not clear how the results from such models can be aggregated. Therefore, a two-step approach is proposed. In the first step, alternative models are identified and used to fit the data. In the second step, a weight is assigned to each model on the basis of goodness-of-fit statistics, and the weighted mean and standard deviation of the desired performance measure are calculated.

Two common model-averaging techniques for hydrologic modeling are *generalized likelihood/uncertainty estimation* (GLUE) and *maximum-likelihood Bayesian-model averaging*. It has been observed that the Bayesian-model averaging approach tends to concentrate model weights on only one or two best-performing models, whereas model weights calculated by the GLUE method are distributed more uniformly across the model space.

The GLUE framework accepts many equally likely parameter realizations or distinct model alternatives as a starting point. The output corresponding to each realization is compared against actual observations. Only those realizations that satisfy some acceptable level of performance, such as a maximum sum-of-squared weighted residuals, also known as the *behavioral threshold,* are retained for further analysis, and the non-behavioral realizations are rejected. Then a likelihood value for each model is computed as a function of the misfit between observations and model predictions. The weights or probabilities for each model are estimated by normalizing the likelihood values.

The GLUE model is flexible with respect to the choice of the likelihood measure. Any reasonable likelihood measure can be used appropriately, providing that it adequately represents the experts' understanding of the relative importance of different data sources used to assess model accuracy.

CASE STUDY: OIL PRODUCTION PREDICTION FOR INFILL WELL

The study generates predictions for a potential range of cumulative production and length of production life for an arbitrary infill well. We implement a workflow that integrates DCA estimation and neural network techniques for a data-driven analysis approach.

Production predictions can assist petroleum engineers in economic forecasts, and the traditional approach necessitates a numerical simulation based on log and core analysis results. However, this process can be technically difficult, time consuming, and expensive in terms of both human and computational resources.

This case study describes a methodology that incorporates both curve fitting and artificial neural network approaches, and offers engineers potential solutions in the range of cumulative production and length of production of an infill well. The benefits of neural networks include its computational efficiency, nonlinear characteristics, generation properties, and ease of working with high-dimensional data.

The groundwork behind the prediction is the well's initial production and its economic cutoff. The assumption adopted in the study is that the production of an infill well is similar to extant wells in the same reservoir; thus, production curves of these wells can provide appropriate knowledge to support forecasted production of an infill well. However, it is also assumed that an engineer with local experience is ideal to judge how relevant the information is from the existing wells.

The five conventional methods of estimating, both physically and economically, remaining reserves of petroleum in an oil well include:

1. *Analogy:* The prediction is based on a well that is expected to perform similarly to the target well. This method is fast, cheap, and can be used before drilling. However, this method is inherently devoid of ostensible accuracy.

2. *Volumetrics:* This estimation of oil-in-place is performed by combining net reservoir volume with additional parameters such as porosity, saturation, and recovery factor. A relatively fast methodology with the requisite input minimal, with the applicability of early adoption in a well's lifecycle. However, this methodology makes assumptions on area of the well and recovery factor, and is thus inherently flawed.

3. *Material balance:* The material balance technique of determining original oil-in-place is based on the law of *conservation of mass*. This method requires information on pressures, production history, fluid properties, and rock properties, and can be used for determining many parameters, such as recovery factor, water influx, and gas cap size. The disadvantages of this approach include its sensitivity to relative permeabilities and its reliance on augmenting the dimension of the input space.

4. *Decline curve analysis:* This method needs only production history. The procedure of generating decline curves is fast and inexpensive but it is empirical by nature and is reliant on Arps' equation to generate type curves. The method can generate production-versus-time predictions and is very accurate under certain circumstances. Its weakness is that the target well must be producing under constant conditions when this method is applied. Moreover, the method involves curve fitting with at least 6 months of historical data; its performance improves if data of between 2 and 10 years are available.

5. *Reservoir simulation:* Reservoir simulation is ostensibly an extension of the material balance technique. It requires much more input data than other methods. The strength of the method is that it can handle different rock and fluid properties in different areas of the reservoir; its weaknesses, however, include the cost and time required to do the study and the amount of input needed. In the process of applying the method, the parameters are adjusted to better fit pressure-production history of the well of interest. However, since often a unique fit cannot be ascertained, it is essential to be diligent so that only acceptable values are used. Moreover, even when a good fit is obtained, assumptions made to obtain the fit may not be true in prediction runs.

Each of these methods can be applied independently and has its strengths and weaknesses. While all five methods can be used for predicting recoverable reserves of a reservoir, the methods have different data requirements.

There is substantial research conducted on estimating oil production using the ANN approach. Aminzadeh, Barhen, and Toomarian[6] adopted the ANN technique in estimating oil field reservoir parameters from remote seismic data. Huang and William[7] developed a model for predicting porosity and permeability from well logs using ANN techniques. Although the core measurements were not used for constructing training examples, the predicted curves and the actual measurements agree except for a few data points. Wong and Taggart[8] described a model similar to that of Huang and William, but which includes information on lithofacies as input. The results showed that the standard neural network method gave lower root mean square error (RMSE) compared to the simulated method, but the simulated method produces better statistics of the actual data, including mean, standard deviation, coefficient of variation, and maximum and minimum values. Wong and Taggart believed data preprocessing to be the most important step in applying the ANN approach to geological problems.

The ANN model showed higher accuracy when compared to any other correlation method; it also produced the lowest errors, the lowest standard deviation, and the highest correlation coefficient for both outputs.

This study adopts two modeling approaches:

1. Curve estimation
2. ANN methodology

Curve Estimation

Data can usually fit more than one type of curve, and the modeling objective is to find a curve with minimal deviation from all the data points. The best-fitting curves can be ascertained based on the method of least squares, which assumes that the best-fitting curve of a given type is the curve that has the minimal sum of the squared deviations from a given set of data. The linear least squares fitting technique is the most fundamental and hence is frequently applied, providing a solution to the problem of determining the best-fit straight line through a set of points. In this study, most equations used to fit the data are linear or linearizable. They include the linear, logarithmic, exponential, and harmonic equations.

ANN Methodology

Neural networks use more advanced nonlinear curve-fitting algorithms than the curve-fitting equations mentioned in curve estimation methodologies. Instead of solving a set of equations to obtain the best coefficients, the neural network model updates weights in the neural networks to reduce the error at each step.

A history-matching step adopts the curve estimation and neural networks techniques already mentioned. Each model takes the month index as input and outputs a predicted monthly production. The matching involves a process of minimizing root mean square error (RMSE) between predicted and observed output values. Neural networks were trained to find the optimal architectures and weights. For the curve estimation methods, a set of curve coefficients were derived.

To reduce the chance of the neural network models over-fitting the data, cross-validation was implemented. During training, the data were divided in different ways into two portions for training and validation; the validation portion was used to measure the performance of the model trained to that point. We also wanted to avoid the neural network spending time learning meaningless correlations among a large input space owing to idiosyncrasies in individual training cases. Thus, diminishing the number of input variables enables the ANN to focus on only the most critical correlations. The problem obviously is to identify those variables implicated as the most significant variables. PCA is the traditional methodology to ascertain if a variable is highly correlated with another. The analysis also indicates those combinations of variables that contain large spreads in the data on average. Another benefit is the surfacing of those variables that are on average approximately constant and can thus be dismissed as significant.

The objective of the history-matching models is not only to retain production curves, but to forecast future values based on the historical dataset. A new well with higher initial production values will likely have a longer production life than an extant well with lower initial production values. Hence, the capacity to determine future values is even more important to make analogue predictions in the case of higher initial production. If the production life of the new well is shorter than that of the existing well, the observed values from the existing well can be used directly to make analogue predictions and no future value needs to be generated. However, if the life of the new well is longer than that of the existing well, the observed values are insufficient, and future predictions are needed.

The study implemented the analogue methodology to ascertain the production of a new well based on decline curves of existing wells. Implicit in this adoption of the analogue method is the assumption that the production decline curve is similar to those of the existing wells in the same area. Another heuristic adopted was developed based on the study of the historical data on a well. It was noted that while the shape of two production curves can be different, the total production volumes of two wells are similar when their initial production volumes are at the same level.

Hence, to make analogue predictions the production curve of an existing well is adjusted to match the new level of initial production. There are several ways to shift the production curve to a new level:

- *Additive:* A constant is added to the monthly production of an existing well.

- *Multiplicative:* A constant is multiplied to the monthly production of an existing well, and the production rate is assumed to be proportional to the initial production.

- *Linear:* The relationship between monthly production and initial production is expressed as a linear function.

- *Nonlinear:* The relationship between monthly production and initial production is expressed as a nonlinear function.

Table 7.1 shows that the multiplicative method generates more accurate results than the additive method since the predicted values are closer to the range of the observed values, and there are no negative values in the prediction. Hence, the multiplicative approach was adopted in this study.

The performance of this solution must be evaluated by the domain experts. In addition, accuracy of the system can be corroborated using the available data. Considerable progress has been made in the development of methods for estimating future production of oil wells. However, these methods are invariably either difficult to use or inaccurate. This methodology does not attempt to invent a novel prediction method. Instead, it is based on several simple available methods and gives users numerical and visual illustrations of the results so that experienced engineers can exercise their judgment and decide which scenario is the more likely.

Table 7.1 Well Analysis for Additive and Multiplicative Methods

	Well A	Well B	Well C	Well D	Well E
Well A	2736.9	−500.71	−268359	3050	2919.5
Well B	11575.8	3838.19	4570.4	11888.9	11758.4
Well C	11058.3	3320.69	4052.9	11371.4	11240.9
Well D	853.2	−6884.41	−6152.2	1166.3	1035.8
Well E	873.9	648.8	−6131.5	1187	1056.5

	Well A	Well B	Well C	Well D	Well E
Well A	2736.9	1257.234	1381.972	2073.422	1862.305
Well B	8355.44	3838.19	4219.002	6329.919	5685.403
Well C	8026	3687	4052.9	6080	5461.98
Well D	1539.65	707.78	777.43	1166.3	1046.98
Well E	1552.78	713.56	784.89	1176	1056.5

NOTES

1. W. W. Cutler and H. R. Johnson, "Estimating Recoverable Oil of Curtailed Wells," *Oil Weekly* (May 27, 1940).

2. J. J. Arps, "Analysis of Decline Curves," *Transactions of the American Institute of Mining Engineers* 160 (1945): 228–247.

3. E. C. Capen, "The Difficulty of Assessing Uncertainty," *Journal of Petroleum Technology* 28, no. 8 (1976): 843–850.

4. V. A. Jochen and J P. Spivey, "Probabilistic Reserves Estimation Using Decline Curve Analysis with the Bootstrap Method," SPE 36633, presented at the SPE Annual Technical Conference and Exhibition, Denver, CO, October 6–9, 1996.

5. M. J. Fetkovich, "Decline Curve Analysis Using Type Curves," *Journal of Petroleum Technology* (June 1980), 1065–1077.

6. F. Aminzadeh, J. Barhen, and N. B. Toomarian, "Estimation of Reservoir Parameter Using a Hybrid Neural Network," *Journal of Petroleum Science and Engineering* 24, no. 1 (1999): 49–56.

7. Z. Huang and M. A. William, "Determination of Porosity and Permeability in Reservoir Intervals by Artificial Neural Network Modeling: Offshore Eastern Canada," *Petroleum Geoscience* 3, no. 3 (1997): 245–258.

8. P. M. Wong and I. J. Taggart, "Use of Neural Network Methods to Predict Porosity and Permeability of a Petroleum Reservoir," *AI Applications* 9, no. 2 (1995): 27–37.

CHAPTER **8**

Production
Optimization

*I've come loaded with statistics, for I've noticed that
a man can't prove anything without statistics.*

Mark Twain

Production optimization is predicated on facilitating a more efficient decision-making cycle. Only sound and timely judgments on tactics and strategies across the asset can ensure optimized workflows to enhance performance across the well portfolio. Thus production optimization must leverage and scale the experienced workforce and transform the methodologies to ensure collaboration. People, processes, and technologies comprise the triumvirate of effective organizational excellence. Habitual approaches to production optimization need refinement to include data-driven models.

What are some of the benefits attained through activities geared around production optimization? Reduction in unplanned shutdowns and controlled spending to reduce OPEX and CAPEX as well as exploiting more reserves and increasing the asset performance are but a few of the most important consequences.

Strategic assessment that reviews and defines the roadmap for integrated operations and digital oilfields as well as asset surveillance and alerting are underpinned by advanced analytical methodologies that can perform data management and exploratory data analysis, and operationalize predictive models running against a plethora of real-time data consumed from data historians.

Asset simulation and optimization currently employs complex numerical models to maximize production across the three integrated systems: reservoir, well, and surface facilities. Mohaghegh, Modavi, Hafez, and Haajizadeh[1] have

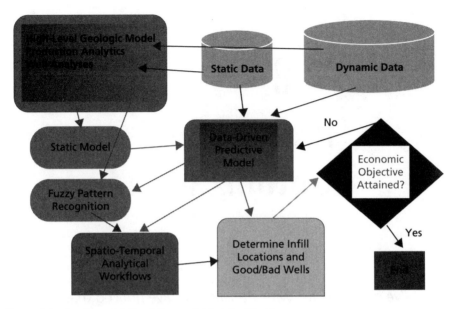

Figure 8.1 Top-Down Intelligent Reservoir Modeling Workflow

introduced the industry to an alternative soft computing suite of techniques that implement neural networks, fuzzy clustering, pattern recognition, and so on, under the guise of a *top-down modeling approach* (Figure 8.1). It is a formalized and comprehensive empirical reservoir simulation methodology that addresses the multivariate, multivariant, multidimensional, and stochastic complexities inherent in the reservoir.

The inverse of a top-down approach underpins the standard reservoir simulation and modeling methodology. The initial geological model is formulated by integrating the optimum extant petrophysical and geophysical data. We then add fluid flow empirical understanding to numerically attain a dynamic reservoir model that is subsequently calibrated with the historical production data. The history-matched model is implemented to ascertain field (re)engineering strategies to attain the objective function: maximize infill drilling, enhance recovery factor, or increase well performance.

The goal of the top-down workflow is to generate a simulation of the reservoir initiated by studying the nuances of the historical well performance. We tend to supplement these data with cores, wireline logs, well tests, and seismic attributes so as to enhance the accuracy of the top-down modeling technique. Thus this approach is deemed not as a replacement to conventional reservoir simulation and modeling, but as an adjuvant methodology, especially pertinent when numerical models are cost and resource prohibitive.

The top-down workflow should consist of but not be limited by some of the following de facto standard protocols in numerical modeling:

- Decline curve analysis
- Type curve matching
- History matching
- Volumetric reserve estimation
- Recovery factors determination

Adopting simple linear regression techniques it is feasible to generate a suite of multiple production indicators (3, 6, and 9 months cumulative liquid production as well as 1-, 3-, 5-, and 10-year cumulative oil, gas, and water production in addition to smoothed gas–oil ratio and water-cut values across a sampled discrete time window). These analyses and statistics generate a large volume of data and information that are snapshots of reservoir behavior in discrete slices of time and space. We can then apply a range of soft computing techniques such as neural networks, genetic algorithms, and fuzzy pattern recognition to ascertain predictive models to forecast well performance. The set of discrete, intelligent models are then integrated using a continuous fuzzy pattern recognition algorithm in order to arrive at a cohesive picture and model of the reservoir as a whole.

The *top-down, intelligent reservoir modeling* is a marriage between the extant trends in artificial intelligence and data mining (AI&DM), reflecting the non-determinism and robust reservoir engineering methodologies and principles based on determinism. You can gain a unique appreciation of the field and reservoir using actual measurements.

EXPLORATION AND PRODUCTION VALUE PROPOSITIONS

Many oil and gas companies realize that their operations could benefit from improved ways of working driven by better-quality information and tools. However, they often struggle to identify what is important and what is just hype. The scope of an assessment varies from a single asset to a complete company's asset portfolio. Typically, a project scope will focus on one or a small number of assets with the intention to structure a program in a way that it can be easily extended to other assets.

The inherent value and benefits of optimizing production are obvious, but at what expense? In light of the avalanche of E&P data with multiple varieties across the disparate and siloed engineering disciplines, it is critical to develop automated and semi-automated methodologies that implement soft computing techniques. Data management, quantifying uncertainty, and assessing risks associated with the operational models must be addressed to effect successful (re)engineering strategies that focus on the objective function: optimized production.

Let us walk through some case studies that explicate the tangible benefits of applying data-driven models and advanced analytical methodologies to a dataset representative of a complex system so as to achieve improved portfolio performance.

CASE STUDIES

The following case studies illustrate the effectiveness and validity of applying advanced analytical workflows to optimize production in both conventional and unconventional reservoirs.

Artificial Lift: Optimization of Gas-Injected Oil Wells[2]

Of the approximately 1 million oil and gas wells producing globally, approximately 1 in 20 flow naturally, leaving the majority of oil and gas production reliant on effective artificial lift operations. A mature field has a relatively long production history with multiple aging wells. To increase production rates, we need to increase reservoir pressures. When gas flows are constrained across multiple wells it is a problematic situation to resolve in a timely and effective manner. Let us explore a scalable solution that offers efficient and potent results.

Electronic submersible pumps (ESP) and artificial gas injection are two techniques that strive to maintain production performance in a mature reservoir. Implementing the latter methodology is prevalent in many production wells. We can generate a complex suite of partial differential equations to be numerically solved so as to render a physical model representing the phenomena associated with gas lift. The equations are derived from fundamental mass and momentum balances and hinge on the physical properties inherent in the gas lift system.

Figure 8.2 illustrates a graphic portrayal of a continuous gas lift (CGL) oil field system.

When reengineering the tactics and strategies across a mature field, determining the optimized artificial lift system in the well portfolio, it is obviously complicated by the interference patterns between wells across the reservoir. Not only is field segmentation a contributing factor but also other influences such as the gas–oil ratio and temperature for each well and the type of gas lift valves and the capacities of the surface processing facilities (compressed gas availability and gas–oil separation). There is an unstable, optimum, and stable gas injection pressure range ascertained for each well; Figure 8.3 graphically portrays a typical gas lift optimization curve.

The unstable area yields a "heading" characterized by wide variations in injection pressure owing to the physical dynamics of the fluid flow. We invariably notice higher injection rates in the stable region. Predominantly the most

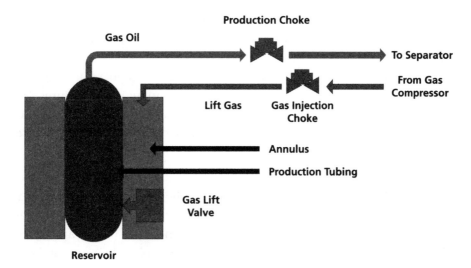

Figure 8.2 Continuous Gas Lift (CGL)

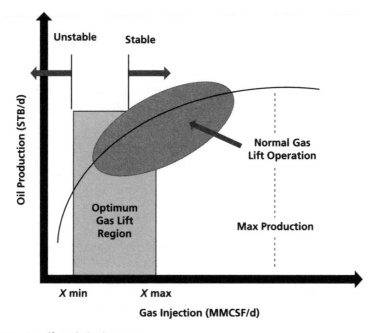

Figure 8.3 Gas Lift Optimization Curve

favorable gas lift area is between 40 and 60 percent of the gas injection rate at the peak oil production mark.

Invariably gas lift optimization curves for each well in the portfolio are calculated via measurement of gas–oil production across a range of injection pressures. These curves can be determined in real time as data from surveillance sensors continuously stream into an advanced analytical workflow.

The results can be implemented to optimize *enhanced oil recovery* techniques that address well interaction and also fine-tune important operational parameters.

For a specific suite of gas lift optimization curves, computation of optimal gas injection pressures can be attained by a variety of numerical procedures. The majority of these techniques necessitate substantial computational resources and thus it is imperative to implement the solution in a distributed architecture.

Modeling Methodology

The first step in the analytical workflow involves the generation of a suite of gas lift optimization curves based on the aggregated data across the well portfolio. The independent variable is the gas injection rate and when plotted against the well production or dependent variable, we can determine the response function. The extant operating conditions in each well are inherent in the curves. In order to address the optimization problem associated with the distribution of gas flows across a range of wells, there have been multiple models and complex methodologies positioned. Let us analyze the discrete gas lift optimization data points and fit them to generate a continuous function with the independent variable in gas injection flow.

A simple polynomial (independent variable) with varying degrees can be fitted to the data using a least squares methodology by assessing the statistical measures relating to the goodness of the best-fit polynomial.

Polynomial in X:

$$f(x) = a_0 + a_1 x + a_2 x^2 + a_3 x^3 + a_4 x^4 \qquad \text{Equation (1)}$$

where:

- x is the independent variable.
- a_0, a_1, a_2, a_3, and a_4 are coefficients of their respective polynomial independent variables.

Fitting of polynomial equations to the general shape of the gas lift curve (Figure 8.3) calls for a higher-order polynomial to approximate the shape of the curve. The fit statistics resulting from a least squares regression and the poor general shape fit indicate that a high-order polynomial form is not satisfactory. Other forms of the function can be used to fit the data and the statistical measures and resultant shape of the curve can be assessed to better match the gas lift optimization relationship. Of several alternatives, the following seems to best fit generalized gas lift curves.

Exponential in X:

$$f(x) = a_3 + [a_2 / (a_0 / a_1 - 1)]\{e^{-a_1 x+} - e^{-a_0 x}\} \qquad \text{Equation (2)}$$

where:

- x is the independent variable, the gas injection rate.
- a_0, a_1, a_2, a_3, and a_4 are coefficients in exponential equation.

Optimize Production Formulation

The most fundamental and constrained production optimization problem can be expressed thus:

Maximize

$$\text{Production} = \sum f(x_i) = \sum a3 + \left| \frac{a2}{\frac{a0}{a1} - 1} \right| \left\{ e^{-a1x} - e^{-a0x} \right\} \qquad \text{Equation (3)}$$

subject to:

Maximum gas injectioin volume $= \Sigma_n^i x_i \Leftarrow$ Total gas available   Equation (4)

For each well, $i = 1$ to number of wells:

$$x_i >= 0 \text{ (Non-negativity of gas injection rates)} \qquad \text{Equation (5)}$$

We can add further constraint criteria such as minimum and maximum injection rates per well. This suite of constraints enables the optimization of each gas lift curve in the *optimal gas lift* region (Figure 8.3). Note equations 6 and 7, ahead.

Computational formulation of the constrained optimization problem and its final solution constitute the next step in the methodology.

It is sufficient for the polynomial in x form (equation 1) to be represented by a linear equation solver while the exponential form (equation 2) necessitates a nonlinear equation solver.

It was determined that the exponential form of the gas lift curve was optimum and thus it was implemented to solve the constrained optimization problem. The sparse *nonlinear optimization solver* using the conjugate gradient method, a Newton-type method with line search, trust region method, or quasi-Newton method) was chosen to solve this problem.

Additional constraints to equations 1, 2, and 3 yield the following formulation:

Optimize production formulation for optimal gas lift area

Supplementary to equations 3, 4 and 5 the following two additional constraints address the optimal gas lift area.

For each well, $i = 1$ to number of wells:

$$x_i <= 60\% \quad x_i \max \qquad \text{Equation (6)}$$

$$x_i > = 40\% \quad x_i \max \qquad\qquad \text{Equation (7)}$$

Constraints equations 6 and 7 ensure that the gas lift injection rate is in the optimal area as in Figure 8.3.

If the optimal gas lift area cannot be attained (owing to total gas injection capacity) for a specific well, the general protocol is to establish the gas lift flow rate at 0 to minimize heading effects.

Selection of Producing Wells

In an operating oil field, maintenance may require particular oil wells to be shut down. A logical extension of the above optimization would be the capability to select those wells operating and subsequently to optimize the gas injection rate for each operating well. This may be attained by including a Boolean (well on/off) parameter in the formulation of either equation 3 or 8.

Five wells are sampled tabulating the gas injection flow (Qg – MMCF/D) against the gas–oil production (Qo STB/D), as in Figure 8.4.

Figure 8.5 graphically illustrates the data depicted in Figure 8.4 underlining the gas lift optimization curve for each of the five wells.

The computed coefficients for exponentials across a hundred wells were captured implementing a nonlinear algorithm for each well. These are used in the computer optimization. These coefficients can be quickly recomputed based on streaming data on production/gas injection rates provided by Supervisory Control and Data Acquisition (SCADA) systems or otherwise collected by field data technicians. This would allow an almost real-time optimization of gas injection rates.

A series of optimizations were completed for gas injection rates between 10 and 100 MMCF/D availability across the 100 wells. The results are shown in Figures 8.6 and 8.7. At the lowest injection gas availability rate (10 MMCF/D) many wells were not allocated any gas injection. At the highest available injection rate (100 MMCF/D) the optimal production was 121,830.9452 STB/D.

One of a number of processes is used to artificially lift oil or water from wells where there is insufficient reservoir pressure to produce the well. The process involves injecting gas through the tubing casing annulus. Injected gas aerates the fluid to reduce its density; the formation pressure is then able to lift the oil column and forces the fluid out of the wellbore. Gas may be injected continuously or intermittently, depending on the producing characteristics of the well and the arrangement of the gas lift equipment.

Gas lift is a form of artificial lift where gas bubbles lift the oil from the well. The amount of gas to be injected to maximize oil production varies based on well conditions and geometries. Too much or too little injected gas will result in less-than-maximum production. Generally, the optimal amount of injected gas is determined by well tests, where the rate of injection is varied and liquid production (oil and perhaps water) is measured.

Well 1		Well 2		Well 3		Well 4		Well 5	
Qg	Qo	Qg	Qo	Qg	Qo	Qg	Qo	Qg	Qo
0	175	0	271	0	321	0	432	0	460
0.06125	187	0.2	307.2	0.2	400	0.263	500	0.3	532.7
0.125	200	0.3	325.8	0.31	425.9	0.427	540	0.444	567.3
0.1825	212	0.4	345.9	0.445	450.6	0.52	560	0.54	588.4
0.25	222	0.52	363.1	0.51	460	0.636	585.9	0.626	610
0.375	238	0.642	376.9	0.6	469	0.714	600	0.728	632.4
0.5	248	0.763	388.8	0.75	482.9	0.8	614	0.809	649.4
0.756	258.7	0.85	397.4	0.87	492	0.926	633.9	0.92	667
1	265	1	407.4	1.045	501.7	1.1	653	1	678
1.385	269.7	1.15	414.6	1.255	509.2	1.289	668.8	1.08	687
1.724	270.46	1.25	418.4	1.455	513.7	1.421	675.6	1.23	704
2	269.2	1.371	421.3	1.62	515.8	1.54	682	1.379	715.5
2.5	266	1.484	423.1	1.818	517.8	1.724	687.9	1.52	726
3	261.5	1.69	425.1	2	517.5	1.9	693	1.669	734
3.5	257	1.838	425.3	2.132	517	2.134	696.1	1.85	740
4	252.8	2.1	424.8	2.273	516.4	2.4	698.5	2	744
4.5	247.5	2.439	422.2	2.478	514.4	2.642	700	2.2	749
5	242.5	2.73	419	2.673	510.9	3.06	701.6	2.494	752.82
5.5	238	3.113	412	3.118	504.1	3.601	702.39	3	751
6	234	3.601	404	3.601	495.9	4.206	701	3.601	749
6.5	230	4	396.8	4.145	484.2	5	696	4.29	743.6
7	225	5	380	5	465	6	688	5	737
7.5	220	6	361.1	6	440	7	680	6	723.6
8	215	7	340	7	414	8	671	7	710
		8	321	8	384.9			8	695.5

Figure 8.4 Sample Gas Lift Curves Data

Although the gas is recovered from the oil at a later separation stage, the process requires energy to drive a compressor in order to raise the pressure of the gas to a level where it can be re-injected.

The *gas lift mandrel* is a device installed in the tubing string of a gas lift well onto which or into which a gas lift valve is fitted. There are two common types

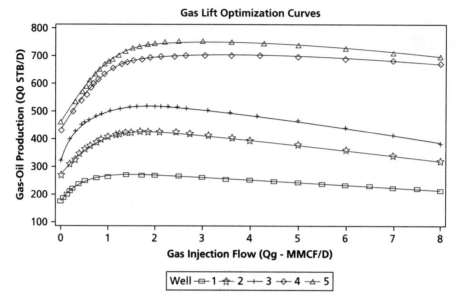

Figure 8.5 Sample Gas Lift Curves

Gas Injection Rate (MMCF/D)	Total Production (STB/D)
0	25,562.73223
10	68,356.17876
20	88,908.82123
30	101,085.27084
40	108,455.77364
50	113,150.24474
60	116,317.92018
70	118,541.69936
80	120,098.28288
90	121,152.89875
100	121,830,9452

Figure 8.6 Optimization Results and Optimal Gas Usage

of mandrels. In a conventional gas lift mandrel, a gas lift valve is installed as the tubing is placed in the well. Thus, to replace or repair the valve, the tubing string must be pulled. In the side-pocket mandrel, however, the valve is installed and removed by wireline while the mandrel is still in the well, eliminating the need to pull the tubing to repair or replace the valve.

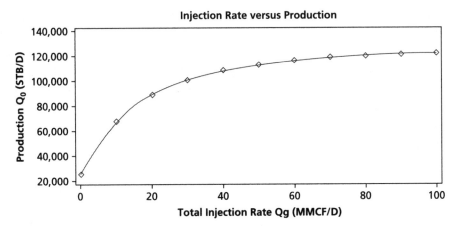

Figure 8.7 Optimization Results for Gas Injection Rates from 0 to 100 MMCF/D

A *gas lift valve* is a device installed on (or in) a gas lift mandrel, which in turn is put on the production tubing of a gas lift well. Tubing and casing pressures cause the valve to open and close, thus allowing gas to be injected into the fluid in the tubing to cause the fluid to rise to the surface. In the lexicon of the industry, gas lift mandrels are said to be "tubing retrievable" wherein they are deployed and retrieved attached to the production tubing.

Maximize Production in Unconventional Reservoirs

Over the past decade significant supplies of natural gas have been discovered in shale. While the development of new technologies has driven down the cost of gas extraction, pursuing natural gas in shale continues to be risky and capital intensive.

Producers seek the most productive zones in their shale basins, as well as continued improvement in hydraulic fracturing processes. Decreasing costs and reducing risk while maximizing shale gas production necessitates innovative, advanced analytical capabilities that can give you a comprehensive understanding of the reservoir heterogeneity in order to extract hidden predictive information, identify drivers and leading indicators of efficient well production, determine the best intervals for stimulation, and recommend optimum stimulation processes and frequencies. Modeling, simulating, and predicting well productivity requires integrated exploratory, predictive, and forecasting capabilities underpinned by advanced analytical models to unlock the true potential of each wellbore. Without the critical insight enabled by integrated analysis to pair productivity analysis with economic feasibility, companies face significant risk and uncertainty when developing new wells or optimizing production of extant wellbores.

It is critical to assess via data-mining methodologies the variability in and potential of well performance in order to formulate an optimized suite of well completion and reservoir development strategies. Owing to the inherent complexity of subsurface systems, a data-driven set of advanced analytical workflows that embrace exploratory data analysis in a multivariate perspective and predictive data analysis must be implemented in order to complement the first principles that underpin the array of geoscientific schools of thought.

Bakken Formation

The Bakken formation is a rock unit of the Late Devonian to Early Mississippian age that stretches beneath areas of Montana and North Dakota in the United States and Manitoba and Saskatchewan in Canada. The most recent estimates of technically recoverable and nonrecoverable with extant technology top out at 18 billion barrels of oil equivalent (BOE). Porosities in the Bakken average about 5 percent, and permeabilities are very low, averaging 0.04 millidarcies, but the presence of vertical to sub-vertical natural fractures makes the Bakken an excellent candidate for horizontal drilling techniques and hydraulic fracturing.

The typical well profile proposed by operators in the Bakken is overly optimistic. We observe a predominantly exponential (weak-to-moderate hyperbolic) decline in most of the individual well decline trends, rather than steadily flattening hyperbolic decline. A prevalent two-stage exponential decline based on decline curve analysis (DCA) of individual wells is thus noted within the Bakken Shale play. A two-stage exponential decline is characterized by an initial 12-to-18-month period of steep decline followed by a stable, shallower rate of decline that continues up to the current status of the wells (commonly over four or more years to date in the Bakken Shale). Our emphasis is on matching the relatively stable, shallower second stage, because that is the portion of the decline history that best predicts future performance. Determining performance trends, (Arps coefficient, b^3) and initial rates of decline (D_i) enables the aggregation of several key production indicators (KPIs). Implementing the values of these KPIs in a cluster analysis generates well profiles that suggest field compartmentalization or segregation.

Clustering is a data-mining tool for categorizing and analyzing groups of these data dimensions having similar attribute characteristics or properties. For wells' analysis this methodology consists in classifying wells by dividing the field into areas. This method determines the most similar wells and generates a first set of clusters; then it compares the average of the clusters to the remaining wells to form a second set of clusters, and so on. There are several ways to aggregate wells but the above method is more stable than the K-means procedure and provides more detailed results; moreover, the displayed tree is useful to visualize the results or to choose the number of clusters. It requires more computing time, but the calculating capacity of current computing units allows processing a thousand wells in a few minutes.

The following wells' properties could be used as parameters for clustering:

- Cumulative liquid production
- Cumulative oil or gas production
- Water cut (percentage determined by water production/liquid production)
- B exponent (decline type curve)
- Initial rate of decline
- Initial rate of production
- Average liquid production

Additional data points such as the operational parameters proppant quantity, proppant type, proppant roundness and sphericity, mesh sizes, fracture fluid volume, and gross perforated interval are also very important independent variables that, when explored in a visual data analytical tool as demonstrated in Figures 8.8, 8.9, and 8.10, can surface trends and hidden patterns. Subsequently it is important to integrate geomechanical environment parameters such as those related to rock mass characterization and rock mass mechanics, and significant data points that reflect lithology, formation properties, dip and heterogeneity, well trajectory, and compressive strength of the rock. Brittleness and ductility with the former being one of the most important rock properties that impact drill-ability of rocks, are also key parameters when striving to identify

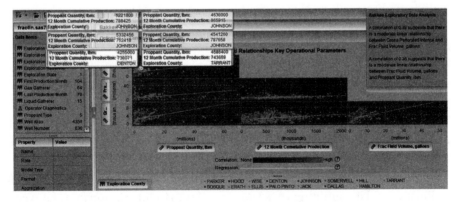

Figure 8.8   Correlations and Regressions in Bakken Proppant Parameters

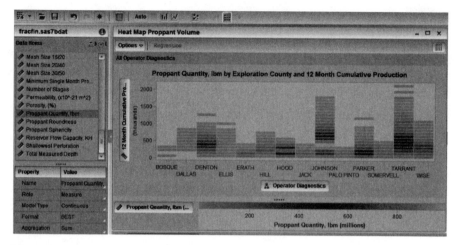

Figure 8.9 Heat Map Detailing Cumulative Production by County

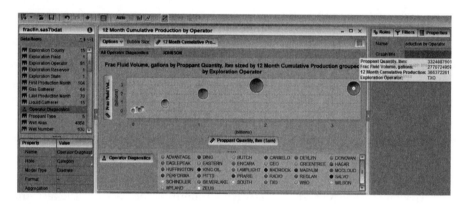

Figure 8.10 Bubble Plot Detailing Frac Fluid Volume and Proppant Quantity

field development strategies around well placement and optimized production. Analysis in offset wells and a good knowledge of the field geology is the best way to realize a realistic forecast of the future well's formations and their geomechanical properties.

The majority of wells drilled in the Bakken are horizontal with laterals ranging from 8,500 to 10,000 feet at vertical depths close to 10,000 feet. To optimize production, it is essential to ascertain the most effective fracture treatment designs and to determine well completion fracture stages introducing PLT data. We shall discuss such studies in the next case study, carried out in the Pinedale Anticline asset.

AI-based reservoir models use pattern-recognition capabilities of artificial intelligence and data mining (AI&DM) in order to build relationships between fluid production, reservoir characteristics, and operational constraints. This is indeed a new way of looking at a reservoir and its fluid-flow behavior. This is a technology at its infancy. It requires input from major players, including scientists, engineers, academicians, service companies, IOCs, NOCs, and independents to grow and mature. This technology has the potential to contribute to the art and science of reservoir simulation and modeling and add to the existing set of tools that are currently used in our industry for reservoir management.

Producers seek the most productive zones in their shale basins, as well as continued improvement in hydraulic fracturing processes. Decreasing costs and reducing risk while maximizing shale gas production necessitates innovative, advanced analytical capabilities that can give you a comprehensive understanding of the reservoir heterogeneity with the following benefits:

■ Extract hidden predictive information.

■ Identify drivers and leading indicators of efficient well production and well placement.

■ Determine the best intervals for stimulation.

■ Recommend optimum stimulation processes and frequencies.

Modeling, simulating, and predicting well productivity requires integrated exploratory, predictive, and forecasting capabilities underpinned by advanced analytical models to unlock the true potential of each wellbore. Without the critical insight enabled by integrated analysis to pair productivity analysis with economic feasibility, companies face significant risk and uncertainty when developing new wells or optimizing production of extant wellbores.

Pinedale Asset

To attain the most efficient completion strategy in the unconventional reservoirs such as the Bakken and the Pinedale assets, it is necessary to perform a multivariate analytical suite of workflows that identify the most important parameters to impact performance. Where do we drill the next wellbore? Can we implement the historical data observed in other wellbores across the same structure—an anticline in the case of the Pinedale asset in Wyoming?

Huckabee and Minquan[4] discuss the use of multivariate analysis (MVA) to evaluate critical performance variables important in optimizing hydraulic fracture treatment. Their paper (SPE 135523) discusses the challenges associated with single variable analysis (SVA) and the successful use of multivariant neural network models for optimizing tight gas completion techniques. This work was done with data from 2009 development activities at the Pinedale Anticline Field in western Wyoming.

The analysis used information from over 50 fluvial sand packages in a single wellbore over 5000 feet of vertical section. Single variable analysis had been performed previously to identify correlations and trends impacting fracture stimulation performance. These techniques proved unsatisfactory as an approach to understanding fracture optimization. The MVA approach addressed the complexity inherent in the data's coincident variation in multiple parameters.

A neural network was chosen among many MVA techniques to evaluate both reservoir parameters as well as variables that are controlled by the operator, such as proppant volume and flowback methods. Current computational capabilities and easy-to-use predictive modeling software were components in the decision to use this approach.

Input data included general well information from 211 wells and 2399 stages, production logging tool (PLT) data, stimulation treatment data, petrophysical data for formations and sands, flowback data, proppant type, proppant volume, and well production data. Details of each of these categories of data are outlined in the SPE paper 135523. The purpose of the analysis was to identify patterns among the poor and exceptional wells and thus appreciate the decreasing trend of stage production performance over time, identifying those factors that have the most impact on production. The disparate data systems had to be aggregated to produce a managed robust dataset conducive to effective exploratory data analysis. These two important steps are essential to identify plausible and efficient hypotheses worth testing and steer the decision makers toward sound modeling techniques.

Neural networks were developed to optimize fracture design and identify geologic sweet-spots (Figure 8.11). Data were grouped into nonoperational

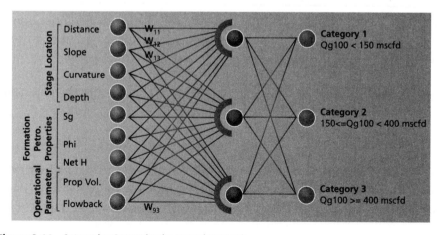

Figure 8.11 Categories Output by the Neural Network

geologic and petrophysical variables and operational completion variables. Some specific variables included distance, slope, curvature, depth, gas saturation (Sg), porosity (phi), net feet of petrophysical pay (NetH), proppant volume, and flowback.

Data clustering[5] was used to create different models and assess different parameters. Models were able to identify the relative impact of the most significant variables affecting stage production performance, and develop probability distributions for potential outcomes at different categories of production. The probability distributions provided a basis for completion optimization. Findings included identification of the impact of flowback procedures in total well performance, and the probable sensitivity to key geologic and petrophysical parameters that most affected performance. The stage gas rate at 100 days (Qg100) was determined to be the ideal comparison metric when analyzing the different partitions and/or categories of data focus, such as geologic subintervals, geographical areas, and proppant types.

There were three buckets that served as the output categories across the suite of neural networks, based on the comparable parameter, Qg100, which quantified the stage performance as a measure of gas production.

It was concluded that 80 percent of the influential parameters having the most impact on stage performance were nonoperational by nature. The remaining 20 percent were under the direct control of engineers formulating a hydraulic fracture strategy, deemed as operational (Figure 8.12).

The completion process discussed in this case study is limited to proppant volume optimization, and has currently not been applied to flowback methods, proppant type, or other operational variables. These areas represent additional opportunities to apply advanced MVA techniques. The process for completion application included initial data collection, calculation of physical properties, a multidisciplinary team "stage-out" meeting, simulation to determine stages, and the output of the exploratory data analysis into an analytical workflow to calculate sensitivity probability distributions for proppant volume.

Evaluation was conducted on 195 stages with 49 stages identified for increase in proppant volume. Through this process the authors identified a need to update the predictive model to include the impact of pressure depletion from down-spacing. Even in the absence of accounting for pressure depletion the team experienced excellent results.

The three key input parameters determined by the neural networks applied across the integrated datasets are:

1. Geological parameters used to characterize the stage location across the anticline
    a. *Distance:* How far away from the global maximum location at the peak of the anticline

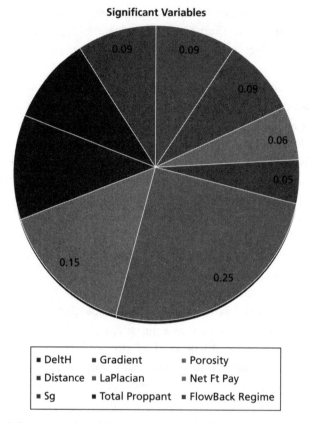

Significant Variables

- ▪ DeltH
- ▪ Gradient
- ▪ Porosity
- ▪ Distance
- ▪ LaPlacian
- ▪ Net Ft Pay
- ▪ Sg
- ▪ Total Proppant
- ▪ FlowBack Regime

Figure 8.12 Relative Impact of Most Significant Parameters on Stage Performance

    b. *Gradient:* Slope of structure gradient (first derivative)

    c. *LaPlacian:* LaPlace operator given by the divergence of the gradient of a function on Euclidean space; measure of concave or convex curvature (second derivative)

    d. *DeltH:* True vertical depth (TVD) from the top surface of the structure

2. Formation petrophysical properties impacting stage production

    a. Sg: Gas saturation

    b. Porosity

    c. Net ft of petrophysical pay

3. Operational parameters

    a. Total proppant

    b. Flowback regime

How do we design an optimized completions strategy for another wellbore across the anticline?

First, we must perform a sequence of exploratory data analysis visualizations to surface hidden patterns and fully comprehend the relationships or trends in the significant variables enumerated in Figure 8.12.

If we study the stage performance based on the formation petrophysical parameters alone (Figure 8.13), we note that the greatest impact on stage productivity is witnessed in stages 4, 5, 7, and 9; conversely, the worst stages are 1, 2, and 3. The objective function total proppant dictates the size of the bubbles and the comparable normalized parameter, Qg100, determines the color.

The petrophysical parameters visualized in Figure 8.14 underline the similarities in distribution across all stages when seen from a category or production perspective. Again, the size and color of the bubble reflect the total proppant and Qg100, respectively. The bubble plot endorses the variance in stage production rate across the categorical buckets but emphasizes the even distribution as expected.

As we shift our attention to the study of each of the geological parameters we start to develop the predictive model that will identify the optimum functional relationship of those parameters that enable best practices for completion across the anticline. Figure 8.15 visualizes two of the geological parameters, LaPlacian and the distance from the peak of the anticline from a stage and wellbore perspective. It is very interesting to note those stages that reflect the best and worst performance as well as the associated total proppant for each wellbore.

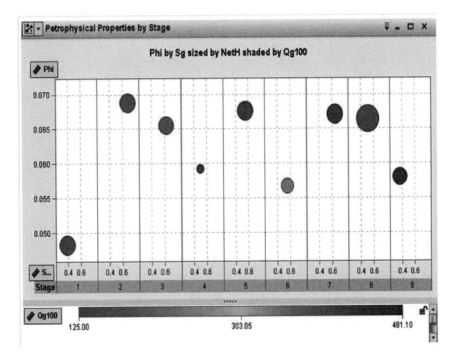

Figure 8.13 Study of the Petrophysical Parameters by Stage

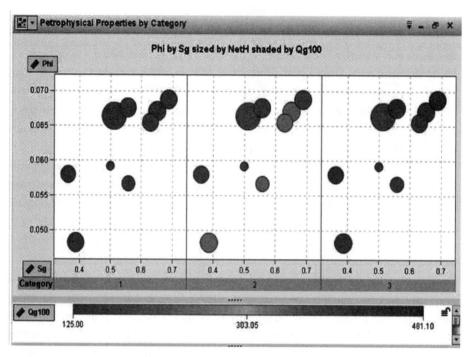

Figure 8.14 Study of the Petrophysical Parameters by Category

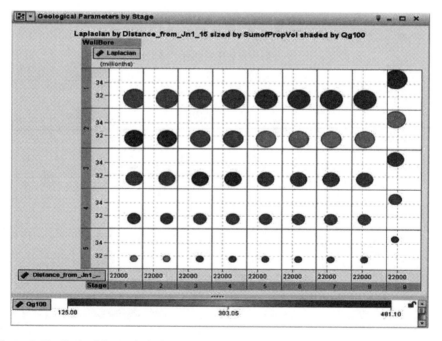

Figure 8.15 Study of the Geological Parameters across the Anticline

Best Wellbore/Stages Production Rates:

- Wellbore 2, stages 1 and 2
- Wellbore 9, stages 5–9

Worst Wellbore/Stages Production Rates:

- Wellbore 3, stages 5–9
- Wellbore 5, stages 5–9
- Wellbores 6 and 8, stages 1 and 2
- Wellbore 9, stages 3 and 4

Remember that the geological parameters represent characteristics locating the wellbore across the anticline. We can quickly identify via a suite of visualizations similar to Figure 8.15 what the location parameters and their intrinsic values are for an optimum stage production based on an optimum amount of proppant for future wellbores.

Let us now visualize the stage performance across all wellbores within a single well to identify those wellbores that not only reflect high or low gas production normalized to the PLT data but also identify the correlated trends

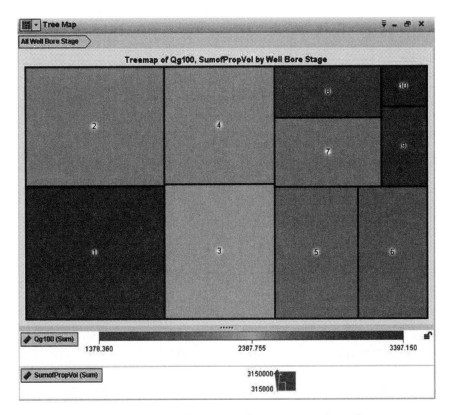

Figure 8.16 Tree Map for the Stage Performance and Proppant Usage by Wellbore

in proppant usage. Figure 8.16 details such a visualization in the form of a tree map. Note the two best performing wellbores: 1 and 10. The antithesis of these wellbores can be seen clearly in wellbore 8. Figure 8.16 allows us to drill into the area named "10" that obviously not only represents the best stage performance but also effectively utilizes the smaller quantity of proppant compared to wellbore 1. This drilling process enables Figure 8.17 to be viewed.

From Figure 8.17 it is apparent which stages in wellbore 10 generate the most cumulative gas (5–9) and which stage is ostensibly a very poor performer (1). Can we close in stage 1 when drilling across this part of the anticline?

It is now feasible to optimize a completion strategy based on the values of the geological parameters used to characterize stage location:

- Distance away from global maximum location at the peak of the anticline
- Slope of the structure gradient
- Curvature measured as a second derivative
- True vertical depth from the top of the structure

To supplement the completion strategy from an operational perspective, we can identify a range of optimum values for said parameters in wellbore 10 and

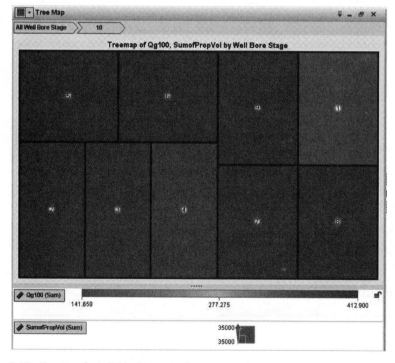

Figure 8.17 Tree Map for Individual Stage Performance and Proppant in Wellbore 10

couple that with the understanding that stage 1 could be closed and the ideal proppant volume could be established from Figure 8.17 for all the remaining stages.

The final step in the analytical workflow is the most important. It takes the study beyond an academic exercise. Let us operationalize the model based on the results in the exploratory data analysis steps.

Operationalize the Model

Some of the inherent soft computing techniques adopted to optimize a completion strategy are:

- Linear and nonlinear models
- Integer and mixed integer programming
- Quadratic models
- Stochastic and dynamic programming

Having explored the data to surface hidden relationships and trends, we developed hypotheses worth modeling. The individual independent variables were ranked in accordance to the correlations visualized and the results of the parametric modeling.

Identifying the most important variables that have a major statistical impact on the objective function, we can position those operational parameters such as proppant volume and number of stages in unison with wellbore location parameters that characterize the geological environment for maximum reservoir contact.

Formulating a function $f(x)$ where x reflects the key production indicators (operational and geologic parameters) it is possible to attain a workable model that can answer *what-if* questions and provide values of said parameters optimized for performance and completion strategy. The engineer submits values for those independent parameters that influence $f(x)$ (proppant volumes in this instance) and designs a completion strategy based on the geological parameters used to characterize the stage location across the anticline, determining maximum reservoir contact and the number of stages conducive with maximum hydrocarbon production.

Innovative Analytical Workflow in Mature Fields

What is a *mature field*? Let us assume that we have a long production history with multiple wells drilled. Some of the aging fields across the globe, for example in Saudi Arabia, feature well numbers in their thousands with 50+ years of continuous production. In the early stages of the well lifecycle few data are available save production owing to the lack of sensors and infrequency of well logs and core data. Essentially, we need to optimize reengineering strategies based on a suite of advanced analytical methodologies that mine the production data.

The approach embraces the following workflows:

- Exploratory data analysis
- Nonlinear regression and transformation
- Extraction of key indicators of production
- Multivariate statistical analysis
- Hierarchical clustering
- Field segmentation

Exploratory Data Analysis

The long production history inherently results in multiple development and drilling campaigns characterized by the different technology stacks, both in hardware and software, contemporaneous to the period under study. This continuously evolving process challenges the interpretation and deterministic evaluations of the historical data. It is essential to aggregate all pertinent data; invariably this is exclusively production data collated across multiple temporal stages in the well's lifecycle.

The exploratory data analysis step identifies patterns and surfaces hidden relationships among the temporal data: rates of fluids and cumulative volumes for each well. Spatial data are scarce but if available should be integrated to enrich the data under study.

Adopting the suite of Tukey visualizations discussed at length in Chapters 3, 4, and 9, it is feasible to segment the temporal data to identify outliers, impute missing data, and correlate those periods of good performance with any hard data associated with wells, including reservoir characteristics and formation petrophysical parameters such as porosity and net feet of pay.

Nonlinear Regression and Transformation

Studying the available production data, we concentrate on the daily quantity of produced oil as well as the water cut and any daily gas production. Owing to historical mechanical problems across the well portfolio and the frequency of remediation strategies and/or interference patterns across neighboring wells, it is clear that fundamental modeling is requisite prior to adoption of any multivariate analysis.

The next step studies the type curves across the segmented temporal data to identify predicted values and ascertain intervals of confidence.

$$Qo = QoMax / (1 + b\,Di\,(date - firstDate))^b$$

$$\text{Or } Qo = QoMax / (1 + EXPR)^a$$

where $EXPR = derQo * (date - firstDate) / a$

The values QoMax are found in the data; a and derQo are yielded by the nonlinear regression procedure. The differences between the observed production data values and those values predicted via the type curves (the hyperbolic model gave the best fit) resulted in the residuals that provided indicators of good and poor performance for each well under study.

The water cut evolution is challenging, especially in heterogeneous reservoirs with long WAG or water-flooding strategies. A LOWESS smoothing methodology that implements a nonlinear regression algorithm in a mobile window was introduced to interpolate and extrapolate a smoothed set of water-cut values. The gas–oil ratio (GOR) trends were smoothed adopting a similar workflow.

Extraction of Key Indicators of Production

We extracted attributes from the models described thus far to compile a suite of two-dimensional parameters conducive to a multivariate analytical workflow. Some of the attributes included the maximum of the Qo values, Qo_{max}, the Qo value uncovered one, two, or three years after Qo_{max}, the ratio between the Qo_{max} and the final Qo, and so on. Other derived attributes included initial and final values for the smoothed curves (water cut and GOR) the time to obtain different levels such as 1, 10, 25, and 50 percent, and so on.

From the initial raw datasets that included wells and temporal readings for liquid rates, a two-dimensional tabulation of wells against attributes is ascertained. The temporal component has been removed ostensibly even though it is integrated indirectly into a few of the key production indicators studied in the next step, which implements a multivariate analysis.

Multivariate Statistical Analysis

The first step in an MVS workflow is a factor analysis process such as principal component analysis (PCA) to reduce the number of attributes and thus condense the input space. PCA is a statistical approach to convert a set of observations of possibly correlated variables into a corresponding set of values of linearly uncorrelated variables. This transformation is enacted such that the first principal component has the largest possible variance to reflect as much of the variability in the data as possible, with subsequent components in turn representing the highest variance possible vis-à-vis the constraint that it be orthogonal to and thus uncorrelated with the preceding components.

Hierarchical Clustering

The table of data established is then analyzed using a hierarchical clustering algorithm. The methodology establishes the most similar wells based on characteristics defined in the algorithm (Figure 8.18). Hierarchical clustering[6] is a process that starts with each point in its own cluster. At each step, the two clusters that are closest together are combined into a single cluster. This process continues until there is only one cluster containing all the points. This type of clustering is good for smaller datasets (a few thousand observations) as generated by the set of wells, attributes pairs in the previous steps.

To enhance the clustering process a discriminant analysis is performed to provide the probabilities of each well's membership in its given cluster.

Field Segmentation

The clusters are mapped and cross-validated with conclusions established from other studies such as sedimentology or structural models. The statistical results enable determination of the most representative well in each cluster. Any summation per cluster is indicative of the net contribution of each well to the cumulative production across the field. The good and bad performers are thus

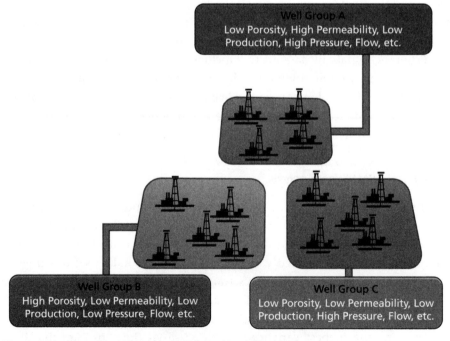

Figure 8.18 Hierarchical Clustering of Wells and Associated Attributes

mapped across the static model and corroborate the reservoir characteristics and reliability of fracture networks as the field is compartmentalized based on the fluid rates that profile each well in each cluster. This methodology corroborates the environment of deposition, sequence stratigraphy, framework, compartmentalization, and reservoir quality.

Recovery Factor Analysis

What are the most influential factors on the recovery of oil in conventional reservoirs?

- The characteristics of the producing formation, such as the porosity, permeability, interstitial or connate water content; and the uniformity, continuity, and structural configuration
- The properties of the reservoir oil, including its viscosity, shrinkage, and quantity of gas in solution
- The operating controls, including control of the available expulsive forces, the rate of oil production, gas and water production, and the pressure behavior
- The well conditions, structural location, and spacing

Volumetric Estimation of OOIP

Adopting a probabilistic approach to calculate original oil in place is desirable in addition to the deterministic methodology. Invariably there are never enough data from well logs or cores to accurately determine the average input values such as porosity, permeability, and fluid saturation. Adopting a probabilistic methodology encompasses a range of values for each variable. Thus there is a range from a minimum to a maximum with some statistical distribution to compute the probability of potential answers. It is widely accepted that reservoir properties such as porosity and net thickness fall into particular quantifiable probability distribution patterns. And such patterns could be triangular, random, normal, or log-normal. Thus it may be advantageous to implement a Monte Carlo simulation based on distributions of reservoir parameters. Such a simulation can generate a large array of values for the target result, such as OOIP, and then assign a range of probability values to it. It is also observed frequently that reservoir properties tend to follow a log-normal distribution when implementing probabilistic analysis.

It is customary to report predicted answers for the 10, 50, and 90 percent cumulative probabilities. However, this technique necessitates a large amount of data.

The probabilistic approach encompasses the following:

- An S-curve plot of all the results assigns a probability to each of the possible answers.
- The confidence envelope surrounding the probabilities is dependent on number of simulations.
- The analysis generally requires 500 to 10,000 simulations.
- Variables are constrained to limited ranges.
- Random numbers are used to assign precise values for each input variable.
- A different set of random numbers is used for each successive calculation.

Having determined OOIP via Monte Carlo simulation in order to discover the 10, 50, and 90 percent probabilities, and implementing the same data along with the following reservoir and fluid properties:

- Permeability
- Oil viscosity
- Bubble-point pressure
- Oil formation volume factor at bubble-point pressure

Estimate the various probabilities associated with the recovery factor and oil reserve.

Other Models under Consideration

Neural net models are not really interpretable. They are a way to form a complex predictive model, but the parameters cannot easily be interpreted. Neural networks are particularly useful for solving problems that cannot be expressed as a series of steps, such as recognizing patterns, classifying into groups, series prediction, and data mining. Pattern recognition is perhaps the most common use for neural networks. Adopting a possible filtered Monte Carlo simulation for inverse design, of which running an artificial neural network is one component step, is also a possibility to determine the constraints of those reservoir properties that influence the recovery factor *a priori*.

Stepwise Regression Model

A multivariable, stepwise, linear regression program was employed that successively sought to add independent variables, which represent reservoir data in a stepwise manner so as to progressively increase the quality of the fit of the regression equation to the data.

The *stepwise procedure* is ideal when there are many independent variables to choose from in developing a regression model. The stepwise procedure is most helpful for exploratory analysis because it can give insight into the relationships between the independent variables and the dependent or response variable. However, the stepwise procedure is not guaranteed to give the "best" model for your data, or even the model with the largest R^2. In the stepwise procedure variables are added one by one to the model. The F-statistic for variable screening must be significant for variables to enter the model. After a new variable is added, the stepwise method looks at all the variables already included in the model and removes any variable that does not produce a significant F-statistic (significance is determined by entry and exit parameters set in the algorithm). Only after this check is made and the necessary deletions accomplished can another variable be added to the model. The stepwise process ends when none of the variables outside the model has an F-statistic significant at the entry parameter setting and every variable already included in the model is significant at the stay parameter setting. The stepwise procedure can also end when the variable to be added to the model is the variable just deleted from the model.

The F-statistic is given by:

$$F = \frac{SSR / k}{SSE/(n-k-1)} = \frac{SSR / k}{s^2} = \frac{MSR}{MSE}$$

for $F_{K.}, n-k-1$.

Criteria for Choice of Best Model

Selecting the best regression model from a candidate pool of developed models can be complicated due to the uncertainty of choosing the terms to be included in the model.

The model builder should consider prior views and prejudices regarding the importance of individual variables. In addition, the model builder should learn something about the system from which the data are taken. This may involve nothing more than the knowledge of the "sign" of a coefficient and can be accounted for by conducting a variable selection or variable screening exercise.

Prediction Criteria

The goal is to combine "selection of best model" with model validation.

- Coefficient of determination (R^2)

$$R^2 = \frac{SS_{reg}}{SS_{total}} = \frac{\sum_{i=1}^{n}(\hat{y}_i - \bar{y})^2}{\sum_{i=1}^{n}(y_i - \bar{y})^2}$$

- Proportion of variation in the response data that is explained by the model.

- An increase in R^2 does not imply that the additional model term is needed, R^2 can be made artificially high by over-fitting (by including too many model terms).

- Mean squared error : s^2 (MSE)

$$MSE = SSE / (n - k - 1)$$

MSE plays an important role in hypothesis testing and confidence bounds. To get narrow confidence intervals and accurate estimates s^2 must be as small as possible. The value R^2 can be increased by adding more terms to the model. However, the addition of unnecessary variables may result in an increase in MSE. Thus, the real task is to balance R^2 and MSE.

- PRESS statistic (prediction sum of squares)

$$\mathbf{PRESS} = \sum_{i=1}^{n}(y_i - \hat{y}_{i,-i})^2$$
$$= \sum_{i=1}^{n}(\varepsilon_{i,-i})^2$$

The PRESS statistic is used with a set of data in which we withhold or set aside the first observation from the sample and use the remaining n–1 observations to estimate the coefficients for a particular candidate model. PRESS residuals are true prediction errors with $\hat{y}_{i,-i}$ being independent y_i. The observation y_i was not simultaneously used for fit and model assessment. The PRESS residuals give separate measures of the stability of the regression and they can help the analyst to isolate which data points have a sizable influence on the outcome of the regression.

- Mallow's Cp

    Cp is a measure of total squared error defined as:

$$Cp = \frac{SSE}{s^2} - (n - 2p) \quad \text{where } p = k + 1$$

where s^2 is the MSE for the full model and SSE is the sum-of-squares error for a model with p variables plus the intercept. If Cp is graphed with p, Mallows recommends the model where Cp first approaches p.

Four criteria (in order of importance with 1 most important):

1. PRESS (want small)

2. Cp (near $k + 1$) (small)

3. MSE, s^2 (small; if a model is underspecified, s^2 is overestimated)

4. R^2 (large)

The stepwise procedure will generate Cp, MSE, R^2, and the F-statistic as output data. The relative size of the PRESS statistic, Cp, MSE, and R^2 is used to develop a more statistically correct model. In addition, a more complete analysis of residuals is necessary for the detection of violation of assumptions. For example, residuals must be independent of the independent variables. Most importantly, the parameters included in the regression models developed should make sense from a petroleum engineering perspective. The developed equations are formulated from the respective original variable lists representative of carbonate and sandstone reservoirs and the associated drive mechanism, be it water drive or solution-gas drive. The four criteria select the important variables that would most influence the recovery factor for each scenario, with the coefficients for each variable identified as the values ascertained from the stepwise algorithm.

NOTES

1. S. Mohaghegh, A. Modavi, Hafez H. Hafez, and Masoud Haajizadeh, "Development of Surrogate Reservoir Models for Fast Track Analysis of Complex Reservoirs," SPE 99667, Intelligent Energy Conference and Exhibition, Amsterdam, The Netherlands, April 11–13, 2006.

2. Robert N. Hatton, Ken Porter, "Optimization of Gas-Injected Oil Wells," SAS Global Forum, Paper 195–2011, Caesars Palace, Las Vegas, April 4–7, 2011.

3. J. J. Arps, "Analysis of Decline Curves," *Transactions of the American Institute of Mining Engineers* 160 (1945): 228–247.

4. P. Huckabee, J. Minquan, R. Lund, D. Nasse, and K. Williams, "Tight Gas Well Performance Evaluation with Neural Network Analysis for Hydraulic Propped Fracture Treatment Optimization," SPE 135523, ATCE, September 2010.

5. K. A. Jain, and R. C. Dubes, *Algorithms for Clustering Data* (Upper Saddle River, NJ: Prentice Hall, 1988), 319.

6. J.-P. Valois, "Robust Approach in Hierarchical Clustering: Application to the Sectorization of an Oil Field," paper presented at the *7th Internal Federation of Classification Soc.*, Namur, Belgium, July 2000 (to be published by Springer Verlag, Berlin).

CHAPTER 9

Exploratory and Predictive Data Analysis

We are overwhelmed by information, not because there is too much, but because we don't know how to tame it. Information lies stagnant in rapidly expanding pools as our ability to collect and warehouse it increases, but our ability to make sense of and communicate it remains inert, largely without notice.

Stephen Few, *Now You See It*

*E*xploratory data analysis is an approach to analyzing data for the purpose of formulating hypotheses worth testing, complementing the tools of conventional statistics for testing hypotheses. It was so named by John Tukey to contrast with *confirmatory data analysis*, the term used for the set of ideas about hypothesis testing, *p*-values, and confidence intervals (CIs).

Tukey suggested that too much emphasis in statistics was placed on statistical hypothesis testing (confirmatory data analysis); essentially more emphasis had to be placed on enabling data to suggest hypotheses worth testing (exploratory data analysis). We must not muddle the two types of analyses; formulating workflows that convolve them on the same set of data can lead to systematic bias owing to the issues inherent in testing hypotheses suggested by the data.

The exploratory phase "isolates patterns and features of the data and reveals these forcefully to the analyst."[1] If a model is fit to the data, exploratory analysis finds patterns that represent deviations from the model. These patterns lead the analyst to revise the model via an iterative approach. In contrast, confirmatory data analysis "quantifies the extent to which deviations from a model could be expected to occur by chance."[2] Confirmatory analysis uses the traditional statistical tools of inference, significance, and confidence. Exploratory data analysis is sometimes compared to detective work: It is the process of gathering evidence. Confirmatory data analysis is comparable to a court trial: It is the process of evaluating evidence. Exploratory analysis and confirmatory analysis "can—and should—proceed side by side."[3]

Modern computer technology with its attendant high-powered graphic screens displaying multiple, linkable windows enables dynamic, simultaneous views on the data. A map of the position of sample data in space or representations along the time axis can be linked with histograms, correlation diagrams, variogram clouds, and experimental variograms. It is thus feasible to garner important spatial, time, and multivariate structure ideas from a host of simple but powerful displays. The data typically analyzed in reservoir characterization projects can be visualized in one, two, and three dimensions, with the one-dimensional perspective leading inexorably and logically to the next dimension, and so forth, until a comprehensive appreciation of the underlying structure of the data explicates and corroborates appropriate modeling techniques whence viable and reliable conclusions can be ascertained for efficient field management strategies to exploit extant reservoirs.

Predictive analytics enable you to quickly derive evidence-based insights, take impactful decisions, and improve performance across the E&P value chain. Running your processing, refining, or petrochemical plant at peak performance is a critical factor for success, but there are times when events or special unforeseen factors prevent operators from achieving this goal. The trick is to learn how to predict when outages may occur, using data that are available for the wide range of variables that impact these processes, such as temperature, chemical composition degradation, mechanical wear and tear, or the simple life expectancy of a valve seal. By integrating data from a variety of process sources with knowledge and experience databases, operations can boost uptime, performance, and productivity while lowering maintenance costs and downtime. This is attainable by building a predictive model, calibrated by a root-cause analytical methodology that starts with a data quality control workflow, followed by development of an appropriate spatiotemporal data mart, and finally an exploratory data analysis step.

EXPLORATION AND PRODUCTION VALUE PROPOSITIONS

Statistical thinking will one day be as necessary for efficient citizenship as the ability to read and write.

H. G. Wells

Producers seek the most productive zones in their unconventional basins, as well as continued improvement in hydraulic fracturing processes, as they explore and drill new wells into a resource that requires careful strategic planning not only to increase performance but to reduce negative impacts on the environment. Decreasing costs and reducing risk while maximizing gas production necessitates innovative, advanced analytical capabilities that can give you a comprehensive understanding of the reservoir heterogeneity in order to extract hidden predictive information, identify drivers and leading indicators of efficient well production, determine the best intervals for stimulation, and recommend optimum stimulation processes and frequencies.

Following are some high-level steps in a study for an unconventional reservoir that concentrated on the influence of proppant and fracture fluid volumes, with extended analytical projects around other operational parameters to determine an ideal hydraulic fracture treatment strategy that could be used as an analog in new wells.

The operator in the unconventional reservoir wished to identify the impact of the proppant and fracture fluid volumes on performance across some 11,000 wells, of which some 8000 wells were in the public domain. Is there a correlation, and if so, how strong is the relationship between proppant/fracture fluid volumes and performance?

The adoption of data management workflows, exploratory data analysis (EDA), and predictive modeling enabled them to cluster the operational and nonoperational variables that most impacted each well's performance and hence identify characteristics of good and bad wells. How were these good/bad wells distributed across the asset? Did the wells map to the current geologic model? Who operated the good and bad wells? Some of the questions were answered through a data-driven methodology that could throw light on business issues when exploiting unconventional reservoirs.

The operator faced many challenges, such as the inability to:

■ Understand impact of proppant and fracture fluid volumes on production and enumerate key production indicators that increase performance.

■ Isolate significant variables impacting the hydraulic fracture process.

■ Understand interaction of multiple variables and quantify uncertainty in those variables.

■ Understand why some oil/gas wells are deemed good and others poor, although they are drilled with similar tactics in ostensibly similar geologic strata.

The study demanded an exploration of the volumes of proppant and fracture fluid utilized by various operators traversing multiple counties, geographically distributed across the asset. A target variable or objective function of cumulative gas is defined and an EDA performed to understand the influence of operational parameters upon the target variable. Hidden patterns and trends in those parameters deemed important as influencers on the cumulative production, either as an agent of increase or decrease in gas production, are identified or further investigated. The main objective is to understand the relationship between proppant usage (volumes and type), well profiles, and geospatial location with production levels. The premise is that advanced analytics can provide insight into the complexity of how selected proppants relate to production in a variety of wells. Proppant is a large cost factor in the unconventional drilling process; the optimization of proppant usage will lead to substantial savings. Currently, the operator has a basic understanding of the effects of these types on production variables (bivariate analysis). It was proposed that an advanced statistical multivariate analysis be studied to find patterns that can lead to deeper understanding on how proppant factors can impact (or not) production levels.

The solution enabled descriptive analysis of the analytical data warehouse, plus workflows to analyze the impact of the different variables on production, using bivariate correlation analysis and multivariate predictive models using techniques such as decision trees, regression, and supervised neural networks. Additional techniques like SOM and unsupervised neural networks enabled insight to the relationships between performance and the operational parameters of a hydraulic fracture treatment plan.

The study resulted in a reduction in proppant volume across multiple wells, controlling costs and indirectly having a positive impact on the topside footprint. Thus, optimizing well performance has a positive impact from an environmental perspective. The objective function, cumulative production, may not have been improved across some wells, but a 30 percent decrease in proppant for those wells was shown to be ideal to exploit similar gas production, resulting in massive savings annually in operational expenditure.

EDA COMPONENTS

EDA itself can be partitioned into five discrete component steps:

1. Univariate analysis
2. Bivariate analysis
3. Multivariate analysis
4. Data transformation
5. Discretization

Univariate Analysis

The univariate analysis sketches the data and enumerates the traditional descriptors such as mean, median, mode, and standard deviation. In analyzing sets of numbers you first want to get a feel for the dataset at hand and ask such questions as the following: What are the smallest and largest values? What

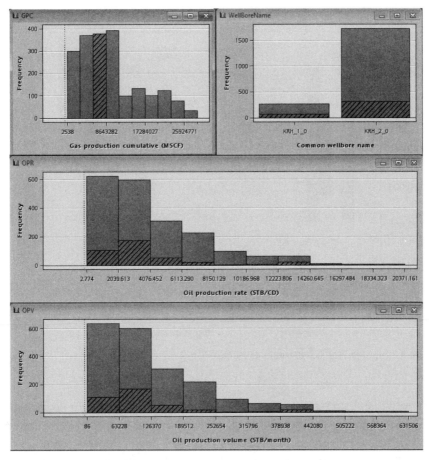

Figure 9.1 Histograms Depicting Dynamic Relationships between Gas Production, Wellbore, Oil Production Rate, and Oil Production Volume

might be a good single representative number for this set of data? What is the amount of variation or spread? Are the data clustered around one or more values, or are they spread uniformly over some interval? Can they be considered symmetric? You can explore the distributions of nominal variables by using bar charts. You can explore the univariate distributions of interval variables by using histograms and box plots.

A histogram is an estimate of the density or the distribution of values for a single measure of data (Figure 9.1). The range of the variable is divided into a certain number of subintervals, or bins. The height of the bar in each bin is proportional to the number of data points that have values in that bin. A series of bars represents the number of observations in the measure that match a specific value or value range. The bar height can represent either the exact number of observations or the percentage of all observations for each value range.

Descriptive statistics embrace the quantitative appreciation inherent in a dataset. To be distinguished from both inferential and inductive statistics,

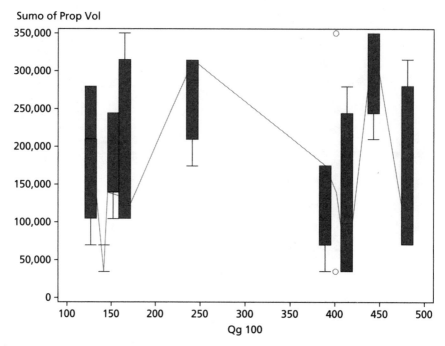

Figure 9.2 Outlier Detection Implementing a Box Plot

descriptive statistics strive to summarize a data sample taken from a population and hence are not evolved on the basis of probability theory. The measures generally used to describe a dataset depict central tendency and variability. Measures of central tendency include the mean, median, and mode while measures of variability include the standard deviation (or variance), the minimum and maximum values of the variables, kurtosis, and skewness. *Kurtosis* reflects the "peakedness" of a probability distribution describing its shape. A high kurtosis distribution has a sharper peak and longer, fatter tails while a low kurtosis distribution has a more rounded peak and shorter, thinner tails. *Skewness* is a measure of the extent to which a probability distribution "favors" one side of the mean. Thus its value can be either positive or negative.

A box plot as depicted in Figures 9.2 and 9.3 summarizes the distribution of data sampled from a continuous numeric variable. The central line in a box plot indicates the median of the data while the edges of the box indicate the first and third quartiles (i.e., the 25th and 75th percentiles). Extending from the box are whiskers that represent data that are a certain distance from the median. Beyond the whiskers are outliers: observations that are relatively far from the median.

Quantitative terms of operational and nonoperational parameters in E&P are essential to tabulate, in addition to pictorial representation. In Figure 9.3

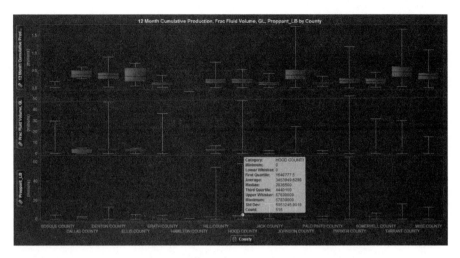

Figure 9.3 Box and Whiskers for Descriptive Statistics of Operational Parameters

we see the average, mean, minimum, and maximum as well as the first and third quartile of cumulative production, fracture fluid, and proppant volumes.

Bivariate Analysis

One can explore the relationship between two (or more) nominal variables by using a mosaic chart. One can also explore the relationship between two variables by using a scatterplot. Usually the variables in a scatterplot are interval variables. If one has a time variable, one can observe the behavior of one or more variables over time with a line plot. One can also use line plots to visualize a response variable (and, optionally, fitted curves and confidence bands) versus values of an explanatory variable. One can create and explore maps with a polygon plot.

The rank correlation coefficient depicted in Figure 9.4 is a useful statistical tool for comparing two variables. Unlike the correlation coefficient, which can be influenced by extreme values within the dataset (impacting the mean and variance), the rank correlation coefficient is not affected significantly. Therefore, it is a relatively robust measure and may enable detection of any measurement errors, especially if there is a noticeable difference between the values. The correlation coefficient is 0.9272 and the rank correlation coefficient is 0.8971, indicating very little local bias in this relationship.

A mosaic plot is a set of adjacent bar plots formed first by dividing the horizontal axis according to the proportion of observations in each category of the first variable and then by dividing the vertical axis according to the proportion of observations in the second variable. For more than two nominal variables, this process can be continued by further horizontal or vertical subdivision. The area of each block is proportional to the number of observations it represents.

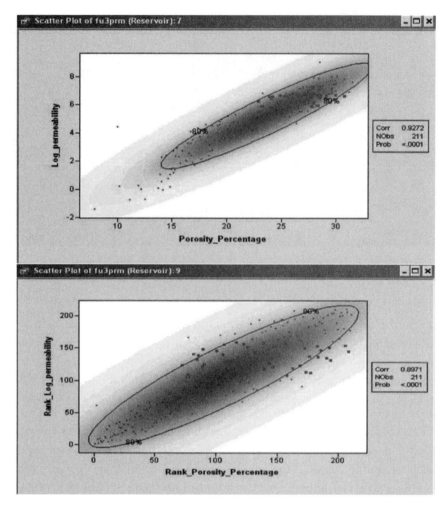

Figure 9.4 3D Scatterplot Surfacing Relationship between Porosity, Permeability, and Water Saturation

The polygon plot can display arbitrary polylines and polygons. To create a polygon plot, you need to specify at least three variables. The coordinates of vertices of each polygon (or vertices of a piecewise-linear polyline) are specified with X and Y variables. The polygon is drawn in the order in which the coordinates are specified. A third nominal variable specifies an identifier to which each coordinate belongs.

Multivariate Analysis

Multivariate analysis examines relationships between two or more variables, implementing algorithms such as linear or multiple regression, correlation coefficient, cluster analysis, and discriminant analysis.

One can explore the relationships between three variables by using a rotating scatterplot. Often the three variables are interval variables. If one of the variables can be modeled as a function of the other two variables, then you can add a response surface to the rotating plot. Similarly, you can visualize contours of the response variable by using a contour plot.

A contour plot as shown in Figure 9.5 assumes that the Z variable is functionally related to the X and Y variables. That is, the Z variable can be modeled as a response variable of X and Y. A typical use of a contour plot is to visualize the response for a regression model of two continuous variables. Contour plots are most useful when the X and Y variables are nearly uncorrelated. The contour plot fits a piecewise-linear surface to the data, modeling Z as a response function of X and Y. The contours are level curves of the response function. By default, the minimum and maximum values of the Z variable are used to compute the contour levels.

Figure 9.5 also depicts a rotating plot in which one assumes that the Z variable is functionally related to the X and Y variables. That is, the Z variable can be modeled as a response variable of X and Y. A typical use of the rotating surface plot is to visualize the response surface for a regression model of two continuous variables. One can add the predicted values of the model to the data table. Then one can plot the predicted values as a function of the two regressor variables.

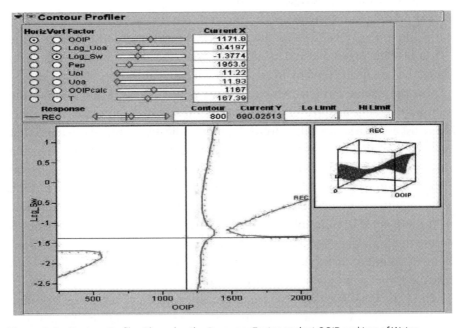

Figure 9.5 Contour Profiler Observing the Recovery Factor against OOIP and Log of Water Saturation

Data Transformation

The data transformation methodology encompasses the convenience of placing the data temporarily into a format applicable to particular types of analysis; for example, permeability is often transferred into logarithmic space to abide its relationship with porosity.

Discretization

Discretization embraces the process of coarsening or blocking data into layers consistent within a sequence-stratigraphic framework. Thus, well-log data or core properties can be resampled into this space.

EDA STATISTICAL GRAPHS AND PLOTS

There is a vast array of graphs and plots that can be utilized during the discovery phase of raw data. It is essential to know the relevance of these visualization techniques so as to garner maximum insight during the exploratory data analysis phase of data-driven modeling. Let us walk through several of the most important and useful visuals to enable an intuitive feel for the upstream data.

Box and Whiskers

The box plot in Figure 9.6 displays the distribution of data values by using a rectangular box and lines called "whiskers."

The bottom and top edges of the box indicate the *interquartile range* (IQR), that is, the range of values that are between the first and third quartiles (the 25th and 75th percentiles). The marker inside the box indicates the mean value. The line inside the box indicates the median value.

You can enable outliers, which are data points whose distances from the interquartile range are greater than 1.5 times the size of the interquartile range. The whiskers (lines protruding from the box) indicate the range of values that are outside of the interquartile range. If you do not enable outliers, then the whiskers extend to the maximum and minimum values in the plot. If you enable outliers, then the whiskers indicate the range of values that are outside of the interquartile range, but are close enough not to be considered outliers.

If there are a large number of outliers, then the range of outlier values is represented by a bar. The data tip for the bar displays additional information about the outliers. To explore the outliers, double-click on the outlier bar to view the values as a new histogram visualization.

The basic data roles for a box plot are categories and measures. You can assign one category only, and the category values are plotted on the category axis. You can assign many measures, and the measure values are plotted on the response axis. At least one measure is required.

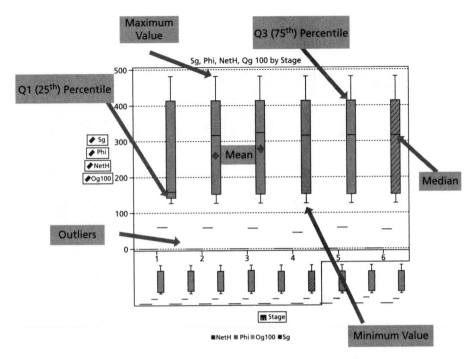

Figure 9.6 Box and Whiskers

Histograms

The principal utility of the histogram (Figure 9.7) is that it shows the relative class frequencies in the data and therefore provides information on the data density function. A widely used graphical display of univariate data is the histogram, which is essentially a bar plot of a frequency distribution that is organized in intervals or classes. The important visual information that can be gleaned from histograms encompasses central tendency, the dispersion, and the general shape of the distribution. However, quantitative summary or descriptive statistics provide a more accurate methodology of describing the reservoir data. In purely quantitative terms, the mean and the median define the central tendency, while data dispersion is expressed in terms of the range and the standard deviation.

Parameters of central tendency or location represent the most important measures for characterizing an empirical distribution. These values help locate the data on a linear scale. The most popular indicator of central tendency is the arithmetic mean, which is the sum of all data points divided by the number of observations. The median is often used as an alternative measure of the central tendency since the arithmetic mean is sensitive to outliers. Although outliers also affect the median, their absolute values do not influence it. Quantiles are a more general way of dividing the data sample into groups containing equal numbers of observations.

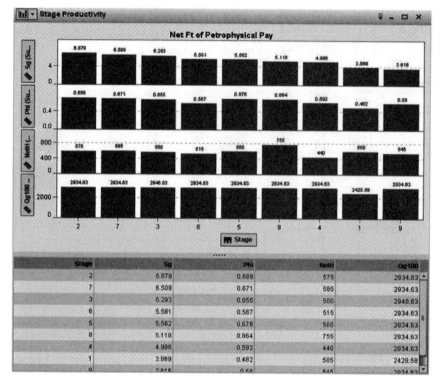

Figure 9.7 Histograms

Probability Plots

The graphical techniques described so far provide a reasonably good idea about the shape of the distribution of the data under investigation but do not determine how well a dataset conforms to a given theoretical distribution. A goodness-of-fit test could be used to decide if the data are significantly different from a given theoretical distribution; however, such a test would not tell us where and why the data differ from that distribution. A probability plot, on the other hand, not only demonstrates how well an empirical distribution fits a given distribution overall but also shows at a glance where the fit is acceptable and where it is not. There are two basic types of probability plots: P-P plots and Q-Q plots. Both can be used to compare two distributions with each other. The basic principles remain the same if one wants to compare two theoretical distributions, an empirical (or sample) distribution with a theoretical distribution, or two empirical distributions.

Let us follow a case study to optimize a hydraulic fracture strategy in an unconventional reservoir where the EDA techniques are enumerated and graphically detailed as we strive to increase production performance based on operational parameters that must be customized to the reservoir characteristics across the shale play.

Scatterplots

A scatterplot is a two- or three-dimensional visualization that shows the relationship of two- or three-measure data items. Each marker (represented by a symbol such as a dot, a square, or a plus sign) serves as an observation. The marker's position indicates the value for each observation. Use a scatterplot to examine the relationship between numeric data items.

The 3D scatter-graphs in Figure 9.8 are frequently used when the data are not arranged on a rectangular grid. Simple 3D scatter-graphs display an object or marker corresponding to each datum. More complicated scatter-graphs include datum-specific marker attributes, drop-lines, and combinations of the scatter data with additional objects such as a fitted surface.

3D scatterplots are used to plot data points on three axes in the attempt to show the relationship between three variables. Each row in the data table is represented by a marker whose position depends on its values in the columns set on the X, Y, and Z axes.

A fourth variable can be set to correspond to the color or size of the markers, thus adding yet another dimension to the plot.

The relationship between different variables is called *correlation*. If the markers are close to making a straight line in any direction in the three-dimensional

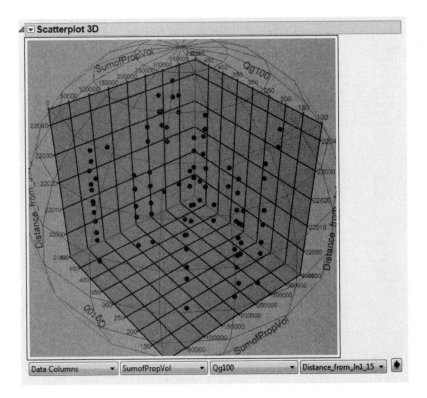

Figure 9.8 3D Scatterplot

space of the 3D scatterplot, the correlation between the corresponding variables is high. If the markers are equally distributed in the 3D scatterplot, the correlation is low, or zero. However, even though a correlation may seem to be present, this might not always be the case. The variables could be related to some fourth variable, thus explaining their variation, or pure coincidence might cause an apparent correlation.

You can change how the 3D scatterplot is viewed by zooming in and out as well as rotating it by using the navigation controls located in the top-right part of the visualization.

Heat Maps

Heat maps are a great way to compare data across two categories using color. The effect is to quickly see where the intersection of the categories is strongest and weakest. A heat map essentially displays the distribution of values for two data items by using a table with colored cells.

We use heat maps when we want to show the relationship between two factors. We could study segmentation analysis of a well portfolio, garner insight into well performance across reservoirs, or understand rig productivity based on engineering experience and rate of penetration.

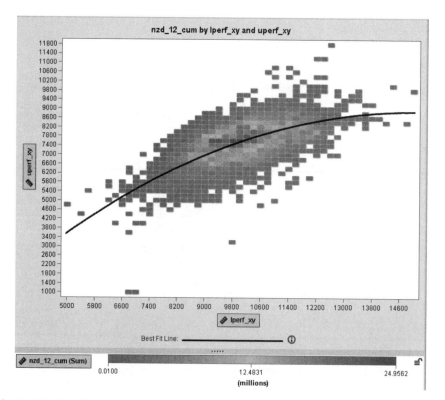

Figure 9.9 Heat Map

Figure 9.9 illustrates the potential comprehension surfaced by studying visually the 12-month cumulative gas production across an unconventional reservoir, noting the optimum upper and lower perforated stages. We also note the "best-fit line" that results in a quadratic fit plotted across the heat map to describe the relationship between the two variables when that relationship exhibits the "bowl shape" curvature typically defined by a quadratic function. If the points on the scatterplot are tightly clustered around the line, then it likely provides a good approximation for the relationship. If not, another fit line should be considered to represent the relationship.

Bubble Plots

A bubble plot (Figure 9.10) is a variation of a scatterplot in which the markers are replaced with bubbles. A bubble plot displays the relationships among at least three measures. Two measures are represented by the plot axes, and the third measure is represented by the size of the plot markers. Each bubble represents an observation. A bubble plot is useful for datasets with dozens to hundreds of values. A bubble's size is scaled relative to the minimum and maximum values of the size variable. The minimum and maximum sizes are illustrated in the plot legend.

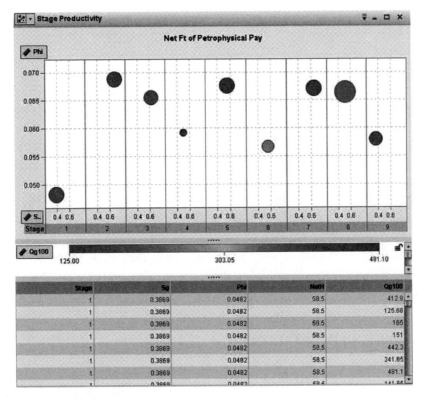

Figure 9.10 Bubble Plot

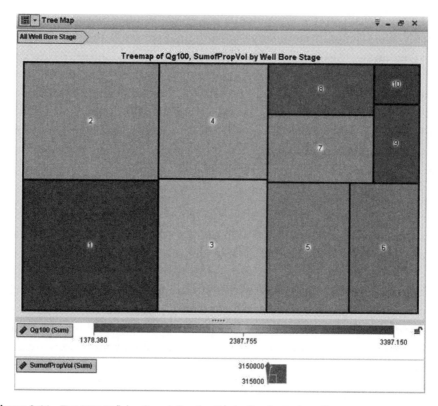

Figure 9.11 Tree Map Defining Cumulative Gas Production for Each Wellbore Stage

Tree Maps

A tree map (Figure 9.11) displays a hierarchy or a category as a set of rectangular tiles. Each branch of the tree is given a rectangle, which is then tiled with smaller rectangles representing sub-branches. A leaf node's rectangle has an area proportional to a specified dimension on the data. Often the leaf nodes are colored to show a separate dimension of the data.

When the color and size dimensions are correlated in some way with the tree structure, one can often easily see patterns that would be difficult to spot in other ways, such as if a certain color is particularly relevant. A second advantage of tree maps is that, by construction, they make efficient use of space. As a result, they can legibly display thousands of items on the screen simultaneously.

ENSEMBLE SEGMENTATIONS

Segmenting wells across an asset portfolio based on their performance or their geomechanical attributes is the mainstream of reservoir segmentation basics; however, until recently the idea of combining these different reservoir segmentations has not been reported in literature. The ability to combine groups of segments together actually stems from a Bayesian methodology for combining information from different sources together to form a new insight not found in the uncombined information sources alone. The algorithm to perform these combinations, however, can take on a Bayesian approach or a more traditional approach, such as K-means clustering.

What exactly is *ensemble segmentation*? In order to answer that question, it is prudent to answer what a predictive ensemble model is first. *Ensemble* means to combine, collect, or collaborate; for instance, a music ensemble is a small group of musicians performing a single manuscript of music together. Thus segmentation is the process of placing observations that are classified into groups that share similar characteristics. In predictive modeling, an *ensemble model* is the combination of two or more predecessor models, and a combination function defines how the models are to be combined. An example of an ensemble model might be a response such as well production rate and a regression tree and a least squares regression combined as the average of both models as points along the data space. Another example might be a model to predict water cut where the training dataset contains high water cuts as 1's and low water cuts as 0's. A decision tree and a logistic regression and possibly a neural network could predict the probability of high water cuts (1's) and the combination function could be a voting of the maximum probability for each of the input models along the data space.

Ensemble Methods

Typical methods for combining different models of the same target variable have been reported, such as bagging and boosting. *Bagging* stands for *bootstrap aggregation*. In a bagging model, the following steps are taken in the algorithm:

Step 1. A random sample of the observations is done with a size of n with replacement (meaning that once a draw has been made, if an observation has been drawn before, a replacement is done).

Step 2. A model is constructed to classify the target response variable, such as a decision tree, logistic regression, or neural network. If a decision tree is used, the pruning part is omitted.

Step 3. Steps 1 and 2 are repeated a relatively large number of times.

Step 4. For each observation in the dataset, the number of times a model type is used in step 2 acts as a classification for each level of the target or response variable.

Step 5. Each observation is assigned to a category by voting with the majority vote from the combination of predecessor models.

Step 6. The model is selected that has the highest majority vote of correct classifications of the response. This is an ensemble of repeated samples and model building and the combination function is a vote with the best classification of the response variable.

Boosting is another ensemble model algorithm that boosts a classifier model that is weak or poorly developed.

Ensemble Clusters

In ensemble clusters, the goal is to combine cluster labels that are symbolic, and therefore one must also solve a correspondence problem as well. This correspondence problem occurs when there are two or more segmentations/clusters that are being combined. The objective is to find the best method to combine them so that final segmentation has better quality and/or features not found in the original uncombined segments alone. Strehl and Ghosh[4] used a couple of methods to combine the results of multiple cluster solutions. One method is called *cluster-based similarity partitioning* (CSPA) and another is called *meta-clustering algorithm* (MCLA).

Ensemble Segments

How do ensemble segments add value to upstream business issues? Let us enumerate some of the more tangible and important benefits:

- Customer data is complex: Segmentations simplify the complex nature of the data.
- Ensemble segments further simplify multiple segmentations.
- Ensemble segmentation is conceptually just as simple as originally grouping customers into segments.
- Combining segmentations allows the fusing of multiple business needs/objectives into a single segmentation objective.
- Method enables merging of business knowledge and analytics together.
- Ensemble segmentation is simple to implement.

DATA VISUALIZATION

Despite the fact that predecessors to data visualization date back to the second century A.D., most developments have occurred in the last two-and-a-half centuries, predominantly during the last 30 years. The earliest table that has

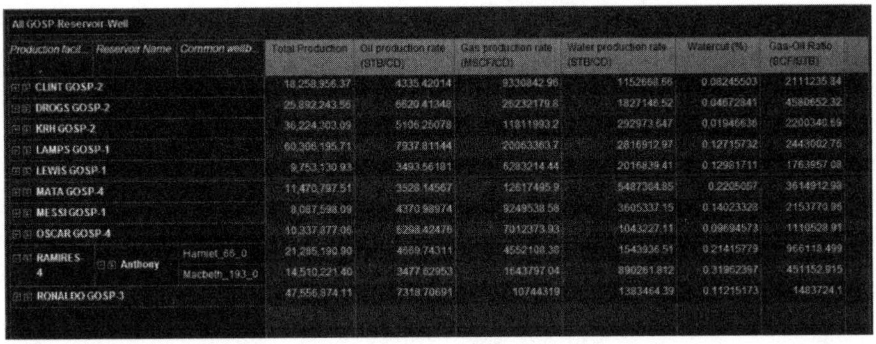

All GOSP Reservoir Well

Production facil...	Reservoir Name	Common wellb...	Total Production	Oil production rate (STB/CD)	Gas production rate (MSCF/CD)	Water production rate (STB/CD)	Watercut (%)	Gas-Oil Ratio (SCF/STB)
CLINT GOSP-2			18,258,956.37	4335.42014	9330842.96	1152668.56	0.08245503	2111235.84
DROGS GOSP-2			25,892,243.56	6620.41348	26232179.8	1827146.52	0.04672841	4580652.32
KRH GOSP-2			36,224,303.09	5106.25078	11811993.2	292973.647	0.01946636	2200340.69
LAMPS GOSP-1			60,306,195.71	7937.81144	20063363.7	2816912.97	0.12715732	2443002.76
LEWIS GOSP-1			9,753,130.93	3493.56181	6283214.44	2016839.41	0.12981711	1763957.08
MATA GOSP-4			11,470,797.51	3528.14567	12617495.9	5487304.85	0.2205057	3614912.98
MESSI GOSP-1			8,087,598.09	4370.98974	9249538.58	3605337.15	0.14023328	2153770.96
OSCAR GOSP-4			10,337,877.06	5298.42476	7012373.93	1043227.11	0.09694573	1110528.91
RAMIRES 4	Anthony	Hamlet_66_0	21,285,190.90	4669.74311	4552108.38	1543936.51	0.21415779	966118.499
		Macbeth_193_0	14,510,221.40	3477.62953	1643797.04	890261.812	0.31962397	451152.915
RONALDO GOSP-3			47,556,874.11	7318.70691	10744319	1383464.39	0.11215173	1483724.1

Figure 9.12 Tabular Format for Depicting Production Data

been preserved was created in the second century in Egypt to organize astronomical information as a tool for navigation. A table is primarily a textual representation of data, but it uses the visual attributes of alignment, whitespace, and at times rules (vertical or horizontal lines) to arrange data into columns and rows. Tables, along with graphs and diagrams, all fall into the class of data representations called charts.

Although tables are predominantly textual, their visual arrangement of data into columns and rows was a powerful first step toward later developments, which shifted the balance from textual and visual representations of data (Figure 9.12).

The visual representation of quantitative data in relation to two-dimensional coordinate scales, the most common form of what we call graphs, didn't arise until much later, in the seventeenth century. Rene Descartes, the French philosopher and mathematician probably best known for the words *Cogito ergo sum* ("I think; therefore, I am"), invented this method of representing quantitative data originally, not for presenting data, but for performing a type of mathematics based on a system of coordinates. Later, however, this representation was recognized as an effective means to present information to others as well.

Following Descartes' innovation, it wasn't until the late eighteenth and early nineteenth centuries that many of the graphs that we use today, including bar charts and pie charts, were invented or dramatically improved by a Scottish social scientist named William Playfair.

Over a century passed, however, before the value of these techniques became recognized to the point that academic courses in graphing data were finally introduced, originally at Iowa State University in 1913.

The person who introduced us to the power of data visualization as a means of exploring and making sense of data was the statistics professor, John Tukey of Princeton, who in 1977 developed a predominantly visual approach to exploring and analyzing data called *exploratory data analysis.*

No example of data visualization occupies a more prominent place in the consciousness of businesspeople today than the *dashboard*. These displays, which combine the information that's needed to rapidly monitor an aspect of the business on a single screen, are powerful additions to the business intelligence arsenal. When properly designed for effective visual communication, dashboards support a level of awareness that could never be stitched together from traditional reports.

Another expression of data visualization that has captured the imagination of many in the business world in recent years is *geospatial visualization*. The popularity of Google Earth and other similar web services has contributed a great deal to this interest. Much of the information that businesses must monitor and understand is tied to geographical locations.

Another trend that has made the journey in recent years from the academic research community to commercial software tackles the problem of displaying large sets of quantitative data in the limited space of a screen. The most popular example of this is the tree map (Figure 9.13), which was initially created by Ben Shneiderman of the University of Maryland. Tree maps are designed to display two different quantitative variables at different levels of a hierarchy.

High-quality immersive visualization can enhance the understanding, interpretation, and modeling of Big Data in the oil and gas industry; the combination of advanced analytical methodologies and a flexible visualization toolkit for the O&G industry deliver efficient and effective insight, characterization, and control of a very complex heterogeneous system that is an oil and gas reservoir.

The fundamental goal is to present, transform, and convert data into an efficient and effective visual representation that users can rapidly, intuitively, and easily explore, understand, analyze, and comprehend. As a result, the raw data are transformed into information and ultimately into knowledge to

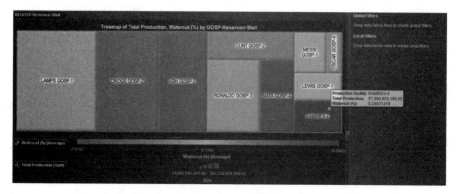

Figure 9.13 Tree Maps Explain Production of Hydrocarbons and Water by GOSP

quantify the uncertainty in a complex, heterogeneous subsurface system to mitigate risks in field (re)development strategies and tactics.

Existing reservoir visualizations can be complex, difficult to interpret, and not completely applicable to the available information and visualization requirements of the different states and characteristics of the field development cycle:

■ Early exploration, with limited data availability, high level of uncertainty, and the requirement of visualizing and interpreting the big picture

■ Exploration and drilling appraisal and field development, with medium levels of data availability, uncertainty, and details to be visualized

■ Production, with large data availability, a reduced level of uncertainty, and requiring visualizations for insight and interpretation over a multitude of details

To meet this challenge, novel types of interactive visualization systems and techniques are required to reflect the state of field development and available (increasingly more complex) data and information. Figure 9.14 illustrates a bivariate correlation of operational parameters in an unconventional shale reservoir, illuminating the important parameters that statistically impact well performance.

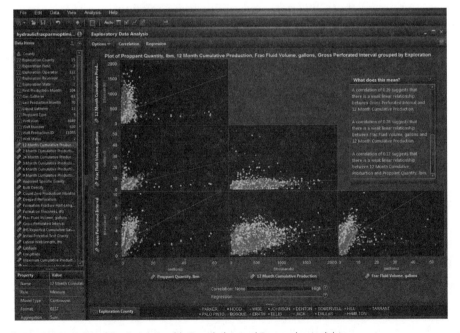

Figure 9.14   Suite of Scatterplots with Correlation and Regression Insights

CASE STUDIES

The following case studies illustrate the practical application of graphs and plots to uncover knowledge from upstream data across unconventional reservoirs.

Unconventional Reservoir Characterization

It is important to ascertain a more robust reservoir model and appreciate the subtle changes in geomechanics across an unconventional asset as drilling and completions strategies become more cost prohibitive to exploit these resources.

Again, marrying a data-driven methodology with traditional interpretive workflows enables more insight, and adopting EDA to surface hidden patterns culminates in hypotheses worth modeling under uncertainty.

To abide by Tukey's dictates we must generate a comprehensive suite of visualization techniques, preferably via an auto-charting methodology that is optimum for the datasets construed as essential for the business problem under study. We can progress through the iterative process of farming knowledge from our raw data. With the advent of Big Data as intelligent wells and digital oilfields are becoming more popular on the asset surveillance and optimization landscape, we need to handle terabytes of raw data as aggregation across engineering silos enables geoscientists to interpret data without the inherent issues associated with sampling these data.

Exploratory data analysis is the key to unlock the pattern-searching workflow, identifying those bivariate and multivariate relationships that enhance the engineers' understanding of the reservoir dynamics. Why use EDA?

- EDA is an iterative process that surfaces by trial-and-error insights and these intuitive observations garnered from each successive step are the platform for the subsequent steps.

- A model should be built at each EDA step, but not too much onus should be attributed to the model. Keep an open mind and flirt with skepticism regarding any potential relationships between the reservoir attributes.

- Look at the data from several perspectives. Do not preclude the EDA step in the reservoir characterization cycle if no immediate or apparent value appears to surface.

- EDA typically encompasses a suite of robust and resistant statistics and relies heavily on graphical techniques.

Maximize Insight

The main objective of any EDA study is to "maximize insight into a dataset."[5] Insight connotes ascertaining and disclosing underlying structure in the data. Such underlying structure may not be surfaced by the enumerated list of items above; such items assist to distinguish goals of an analysis, but the significant and concrete insight for a dataset surfaces as the analyst aptly scrutinizes and explores the various nuances of the data. Any appreciation for the data is derived almost singularly from the use of various graphical techniques that yield the essence of the data. Thus, well-chosen graphics are not only irreplaceable, but also are at the heart of all insightful determinations as there are no quantitative analogues as adopted in a more classical approach. It is essential to draw upon your own pattern-recognition and correlative abilities while studying the graphical depictions of the data under study, and steer away from quantitative techniques that are classical in nature. However, EDA and classical schools of thought are not mutually exclusive and thus can complement each other during a reservoir characterization project.

Surface Underlying Structure

We collected about 2500 individual well datasets in the Barnett from a major operator and integrated them with publicly available well data from the same region, resulting in an aggregated analytical data warehouse (ADW) containing both production and operational data from 11,000 wells that define the important hydraulic fracture parameters for each well's strategy. The primary goal was to understand which independent operational variables most impacted well performance with an initial focus on both proppant and fracture fluid volumes.

The target variable or objective function we agreed upon was the 12-month non-zero cumulative gas production. Let us explore its correlation with some of the operational parameters.

A correlation matrix displays the degree of correlation between multiple intersections of measures as a matrix of rectangular cells. Each cell in the matrix represents the intersection of two measures, and the color of the cell indicates the degree of correlation between those two measures.

The stronger correlations appear to be with the shallowest and deepest perforation, so we shall have to investigate further to identify the sweet-spot as regards minimum/maximum depths for 12-month non-zero cumulative gas production.

Further reading of the correlation matrix illustrates the low correlations between our two study parameters, proppant and fracture fluid volumes and the target variable. Already we have identified potential savings in OPEX by a reduction in these operational parameters with comparable gas production. Another beneficial consequence is the positive impact on the environment as the hydraulic fracture strategy would necessitate less sand and water, resulting in fewer truck trips and smaller surface footprint. These deductions must be studied further with more visualization to fully understand an optimized hydraulic fracture strategy.

We can identify and quantify the influence of the operational parameters upon the target variable. This will enable us to build more precise models in the next stage of the study.

Extract Important Variables

From the correlation matrix in the previous visualization we can start an itera-tive analytical process for each cell and study further the bivariate relation-ships to identify possible operational parameters that may have an impact on gas production. Let us take the shallowest and deepest perforation cell in the matrix and note those cells that correlate with best performance according to the target variable in this visualization, the heat map shown in Figure 9.15.

A *heat map* displays the distribution of values for two data items by using a table with colored cells. If you do not assign a measure to the color data role, then the cell colors represents the frequency of each intersection of values. If you assign a measure to the color data role, then the cell colors represent the aggregated measure value for each intersection of values.

Auto-charting enables users to create the best possible visualizations. Normally, with two numerical variables a scatterplot is rendered, but owing to the large number of data points, we witness the software modifying how the data are represented, producing in this case a heat map that shows the frequency or density of the data in each cell, here representing the objective function.

Initial reading of this visualization leads us to believe optimum average 12-month cumulative production occurs between the shallowest perforation depths of 6,625 and 8,125 feet, and between the deepest perforation depths of 11,900 and 12,900 feet (see inset, Figure 9.15). We shall also have to investigate

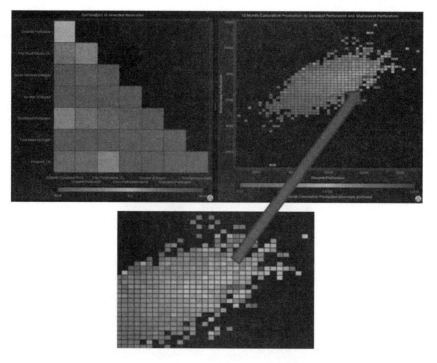

Figure 9.15   Heat Map Enables Identification of Sweet-Spot for Perforation

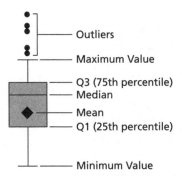

Figure 9.16 Box-Whiskers Chart Detailing Twenty-Fifth and Seventy-Fifth Percentiles

the outliers for high production by drilling down to identify which wells contributed to those cells.

Detect Outliers and Anomalies

The box-whiskers visualization is ideal to highlight the descriptive statistics for the independent variables as we try to establish potential values for each parameter that is important as we build the predictive model. It is a convenient way of graphically depicting groups of numerical data through their quartiles. Box plots usually have lines extending vertically from the boxes (whiskers) indicating variability outside the upper and lower quartiles. Box plots display differences between populations without making any assumptions of the underlying statistical distribution: they are nonparametric. The spacing between the different parts of the box helps indicate the degree of dispersion (spread) and skewness in the data, and identify outliers. It is a convenient way to visually Quality Control your data prior to building a predictive model.

A box plot (Figure 9.16) displays the distribution of values for a measure by using a box and whiskers. The size and location of the box indicate the range of values that are between the twenty-fifth and seventy-fifth percentile. Additional statistical information is represented by other visual features.

You can create lattices, and select whether the average (mean) value and outliers are displayed for each box.

Test Underlying Assumptions

A bubble plot represents the values of three measures by using differently sized markers (bubbles) in a scatterplot. The values of two measures are represented by the position on the graph axes, and the value of the third measure is represented by the marker size.

An animated bubble plot (Figure 9.17) displays the changes in your data values over time. Each frame of the animation represents a value of the date-time data item that is assigned to the *animation* data role.

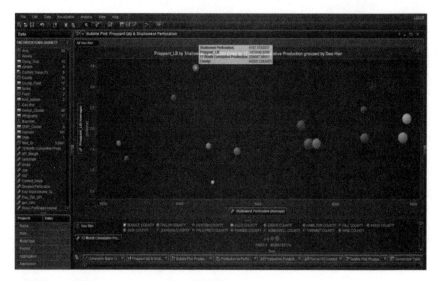

Figure 9.17 Animated Bubble Plot Offers Insight across a Temporal Slice of the Data

If we look at the average shallowest perforation, we see that both Johnson and Tarrant counties, red and dark blue respectively, have the highest average gas production in addition to Dallas, exhibiting the average optimum depths of 7621 to 7722 feet, respectively, which is consistent with our earlier findings on the heat map. Dallas reflects an average shallowest perforation of 8888 feet that falls outside the sweet-spot previously identified. Is this an outlier or reflective of the geologic dip of the producing zone of interest across the region? These depths across counties suggest a geologic characteristic that must be compared to a current static geologic model for the asset. These values seem important as indicators of high gas production, which is something we need to be aware of as we build a decision tree or neural network in our modeling phase.

This bubble plot representation also underlines that Hood County utilizes a large amount of proppant but the corresponding gas production is low by comparison with other counties. Also, note the shallowest perforation is about 6150 ft. Does this correlate with the dip of the shale zone across the Barnett? At this point we can drill down and surface which operators are inefficient in Hood County. Remember, not only do we wish to identify an optimized hydraulic fracture strategy that can be implemented in future wells by way of analogues, we are also trying to reduce the proppant and fracture fluid volumes so as to reduce OPEX without impacting performance.

Figure 9.18 underlines the poor performance in Hood County and enables the identification of those operators that perform poorly as the main contributors to overall low gas production vis-à-vis proppant volumes. For instance, we can observe that Enervest Operating LLC is using the highest amount of proppant for a fairly average production of oil. We should investigate their best practices and compare to other operators in a comparable geographic area.

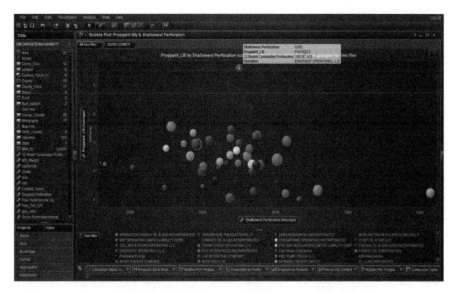

Figure 9.18 Bubble Plot Can Drill into a Hierarchy to Identify Well Performance

One of the major functionalities implemented in this visualization is the usage of the hierarchy that facilitates the drill-down of parameters based on a user-controlled characterization of the data. It is essentially OLAP cubes on-the-fly, a very simple methodology to cascade through a layered set of data that fall into a natural hierarchy such as Field: Reservoir: Well.

We are now establishing a more comprehensive understanding of each operator's usage of one of our study operational parameters, proppant volume. Which companies are underperforming by implementing too much proppant in their hydraulic fracture strategy? And what is the best practice as regards proppant volume for each respective fracture strategy across the geologic strata? Similar visualizations can be built to study fracture fluid. We are now moving toward defining the important parameters in our predictive model.

Drilling down we arrive at the well level and see that well #242090238900 is the one that uses the highest amount of proppant, but with relatively high gas production. Is this an outlier, or is it representative of the geologic characterization in this area of the Barnett? We must determine if the performance is acceptable, falling between confidence limits for cumulative gas production. This visualization details some much better performing wells with much smaller amounts of proppant; what key production indicators differentiate these good wells from the bad well in Hood County operated by Enervest Operating LLC?

We are building some identifying characteristics for good and bad well performance. We can subsequently ratify these findings by running a cluster analysis.

High volumes of proppant are being used in Hood County with relatively little return in 12-month cumulative production when compared to other counties, such as Tarrant and Johnson, where less proppant is used on average

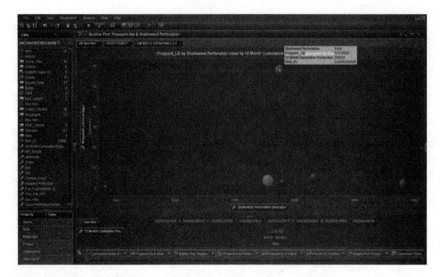

Figure 9.19 Animated Plot Investigating Proppant Quantities against Performance

with improved average performance. We have not been convinced that the associated gas production in Hood warrants such a large quantity of proppant. Perhaps the varying proppant quantities and gas production we see in the animation in Figure 9.19 across the GPI from 2200 to 2400 can be explained by *thief zones* in Hood County: faults/fractures not identified, consuming the fracture fluid and proppant with no impact on performance.

Or is poor performance related to poor operator practices? The visualizations associated with exploratory data analysis enables the identification of hypotheses worth modeling. We are quantifying the uncertainty in the underlying parameters.

For a more effective analysis of the efficiency at well level we can compare two maps (Figure 9.20), where in the first we show the amount of proppant and production across the region and in the second the content value (where 6 represents oil and 1 gas/condensate). We can see, for instance, in the first map that well #242090242813 in Hood County has definitely some issues with proppant quantity and efficiency. In fact, adjacent wells that have the same level of gas production utilize far less volumes of proppant. This is definitely indicative of poor practices and hydraulic fracture treatment strategy as the geologic model is fairly homogeneous as borne out by the wells in close proximity that show comparable performance.

The distribution of the wells' content value in the second map reflects a fuzzy understanding of where the oil and condensates are located. Do these map to the overlying geologic expectation? What are the reservoir characteristics at these well locations? We could cluster the wells by content value and include reservoir characteristics and geomechanical data, and tying these well properties to the static geologic model we can ascertain localized geologic structure/ stratigraphic characteristics. Do they reflect comparable well production?

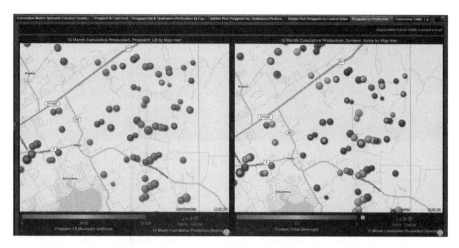

Figure 9.20 Bubble Plot Mapped across the Well Locations

Here we look again at Hood County in terms of proppant per fluid per GPI used and content value (we see that it is > 4.8 representing oil).

Which hydraulic fracture strategy is best for oil as opposed to gas production? What are the best practices in Johnson County that appear to produce more efficiently with comparable average proppant per fluid per GPI?

We must investigate whether proppant is being used efficiently, and if so, whether we could attain a similar level of production with a much lower amount of proppant, as implied by previous visualizations.

A crosstab shows the intersections of category values and measure values as text. If your crosstab contains measures, then each cell of the crosstab contains the aggregated measure values for a specific intersection of category values. If the crosstab does not contain measures, then each cell contains the frequency of an intersection of category values.

In the cross-tab visualization in Figure 9.21, we take into consideration two wells that in Hood County have approximately similar amounts of cumulative production but with a radically different amount of proppant volume. In fact, the well that seems highly inefficient is well #242090242813, which is operated by Chesapeake Operating Inc. This visualization can be built out to quickly identify best and worst practices across different wells in various counties. This process will throw light again on identifying the ideal values for important operational parameters deemed most influential in a hydraulic fracture strategy treatment plan. The results read from this visualization will help build future predictive models.

The data roles for a crosstab are columns, rows, and measures. You can assign either a single hierarchy or any number of categories to each of the columns and rows roles. If you assign measures to the crosstab, then the measure values are displayed in the cells of the crosstab. If you do not assign measures, then the cells of the crosstab show the frequency of each intersection of values.

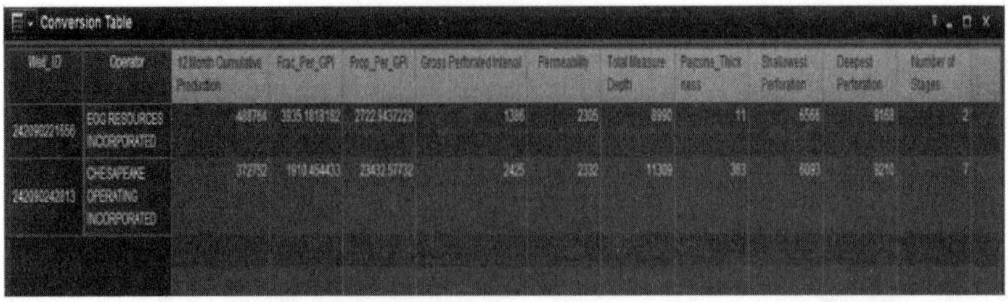

Figure 9.21 Crosstab Display Detailing Specific Measures

Early Warning Detection System

Oil and gas companies traditionally implement rudimentary monitoring consoles and surveillance systems that are at best *case-based reasoning* by nature. They offer isolated perspectives and tend to be predominantly reactive. With the proliferation of predictive analytical methodologies across many business verticals, it is paramount that the O&G industry adopt an analytics-based framework to improve uptimes, performance, and availability of crucial assets while reducing the amount of unscheduled maintenance, thus minimizing maintenance-related costs and operation disruptions. With state-of-the-art analytics and reporting, you can predict maintenance problems before they happen and determine root causes in order to update processes for future prevention. The approach reduces downtimes, optimizes maintenance cycles, reduces unscheduled maintenance, and gains greater visibility into maintenance issues.

There are multiple sensors on O&G facilities generating a tsunami of data points in real time. These data are invariably collated on a data historian, compressed, and then batch-processed by an analytical workflow. Figure 9.22 depicts a possible flow of data streams from sensors aggregated with other disparate datasets into an event stream processing engine. Such an engine focuses on analyzing and processing events in motion or "event streams." Instead of storing data and running queries against the stored data, it stores queries and streams data through them. It allows continuous analysis of data as they are received, and enables you to incrementally update intelligence as new events occur. An innate pattern-matching facility allows you to define sequential or temporal (time-based) events, which can then be used to monitor breaks in patterns so actions can be taken immediately. The engine processes large volumes of data extremely quickly, providing the ability to analyze events in motion even as they are generated.

Incoming data are read through adapters that are part of a publish-and-subscribe architecture used to read data feeds (Figure 9.23). An early warning detection system takes advantage of predictive analytical methodologies that house a predictive model. How is that model built and operationalized? First, we need to identify signatures and patterns in a multivariate, multidimensional complex system that are precursors to an event; that event could be a failure in

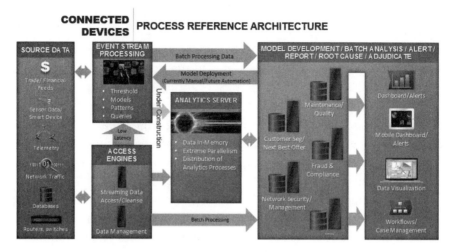

Figure 9.22 Data Stream Flows Generated by Sensors

Figure 9.23 Event Stream Processing Engine and Associated Data Flows

a pump or a liquid carryover occurrence. A root-cause analytical workflow that mines all the aggregated datasets deemed relevant to the study is performed to identify those signatures and patterns that occur prior to the event. The root-cause analysis determines leading and lagging indicators to characterize the performance of the system in real time. The objective is to identify the rules that are harbingers to the event under study based on the occurrences of other events in the transactions. Once established we can build a predictive model, be it a neural network, a decision tree, or a vanilla nonlinear regression model. A hybrid of said models could also be deployed. Having operationalized the predictive model, we can open the gates to the flood of real-time data from sensors via the historians into a complex event processing engine. The engine handles data streams in real time. First principles or engineering concepts can be built into the engine's logic as the streaming data are analyzed and broken down into succinct events. Those data are then passed into the predictive model to monitor the signatures and patterns identified as precursors to an impending event.

The basic principle of a model-based early warning fault detection scheme is to generate residuals that are defined as the differences between the measured and the model predicted outputs. The system model could be a first principles–based physics model or an empirical model of the actual system being monitored. The model defines the relationship between the system outputs, system faults, system disturbances, and system inputs. Ideally, the residuals that are generated are only affected by the system faults and are not affected by any changes in the operating conditions due to changes in the system inputs and/ or disturbances. That is, the residuals are only sensitive to faults while being insensitive to system input or disturbance changes.[6] If the system is "healthy," then the residuals would be approximated by white noise. Any deviations of the residuals from the white noise behavior could be interpreted as a fault in the system.

Thus, predictive models are at the core of any *predictive asset maintenance* workflow. It is an analytics-driven solution designed to improve uptimes of crucial assets and reduce unscheduled maintenance, thus lowering maintenance and operating costs and minimizing maintenance-related production disruptions. To get answers to complex E&P questions it is necessary to adopt a multipurpose and easy-to-use descriptive and predictive analytics suite of workflows. Adopting EDA and predictive analytics you can:

- Discover relevant, new patterns with speed and flexibility.
- Analyze data to find useful insights.
- Make better decisions and act quickly.
- Monitor models to verify continued relevance and accuracy.
- Manage a growing portfolio of predictive assets effectively.

The case study in Chapter 10, "Deepwater Electric Submersible Pumps," expands on an opportunity to apply a predictive model to preclude failures in electric submersible pumps.

A potential suite of workflows that illustrates implementing predictive models on real-time data is depicted in Figure 9.24.

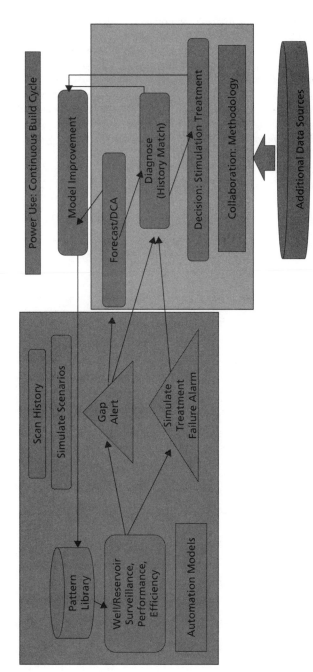

Figure 9.24 Workflows to Implement Predictive Models

NOTES

1. D. C. Hoaglin, F. Mosteller, and J. W. Tukey, eds., *Understanding Robust and Exploratory Data Analysis* (New York: John Wiley & Sons, 1983).

2. A. Gelman, "Exploratory Data Analysis for Complex Models," *Journal of Computational and Graphical Statistics* 13, no. 4 (2004): 755–779.

3. J. W. Tukey, *Exploratory Data Analysis* (Reading, MA: Addison-Wesley, 1977).

4. A. Strehl and J. Ghosh, "Cluster Ensembles: A Knowledge Reuse Framework for Combining Partitionings," *Journal of Machine Learning Research* 3 (2002): 583–617.

5. J.-F. Coste and J.-P. Valois, "An Innovative Approach for the Analysis of Production History in Mature Fields: A Key Stage for Field Re-Engineering," SPE 62880, presented at the SPE Annual Technical Conference and Exhibition, Dallas, TX, October 1–4, 2000.

6. R. J. Patton and J. Chen, *Robust Model-based Fault Diagnosis for Dynamic Systems* (Norwell, MA: Kluwer Academic, 1999).

CHAPTER **10**

Big Data: Structured and Unstructured

Any enterprise CEO really ought to be able to ask a question that involves connecting data across the organization, be able to run a company effectively, and especially be able to respond to unexpected events. Most organizations are missing this ability to connect all the data together.

Tim Berners Lee

The oil and gas industry, a sector known for its rapid adoption and ability to adapt to challenges of the digital age, is entering a new generation of digital transformation. As assets' yields become harder to access and even harder to forecast, it is imperative that the industry is collecting and maintaining its data efficiently.

As companies take in petabytes of data daily, it is the ability to understand analytical trends, to accurately interpret all geological, engineering, production, and equipment data efficiently and in real time that ensures success. The capacity to access and draw rich insights from your datasets is at the heart of profitability in this industry where your success relies on how quickly you can forecast potential while keeping costs low to actualize that success; you can't afford to get lost in datasets.

Big Data is a popular term used to describe the exponential growth and availability of data, both structured and unstructured. And Big Data may be as important to the oil and gas industry as the Internet has become to society. Why is this so? More data may lead to more accurate analyses. More accurate analyses may lead to more confident decision making. And better decisions can mean greater operational efficiencies, cost reductions, and reduced risk. The real-time dimension compounds the criticality driving adoption of soft computing techniques that when implemented in advanced analytical methodologies enable Big Data knowledge aggregated across disparate engineering silos.

As far back as 2001, industry analyst Doug Laney articulated the now-mainstream definition of *Big Data* as the three *V*s: volume, velocity, and variety:

1. *Volume:* Many factors contribute to the increase in data volume. Transaction-based data are stored through the years. Unstructured data are streaming in from social media. Increasing amounts of sensor and machine-to-machine data are being collected. In the past, excessive data volume was a storage issue. But with decreasing storage costs, other issues emerge, including how to determine importance within large data volumes and how to use analytics to create value from germane data.

2. *Velocity:* Data are streaming in at unprecedented frequencies and must be dealt with in a timely manner. Radio-frequency identification (RFID) tags, sensors, and smart metering are driving the need to deal with tsunamis of data in near real time. Reacting quickly enough to deal with data velocity is a challenge for most organizations.

3. *Variety:* Data today come in all types of formats. Traditional databases house structured alphanumeric data. There is information created from line-of-business applications. Unstructured text documents in the form of daily drilling reports, e-mail, video, audio, and financial transactions proliferate as the digital oilfield expands its footprint in the industry. Managing, merging, and governing different varieties of data is a burdensome task the majority of E&P companies still grapple with as upstream siloed data explodes with emerging intelligent wells and digital oilfield initiatives.

There are two further dimensions to consider when discussing Big Data:

1. *Variability:* In addition to the increasing velocities and varieties of data, data flows can be highly inconsistent with periodic peaks. Is something trending in social media? Daily, seasonal, and event-triggered peak data loads can be challenging to manage, even more so with unstructured data involved.

2. *Complexity:* Today's data come from multiple sources. And it is still an undertaking to link, match, cleanse, and transform data across systems. However, it is necessary to connect and correlate relationships, hierarchies, and multiple data linkages or your data can quickly spiral out of control.

The real issue is not that oil and gas companies are acquiring large amounts of data. It is what you do with the data that counts. The hopeful vision is that

E&P departments will be able to take data from any source, harness relevant data, and analyze them to find answers that enable:

- CAPEX and OPEX reduction
- Resource time maximization
- Exploration and production optimization
- Smarter business decision making
- Accurate quantification of uncertainty
- Mitigating risk across engineering decisions

For instance, by combining Big Data and high-powered analytics, it is possible to:

- Determine root-causes of failures, issues, and defects in near-real time, potentially saving billions of dollars annually.
- Optimize drilling parameters and increase ROP as well as reduce NPT.
- Maximize performance across a portfolio of wells by identifying candidate wells for remediation.

Finding value in Big Data does not stop at applying analytics to masses of static information. Today, organizations need to pull immediate insight from real-time, streaming data. Traditional approaches, which apply analytics after data are stored, may provide insight too late to act.

Event stream processing analyzes high-velocity Big Data as they are received. This drastically reduces time to decision so that you can make those critical decisions in time to be the most effective. We shall discuss a case study from a deepwater field to optimize electrical submersible pumps and ultimately increase production and preclude periods of deferment.

Structured data are relational, orderly, consistent, and easily stored in spreadsheets and database tables. Unstructured data are their inverse. They are big, non-relational, messy, text laden, and not easily represented in traditional tables.

Let us move on to *metadata*, a term that is increasingly entering the business vernacular. The term *metadata* means, quite simply, data about data. *Meta* is a prefix that in most information technology usages means "an underlying definition or description." Metadata summarize basic information about data, which can make finding and working with particular instances of data easier. For example, pump type, pressure, temperature, and date created represent very rudimentary metadata collated from an electric submersible pump. Having the ability to filter through that metadata makes it much easier for an engineer to locate a specific report that may be critical to detail the signatures of an event such as a failure.

Text analytics (TA) enable oil and gas companies to maximize the value of unstructured electronic text sourced from documents, Web pages, rig communications, online discussions, blogs and other social media, daily reports, and e-mails. Using natural language processing (NLP), TA reveal the relevant information buried within large quantities of documents.

TA are useful in virtually every industry where time is spent manually tagging, assigning categories, or reading through volumes of documents. It is imperative to efficiently process massive volumes of text sometimes in an extensive array of languages and to fully integrate with other business intelligence capabilities. Text analytics also extend the value of existing investments in document management systems and search engines. TA support a number of traditional business units/operations that are highly dependent on document-centric workflows and processes, through standalone offerings or embedded within industry and line-of-business solutions.

Confronted with Big Data issues arising from the deluge of unstructured content, many organizations struggle to get the optimum possible value from text data. Because of the ambiguity and numerous ways that text can be interpreted, it's not easy to discern, quantify, analyze, or exploit insights from text-based data. And many organizations cannot combine text-based information with structured data, so it's impossible to get a full, accurate view of the asset.

Text analytics turn text data into an organizational asset by helping you automatically assess, analyze, understand, and act upon the insight buried in electronic text. Integrated capabilities enable you to incorporate the new information from text analytics into real-time intelligence—as new variables for visualization and predictive analysis, and as metadata for other specialized document retrieval applications. As a result, you can make more effective, proactive business decisions, streamline priorities, and produce more meaningful reports.

Predictive analytics and sentiment analysis are not only providing insights into existing problems, but addressing unforeseen ones. In effect, they are suggesting new and important questions, as well as their answers. Through Big Data, oil and gas companies are identifying issues, trends, problems, and opportunities that engineers and geoscientists simply cannot.

EXPLORATION AND PRODUCTION VALUE PROPOSITIONS

In God we trust. All others must bring data.

William Edwards Deming

Event stream processing allows the continuous analysis of events as they occur. This incremental updating of information enables the real-time analysis of trends to detect anomalies immediately. These capabilities help capture value that could otherwise be lost through information lag. It provides increased performance for real-time decision management. An *event stream processing engine* invariably incorporates extant technologies, such as parallel processing, threaded kernel processing, and customizable data filters. It also provides native support for updates, deletions, and insertions for easy modeling with improved performance. It is essential to handle complex logic and improve storage latency. The ability to split incoming events enables you to conserve bandwidth for better performance as well as generate multiple processing paths for complex events. A powerful expression language and procedural windows provide better methods for handling complex processing logic. A sophisticated pattern-matching facility allows you to define sequential or temporal (time-based) events, which can then be used to monitor breaks in patterns so corrective action can be taken immediately. You do not have to wait for batch jobs to run before receiving critical information.

Studies have shown that the oil and gas industry has experienced substantial growth in unconventional resources markets. This increase in focus has not only brought on greater competition for assets, but a smaller margin for error. With projects demanding more expensive drilling and production technology and profound changes in government regulations and commodities, companies need to exercise operational prudence and strategic foresight to ensure success. Such foresight is attainable by adopting data-driven methodologies across the comprehensive suite of data sources, both structured and unstructured.

Content Categorization

Text analytics uses natural language processing and advanced linguistic techniques to automatically analyze large volumes of content for entities, facts, relationships, and topics. Analysis of the text creates metadata, documented taxonomies, linguistic models, and concept definitions that can be automatically applied to large document collections for fast, accurate classification, topic discovery, sentiment evaluation, and semantic insight and used to trigger real-time business processes.

Managing enterprise content effectively, and as a strategic asset, requires a common underlying informational structure. Content categorization applies natural language processing and advanced linguistic techniques to identify key topics and phrases in electronic text so you can automatically categorize large volumes of multilingual content that is acquired, generated, or exists in a repository. It correctly parses, analyzes, and extracts content for entities, facts, and events to create metadata tags that index documents—all in a collaborative taxonomy management environment. As a result, people across the engineering disciplines can quickly find the relevant content they need, when they need it, at the level of granularity required. It is feasible to define sophisticated linguistic rules to consistently organize, index, and trigger dependent information activities in real time. This drives faster, more efficient document organization, access, findability, and knowledge sharing and reduces overhead associated with processes such as manual tagging and retrospective indexing.

With a rich suite of tools, your text data are transformed into a reusable asset. This helps to facilitate document classification, discover explicit associations between terms and documents, cluster documents into categories, and discover linguistic rules for new insights across collections.

Advanced linguistic and parsing technologies can standardize your organization's subject-matter expertise. When defined to the system, documents are automatically processed to these knowledge-driven rules and concepts. Then, documents can be evaluated in real time, used in existing workflows, reports, and notification systems, and updated to transaction systems, automating information classification.

By defining semantic terms, the relationships between disparate collections can be consistently assigned to existing text repositories and assets. This maximizes the value of your organization's text collections by creating a knowledge lens for the information stores, enforcing data quality, and bringing meaningful content to the forefront when related information is examined. When used with categorization, it improves information retrieval activities and automates the delivery of related topics.

Abstraction from a large set of documents across multiple enterprise repositories enables focus on the content value to recognize what is irrelevant noise and what is relevant noise. Removing duplicates and focusing on what matters provides effective version control, as well as confidence in organizational assets through the entire content lifecycle from creation or acquisition through retention and disposition.

Content categorization, for example, is key when developing a hybrid solution to an E&P issue, such as identifying appropriate artificial lift mechanisms in a brownfield (see the section ahead, "Artificial Lift").

Ontology Management

Using advanced linguistic technologies to collaboratively define and manage semantic terms, an *ontology* management system associates text from different sources, file systems, and topical areas. It enables you to create relationships among entities, including preexisting and siloed taxonomies, so that subject-matter expertise about use and meaning can be systematically built into rules. When these rules are used in conjunction with categorization processing, related content is retrieved so queries will return relevant, comprehensive, and meaningful answers.

Sentiment Analysis

Analyzing information from the Web can be labor intensive, but businesses increasingly rely on these sources to discover trends, opportunities, and risks related to their products and services at a detailed level.

Sentiment analysis helps your organization to quickly understand customers' and constituents' opinions from across multiple sources of digital content: websites, communication centers, e-mails, forms, surveys, internal files, and reports. It automatically locates and analyzes digital content in real time, then combines statistical learning with advanced linguistic rules to accurately reveal the core sentiments expressed in textual data, evaluating text for positive and negative connotations, including subtle emotional content, and providing a detailed breakdown that you can graph to easily communicate exactly what comments mean in relation to overall sentiment and changes. As a result, you can spot trends before they become viral, and better identify your customers' priorities. Are all drilling reports written to a standard vocabulary or dictionary? Perhaps rig efficiency is a direct correlation to individual performance that may be surfaced through individual daily reports?

Text Mining

Text mining workflows help you discover information buried in unstructured text collections. The solution saves time and resources by automating the tasks of reading and comprehending text for new insight. The technology automatically parses text, identifies synonyms, creates frequency term counts, and can be mined to discover common topics, themes, and linguistic rules. You can jumpstart taxonomy development by using automated Boolean rule discovery in your categorization efforts. Through interactive drill-down reporting and visualizations, you can discover previously unknown patterns in document collections and apply those insights to your taxonomies or corporate dashboards. And as part of a fully integrated data mining environment, text topics and clusters are structured to be included in descriptive or predictive analysis. By consolidating existing structured data with text-based information, you can observe trend details, spot new issues, send alerts about potential problems, predict term influence, and flag new business indicators more efficiently and with less risk.

HYBRID EXPERT AND DATA-DRIVEN SYSTEM

A hybrid expert and data-driven system encompasses a methodology that combines the best practices garnered from experienced engineers and a data-driven workflow capturing salient E&P data.

Artificial Lift

Mature fields with multiple active wells necessitate at some point in the field's lifecycle artificial lift systems. Identifying candidate wells and the appropriate system to be implemented at the optimum time are critical factors to exploit efficiently the asset's resources. Mining historical data through an exploratory data analysis workflow to surface hidden patterns and trends enables efficient understanding of the input space that may entail multiple variables. Invariably these variables describe a multivariant, multidimensional, multivariate, and stochastic environment that is implausible to entrenched first principles advocated by the engineers familiar with the asset's historical performance. However, aggregating the observations noted by experienced engineers with the results ascertained from soft computing techniques provides a comprehensive knowledge base from which to develop timely and efficient EOR strategies made under uncertainty.

Let us look at a highly compartmentalized and unconventional reservoir that requires hydraulic fracture strategies to enhance performance. Prior to building any models that act as harbingers or predictors of performance, it is necessary to integrate relevant datasets in a spatiotemporal data mart on which is predicated a hybrid analytical methodology. We have production data, well test datasets, and historical information detailing prior stimulations as well as reservoir properties.

Figure 10.1 illustrates the key components for the hybrid system.

The user-driven methodology incorporates the knowledge garnered by experienced engineers. A deterministic rules-based leg is essentially built to answer the question: Does the well require an artificial lift system? The Bayesian workflow is by nature stochastic and enables a belief-based probabilistic approach that operates under uncertainty quantification. Each input and output variable is represented by a node with a cause–effect mapping represented by an arc.[1]

The rules-based reasoning methodology encapsulates the engineers' knowledge base within an automated routine implementing a sequence of IF-THEN-ELSE code blocks. The captured reasoning and logic from a user's perspective emulates a surveillance loop that is either scheduled to run in an ad-hoc fashion or implemented in real-time. A suite of operational and nonoperational parameters are identified as significant decision criteria. Such parameters could include the following:

- Tubing diameter
- Choke size
- Well head pressure
- Gas production rate

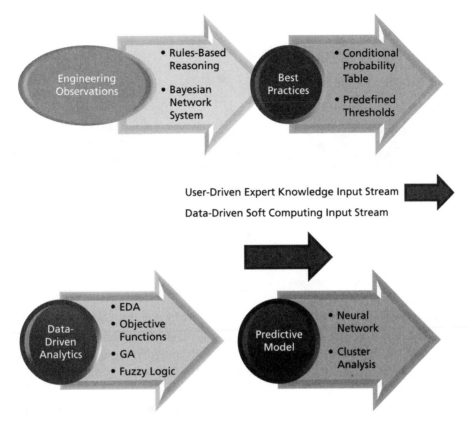

Figure 10.1 Hybrid System Integrating a Data-Driven and Expert Workflow

- Last well test
  - Condensate rate
  - Water rate
- GOR

A unique set of parameters are collated as indicative of a specific artificial lift requirement. The system is flexible to enable an engineer to adapt the parameters and their values customized to a singular reservoir characterization. When a well's behavior is noted to signify via the rules-based logic that a particular type of artificial lift is needed, an alert or notification is communicated to responsible parties. To avoid an avalanche of notifications, a ranking workflow can be introduced that quantifies the number of times each well in the field's portfolio is alerted. The inherent limitations of the rules-based approach are its inadequate handling of missing data points and any duplicity of artificial lift identification based on parameter analysis where more than one EOR methodology is surfaced as appropriate for a specific well. There is no qualitative assessment to determine the optimum artificial lift mechanism when two or more are identified by the rules-based logic.

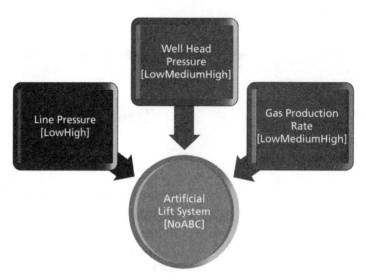

Figure 10.2 Bayesian Belief Network

To address the uncertainties inherent in the aforementioned system, let us detail the *Bayesian network* approach. Essentially it is a belief-based probabilistic methodology that expresses itself under conditions of uncertainty, thus outputting a probabilistic distribution as opposed to a discrete Boolean TRUE or FALSE state.

Figure 10.2 depicts the *Bayesian belief network* (BBN) for the artificial lift advisory system as described by De la Vega, Sandoval, and Garcia.[2] It was ascertained that the three most influential parameters were gas rate, well head, and line pressures. The input nodes are defined by a range of values that are subdivided into states [LowMediumHigh].

The output node maps to the appropriate artificial lift system or is defined as not appropriate owing to adequate well performance. The probabilities of each state [ABC] are detailed in the conditional probability table (CPT) as ascertained by engineering first principles and knowledge garnered from experience.

The data-driven workflow is becoming more prevalent across the E&P value chain as Big Data accumulate in real-time, marrying the soft computing technologies, discussed as a common theme in this book, with the constraints inherent in first principles.

De la Vega, Sandoval, and Garcia advocate an unsupervised clustering technique complemented by a visualization workflow implementing Kohonen's self-organizing maps (SOMs). The SOM uses the Euclidian distance between two points in an input space that is not only multivariate but multidimensional, quantifying a measurement of similarity. The more similar the measurement, the closer the points are located in the maplet or 2D projection space. Thus SOMs are applied to identify a pattern in the historic decision making of

Liquid Level Before　　　　　**Well Head Pressure Before**

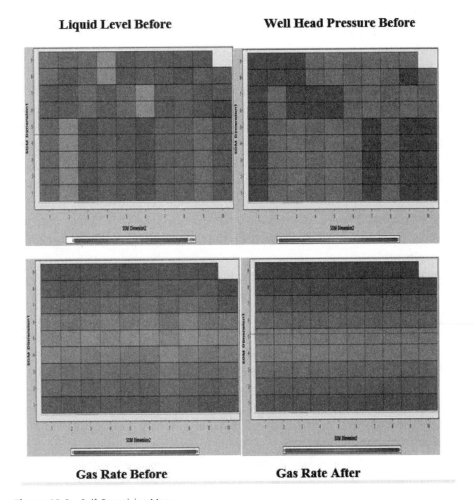

Gas Rate Before　　　　　**Gas Rate After**

Figure 10.3　Self-Organizing Maps

the asset engineers. Can we determine the hidden pattern that is representative of a specific artificial lift selection criterion?

We can see four realizations of the same SOM in Figure 10.3. Each realization or maplet corresponds to a parameter used to calibrate the SOM. The different artificial lift systems under study are represented by the range of colors from Blue to Red echoing the set [NoABC]. It can be noted when Artificial Lift system A [Red] should be used and when it is advisable not to implement [Shades of Blue]. Artificial Lift system A is thus applied for high to relatively high gas rate wells with moderately low static liquid level in the wells.

The data that calibrated the SOM act as the input space for a hierarchical clustering workflow. The individual clusters reflect well profiles with distinctive characteristics. The technique reduces the dimensionality of the input space. Consider how the problem space consisting of several hundred wells can be diminished into a dozen clusters that bin those wells that have similar profiles.

The SOM is a type of neural network based on competitive learning. It can be used for clustering and for visualization of high-dimensional data. Competitive learning embraces a category of algorithms based around the concept of a special data point called a *unit* that gravitates toward the other points in the data. One of the problems with plain competitive learning is that once the units have converged to their final positions, all one can get is the coordinates for cluster centers; one still has no real idea of what feature space looks like and what are the relationships between the different clusters. By tethering the units together in a grid, one can force them to maintain formation. One unit will have some form of relationship in feature space to the units adjacent to it in the grid.

As mentioned, SOMs provide a way of representing multidimensional data in much lower dimensional spaces, usually one or two dimensions. This process of reducing the dimensionality of vectors is essentially a data-compression technique known as *vector quantization*. In addition, the Kohonen technique creates a network that stores information in such a way that any topological relationships within the training set are maintained, and this is an important factor that makes it conducive to the heterogeneity inherent in reservoirs typical of unconventional plays.

Like most artificial neural networks, SOMs operate in two modes: training and mapping. Training builds the map using input examples. It is a competitive process, also called vector quantization. Mapping automatically classifies a new input vector.

A self-organizing map consists of components called *nodes* or *neurons*. Associated with each node is a weight vector of the same dimension as the input data vectors and a position in the map space. The usual arrangement of nodes is a regular spacing in a hexagonal or rectangular grid. The self-organizing map describes a mapping from a higher-dimensional input space to a lower-dimensional map space. The procedure for placing a vector from data space onto the map is to find the node with the closest weight vector to the vector taken from data space and to assign the map coordinates of this node to our vector.

While it is typical to consider this type of network structure as related to feed-forward networks where the nodes are visualized as being attached, this type of architecture is fundamentally different in arrangement and motivation.

The benefit derived by adopting the methodologies in this solution is the reduction of lost production owing to more efficient decision making in identifying an appropriate artificial lift system across an asset's well portfolio. The captured knowledge and experience from engineers provides an automated screening tool that constrains the data-driven workflows with limited first principles. The decision cycles include not just production and process data but also economic data, offering a holistic perspective on tactics and strategies for effective EOR.

CASE STUDIES

The two case studies that follow cover the analysis of structured data to optimize the maintenance of electric submersible pumps and unstructured data to garner important insight in the upstream with text analysis.

Deepwater Electric Submersible Pumps

It is not uncommon to deploy very large electric submersible pumps (ESP) in the world's deepest offshore fields to pump oil to the surface. These pumps will be installed in caissons located on the ocean floor sometimes in excess of 10,000 feet below the platform. Should an ESP fail, the financial impact could be $200 million in revenue loss and $20 million replacement costs. Given the total cost of an ESP failure, the goal must be to define the operating parameters that will preclude catastrophic damage to the ESP, even at the expense of lost or lower production rates.

The principal cause for failure is burnout of motor windings that are designed to be cooled by production oil flowing through the pump. There is a recycle loop that could be used for cooling. The intent of the recycle loop is to maintain the desired feed rate when well production falls below targets. Sometimes there are multiple ESPs but the recycle loop from topsides can be connected to only one ESP at a time.

Gas is invariably produced in the wells and the subsea systems include a gas separator and gas lift capabilities. Variability in gas and well production combined with ESP and gas lift flow rates can cause excess gas or excess liquids to result in problems with the gas separator and ESP. These conditions, known as *gas over* and *gas under*, are avoided by controlling the liquid level in the caisson. If the liquid level is too low, gas will be pulled into the ESP, causing a loss of head and motor windings heating due to loss of cooling effect from oil flow. If the liquid level in the caisson is too high, the liquids will interfere with the gas separator. Foaming caused by the waterfall effect of liquids falling into the caisson can also contribute to gas over and gas under. Other potential motor failures include bearing failure, seal failure, and bellows failure. Bellows are included in the motor to handle the expansion and contraction of motor lubricating oils that is encountered while installing the motors on the sea floor.

There is also concern that "infant mortality" or operator error may lead to premature ESP failure. The anticipated lifespan of an ESP is 3–5 years, but historically, tests have failed to reach that goal.

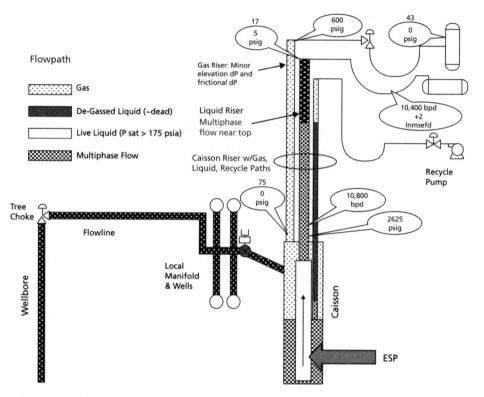

Figure 10.4 Oil and Gas Production Flowpath

In this case study wells are clustered in four areas on the seafloor and connected via flowlines to manifolds that enter at the top of the caisson. Figure 10.4 shows the flowpath of oil and gas, and the ESP is located in the center of the caisson. The caisson is sunk into the ocean floor with the bottom of the caisson resting 350 feet below the mud level of the ocean floor. Gas will separate from liquids in the caisson, with liquids flowing to the bottom of the caisson where the ESP intake is located. Liquid output from the ESP is controlled with motor speed and flows through a check-valve prior to entering the liquids riser, which is connected to the surface equipment. Gas is introduced into the liquids riser between the ESP and the check-valve to assist lifting liquids to the surface. Chemicals are added at the manifold to control foaming in the caisson.

The analytical methodology for event prediction utilizes both data and statistical estimates to surface relationships that explicate why certain conditions or events occur. This enables engineers to supersede domain knowledge and judgment by experience to identify rules and operating parameters that can be integrated into systems to provide automated monitoring and alerting.

The automated processing used by this methodology is ideal for analyzing complex, interdependent systems and environments that may span multiple engineering and job specialties.

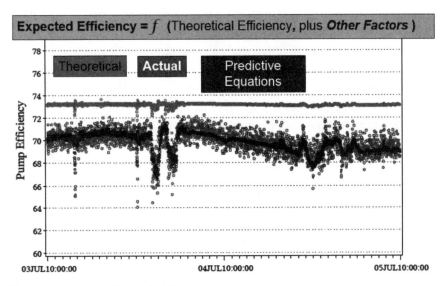

Figure 10.5 Actual and Theoretical Efficiency

The historians that collate the sensor data from the pumps constitute the principal source of data for this analysis.

Specific goals include the following:

- Definition of ESP performance metrics
  - ESP efficiency
  - ESP gas under
  - ESP gas over
- Visualization of performance metrics
- Exploration and identification of operational parameters that impact performance
- Measurement of relative impact imparted by operational parameters
- Development and testing of potential operational rules

The historians contain about 150 sensors that monitor various aspects of the ESP performance. Additional sensors in the system monitor other aspects of the overall system. Other datasets could be aggregated based on the objective function. Many extra variables can be created by simple or complex calculations.

Adopting data-driven multivariate statistical models allows us to capture the effects that explain variation in the actual against the theoretical efficiency as depicted in Figure 10.5. Those effects are a quantification of the correlations explicit in the data. Some of the effects are ostensibly apparent and well understood but some are more subtle, being either short term or long term by nature. Automatically surfacing these effects enables improved surveillance in real time.

The analytical solution provides a framework for continuous modeling of pump efficiency, establishing an automated surveillance system with problem identification and root-cause analyses. Big datasets are quickly aggregated as multiple sensors record high-frequency data points. Integrated with additional data such as the results of spectral analyses modeling to determine the suboptimal signatures resulting in electrical and mechanical harmonics, we quickly accumulate some very big data that must be analyzed effectively and efficiently.

Text Analytics in Oil and Gas

A major oil and gas company implemented a workflow that initiated with text analytics to garner asset and equipment knowledge from the plethora of unstructured raw data detailed in daily reports. Extracting information from the field notes written by drilling engineers enabled more robust knowledge to be ascertained based on mining the symptoms and identifying patterns and hidden relationships not surfaced by casual perusal. Such determinations enabled effective mitigation strategies to be enacted based on a plausible root-cause analytical methodology of the raw data contained in the reports.

A content categorization workflow (Figure 10.6) develops multiple categories; each contains its own set of rules based on keywords, phrases, Boolean logic, proximity based, regular expressions, parts of speech, or combinations thereof. The hierarchy of categories and subcategories can be defined by engineers from a domain perspective or even statistically derived drawn from linear or nonlinear regression methodologies.

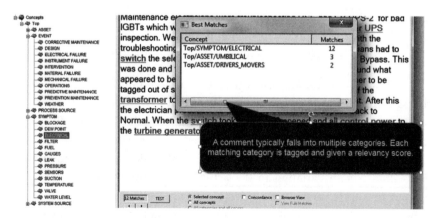

Figure 10.6 Content Categorization Step

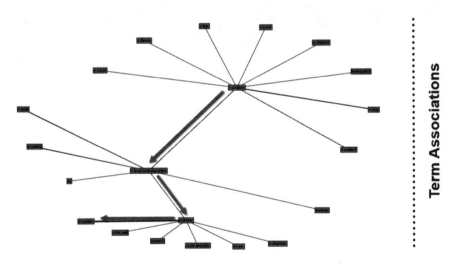

TERM	FREQ	# DOCS	KEEP ▼	WEIGHT	ROLE	ATTRIBUTE
⊞ separator	103	38	☑	0.515		Alpha
⊞ perform	80	38	☑	0.503		Alpha
⊞ bring	88	37	☑	0.508		Alpha
⊞ difference	101	36	☑	0.5		Alpha
⊟ plug	84	35	☑	0.515		Alpha
⊢ pluged	1	1				Alpha
⊢ plug	28	10				Alpha
⊢ plugged	22	11				Alpha
⊢ plugging	32	17				Alpha
⊢ plugs	1	1				Alpha
low	49	33	☑	0.522		Alpha
⊞ slug	63	33	☑	0.525		Alpha
plant	83	32	☑	0.523		Alpha
⊞ problem	66	32	☑	0.527		Alpha
⊞ plan	58	31	☑	0.531		Alpha
⊞ investigation	61	31	☑	0.533		Alpha
cut back	76	31	☑	0.526	Noun Group	Alpha
⊞ result	44	31	☑	0.53		Alpha
⊞ activity	79	30	☑	0.529		Alpha
lift	57	30	☑	0.536		Alpha
a-1	61	30	☑	0.539		Mixed
⊞ t-gen	77	30	☑	0.533		Mixed
⊞ choke	64	29	☑	0.542		Alpha
⊞ pad	61	29	☑	0.554		Alpha
⊞ hold	68	29	☑	0.535		Alpha
s38	79	28	☑	0.535		Mixed

Stemming identifies different tenses of a word as well as misspellings

Figure 10.7 Stemming Process to Identify Roots of Multiple Spellings of a Word

Figure 10.8 Term Associations Implemented to Determine Root Causes for Issues

Often it is necessary to perform a stemming process. In linguistic morphology and information retrieval, stemming is the process for reducing inflected (or sometimes derived) words to their stem, base, or root form, as in Figure 10.7 where we determine misspellings and variable versions of the same word, *plug*.

Term associations (Figure 10.8) are used to discover root causes for identified issues such as a pump failure. The exploration of the context of wording

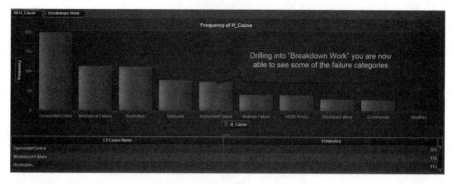

Figure 10.9   Drilling into the Failure Categories

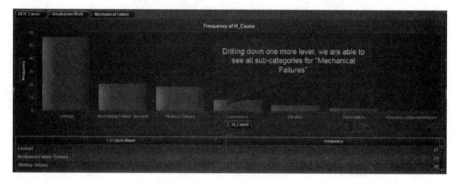

Figure 10.10   Drilling into Subcategories for Mechanical Failures

and specific nomenclature are considered. In this case, the term *problem* is associated to "level control" and ultimately to an issue with the stabilizer and reboiler.

The textual raw data were transformed into a structured format for efficient exploratory data analysis. Compressor reports were mined to build a hierarchical dataset containing categorical variables for events, detailing the assets and the reported symptoms. Were the shutdowns planned or unplanned? Drilling down into the "Breakdown Work" category it was feasible to visualize the failure categories depicted in Figure 10.9.

Further traversal of the hierarchy highlighted the subcategories enumerating the mechanical failures, as depicted in Figure 10.10.

The lowest hierarchical level maps to the raw text taken from the daily field report, showing the original textual comments entered by the engineers. The unstructured data were then merged with disparate structured data from across the upstream engineering silos to yield a richer dataset. Further analytical methodologies could then be implemented using soft

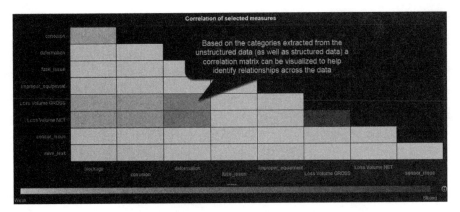

Figure 10.11 Correlation Matrix Surfaces Relationships from a Bivariate Perspective

computing data-driven models to address multiple business problems quantified by uncertainty.

Categories were extracted from the unstructured data and aggregated with the appropriate structured data. A correlation matrix (Figure 10.11) was then generated to visualize identification of important hidden relationships and trends across the input space.

Assets such as valves, piping, compressors, pumps, heat exchangers, and flowlines can be investigated via a text mining workflow capturing all salient data values from daily reports enriched by integration of additional structured datasets. Identifying symptoms of compressor failures in an immersive 2D and 3D visualization tool, exploratory data analytical workflows quickly identify frequency of reported issues such as leakage or high pressures or temperatures. Amassing these critical observations and quantifying the uncertainty and statistical impact on an objective function such as performance, it is plausible to design a model based on the historical signatures of a multivariate system that forecasts or predicts issues. Engineering solutions can then be implemented in a timely fashion having determined the root cause of inherent failures with a lead time surfaced by pattern-matching signatures of multiple independent and dependent parameters.

Figure 10.12 illustrates trend-lines for certain issues/categories under exploration. Forecasting is then a feasible workflow to identify emerging issues before they occur.

Thus text analytics are appropriate to convert unstructured data into structured data following a process flow via categorization, sentiment analysis, and text mining. There are patterns and thematic relationships that need to be surfaced from the plethora of journals, books, daily reports, and e-mails

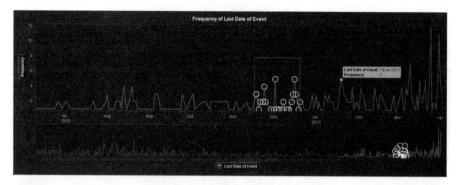

Figure 10.12 Forecasting Capability on Unstructured Data

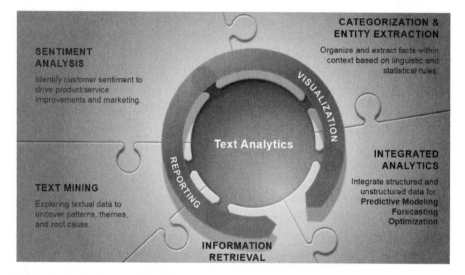

Figure 10.13 Text Analytical Workflow

amassed daily on remote rigs and in collaboration centers in upstream oil and gas companies.

A typical text analytical process flow is defined in Figure 10.13.

Figure 10.14 shows the value collating the disparate sources of unstructured data across the E&P siloed engineering disciplines; we can perform text mining and convert to a structured dataset [1]. The text mining workflow includes categorization and sentiment analysis [2, 3A, and 3B]. Once a robust analytical data warehouse has been established, enriched by the unstructured data patterns garnered from textual sources [4], it is important to define several analytical methodologies [5] that enact the exploratory data analysis steps in a visualization tool to reduce the dimensionality of the input space and identify salient independent parameters that have statistical

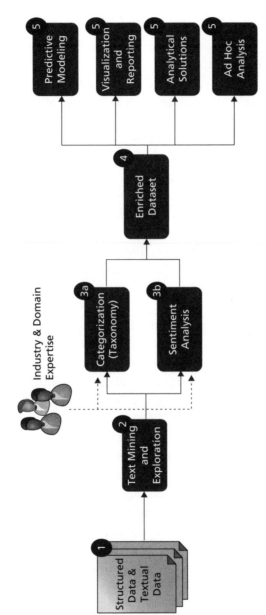

Figure 10.14 Unstructured Data Analytical Process Workflow

329

impact on the objective function determined *a priori* to reflect the business problem(s) under study.

MULTIVARIATE GEOSTATISTICS

The application of statistics to problems in geology and mining as well as to hydrology date back a considerable time. Invariably, geostatistics meant statistics applied to geology or perhaps more generally to problems in the earth sciences. Beginning in the mid-1960s and especially in the mid-1970s, it became much more closely affiliated with the work of Georges Matheron[3] and perhaps that connection is still the prevailing one today.

Professor Matheron was at the Ecole Normale Superieure des Mines de Paris (School of Mines), one of the Grande Ecoles. Matheron established the Centre de Morphologie Mathematique. Jean Serra's two-volume series on mathematical morphology and image analysis is well-known and is based on Matheron's earlier book on random set theory. Two of Matheron's students were instrumental in implanting geostatistics in North America. André Journel moved to Stanford University in 1978 and also co-authored Mining Geostatistics with Ch. Huijbrechts. Michel David had earlier moved to the Ecole Polytechnique in Montreal and in 1977 published "Geostatistical Ore Reserve Estimation."

Geostatistics is very much an applied discipline and its evolution has been the work of mining engineers, petroleum engineers, hydrologists, soil scientists, and geologists as well as statisticians. There is some overlap with geographic information systems (GISs) and spatial statistics in general.

In one respect, geostatistics might be viewed as simply a methodology for interpolating data on an irregular pattern, but this is too simplistic. A number of interpolation methods/algorithms were already well-known when geostatistics began to be popular. *Inverse distance weighting* and *trend surface analysis* as well as the much simpler *nearest-neighbor algorithm* were prevalent methods.

Geostatistics thus is a branch of statistics focusing on spatial or spatiotemporal datasets. Developed originally to predict probability distributions of ore grades for mining operations, it is currently applied in diverse disciplines, including petroleum geology, hydrogeology, hydrology, meteorology, oceanography, geochemistry, geometallurgy, geography, forestry, environmental control, landscape ecology, soil science, and agriculture. Geostatistics is applied in varied branches of geography, particularly those involving the spread of diseases (epidemiology), the practice of commerce and military planning (logistics), and the development of efficient spatial networks.

Interpolation algorithms must address the basic principle inherent in the majority of depositional environments where both geological features and associated petrophysical properties are distributed anisotropically, exhibiting variance in those properties when measured in different directions. Geostatistics provide a methodology for both identifying and quantifying anisotropic behavior in data. This methodology is termed *variography*, and the suite of metrics generated is encapsulated in a *semivariogram*. A variogram algorithm produces a set of metrics that are subsequently implemented during interpolation and simulation to preserve directions and scales of continuity by the kriging and simulation methods, respectively.

Thus anisotropy identification is performed empirically on the basis of the given data and observations. It is up to the geologist, geophysicist, or petrophysicist to assess whether anisotropy is present and to identify its metrics (i.e., the anisotropy axes angles and the anisotropy range ratios compared to the main direction). Once the user specifies the anisotropy metrics, spatial procedures can account for the identified anisotropy in semivariance computations, as well as in prediction and simulation.

It is paramount that variables of interest in the oil and gas industry, such as porosity, permeability, saturation, and sand/shale volumes, are understood from both a scale and a directional perspective.

Having cleansed and prepared the data and generated variograms or spatial models, we can then interpolate the key reservoir variables onto a defined grid using the kriging technique. Thus, the description of anisotropy in a problem is integrated in the continuity measure or semivariance. The kriging algorithm makes use of this measure to describe continuity characteristics across all distances and azimuths, allowing algorithms to compute variance between any two given locations. The kriging algorithm internally executes the variance computations at a set of user-specified locations, at which the algorithm executes internally the variance computations.

Simulation algorithms invariably offer both conditional and unconditional Gaussian simulation. It is the former implementation of the algorithm that provides reservoir engineers and geologists the means to generate practical reservoir models that are a true reflection of the spatial relationships between geological elements and their petrophysical properties, regardless of whether they are anisotropic or isotropic in nature.

Additionally, the results can be expressed from a probabilistic perspective, enabling quantification of uncertainty, provision of fundamental and imperative flow simulation input, and mitigation of potential risk. And this is the great value of simulation: It allows you to try different scenarios and investigate a reservoir property behavior for a variety of continuity configurations and under different parameter selections.

With the numerous realizations that can be potentially produced from a single dataset, you can rank and do post-processing to determine the degree of uncertainty in the models.

Thus conditional simulation is fundamentally an extension of kriging, reintroducing variance into the equation.

You can determine the degree of uncertainty in a model with the many realizations generated by simulation, drawing stochastic characteristics out of the data. Having measured the degree of difference from one realization to the next, you can compile a synopsis of statistical metrics and then render appropriate displays to garner the full potential of geostatistics in a reservoir characterization project. Better quantification of uncertainty at all levels, from input data to model assumptions and model parameters, is sought. By appreciating the boundaries of uncertainty in developing a geostatistical reservoir-characterization model, it is plausible to offer techniques to alleviate some of the risk underpinned by uncertainty. The results enable more reliable drilling plans, improved secondary and tertiary recovery strategies, and a more comprehensive portfolio analysis of upstream assets.

BIG DATA WORKFLOWS

The closed loop illustrated in Figure 10.15 reflects an efficient iteration of steps in a Big Data workflow.

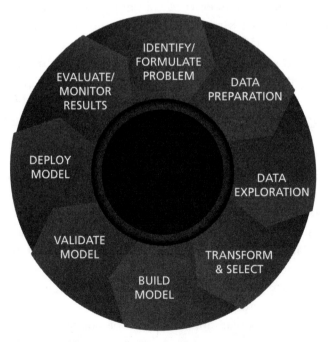

Figure 10.15 Big Data Workflows

Formulate Problem

It is necessary to identify an E&P business issue that collaboratively integrates disparate and siloed datasets. Big Data embrace structured as well as unstructured data. The first step enables a cross-pollinated group of engineers and business experts to aggregate the requisite data and experience to address the business issue and translate it into an objective function.

Data Preparation

The data must be run through some data quality control workflows to impute missing values, segregate outliers, filter any noise (be it coherent or random), and generate additional soft data parameters from the hard data measured in the field. Experienced and user-driven data points must be encapsulated as the data-driven methodologies employed subsequently must be constrained by first principles and engineering concepts. Big datasets invariably run into the petabytes and thus an architecture that enables upload of said data into memory ameliorates the subsequent analysis, be it exploratory or predictive in nature.

Data Exploration

During the exploratory data analysis step we must employ several workflows that implement the Tukey immersive visualization suite of charts and plots to surface hidden patterns and identify correlations. Essentially a sensitivity study, it allows us to reduce the dimensionality of the complex, multivariate, and multivariant input space. We need to understand those parameters that have the most influence and statistical impact on the objective function reflected by one or more dependent variables.

Transform and Select

This step supplements the data preparation workflow post exploratory data analysis. It provides the opportunity to transform individual parameters from a normal distribution to log-normal, and so forth. The selection step implements workflows based on PCA or factor analysis that enable us to hone in on the most important independent variables.

Build Model

The building of a model or models opens the door to multiple solutions that must be assessed to determine the most appropriate model. These models are data driven, incorporating any constraints introduced by first principles. We should implement several diverse models as data quality and size influence the success of certain types of soft computing techniques and models:

- Logistic regression
- Regression
- Neural networks
- Nonlinear regressions
- Mixed linear models
- Random forest
- Decision tree

Validate Model

It is of paramount importance to develop a framework to manage the predictive models and ensure the validity of all models, especially after each model is updated with new data. Metadata describing the models ensure their integrity and usefulness.

Deploy Model

Figure 10.16 represents the operational implications of a predictive model deployment. The starting point for the process is *surveillance*, taking data from a number of sources but primarily tag data. Real-time data will be compared with models held by the Failure Model Library. Out of the surveillance process two types of alert are possible:[4]

1. *Performance gaps:* A statistical deviation from long-term operating history. This is not a predictive alert.
2. *Predictive alarm:* A match with a failure model providing advance warning of a problem.

Performance gaps are passed to the engineering community for review. Questions analyzed might be:

1. Has this occurred before?
2. Did it lead to a problem?
3. What remediation actions were taken?
4. Could a predictive model be created and deployed within the Failure Model Library?
5. Do the data show a possible root cause that can be enacted?

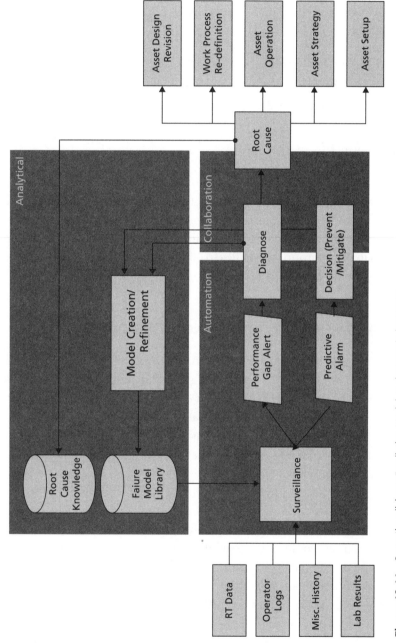

Figure 10.16 Operationalizing a Predictive Model against Real-Time Data

335

Predictive alarms lead to a decision-making process:

1. Are backup operations in place and ready?
2. What remediation activities are recommended from previous occasions?

At the high level, the predictive model is supporting three different categories' capabilities:

1. Automation supporting surveillance
2. Collaboration supporting diagnosis and decision making
3. Analytical—the process of creating and deploying predictive models

Evaluate and Monitor Results

It is ideal to monitor the performance of the predictive model without having to extract data, thus dynamically highlighting those findings based on the extant KPIs or engineering business rules established to ensure correct alerts. It is also important to distribute the results as documents, spreadsheets, or presentations to the appropriate profiles to ensure effective remediation and attention to any alerts.

INTEGRATION OF SOFT COMPUTING TECHNIQUES

Thus far we have discussed several soft computing techniques, such as artificial neural networks (ANN), fuzzy logic (FL), and genetic algorithms (GA). In isolation each has inherent merits, but a combinative power is plausible when studying the different methodologies that implement two or more techniques in a single workflow. Let us summarize both the strengths and the weaknesses native to each approach and feed off that arbitrary scoring to define effective combinations (Figure 10.17).

It is apparent that no single soft computing method stands out as the omnipotent one to address all upstream problems. However, if we can compensate for the weakness in one method by applying an inherent strength of an alternative method, we come closer to achieving that analytical nirvana. Owing to the consequent complexity resulting from the integration of these methods, we should enumerate a few examples that bear fruit and act in adjuvant roles to formulate upstream value propositions. Let us study two examples in the upstream in detail.

Traditional mathematical and statistical methodologies are à propos when probability distributions or highly delineated models are available. Real-time operations such as attaining pipeline flow assurance could be modeled by a recursive methodology such as a Kalman filter.

Issue	ANN	FL	GA
Non-Linearity	A	A	A
Real-Time Analysis	B	A	C
Fault Tolerance	A	A	A
Domain Expertise Integration	B	A	D
Quantifying Uncertainty	A	A	A
Self-Learning Capability	A	D	B
Mathematical Model Integration	D	B	D
Optimization Capability	B	D	A
Ease to Operationalize	A	C	C

Figure 10.17   Scoring ANN, FL, and GA

The first hybrid approach convolves an artificial neural network and fuzzy logic. Both are essentially numerical or mathematical model-free estimators. When the input space is complex, uncertain, multivariant, multivariate, and stochastic, it behooves the engineer to adopt a methodology that marries the benefits of ANNs and FL algorithms. Thus no mathematical model is required *a priori* to describe relationships between the input and output spaces. The resulting *neuro-fuzzy* (NF) system has been implemented to determine *total organic content* (TOC) from an array of well logs. Kamali and Mirshady[5] focused their study to quantify organic matter due to its importance in controlling the hydrocarbon generation.

The following rules were ascertained:

Rule 1. If x_1 is A_1 and x_2 is B_1, then class is 1.

Rule 2. If x_1 is A_2 and x_2 is B_2, then class is 2.

Rule 3. If x_1 is A_1 and x_2 is B_3, then class is 1.

Figure 10.18 illustrates the implementation of the three aforementioned rules followed by three additional layers:

Layer 3. Combination of firing strengths. If several fuzzy rules have the same consequence class, this layer combines their firing strengths. Invariably, the maximum connective is implemented.

Layer 4. This specific layer includes the fuzzy output of the classes. These values reflect the level of match between the input and the classification.

Layer 5. Defuzzification that surfaces the best matching class for the input as the output class.

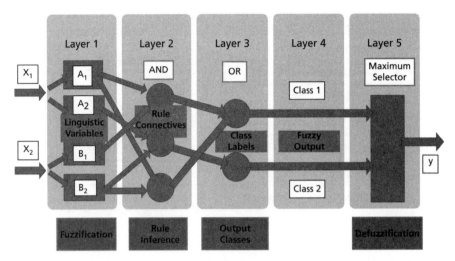

Figure 10.18 Neural Structure of Neuro-Fuzzy System

Batyrshin, Sheremetov, Markov, and Panova[6] implemented a hybrid methodology, aggregating the individual power of a fuzzy logic algorithm, a genetic algorithm, and standard mathematical and statistical approaches to analyze well logging data across a field in Mexico. The standard approaches used principal component analysis (PCA) to reduce the dimensionality of the input space followed by a fuzzy classification and evolutionary optimization. The objective function defined the structure of the porosity space yielded by primary, cavernous, and microfracture porosity classes. The hybrid method was most effective in attaining plausible results, decreasing both the requisite accuracy in well log data and the costs associated with said well log collection.

The porosity segmentation study adopted statistical methodologies to determine mapping between rocks and pore space type, assisted by fuzzy porosity classes composed of several fuzzy granules that yielded a scope of potential intersected porosity classes in the space of studied attributes. The classification of porosity was also achieved, implementing a separation of classes by planes in three-dimensional spaces of attributes. An *evolutionary algorithm* or genetic algorithm was used to construct the optimal planes.

The PCA/factor analysis combination strove to attain through a factor analysis workflow the principal components in the logging data and ascribe an importance factor to each component by way of establishing eigenvalues. The total variability represented by the input log data is examined by PCA and is then defined in terms of a set of factors. Each factor accounts for a proportion of the original variability and will not be correlated with other identified factors. Thus principal components are orthogonal by nature. Invariably the majority of the variability is described by fewer principal factors than the number of input variables. Essentially, PCA was used to encapsulate and approximate log

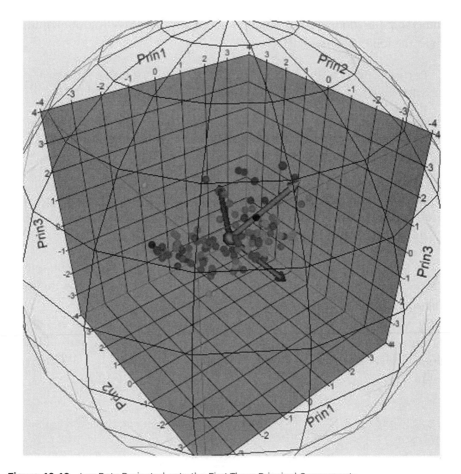

Figure 10.19 Log Data Projected onto the First Three Principal Components

data with fewer dimensions, while factor analysis was introduced to deduce an explanatory model for the correlations among the log data.

Figure 10.19 illustrates the transformation of the well log data into three principal components where the principal component scores have variance equal to the corresponding eigenvalue. The arc-ball enables an easier visualization of the rotated scatterplot in 3D. The three porosity classes are represented: Cavernous, Primary, and Micro-fractures.

The FL part of the workflow created fuzzy membership functions that retained six principal features embracing the main attributes used for describing the porosity structure of the log data. On visualization of the data obtained in the space of the first three principal components we see that the three porosity classes are partially separated and may be deemed as mutually intersected fuzzy classes.

Each fuzzy class was looked on as a union of three fuzzy granules, the fuzzy granules being ascertained as a result of intersection of corresponding membership functions. It is essential to adopt a sound classification definition such as the following nomenclature:

> For each point x that belongs to class C_1 in the training dataset a separability value $Q(x)$ was calculated. The higher the value $Q(x)$, the better is the classification of x. For each class C_1 an average value of the maximization of this criterion was used to surface the optimal parameters of membership values. The true classification on the training dataset was equal to 74, 65, and 88 percent for class C_1, C_2, and C_3. The classification on the validation dataset was equal to 35, 62, and 86 percent. The classification of porosity classes C2 (primary) and C3 (micro-fractures) may be deemed as adequately accurate in light of the high mixture of classes in some regions of the space of parameters.

The fuzzy classification obtained yields a good classification of the micro-fractures porosity class in carbonate formations that are considered the most influential porosity class for oil reservoir exploration.

The GA component in the hybrid methodology is implemented as a global optimizer to create porosity classes by dividing attribute space into different regions. Visual investigation of porosity classes illustrates that C_1 and C_2 may be separated from each other by different planes in 3D (Figure 10.20).

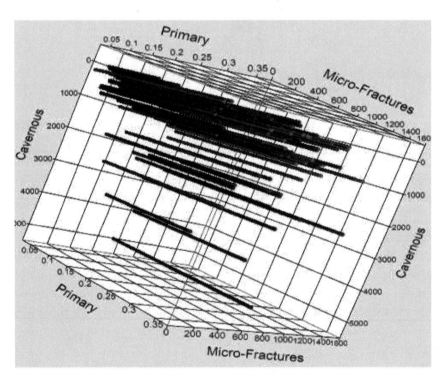

Figure 10.20 3D Visualization of a Scatterplot Reflecting Different Planes

The GA algorithm is implemented to determine the optimum planes that separate different classes. Each plane is defined by three parameters (a, b, c) and for each member of the population, represented by the triplet (a, b, c), a function F_1 and F_2 (associated with C_1, C_3, respectively) is calculated as a fitness function. Approximately 20 triplets with the maximum fitness were selected as the elite group and subsequently a new population was generated by crossover and mutation operations to determine a new elite group. The GA proved to be an effective optimization tool to ascertain the boundaries of different classes.

This hybrid workflow does not necessitate any prior assumptions to build a model from the hard data represented by the well logs. However, as a pattern-recognition technique it is essential to have a quality-controlled input dataset that is representative of the given complexity of a reservoir.

NOTES

1. Kevin B. Korb and Ann E. Nicholson, *Bayesian Artificial Intelligence* (Boca Raton, FL: CRC Press, 2003).

2. E. De la Vega, G. Sandoval, and M. Garcia, "Integrating Data Mining and Expert Knowledge for an Artificial Lift Advisory System," SPE 128636, Intelligent Energy Conference and Exhibition, Utrecht, The Netherlands, 2010.

3. G. Matheron, "Estimating and Choosing: An Essay on Probability in Practice," *Presses de l'Ecole des mines* (September 26, 2013).

4. Horia Orenstein, "Increased Upstream Asset NPV with Forecasting, Prediction and Operational Plan Adaptation in Real Time," SPE 133450, Abu Dhabi International Petroleum Exhibition & Conference, UAE, November 1–4, 2010.

5. M. R. Kamali and A. A. Mirshady, "Total Organic Carbon Content Determined from Well Logs Using DeltaLogR and Neuro-Fuzzy Techniques," *Journal of Petroleum Science and Engineering* (December 2004): 141–148.

6. I. Batyrshin, L. Sheremetov, M. Markov, and A. Panova, "Hybrid Method for Pore Structure Classification in Carbonate Formations," *Journal of Petroleum Science and Engineering* 47 (2005): 35–50.

Glossary

ADW

Analytical data warehouse customized to store those parameters deemed critical for subsequent advanced analytical methodologies.

ANN

In computer science and related fields, artificial neural networks are computational models inspired by animals' central nervous systems (in particular the brain) that are capable of machine learning and pattern recognition. They are usually presented as systems of interconnected "neurons" that can compute values from inputs by feeding information through the network.

ANOVA

Analysis of variance is a collection of statistical models used to analyze the differences between group means and their associated procedures (such as "variation" among and between groups).

AVO

Variation in seismic reflection amplitude with change in distance between shot point and receiver that indicates differences in lithology and fluid content in rocks above and below the reflector. AVO analysis is a technique by which geophysicists attempt to determine thickness, porosity, density, velocity, lithology, and fluid content of rocks.

BHA

A bottom hole assembly is a component of a drilling rig. It is the lower part of the drill string, extending from the bit to the drill pipe. The assembly can consist of drill collars, subs such as stabilizers, reamers, shocks, hole-openers, and the bit sub and bit.

BHP

The pressure, usually measured in pounds per square inch (psi), at the bottom of the hole. This pressure may be calculated in a static, fluid-filled wellbore with the equation:

$$BHP = MW * Depth * 0.052$$

where BHP is the bottom hole pressure in pounds per square inch, MW is the mud weight in pounds per gallon, Depth is the true vertical depth in feet, and 0.052 is a conversion factor if these units of measure are used.

BI

Business intelligence is a set of theories, methodologies, architectures, and technologies that transform raw data into meaningful and useful information for business purposes.

CAPEX

Capital expenditures are expenditures creating future benefits. A capital expenditure is incurred when a business spends money either to buy fixed assets or to add to the value of an existing fixed asset with a useful life extending beyond the taxable year.

CDP

In multichannel seismic acquisition where beds do not dip, the common reflection point at depth on a reflector, or the halfway point when a wave travels from a source to a reflector to a receiver. In the case of flat layers, the common depth point is vertically below the common midpoint.

CEP

Event processing is a method of tracking and analyzing (processing) streams of information (data) about things that happen (events), and deriving a conclusion from them. Complex event processing (CEP) is event processing that combines data from multiple sources to infer events or patterns that suggest more complicated circumstances.

CRM

Customer relationship management is a model for managing a company's interactions with current and future customers. It involves using technology to organize, automate, and synchronize sales, marketing, customer service, and technical support.

DCA

Decline curve analysis is an empirical determination of the type curves based on historical production data to forecast well performance and estimate ultimate recovery.

DHI

In reflection seismology, a bright spot is a local high-amplitude seismic attribute anomaly that can indicate the presence of hydrocarbons and is therefore known as a direct hydrocarbon indicator.

DOFF

Digital oilfields of the future is defined by how the petroleum industry deploys its technology, people, and processes to support optimizing hydrocarbon production, improving operational safety, protecting the environment, and maximizing and discovering reserves.

E&P

Exploration and production chain that covers all the steps in the upstream: exploration, appraisal, development, production, and intervention.

EDA

In statistics, exploratory data analysis is an approach to analyzing datasets to summarize their main characteristics, often with visual methods.

EOR

Enhanced oil recovery is a generic term for techniques for increasing the amount of crude oil that can be extracted from an oil field.

ERP

Enterprise resource planning provides an integrated real-time view of core business processes, using common databases maintained by a database management system.

ETL

In computing, extract, transform, and load refers to a process in database usage and especially in data warehousing that: extracts data from outside sources; transforms it to fit operational needs, which can include quality levels, and loads it into the end target (database, more specifically, operational data store, data mart, or data warehouse).

EUR

Estimated ultimate recovery from a field, reservoir, or well.

FFT

A fast Fourier transform is an algorithm to compute the discrete Fourier transform (DFT) and the inverse. A Fourier transform converts time (or space) to frequency and vice versa; an FFT rapidly computes such transformations.

FL

Fuzzy logic is a form of many-valued logic; it deals with reasoning that is approximate rather than fixed and exact. Compared to traditional binary sets (where variables may take on true or false values) fuzzy logic variables may have a truth value that ranges in degree between 0 and 1.

GA

In the computer science field of artificial intelligence, a genetic algorithm is a search heuristic that mimics the process of natural selection.

GIS

A geographic information system is a system designed to capture, store, manipulate, analyze, manage, and present all types of geographical data.

GOSP

Gas-Oil Separation Plant parts the crude oil from sediments, solids, and sand, removing gases and condensates to enable the crude to be pumped.

HSE

Occupational safety and health is an area concerned with protecting the safety, health, and welfare of people engaged in work or employment.

MDM

In business, master data management comprises the processes, governance, policies, standards, and tools that consistently define and manage the critical data of an organization to provide a single point of reference.

MPP

In computing, massively parallel refers to the use of a large number of processors (or separate computers) to perform a set of coordinated computations in parallel.

NMO

The effect of the separation between receiver and source on the arrival time of a reflection that does not dip.

OLAP

In computing, online analytical processing is an approach to answering multidimensional analytical queries swiftly.

NPT

Nonproductive time.

OOIP

Original oil in place is the total hydrocarbon content of an oil reservoir and is often abbreviated STOOIP, which stands for *stock tank original oil in place*, or STOIIP for *stock tank oil initially in place*, referring to the oil in place before the commencement of production.

OPEX

An operating expense is an ongoing cost for running an oil and gas strategy across the exploration and production value chain.

OWC

Water contact is a term used in the hydrocarbon industry to describe the elevation above which fluids other than water can be found in the pores of a rock. In most situations in the hydrocarbon industry, the term is qualified as being an oil–water contact (OWC) or a gas–water contact (GWC). Often there is also a gas–oil contact (GOC).

PCA

Principal component analysis is a statistical procedure that uses orthogonal transformation to convert a set of observations of possibly correlated variables into a set of values of linearly uncorrelated variables called *principal components*.

PDM

Abbreviation for positive displacement motor, a downhole motor used in the oil field to drive the drill bit or other downhole tools during directional drilling or performance drilling applications.

Q-Q Plot

In statistics, a Q–Q plot (Q stands for *quantile*) is a probability plot that is a graphical method for comparing two probability distributions by plotting their quantiles against each other.

SAGD

Steam assisted gravity drainage is an enhanced oil recovery technology for producing heavy crude oil and bitumen.

SMP

Symmetric multiprocessing involves a multiprocessor computer hardware and software architecture where two or more identical processors connect to a single, shared main memory, have full access to all I/O devices, and are controlled by a single OS instance that treats all processors equally, reserving none for special purposes.

SOM

A self-organizing map or self-organizing feature map (SOFM) is a type of artificial neural network (ANN) that is trained using unsupervised learning to produce a low-dimensional (typically, two-dimensional), discretized representation of the input space of the training samples, called a map.

SOR

The steam–oil ratio is a metric used to quantify the efficiency of oil recovery processes based on types of steam injection.

TOB

Torque on bit.

WAG

The WAG injection process aims to squeeze more oil out of a reservoir. It was originally intended to improve sweep efficiency during gas flooding, with intermittent slugs of water and gas designed by and large to follow the same route through the reservoir.

WOB

Weight on bit is the amount of downward force exerted on the drill bit and is normally measured in thousands of pounds.

About the Author

Keith R. Holdaway is an upstream domain expert and oil and gas business developer at SAS Institute Inc., having worked as a principal software developer. He started his career in 1980 as a geophysicist, performing seismic processing and interpretation in London, Dubai, the Sultanate of Oman, and Houston for several geophysical service companies and oil and gas operators. He received his degrees in mathematics and geophysics in the United Kingdom. Holdaway is also an active member of the Society of Exploration Geophysicists, the European Association of Geoscientists and Engineers, and the Society of Petroleum Engineers (SPE). He has written multiple technical papers and presents at SPE conferences. Holdaway is also a Fellow of the Geological Society of London and an active member of the Petroleum Data Driven Analytics technical group for the SPE.

Index